D1283370

PROACTIVE LEADERSHIP

IN THE 21ST CENTURY CLASSROOM, SCHOOL, AND DISTRICT

Robert L. DeBruyn
Author of *The MASTER Teacher*

© Copyright 1997 by The MASTER Teacher, Inc.

All rights reserved. No part of this book may be reproduced or transmitted in any form or by any means, electronic or mechanical, including photocopying, recording, or by any information storage and retrieval system, without permission in writing from the publisher.

The MASTER Teacher, Inc.
Publisher
Leadership Lane
Manhattan, Kansas 66502-0038

Library of Congress Catalog Card Number: 97-70000
ISBN 0-914607-44-8
First Printing 1997
Printed in the United States of America

This book is dedicated to making leadership as effective and rewarding as the quest for it—with special acknowledgment to four colleagues who helped to make the journey of writing it very satisfying: James Rickabaugh, Shannan Farber, Alice Holle, and Daniel Blea. Thank you.

Robert L. DeBruyn

TABLE OF CONTENTS

PREFACE

Since the original writing on leadership and management in 1976, *Causing Others To Want Your Leadership* has been reprinted six times. During this time, I have had the opportunity to work with thousands of you personally in seminars and workshops in your school districts throughout North America as well as during the leadership and management week of The MASTER Teacher Academy. I have also enjoyed and benefited from your letters and telephone calls.

As the years have gone by, many educators have told me that the original book should have been written for teachers as well as department heads, principals, superintendents, and all of those in positions of appointed leadership. I have agreed with this advice. However, tackling this task presented me with six considerations to reflect upon before writing such an all-inclusive book on leadership and management.

THE MYTH: OTHER LEADERSHIP
POSITIONS ARE DIFFERENT

First, *Causing Others To Want Your Leadership*, written exclusively for administrators, has been widely accepted by principals and superintendents. It has been a highly successful book—by anyone's standards. It still is. Yet, I am very much aware that everybody thinks he or she must have his or her own specialized book when it comes to the subject of leadership. Principals do. Superintendents do. Teachers do. And so do members of the board of education. For a wide assortment of reasons, most people really think their leadership task—in their specific position or with their specific title—is different from that of others. In fact, the higher people go in rank or position within an organization, the more they are apt to believe that their leadership functions are unique and require a distinctive, as well as a more sophisticated, level of expertise. This includes an advanced level of theory and training in addition to more sophisticated methods, techniques, and skills to employ with those being led. Yet, the truth of the matter is that when it comes to leading people, including yourself, the rules of the game are the same.

Second, people with any on-the-job experience always want to start on square ten when it comes to learning about leadership. They tend to say, "I already know that," "Everybody knows that," or "Let's get into more complex teachings." Yet, all these beliefs are more incorrect and dangerous than we might ever believe. In studying leadership, one should always start on square one. We should go to square ten only following review—and after steps one through nine are ingrained into us and have become the functional basis of everything we think and do. Make no mistake: When it comes to leading, we are always functioning on square one, even while we are dealing with high-level and complicated issues. Therefore, the day we start any leadership thought or action without starting on square one, our chances for failure are heightened—immediately and drastically. Without question, most of the leadership mistakes I see, from simple to complex, are caused by foundation problems. They are caused when leaders fail to consider steps one, two, three, etc. That's why this book starts on square one and proceeds from the simple to the complex. In the process, it continually makes the statement that step one is of paramount importance—always.

As a response to these common beliefs, writers who are both students and practitioners of leadership and management have a tendency to avoid fighting these common beliefs, even though such beliefs are myths. We simply give each person his or her own book on leadership—one book for teachers, one for principals, another for superintendents, and yet another for assistants of all kinds. It is an easy task. Yet, more and more I find myself in complete disagreement with this course of action, both professionally and ethically—and for good reason.

No matter who you are or what title you hold, whenever you manage work, you are management. Whenever you manage people who do that work, you are a leader. For instance, the teacher is, without question, the chief executive officer in the classroom. The principal is the chief executive officer in the school. The superintendent is the chief executive officer in the district. We're all on the same team. We all have the same mission. It is only some of our functions that differ on the technical side of management. When it comes to the people side of leadership, however, the laws, principles, theories, rules, and practices are the same. The outcomes are the same whether those being led are students, teachers, administrators—or secretaries, parents, cooks, or custodians. And, of course, teachers, principals, and superintendents often have to lead some of the same people.

For instance, teachers must lead students, but so must administrators. And though administrators must lead teachers, teachers must lead each other as well. That's why the more those of us who work in a school see ourselves as chief executive officers in our respective leadership positions—and function accordingly as leaders—the better we will all do. And if we're into shared decision making, site-based management, collaboration, cooperative learning, team teaching, or any other leadership approach, the more this is true. In fact, without leadership and management training, such objectives as shared decision-making and site-based management will be hard to achieve. Why? Because we simply don't have the leadership and management understanding, knowledge, and skills to make them work.

PRINCIPALS AND SUPERINTENDENTS REVEALED
THE NEED TO INCLUDE TEACHERS

Third, my belief that the second writing of a book on leadership and management should be for teachers and administrators alike has been reinforced by principals and superintendents for a long time in a very direct way. Every time I speak at a state or national convention or a workshop in a school district, administrators say, "My teachers need to hear what you are saying." As a result, principals and superintendents throughout North America have engaged me to present leadership and management seminars for their teachers—and the topics and all materials presented are from the original book, *Causing Others To Want Your Leadership*—which was written for administrators.

Fourth, several years ago we established The MASTER Teacher Academy. The Academy was designed to train teachers in a comprehensive way to be master teachers in the classroom—and administrators to be the instructional leaders in the school. We offered a money-back guarantee if we didn't do the job. Our professional staff ultimately decided that six weeks of training were necessary to achieve this goal, with one entire week being devoted to leadership and management. The other weeks consist of *Results-Oriented Teaching I*, *Results-Oriented Teaching II*, *Discipline and Motivation*, *Climate and Culture*, and *Technology*. The point is this: We did not feel we could train teachers completely and comprehensively to be master teachers or train administrators to be highly effective instructional leaders and offer a money-back guarantee without including leadership and management as part of the curriculum. We use the same curriculum materials for teachers and administrators at The Academy. In fact, we teach both teachers and administrators in the same class so that they can learn together and be better equipped to work together.

Fifth, the laws and principles of leadership and management do, without reservation, apply at every level of appointed leadership. They apply to teachers, principals, and superintendents. They also apply to head cooks, head custodians, and head secretaries. They apply to department heads and curriculum directors. Without question, these laws and principles apply to everyone in a leadership and management position who manages work and leads the people who need to do that work. They apply to those leaders regardless of the title and function they hold—even the student council president, head cheerleader, or team captain. When it comes to leading people, we are all governed by the same rules as appointed leaders. We all need the same knowledge of human behavior. We all need the same professional foundations. We all need the same kinds of understandings and skills. And we all need to know the laws and principles of leadership and management—and how to apply the methods and techniques which facilitate success.

Sixth, it is a tremendous advantage if teachers and administrators can see the leadership and management responsibilities, efforts, and functions each has within our schools. In fact, it is more than an advantage. It is a professional need which must be met if we expect educators and schools to move to higher levels of functioning and find more success and satisfaction in the work we do together. Teachers need to see the roles and efforts of principals and superintendents. Superintendents need to see the function of principals. And administrators need to see teachers functioning as leaders in the classroom, school, and district. In the process, we all need very much to learn from each other—and appreciate the various functions of our colleagues regardless of the titles they hold.

A NEW NEED
OF OUR TIMES

Changes in leadership and management training are, in reality, part of the wholesale school changes that will be taking place in teacher education and inservice training in the 21st century. All educators should embrace the training for a very practical reason. A changing society, as well as parent environment, shared decision making, accountability, and the restructuring of schools, is guaranteed to cause us more problems than solutions unless such training is received. After all, unless teachers and administrators have executive training as managers and leaders, do we honestly believe they will have either the executive attitudes, understandings, or skills to make concepts such as cooperation, site-based management, and shared decision making work? The answer is simple: They won't.

All the changes occurring in society and education tell us that leadership and management training is a must for all educators. When it comes to leading people, ignorance is not bliss. Rather, it is an assurance of misery and failure.

Educators should agree that the education reforms of the past demonstrated that it's futile to try to squeeze high performance from schools by doing more of the same. Without question, the new classroom approach will stress extensive planning, realistic problem solving, cooperation, maximum use of personnel, teamwork that extends beyond the school grounds, student interaction in projects, parent involvement, and higher levels of academic competency, grading, and testing. It will also find more adults who are not certified personnel working with the regular teacher. Teachers of the future will be cast as classroom executives, team leaders, guides, and mentors rather than lecturers who are expected to hold all the answers. And we all know a key component will be comprehensive student assessment. These achievements will simply be impossible without leadership and management training designed to help administrators and teachers alike acquire the knowledge and skills to lead people and perform successfully in these different environments.

WE ALL NEED THE
SAME TRAINING

The internal teaching of leadership and management on all levels in a school can occur only if we all receive the *same* executive training relative to leading people. That means we all need exposure to the same foundations. It means we need to operate with the same core values which are in agreement with the work and mission of the school and hold student learning and success supreme. It means we must acquire more "people skills," know the laws and principles of leadership and management, and practice the methods, techniques, and skills which enhance success. And, at this time in history, when we are moving toward higher standards, greater requirements, empowerment, reorganization, restructuring, and national goals—the joint and comprehensive training of teachers and administrators appears to be a necessity.

It is for these reasons that the new version of this book is called *Proactive Leadership In The 21st Century Classroom, School, And District*. It can be used individually—or as the foundation for group study involving a department or the entire faculty in a school and district. The purpose of this book is fivefold.

First, it will familiarize teachers and administrators with the specific and predictable wants, needs, and motivations of human beings. Acquiring this foundation is an absolute necessity for all in appointed leadership positions.

Second, it will introduce teachers and administrators to the laws, principles, and theories of human management as they relate to leading people and being either classroom teachers or school administrators.

Third, it will give both teachers and administrators leadership foundations which include the attitudes, beliefs, philosophies, and theories upon which their belief systems can be formed and actualized.

Fourth, it will provide teachers and administrators with the practical and workable methods, techniques, and skills needed to lead people in agreement with good management and educational practices.

Fifth, it will help teachers see themselves as the chief executive officers in the classroom, principals see themselves as the chief executive officers in the school, and superintendents see themselves as the chief executive officers in the district—and all to think and act accordingly.

This book will also give teachers and administrators the repertoire of skills they'll need to become as proficient on the "people side" of leadership and management as they are on the technical or academic side. This book is intended to go beyond defining the problem. It is meant to reveal the rules of the game and provide some proactive answers which can be applied—immediately. It is also meant to give teachers and administrators more security and satisfaction in leading.

1

LEADERSHIP AND MANAGEMENT ARE NOT THE SAME

Leadership and *management* are terms which are often used interchangeably. Many people, including teachers and administrators, think these two words are identical in meaning and application. However, nothing could be further from the truth. Every teacher, principal, and superintendent needs to know the difference between these related, but uniquely different, words. Why? Because by definition and in practice, leadership and management are different functions.

To completely understand the different functions of leadership and management, let's look at three words: *manage*, *manager*, and *management*. These definitions are simplified on Review Chart 1. Then, let's examine the words *lead*, *leader*, and *leadership*. These definitions are simplified on Review Chart 2.

THE TECHNICAL SIDE: MANAGE, MANAGER, AND MANAGEMENT

To *manage* means to handle. To manage means to have under control, to conduct, to carry on, and to guide. It means to move or use tools or materials in the desired manner. It also means to be cautious and use good judgment with people and to be concerned with all aspects of the enterprise—of the classroom, the school, or the district.

The *manager* is the one who manages—who guides or directs everything. He or she is the one who is at the head of an undertaking. The head of the classroom. The head of the school. The head of the district.

Management is the act, manner, or practice of managing, handling, directing, or controlling something. It can also be the person or persons who manage a place, business, establishment, organization, or institution. Management is the person or persons with executive ability. Management deals with the technical side of being a teacher or an administrator. For administrators, it deals with acquiring the skills to create master schedules, build buildings, schedule buses, purchase supplies, and balance the budget. For teachers, it deals with acquiring the academic knowledge to teach a course or subject and manage the physical objects contained in the classroom.

A. **MANAGE**
1. To handle
2. To have under control
3. To conduct, carry on, guide
4. To move or use in the desired manner
5. To be cautious and use good judgment with people
6. To be concerned with all aspects of business

B. **MANAGER**
1. The one who manages
2. The one who has the guidance or direction over everything
3. The one who is at the head of an undertaking

C. **MANAGEMENT**
1. The act, manner, or practice of managing, handling, directing, or controlling something
2. The person/persons who manage a place, business, establishment, organization, or institution
3. Skill in managing
4. Executive ability
5. The technical/academic side of being a teacher or administrator

THE PEOPLE SIDE: LEAD, LEADER, LEADERSHIP

On the other hand, to *lead* means to go before and guide or conduct by showing the way. It means to direct and govern and to show the method of attaining an objective. It means to entice, allure, induce, and influence. This is quite different from the definition of *manage*.

The *leader* is the one who leads or conducts. The leader is a guide or point of reference for those being led.

Leadership is the position, office, term, or function of a leader. It includes the capacity to be a leader, the ability to lead, and the act or instance of leading. Leadership deals with the people side of our jobs as teachers and administrators.

Review Chart 2

A. **LEAD**
1. To guide or conduct by showing the way
2. To direct and govern
3. To show the method of attaining an objective
4. To entice, allure, induce, influence
5. To go before and show the way

B. **LEADER**
1. One who leads or conducts
2. A guide or point of reference

C. LEADERSHIP
1. The position, office, term, or function of a leader
2. The capacity to be a leader
3. The ability to lead
4. The act or instance of leading
5. The "people side" of the job

You Need
Both
Skills

As we can see, there is a unique difference between the functions of leadership and the functions of management. They are not the same. Management deals with the "thing" or technical side of our job. Leadership deals with the people side of our work. Management is custodial in nature. Leadership is not. Different skills and actions are revealed in leadership and management. However, both are important functions of teachers in the classroom—as well as department heads, principals, and superintendents. And to have the ability to manage but not lead—or vice versa—will not do when it comes to being an effective educator. An individual must have both competencies. If he or she doesn't, high levels of success are not probable.

A CHECKLIST FOR UNDERSTANDING AND APPLICATION

1. When must you function as a manager?
2. When is it necessary for you to function as a leader?
3. What skills do you need in order to be a manager?
4. What skills do you need in order to be a leader?
5. Discuss why both management and leadership skills are needed for success.
6. Which do you most prefer: managing or leading? Why?
7. How are managing and leading related? Different?

TWO SIDES TO OUR JOBS

We are all managers. We are all leaders. Whenever we manage work, we are a manager. And whenever we direct the people who do that work, we are the leader. The teacher is the manager and the leader in the classroom. The principal is the manager and the leader of a school. The superintendent is the manager and the leader of the district.

Therefore, we need to be aware that there are always two distinct sides to our functions as teachers and administrators. The management side has to do with *things*. It pertains to the technical and academic side of our work. For a teacher, management is the academic side of teaching and has to do with knowledge and expertise related to the subject or subjects being taught. It includes arranging rooms, preparing lessons, gathering materials, and completing reports. The technical side includes managing all the *things* we use in classrooms: paper, pencils, books, computers, supplies, workbooks, desks, and chairs.

For administrators, the list on the technical side of management includes such activities as planning, scheduling, budget preparation, purchasing, physical plant maintenance, and balancing classes. And competency on the technical side of management is very important—for teachers and administrators alike.

The technical side of management is a competency that includes choosing, arranging, deciding, planning, and preparing for the work needing to be done by those being led. The management aspect of our work is a vital task. Yet, when compared to leadership, it is the lower level of functioning. We should never think for a moment that it isn't. After all, if teachers operate only as classroom managers, students may not do what teachers want them to do. Likewise, operating only as managers, teachers may not do what an administrator needs them to do to get all the work of the school accomplished.

We need to be both managers and leaders in the school. In truth, however, a close look may reveal that a teacher or administrator may not be the best or most logical manager in the school. In many situations, the best organizer, arranger, and scheduler may be a secretary or aide, and we wouldn't function very well without him or her. We must also recognize that we may be delegating some or much of our work on the management or technical side of our jobs to aides and secretaries.

As teachers, principals, and superintendents, we are usually well-versed and proficient on the *thing* side of management. We should be, for here we have been well-schooled by colleges, universities, textbooks, suppliers, and professional organizations. In addition, we have kept pace with the *thing* side of management via experience and through programs and studies facilitating learning and self-growth.

LEADERSHIP IS
AROUSING, CONVINCING, PERSUADING...

Two Sides to Our Jobs

The other side of our jobs has to do with people. It involves getting people to do what we want them to do. Leadership includes arousing, convincing, persuading, stimulating, and motivating. Leadership is influencing. Leadership is teaching. Leadership is, whether we like it or not, a form of selling. Leadership is also helping those being led do the right thing, for the right reason, in the right way—whether those being led are students, teachers, staff members, or administrators.

No one can deny that leadership requires extensive foundations in both attitude and skill. When compared to the technical side of management, it is the higher level of executive functioning. It is, without reservation, the difficult side of being a teacher or administrator—and my major concern in this book. Operating only as a manager, a teacher or administrator may never create interest or the desire to succeed in those being led. Whereas management tasks can often be delegated easily, this is not so for leadership. Leadership may come from within a class of students, of course. It may come from within a faculty of a school or district. That's fine, but it's not mandatory. However, it must come from the appointed leader in all places. That is mandatory.

We are most likely to go from being a manager to being a leader when we are aware of the differences between both functions, accept both responsibilities as important, and choose to perfect both our management skills and our leadership skills. In the process, we should accept that being a leader in the classroom, school, or district is the ultimate attainment of the professional educator.

IT'S EASIER TO MANAGE
THINGS THAN TO LEAD PEOPLE

The "people side" is of paramount importance to teachers and administrators because, in the leadership plan, *people* are always more significant to achieving success than *things*. In truth, people can be more constructive and destructive than all the various things which are included on the management side of our work. In the classroom, we don't teach math, science, history, music, or English. We teach these subjects to people. And in the office, we can have the best plans in the world, but if we can't get people to carry out those plans, the plans are worthless.

In the classroom, books don't teach all students—teachers do. Desks, chairs, and chalkboards don't deliver lessons—teachers do. The things we use in schools, from overheads to computers, are used or run by people. And clean floors, nice buildings, new overhead projectors, and expensive computers don't make a great school—people do. The achievement of excellence will come primarily from the efforts of people, not things. And leading people is much harder than managing any of the *things* we use in classrooms, in schools, and in school districts.

When this truth is coupled with the fact that teachers and administrators face the challenge of teaching all students and are being held accountable for the accomplishment of all the work of the classroom and the school, which is increasing continuously, you have the makings of one of the most difficult and demanding positions in appointed leadership. Unlike most leaders in business and industry, a teacher or school administrator does not lead a particular group. He or she is not accountable solely to owners or a board of directors like his or her corporate management counterpart.

For instance, a teacher is not just responsible for teaching only those students who are capable and have great interest in learning. He or she must teach all students—the bright, dull, interested, and disinterested. And a principal and superintendent must lead, and are accountable to, a host of people including students, teachers, counselors, nurses, secretaries, custodians, cooks, and the rest of the wide range of personnel who make up a school and district staff. He or she is also responsible and accountable to the central office, board of education, parents, public, and many, many other interest groups which are concerned with the work, mission, and achievement of the school.

In addition, the full power held by corporate executives is not possessed by the teacher, principal, or superintendent. Due process, student and parent empowerment, teacher organizations, and outside groups limit the power of teachers and administrators and the extension of that power. Even though unions are part of corporate management's power curtailment, educational management does not have the management-employee separation and protection enjoyed by corporate management. Principals and superintendents are much more vulnerable personally and professionally as a result of their position than are the executives in industry. And teachers are responsible for the rights and the welfare of students regardless of student skills or what a student does or does not do. That's why administrators and teachers must be highly skilled on the human side of leadership.

The classroom teacher faces some unique leadership problems. Teachers can't pick and choose their students to the same degree that business and industry can their customers. For instance, if a customer does not pay, business can refuse service. If a student does not study, a teacher does not have the same privilege. All students must be taught and helped to learn. The teacher faces an additional obstacle. Most of the time, he or she must function alone in the classroom as a separate entity within the whole of a school and district. And while it's true that we work more and more with colleagues in the classroom, a teacher still often plans lessons alone, teaches alone, and solves problems alone. In problem situations, the teacher cannot leave the classroom to think, reorganize, regroup, or get private counsel before proceeding like those in business and industry do. Rather, the teacher must stand and face students and the problem immediately. And a teacher must operate most of the day confined to the classroom. When a teacher makes a mistake, the whole class may see, experience, and judge the error. Therefore, even errors are public. In business and industry, not all customers see a mistake made with one customer. That's why the people side of teaching is so tough and demanding— and requires continuous and comprehensive training.

EACH SIDE PRESENTS US
WITH DIFFERENT PROBLEMS

This is not saying that the technical side of management doesn't present us with many big obstacles and difficult problems in both teaching and administration. It does. We may need more desks, more materials, more space, or more tools to aid in getting our job done. But these are entirely different kinds of problems than those related to leading people. Problems on the technical side of management are the same for all organizations, whether the organization is an industry, business, church, school, or family.

A close look will reveal that a lack of money, materials, and personal resources needed for getting the work of the classroom and school accomplished is a problem that many people can readily see—and even understand. However, technical kinds of problems—

regardless of what one might think—are not the primary source of our frustrations, disappointments, and failures as educators. And leadership influence and action are almost always required to get all the various things we need on the technical side of management.

We can even defend choices and decisions pertaining to the technical side of management more easily. It is in working with people that our judgment, ability, integrity, character, and skill will be challenged, questioned, and judged the most. That's why every teacher and administrator must be just as highly competent on the human side of work as he or she is on the academic or technical side. If we are not, we have only half the knowledge and skills we need to get the job done. Worse, the half that gets done will offer few achievements and few leadership rewards. We must know, however, that only when we combine management skills with leadership skills, do we have the combination necessary for functioning successfully as a professional educator.

OUR REWARDS LIE IN OUR LEADERSHIP ABILITIES

The "people side" of leadership and management is where the achievement, satisfaction, and rewards lie. It is also the primary source of acceptance, adherence, and respect for our leadership. The reason is obvious. Success on the people side of our work is what will distinguish us as exceptional—and for good reason.

There are a lot of people who are extremely competent with managing *things*. Many teachers know curriculum. Many are exceptional planners and organizers. And many administrators know how to build a superb master schedule or work miracles with a budget. However, there are not nearly as many educators who are highly competent and repeatedly successful working with different kinds of people with varied interests and priorities—and keeping them productive, satisfied, and fulfilled. If we are successful with the management of *things*, but not successful with the leadership of *people*, we will not be highly successful. It's that simple. Whether we are an accepted, respected, and effective leader depends largely upon whether we have specific leadership characteristics and can apply them in getting people to work, achieve, and find satisfaction in their work.

Make no mistake: *Things* are always easier to manage because they cannot plot, scheme, blame, balk, second-guess, stall, procrastinate, destroy, or criticize. People do these things. It's true, "things" can help us do work. Things can help us do more work. Things can even do some work more accurately. But it is people who make the tools we use work. And things cannot inspire, motivate, stimulate, influence, care, or share. But people can. And leaders must.

A MANAGER CAPITALIZES UPON INTEREST—A LEADER CREATES IT

If we are a good manager, we can capitalize upon individual interest, desire, and the needs of those being led. If we are the leader, we will actually create interest, desire, and need for learning and achieving. This is not an easy task. But then, being an effective leader never has been easy—and it never will be. And it's going to get harder as we raise the requirements and standards and strive to keep all students and all educators functioning successfully in school.

Winston Churchill said during the crisis of war, "We are confronted with insurmountable opportunities." The manager who was not a leader probably would have said, "We are confronted with the insurmountable." Leadership competency has always been the key to turning problems and challenges into success.

This process of becoming a manager and leader will not just happen. And it won't happen by experience alone. Rather, it will begin when we acquire a knowledge of the two sides of leadership and management: the technical side and the people side. It will continue by discovering how students learn best and what teachers, principals, and superintendents need to learn and do to be effective. Then we must add the skills necessary to manage work in addition to acquiring the ability to manage the people who must do that work while providing the leadership to make those being led want to do it. What we need to know is this: Each of us can be a highly effective leader. After all, leaders aren't born. They are developed. This development is the purpose of this book.

A BIG PROBLEM: HOW WE CHOOSE OUR LEADERS

Leadership is a social science. And we're learning more and more regarding how to lead people to get work accomplished as well as how to get the objectives of the organization accomplished—and help leaders and followers alike find high productivity and high satisfaction in the process.

What we know about leading people isn't the problem when it comes to developing effective leaders. The problem is that too many people in leadership positions have never been taught how to lead. Worse, some don't see themselves as leaders of people, and some simply aren't coachable. They won't learn or practice what they've been taught so that they can develop into highly accepted and successful leaders. To a large degree, this reality is caused by how we choose leaders.

We often choose our leaders from the ranks of those who are successful doers. Academically, they were good students in college, so we hire them as teachers to be the learning leaders in the classroom. They were knowledgeable or personable teachers, counselors, or coaches, so we make them the appointed leaders of departments or schools. By and large, the chances are great that one may get to be a leader because he or she proved to be a very good doer. Therefore, someone is likely to promote our *potential* to lead rather than our actual *ability* to lead people.

But being a good leader is not being a good doer. *Doing* for those being led is not *leading*. The roles and functions of a leader and a doer are different. People who get to be leaders but who do not understand this reality are not likely to lead people very well.

A close look will reveal that far too many who get to be leaders are prone to remain good doers. They may even become super doers. There is a simple reason for this reality. They have been successful as doers. They think of themselves as doers rather than leaders. They usually function out of the belief that "I've got to do it if it's going to be done" or "Nobody can do it like I do"—so they continue being leaders who do the work of a doer. It's easy to see why. They are better at doing work than getting others to do work. They are inspired, but can't inspire others as easily. Therefore, they perpetuate a self-fulfilling prophecy: It will continue to be true that no one can do it like they do because they never give anyone else a chance to do the work any differently—or any better.

We should all recognize that those we lead can *do*. In fact, those we lead must do. And those being led may be able to do any given job better than the leader who is a doer—even though these people may approach or do the job differently. Unfortunately, leaders who are doers keep doing rather than teaching people how to do. They often end up being "mechanical managers" who are not leaders by any stretch of the imagination. Therefore, they remain super doers instead of developing into super leaders.

These mechanical managers run around all day being involved in everything. They spend their day "fixing" everything. Whatever the task, they say, "It's easier and quicker to do it myself." And even though they get worked up and stressed out occasionally, they wouldn't have it any other way. Why? Because this kind of functioning makes them feel good. They feel wanted. They feel needed. They feel successful. They don't think anything could run without them. They feel very secure being a mechanical manager. In the process, unfortunately, they often feel they are leading. They are not.

There are parents who are doers or mechanical managers. They do everything for their children. Their children couldn't fix a meal or iron a shirt. Likewise, there are teachers, principals, and superintendents who are mechanical managers. They do the work that those being led are supposed to do—from decorating for a school party to handling every problem phone call. In fact, these teachers and administrators have their hand in everything that is being done. Unfortunately, the whole doesn't run well with these people in charge because people in their charge don't learn or get better. They just get more dependent. Worse, these kinds of leaders tend to be crisis managers who spend most of their time running around "putting out brush fires" for those being led rather than teaching people how to function or solve their own problems. In addition, doers or mechanical managers are likely to be governed by destructive myths and carry—as well as spread—the "disease" of four management myths.

A BELIEF IN
THE MYTHS...

Many people in leadership positions honestly believe "My people are different" or "Our situation is different." They say "What is known about being a leader may work elsewhere, but it won't work here, with my people, in our situation, and in this community." So they discount or ignore what is known about leadership and choose to lead in the classroom, school, or district in a wide assortment of individualized and random ways.

They don't learn how to lead because of a self-imposed learning and application void. They are not students of the science of leadership because they don't think the knowledge or training applies to those they are leading, they don't want to learn, they don't think that they have time, or they don't think it's necessary. They are practitioners of the science by happenstance and trial-and-error experience.

These leaders are prone to give "yes—but" responses when it comes to accepting tested leadership attitudes and behaviors. They say "Yes, it may work—but not with my students or with my teachers." Unfortunately, these "yes—but" reactions can result in four pitfalls. These pitfalls tend to spring up and govern in any place in which leaders hold "yes—but" beliefs.

MYTH NUMBER ONE:
MANAGEMENT PARANOIA

Leaders suffering from management paranoia believe that everybody is watching them all the time—and everyone is out to get them. They think everyone is just waiting for them to make a mistake—and will pounce on them once they do. In a wide variety of ways, by both their words and actions, they are saying "I can't be the leader because nobody will let me lead." They are saying "If I do anything, I will surely be criticized." As a result, they procrastinate. They stall. They protect. They do nothing.

In the process of leading, they almost always protect information, including what they know as well as information regarding what they are doing—and why they are doing it. Both isolation and secrecy are the constant companions of leaders suffering from management paranoia. And fear is with them all the time, and they will never deny that it is. They will begin many sentences with "Yes, but...." They are also prone to say, "Do you know what would happen to us if we did that?"

MYTH NUMBER TWO:
GREENER GRASS SYNDROME

It's easy to recognize leaders suffering from the greener grass syndrome. They always believe that other leadership positions and functions are better and easier. They usually think they have the impossible job. "My classes are harder," they say, or "More is required of teachers in our school." "Nobody could work with this board of education," they believe. They talk about how much more money people make in other places, how little those people do, and how much cooperation and appreciation other teachers and administrators in other communities get in comparison to them.

Envy is the constant companion of leaders suffering from the greener grass syndrome. Worse, these leaders always miss opportunity because they really never see it or purposely avoid it. Instead, they look down on the possibilities in the job they hold as well as on the potential of those they lead. And they always hold low expectations for themselves and those they lead. And, obviously, they do not feel that they have much influence with those being led. Needless to say, all these beliefs are self-defeating myths.

MYTH NUMBER THREE:
STATUS QUO PROJECTION

The status quo projection is very common and very dangerous. Here, the appointed leader says to students in a classroom or teachers in a school, "If you don't rock my boat, I won't rock yours. If you don't criticize me, I won't criticize you. If you don't ask or expect me to do anything, I won't ask or expect you to do anything." In the process, these leaders operate in a state of denial and pretend everything is going well and smoothly—no matter what the reality.

They measure everything by calm waters and "everything staying the same." They radiate "all is perfect" so they can avoid work, conflict, change, or decision making. Most of us know those who abide by the status quo projection as the "buddy" or "good old boy" leader.

Some teachers try to be a buddy to their students. In fact, they may act more like students than professional classroom teachers. If they are administrators, they don't ask much of themselves or those they lead. They wait to be led by staff consensus rather than do any leading themselves. In these cases, the leaders are lazy, weak, and insecure. They operate with various forms of low-level fear as a constant companion. They try to instill a hear-no-bad, see-no-bad, do-no-bad climate—and any effort to correct anything or anyone is avoided at almost any cost. Why? Because if someone else gets corrected, someone is going to correct them. It's easy to see that these leaders neither lead nor do the things a good and effective leader is supposed to do. To project the status quo, they often begin or end conversations with, "Yes, but...."

MYTH NUMBER FOUR:
MANAGEMENT FEAR COMPLEX

Individuals who work under this myth usually fear certain people: students, staff members, parents, or board members. And they are always looking for the signs which tell them to withdraw, cover their backside, or put up their guard. They may work continually gathering their supporters—and trying to avoid or exclude all others. And their supporters usually offer "blind support."

For instance, some teachers may have a group of students and parents who are totally loyal and who always back them. These leaders often try to operate by granting favors, having favorites, or creating exclusive or privileged relationships. But they spend all their time promoting themselves with certain people or protecting their backside. As a result, they don't do much progressive leading or much achieving in a meaningful way. And, because of their fears, they avoid anything new or challenging—including goals and change.

All teachers, principals, and superintendents who fall into any of these traps need to develop a new sense of awareness. There is only one "yes—but" when it comes to learning and practicing leadership successfully. *Yes*, what we know about leadership and management will work with our people in our classroom, in our school, and in our district—*but* we have to learn and apply what has been learned about leadership to be highly successful.

A CHECKLIST FOR UNDERSTANDING
AND APPLICATION

1. List the tasks you must perform on the technical side of being a (teacher) (administrator).
2. List the functions you must perform on the people side of being a (teacher) (administrator).
3. What problems are experienced on the (technical side of your job) (the people side)?
4. How should we choose people to be teachers?
5. How should we choose people to be administrators?
6. Discuss why leading people successfully requires universal skills.
7. How are those you lead (like) (different from) people everywhere?
8. Discuss the myths and fears relative to leading and how each affects you.

WHAT IS LEADERSHIP—
ARE YOU A LEADER?

The actual effectiveness of leadership is the real standard by which leaders should be judged. That's why this book stresses ways for a leader to be effective. A close look will reveal that focusing on typical leadership actions while ignoring effectiveness as the measuring stick is an ongoing problem discussed often in leadership studies.

If we intend to be effective, there are two important questions that need answering by everyone in or aspiring to hold a teaching or administrative position of appointed leadership. The first question I will answer for you. The second, you will have to answer yourself. The questions are: What is leadership?

Are you a leader?

As certainly as some men and women have aspired to be leaders, others have been inspired by leadership. At some point in our lives, many of us have had someone who influenced, added to, and maybe even changed our lives in either a positive, constructive way—or a negative, destructive way. Without doubt, those who inspire in constructive, productive, and effective ways are those with a special ability to relate to and motivate others to higher levels of performance. Above all else, they realize that leadership is a function of showing the way, rather than simply a position or title.

Being a teacher is not a position; it is a function. It requires getting the job done. The principalship is not a position; it is a function. It requires getting the job done. The superintendency is not a position; it is a function. It requires getting the job done.

There are many long and complex definitions of the word *leadership*. People have argued endlessly for centuries over minor points in the definition. Leaders and those being led have made long lists of what a leader is and is not and what a leader should or should not be. Unfortunately, too many people in leadership positions never arrive at a workable definition which holds effectiveness as the primary test and objective.

THE FIRST QUESTION:
WHAT IS LEADERSHIP?

I choose to define *leadership* simply as: "Causing others to want what you are doing to accomplish the work of the classroom, the school, and the district." Close examination should prove that this definition is all-inclusive. It is assumed, of course, that the leader is striving to meet the needs, goals, and mission of the institution. Within this definition, it is also assumed that a leader is doing nothing by word or deed which is contrary to the reasons for the creation or existence of the institution. And these assumptions can be made very easily because of two words in this definition of leadership: *want* and *causing*.

For example, a classroom, school, and district must be totally student-centered. Meeting the needs of students is the reason for the creation and existence of schools. Schools employ teachers, nurses, counselors, administrators, cooks, custodians, and many others. But the workers of the school are not employed to serve themselves. They are employed to meet the needs of students. Therefore, leaders should not and cannot expect to *cause others to want what they are doing* if their actions are self-serving and not in the best interest of students. Leadership efforts must be in agreement with the reason for the existence of the institution, or leadership efforts will not be accepted. They may not even be tolerated.

WANT IS THE KEY WORD

The key word in this definition of leadership is *want*. This word in the body of the definition makes both leading and being led a rewarding experience. The word *want* automatically excludes such leadership practices as being mean, hard-nosed, dictatorial, self-centered, obstinate, belligerent, or protecting of the status quo. Why? Because those being led do not and will not ever come to a point of *wanting* what you are doing as a leader when these leadership characteristics are present.

The word *want* in this definition also changes the meaning of another word in the definition. Without the word *want*, one could easily be misled by or misinterpret the intent of the word *causing*. In the day-to-day application of leadership, many teachers and administrators practice this definition without the word *want*—and it gets them into trouble.

Without the word *want*, the powerful and necessary word *causing* can imply pressure, force, coercion, and even threats. However, the word *want* allows the positive power of the word *causing* in this definition, yet eliminates all of the negative possibilities in leadership practices. *Want* is an important word—it's a word that one aspiring to lead other human beings to a higher level of performance cannot forget. Without this one word, traits such as caring, concern, kindness, and consideration might not be included in either leadership attitudes or practices.

It is also essential to realize that this definition of leadership is one that teachers and administrators need very much to adopt and live by. Equally important, the definition is one that those we lead will need to live by too. After all, application of the definition ensures that both leading and being led will be satisfying, rewarding, productive, and effective experiences—personally and professionally.

It's a fact: Leading students or staff can be a totally and overwhelmingly miserable experience. As we all know well, there are far too many educators wishing they were out of the profession or wanting to find a job outside education with less pressure and fewer problems. In large measure, much of the despair is the product of being unprepared as a teacher or administrator to *cause others to want our leadership*. When we learned to be teachers or administrators, leadership was not a part of the curriculum. As a result, we probably had to learn to lead by trial and error. When such is the case, we usually falter a lot—and we hurt a lot. Worse, we may hurt those we lead a lot. Indeed, trial and error is not the way for any professional to learn. It's not the way for a doctor to learn. It's not the way for a lawyer, an accountant, or an architect to learn. And it's not the way for a teacher or an administrator to learn. The toll on leader and follower alike is too harsh and too destructive, and it results in too much ineffectiveness.

Too, we need to be aware that it's not difficult to take leadership away from a leader. A few students can quickly take leadership influence away from a teacher in the classroom. Likewise, a few teachers can take the leadership away from a principal. And one board member can negate the leadership of the superintendent. Make no mistake: We will lose our leadership when we lack the philosophical foundations as well as the professional knowledge and skills to *cause others to want our leadership.*

Therefore, not trying to *cause others to want what we are doing* can make leading ineffective—and make us pay a heavy price for each of our mistakes. We may still be paying for ones we made years ago. Thankfully, it is never too late to begin anew. The way we choose to *cause others to want our leadership* is important because without guidance we are apt to choose the wrong way to lead and employ very few effective methods and techniques as well. This is important because of a functional leadership fact we would be wise to keep in mind.

ONLY TWO WAYS TO LEAD PEOPLE

Simple observation will reveal that, since time began, many people have believed that there are basically only two ways to lead people. First, make it *pleasant* for those being led to do the things you want them to do or to move in the direction you want them to go. Second, make it *unpleasant* for those being led *not* to do the things you want them to do or not to move in the direction you want them to go. That's it—just two fundamental techniques: Make it pleasant or make it unpleasant. In addition, many leaders try the one-two-three approach, which is a variation of the two fundamental techniques. First, they try to be nice. Second, if that doesn't work, they try to be mean, hard, or tough. Third, when being nice and being mean don't work, they think in terms of getting rid of the insubordinate follower. After trying steps one and two, some teachers will ask a principal to take a student out of their classes—even though they know the student will be placed in the class of colleagues.

My definition of leadership excludes the second and third choice for several reasons. Such action is not effective or acceptable leadership. Motivating by using a wide assortment of methods and techniques which could be classified as negative or unpleasant does not produce high productivity and achievement for the leader or those being led. And I don't believe a leader can get high productivity day in and day out without satisfied followers. In addition, it is impossible for a leader to teach the values or the character traits which facilitate success—or model those values and traits when using negative approaches. When leaders choose the unpleasant stance or "get rid of" mentality, they actually become what they dislike and criticize in those being led. Yet, the weaker our professional foundations and the fewer leadership skills we have, the more likely we are to revert to using unpleasant tactics—especially in problem situations.

I believe that if the attitudes, behaviors, or actions of those being led force a teacher or administrator to be unpleasant continually in order to motivate, a course has been chosen which will result in more negatives than positives, including damaging our reputation, relationship, and influence with those being led. That's why the leader must hold to the attitudes and actions of constructive leadership. Will our efforts always be successful? No. After all, no leader will be successful with every person all the time. Yet, our efforts must be successful the vast majority of the time—and our actions cannot become what we are confronting and correcting in others. If we use negative and unpleasant tactics, we should not be surprised or upset when those we lead do the same. After all, they learn from us—and they will act and react in a manner similar to the way we lead them.

In addition, we simply can't advocate one leadership and management philosophy, standard, and practice when dealing with some people and another when dealing with others. It won't work. For instance, we can't be pleasant when dealing with adults and unpleasant when dealing with young people. It is also dangerous when a leader shifts styles of leading—and begins doing, saying, and acting in a manner which is contrary to what he or she professes to believe in as well as counter to good leadership practices. Such actions can present an enormous problem for the leader, not only with the problem student or employee, but with all students and all employees. That's why the best course lies in choosing the higher road to the positive and pleasant—and *causing others to want your leadership*.

THE SECOND QUESTION: ARE YOU A LEADER?

Only you can answer the second question: Are you a leader? When answering this question, you must recognize some considerations and deal with them honestly and objectively. Remember, the probability is great that you were hired to be a teacher or administrator because you were a good *doer*. But just because you were a good doer does not necessarily mean you are now a good leader. In fact, everything you did to find success as a doer can work against your success in being a good leader.

Leadership requires different abilities—in attitude and thinking as well as work. Unless the *doer* position is dropped and the leadership position is assumed, you can operate in wrong ways and go in wrong directions. This point cannot be stressed too often or too much because too many leaders work very hard in their job in the same ways they did as a doer—while not doing the job they need to do as a leader. They were such good *doers* that they can't be anything else. They like getting involved and digging in and actually doing the work in the trenches. They can't let go. They can't delegate. They can't give up power. They can't take a stand—and they can't teach others *to do*. They can only do themselves. For instance, some teachers can't teach appropriate behavior; they can only correct inappropriate behavior. In every situation, when students don't meet a responsibility, some teachers do it for them—just like some parents do at home. In our own way, like parents, we end up "making beds, picking up clothes, and putting the dishes in the sink." These students don't have a master teacher. They have a master doer.

Just as teachers may be doers rather than leaders, administrators may be doers rather than leaders too. They like returning to do the kinds of things they did so well as doers. In a strange way, the role of doer makes them feel that they are leading. So time and time again, they return to the tasks of a doer. They chair every meeting. They explain every proposal or idea at faculty meetings. They monitor halls, rest rooms, and cafeterias rather than delegate. They do the same job at athletic events. They mistakenly think people will be pleased to see them "doing their job." In truth, schools often have the highest-paid custodian, cafeteria attendant, rest room watcher, and hall monitor in town—the administrator. When we don't choose to lead, we are mechanical managers. We are not leaders.

OUR TASK
IS LEADING

Functioning as mechanical managers, we not only fail to do our jobs, we don't allow others—whether they are students, staff, or faculty—to learn and be fully competent in theirs. For instance, when an administrator continually restores order to a roomful of students in a cafeteria or auditorium, does the staff learn to take effective action? The answer is no. In fact, the staff may keep having the same problem and continue waiting for the administrator to restore order. In effect, administrative *doing* may weaken teachers' position and success with students. Teachers may become dependent rather than self-sufficient because of this kind of administrative action. The same is true for students. They too may become dependent, and teachers can end up doing everything from repeatedly tying shoelaces to chairing student council meetings to decorating for parties. Our task in leading is to teach those being led how to become successful doers.

Unfortunately, mechanical managers often derive far too much satisfaction from *doing*. It can make us feel superior. It can make us believe that those being led couldn't operate without us. And it can make us feel that we are doing a great job because we are *doing* so much. Then, when we are criticized, we can't understand why. We also fail to understand that nothing will ever get any bigger or better than what we have accomplished as long as we function as a mechanical manager. Everything will remain within the dimensions of our own ability and availability of time. As a result, much of what needs to get done will never get approached, much less completed. The more "stretched out" we get, the less will get done under our leadership. And this happens because we continue to think and act more like *doers* than leaders.

We need to understand that the reason our performance does not bring the respect and effectiveness we want and need is that we are still predominantly doing those tasks that gave us the opportunity to be the leaders in the classroom or the school—but we aren't doing those things leaders are supposed to do. And, in many ways, such functioning is degrading to those being led. Rather than appreciate the efforts put forth by the teacher or administrator, those being led are likely to form the opinion that we do not respect or appreciate them—or have much confidence in them or their skills and ability. In the process, they are likely to believe that we don't know how to lead.

We are now the chief executive officer in the classroom or the office. We must concentrate on the tasks of a leader—not just on the tasks of a doer. We must teach those we lead to handle the responsibilities and tasks which they face. We are teachers of doers in our respective positions. If we are in the classroom, we should teach students how to do—and how to be successful in the classroom, the school, and life. If we are administrators, we must be teachers of teachers.

This is not an easy concept to grasp and practice for a simple reason: We must *still* be good doers. After all, whether we are teachers or administrators, there is a *doer* side to our work. There are many things we must do for those being led. There are aspects of our work we must do alone. Yet, a close look will reveal that these "doer responsibilities" are usually on the technical side of our work—not the people side.

As teachers, we don't teach students how to plan and deliver lessons or how to grade papers. As administrators, we don't teach teachers how to prepare budgets, balance classes, or order supplies. Therefore, while there is a *doer* side of our work in which we must excel, it usually does not extend to the people side. On the people side, we must focus on teaching

17

people how to do, rather than do for them. And there are four areas of competency you must master to be a leader.

First, you must know yourself. Second, you must know those being led. Third, you must know your job—including the technical or academic side and the people side. Fourth, you must know the laws and principles of leadership and management as they relate to leading and managing work and the people who do that work. But it all begins with knowing yourself. If you don't know yourself, it's unlikely you'll ever be able to lead others successfully or find satisfaction in being a leader.

DEVELOP BOTH A WILL AND A GENIUS

To reach the highest levels of leadership effectiveness, you must adopt two attitudes to overcome the "doer mentality." First, you must adopt a willingness to lead everyone within the realm of your appointed leadership. That means teachers must willingly lead every student and administrators must willingly lead every teacher and staff member. Second, you must believe in the genius of each person being led. For teachers, that means believing that there is a gift, an ability, and a genius within each student. It means believing all students can learn. It means believing they can all be successful. For administrators, it means believing the same things about teachers that teachers must believe about students. Just as there is a vast untapped potential or genius among students, there is also a vast untapped potential among teachers who serve those students. Superintendents must feel the same about principals—and boards must feel the same about superintendents.

The fundamental leadership problem is that many leaders do not believe this is so. Worse, some do not have the will or the skill to tap the genius of those being led. Paradoxically, in our own hearts, we all know and believe that potential lies within every student, teacher, and administrator. However, a large part of our difficulty has to do with the way we think and the way we act toward this potential for genius in those being led.

The intellectual potential of every student has been dramatically underestimated in the past. As a consequence, we underestimate students and hold expectations for them that are too low. The same can be said of teachers and administrators. If we intend to be successful leaders, we must first look at the fundamental beliefs we have about people. Second, we must consider the expectations we are capable of having. None of our leadership approaches or strategies will mean very much if we don't believe in people and aren't able to hold high expectations for them. Why? It's because if we have programmed ourselves not to believe in people or their potential, our failure to lead people effectively is inevitable.

A CHECKLIST FOR UNDERSTANDING AND APPLICATION

1. Discuss why the only real measure of leadership must be effectiveness.
2. Discuss the implications of the words want and causing in the leadership definition: "causing others to want your leadership."
3. What is the evidence that your (classroom) (school) (district) is totally student-centered?
4. Discuss (practices) (policies) that are not student-centered.

5. Discuss your experiences with the two ways to lead people: pleasant and unpleasant.
6. What are the tasks of a doer that you must do?
7. What are the leadership tasks you must perform?
8. What tasks of "doing" can you delegate from the (classroom) (school) (district)?
9. Discuss the statement: A leader must be a teacher of doers.

Causing
Others to
Want…

4

HUMAN WANTS ARE WITHOUT LIMIT...

The reason we can learn how to be successful managers and leaders is that the functions are a social science. And as a social science, the study of leadership and management is based upon two major facts. Understanding these two facts can save you more time, more grief, and more frustration and give you more insights and the potential for finding more success and peace of mind than anything you can learn about leadership and management. Understanding these two facts will also keep you thinking correctly and going in the right direction rather than fighting, misjudging, and faltering when you attempt to manage things and lead people. These two foundation facts are based upon an economic law.

INDISPUTABLE:
THE FIRST FACT

First, *human wants are without limit—and can never be fully or completely satisfied.* This means that if a teacher gets new desks, it's normal for him or her to want new books, then new chairs. If class size is reduced from 25 to 24, it's normal for teachers to want a class size of 23, then 22, then 21, then 20. If a teacher gets a room painted, it's normal that he or she ask for a closet, then new blinds. The list is endless.

The same is true for everyone, including students, principals, and superintendents. For instance, if you give students five extra minutes for lunch, don't be upset if they ask for ten minutes. It's normal. If you give students three choices for lunch, know that they may ask for four—then five, because the economic law teaches us that *human wants are without limit*.

This leadership teaching tells you that the long and continuing lists of requests you receive from those being led are both normal and predictable. That means the endless list of requests doesn't necessarily make your people bad or wrong. It doesn't necessarily make them selfish or greedy. It doesn't even make them different. It only reveals their normality.

The next time you receive a request and start to "blow up" and start saying "You can't please people," remember this leadership and management fact. It is a foundation fact of leadership and management. It is point one on square one. Therefore, just keep in mind that the minute you stop trying to please those being led by causing them to want your leadership—you will also stop getting high productivity and high satisfaction in effort, work, and achievement.

INDISPUTABLE:
THE SECOND FACT

*Human Wants
Are Without
Limit...*

The second major fact that the study of leadership and management is based upon is equally important. It tells us that *all the resources which are available to satisfy wants, both human and material, are always limited in amount.* Therefore, leadership in the classroom and the office is always concerned with choices. The leader must make decisions regarding what to do—and what not to do because wants are without limit and resources are *always* limited. Therefore, know that as the leader—in the classroom, the school, or the district— you must always make choices regarding how to spend your time, your efforts, your money, and all your other resources. If you make good choices, you'll be successful. If you make bad ones, you'll fail more often than you succeed. This is a foundation fact of leadership and management. It is point two on square one.

These are two foundation facts you can never discount or forget, even for a moment. First, human wants are *without* limit. Second, the resources to satisfy human wants are *always* limited. And these conditions are normal in all people—leaders and followers alike. These are constants. They do not change.

THE TWO MOST IMPORTANT FACTORS:
MONEY AND MANAGEMENT

It's true, money is very important to being successful. But money isn't everything or even the most significant factor in achieving success, because there are *two* "most important" factors—money and management. Yet, many people continue to believe that money is the most important factor in achieving success. But this is simply not true. Of the two, the leadership and management factor is, in reality, the most vital element when it comes to success because of the economic law we just discussed: Wants are always without limit— but the resources to satisfy wants and needs are always limited.

Keep this in mind the next time you believe that a lack of money is at the root of *all* your problems. Never forget this reality the next time you think that just having more money will make you successful. It won't. Instead, remember the facts taught by the social science of leadership and management: *no organization has all the money it wants or needs—no business, no family, no church, no school, no state, and no nation. And if people were given all the money they desired at any given point in time, they would still want more money.* That's what the leadership and management economic law teaches us.

Above all, we need to be aware that even if we have all the money we desire, we can still fail—and we will fail if we make poor choices. And if you focus totally on lack of money as the cause of all your problems, look out. Why? Because you may also start thinking in terms of what you "can't do" rather than what you can do. You may also start lowering expectations for yourself and those being led. Then various forms of ineffectiveness are sure to follow.

Is money important? Absolutely. Does money help make the job of leadership and management easier for teachers and administrators? Yes. However, with all the money you desire, you will fail with poor leadership and management. And, of course, it needs to be said: The less money a person, classroom, school, or district has, the better and more highly skilled the manager or leader must be. After all, the fewer the resources, the fewer bad choices and mistakes one can make. The wealthy can make more mistakes than the poor and survive. This reality applies at every level of leadership. The teacher of low-ability students can't waste time in the classroom. The understaffed administrator can't squander the time of secretaries, cooks, custodians, or teachers. Therefore, reality points out the overwhelming importance of leadership and management.

Effective leadership is the result of making good choices. And these good choices begin when effective leaders know the realities and know where they're going. This means they have goals and objectives—and know how they intend to reach their goals. They have workable plans and strategies and are able to persuade people to work—in addition to showing them the way to reach goals and achieve results. They function out of specific foundations and utilize the methods, techniques, and skills which enhance the success of those being led.

The way a teacher or administrator leads is important. And we all choose how we will lead. Make no mistake regarding this reality. But how we choose to lead in the classroom or the office determines our chances for success. It also determines the success of those we lead. How we choose to lead determines our leadership rewards. And it determines whether leading and being led are constructive, productive, and rewarding experiences. That's why the choice we make regarding how we will lead is vital to everyone. And we can't say, "I'm the only one who can get hurt by my choice." That's not true. We may get hurt, but so does the organization. Those we lead and those we work with get hurt as well.

When it comes to leading, we need to be aware that there are basically three kinds of leaders: the creators, the maintainers, and the destroyers. We need to know which one best describes us. And we need to be aware that, at times, we may be one or another—or all three.

THE CREATORS

The creators choose to take responsibility. They choose to make things happen. They choose to help people be successful—and they know those they lead are their biggest responsibility and biggest asset. They are action- and results-oriented. They work continually to generate interest, enthusiasm, and achievement.

Creators are both the receivers and the initiators of ideas, suggestions, aspirations, actions, and results. They are geared to meet the needs of students and help everyone get the work and mission of the school accomplished. They do so by choosing to be positive, proactive, progressive, mission-oriented people who try to maximize the strengths of those being led. They focus continually on helping people get better. The creators choose to position themselves to be the guidepost or point of reference for those being led. Creators make excellent teachers. They also make excellent principals and superintendents.

THE MAINTAINERS

The maintainers choose to function from a different platform. They can keep something going—and keep it going very well. But they can't and don't initiate much of anything on their own. And they can't add to, create, or improve without the input, approval, and assistance of others. Rather than continually trying to improve on what's being done, they simply choose to keep the same things going in the same way. They use last year's lesson plans and last year's tests. They operate a club or the school in the same way it has always been operated—regardless of the results of such functioning.

They make great assistants, but they don't do well as chief executive officers. They make great teachers' aides, but not very good classroom teachers. In fact, they may be great in support positions, but not good as the head of anything. However, we need to be aware that maintaining is a great asset—and maintainers fill a vital need in any organization.

We need maintainers. We must have them. It's one thing to start or create something—it's quite another to keep it going. We all know well that when we give maintainers an ongoing task or responsibility, it is in good hands. And if maintainers need help in improving a task or adding to a service, the leader can provide the input—and the maintainer will keep things going. Therefore, maintainers are a positive factor in the classroom, school, or district. But a close look will reveal that they are better *doers*, followers, and managers than leaders.

THE DESTROYERS

Fortunately, the destroyers are the only real danger. And some in leadership positions do choose to lead from this platform. They believe sorting out and eliminating will solve any problems being experienced. They are master "cutters"—of projects, tasks, opportunities, services, duties, responsibilities, and jobs. If students misbehave at a party, for instance, destroyers will vote to eliminate all school parties. If two students are talking too much in class, destroyers will impose a "no talking at any time" rule for everyone—or make the whole class stay after school.

These leaders never choose to create, build, or improve. They never choose to add service. They can't. In fact, they usually don't think too much about what students, teachers, administrators, or the school can or should be doing. Rather, they only choose to think about what the school or the staff shouldn't be doing, shouldn't have to do, doesn't need to do, or can't do.

The destroyers choose to believe that *not doing* is the answer to all problems. And they try to convince others that "cutting" is the best course of action. Unfortunately, they will wake up one morning and find out that they—as well as the part of the organization they are leading—aren't doing very much of anything anymore. Why? Termination has been their approach to leadership.

CHOOSING THE RIGHT STANCE

To be a successful leader, one must choose to be a creator as well as a maintainer. And there are times and situations where we must serve well in both roles. And of course, there are times when we will be required to eliminate and discard the old for the new—and something that doesn't work for something that does. Yet, we need to know that there is a big difference between "making changes" and being a destroyer. If we have any experience at all, the destroyers in our ranks are easy to identify.

Success in leadership is achieved by reaching one's potential and helping others do the same. First and foremost, however, one must be able to be a creator and maintainer. A

leader must choose to identify the needs and acquire the abilities to make things happen—
and cause others to want to do the same.

A CHECKLIST FOR UNDERSTANDING AND APPLICATION

Resources to
Satisfy Wants
Are Always
Limited

1. From experience, relate how the wants of (students) (educators) (parents) are without limit.
2. Because resources are always limited, share choices you are faced with making.
3. Between the two factors, money and management, discuss why management is the more important.
4. What kind of leader best describes you?
6. Share insights pertaining to your role as a maintainer.
6. Share insights pertaining to your role as a creator.
7. Discuss examples of functioning as a destroyer.

5

21ST CENTURY LEADERSHIP REQUIRES BLENDING

It's not uncommon to hear an educator say, "Being a teacher, principal, or superintendent isn't the same as it used to be." And one may quickly add, "It's hard to know what you should do or can do, or what people will let you do." This perception is causing many teachers, principals, and superintendents both frustration and confusion. It is also making many leaders "back away" as well as "watch their step" as they approach their functional responsibilities in a classroom, school, or district. Yet, if we stand back and examine what has really happened with the nature of leadership in the past decade, we may see that our functions as leaders remain clear. Too, we may see that the change in the nature of leadership is not indicating that one approach is out and another approach is in. Rather, it's reflecting a blending of two approaches: the new approach and the traditional approach. This means, of course, that we can't hold on to old ways exclusively—or choose only the new approaches. Let's discuss this fact, because choosing one leadership approach over the other will surely alter our effectiveness in the years to come. It may also cause our demise.

THE NEW APPROACHES
REVEAL SPECIFIC COMMONALTIES

There's no question that the new approaches to leadership are revealed by shifts in attitudes, actions, and sources of power. The fact that a shift is occurring is evidenced by the fact that leadership today is called by many names. Some call it *cooperative* or *collaborative leadership*. Others call the new approach *democratic leadership*. Others call it *participatory* or *stakeholder leadership* and stress the need for initiating feelings of ownership. All these terms are used to describe and define both a vision of leadership and a process of practicing leadership which is taking place in many organizations in many communities.

These new names or descriptions reflecting the new nature of leadership have some similarities. There's the recognition that within the organization a broad scope of diverse individuals with a wide range of talents are being led. All approaches or strategies include the recognition that a wide assortment of needs must be met. The new approaches all include those being led taking part in identifying needs, developing plans, making decisions, and solving problems. And all these new approaches give special consideration to the belief that students, parents, and employees should participate in activities that affect them, their work, and their lives. This means, of course, the new approaches to leadership recognize that factors such as varied needs, interests, and priorities must be sorted out and worked through until agreement is reached and everyone can have ownership in creating acceptable solutions.

The evidence of this new nature of leadership abounds in many schools. We have advisory groups for every conceivable interest of parents and citizens in our community. We use staff committees and councils for a wide range of tasks. And the need for a bond election will cause the board of education to turn to the new leadership approach very quickly to gain citizen involvement and support. In many cases, the new participatory, collaborative, or democratic approach is very effective. But with other leadership tasks and responsibilities, it may not work at all. Without question, the teacher or administrator who tries to employ these new approaches in every area of responsibility in a classroom, school, or district is not likely to find much success. And the truth of the matter is that many leaders are trying to employ these new leadership approaches in all that they do. Unfortunately, such a leadership stance will not prove successful in getting the work of the classroom, school, and district accomplished.

THE TRADITIONAL APPROACH
IS STILL WIDELY USED

The traditional approach to leadership is one we all know well. And a close look will reveal that, while the new approaches are being uncovered, discovered, understood, and practiced, the traditional approach—even with an assortment of individual leader styles and variations—is the most widely accepted and practiced in classrooms and schools as well as in business and industry.

Make no mistake: Traditional leadership is not outdated. It is not passé. It is defined by specific characteristics which are held by those in authority—those who have the position, and those who, by law and function, have the responsibility, the authority, and the power, and are held accountable for the success of those being led in the classroom, school, or district. The traditional approach relies heavily on the top-down method for leading individuals, groups, and organizations. In recent years, however, the traditional approach has added caring and consideration and stepped away from the hard-nosed, autocratic practices of the past. And it's unlikely that these past practices will ever be acceptable again.

Traditional leadership is found in most organizations today. Because of its reliance on people in positions of authority, this form of leadership exists in all line-chart, bureaucratic organizations. Business, industry, educational institutions, and religious institutions continue to use traditional leadership. Likewise, large corporations, as well as state and national government, use traditional leadership more than the new approaches. Today, most local governments continue to use traditional leadership even though the number of local governments considering and applying the new approaches is growing.

EACH APPROACH HAS ADVANTAGES
AND DISADVANTAGES

Fortunately, most leaders are looking for better and more effective ways to lead. At this point, however, it should be easy to see that the need is not to choose one approach over the other, but to perfect the use of both. The teacher or administrator who is remaining fixed on the traditional approach will feel enormous pressures in the future. And the teacher or administrator who chooses the new leadership approach and abandons the traditional method entirely will encounter serious problems as well. After all, the new approach works best for some things and situations—and not at all for others. And where the traditional approach will run into a brick wall, the new approach will open doors. Each approach has practical and common sense advantages and obvious disadvantages. In truth, both approaches are appropriate and effective in the right place at the right time—and with the right issue or problem. And, in any given situation, one approach has the best chance to succeed while the other has a higher probability for failure.

When a decision must be made quickly and with certainty—traditional leadership must be employed or the results could be disastrous. Issues relating to safety, legality, and budgetary matters all fall within this realm. If there is a fire in the building, it is not the time to call a meeting to come to consensus on what should be done.

We may use traditional leadership more in the classroom with students, but the new approach more when working with the student council. Likewise, using the traditional approach to leadership exclusively may be viewed by patrons of the district as misdirected or ignorant in a school or district with a varied socioeconomic public. And traditional leadership may not work well for solving complex problems in which the solutions to problems must be created. And, of course, we may find countless situations in which a combination of both approaches is advisable.

CAUSING OTHERS TO WANT APPLIES TO BOTH LEADERSHIP DEFINITIONS

An examination will show that the leadership change in concept and approach simply reflects the changing conditions of the postindustrial age. The meaning and nature of work and achieving high productivity as well as satisfaction with work are undergoing a major change. The expected competition for jobs in the 21st century has aroused new concerns, and the new shift in leadership perception and practice reflects the attitudes of an information-based, service-oriented, and highly competitive work society.

As we learn more and more about leading people—and as the workplace continues to change—we can expect more changes in leadership. We will use the leadership approach that best suits the people, the situation, and the work at hand. We will use the leadership approach that fits the opportunities and the needs at hand. We will use the approach that produces the highest productivity and effectiveness as well as the highest satisfaction for the leader and those being led, and which meets the needs of those the institution serves. Therefore, leaders will use both leadership approaches—and the blend of both approaches will be regarded as "true" leadership.

As we learn about the new approaches to leadership, we would be wise not to forget what we know about traditional leadership. In the process, however, we need to remember that our task remains: to cause others to want what we are doing to get the work of the classroom, the school, and the district accomplished. This objective should guide our decision to choose the new or the traditional. Remember, our task as leaders is to arouse, motivate, persuade, convince, and move people to higher and higher levels of performance. This is not likely to happen with students, teachers, or administrators who do not receive a high degree of stimulation and satisfaction from their work, the people they work with, those being served, and their leaders.

A CHECKLIST FOR UNDERSTANDING AND APPLICATION

1. What tasks are best achieved by the traditional leadership approach?

2. Which approach—new or traditional—do you like best? Which do you use the most?
3. Discuss the (advantages) (disadvantages) of each approach.
4. Discuss how leadership has changed since you began your career.
5. How (do you) (can you) use both approaches?
6. How does caring and consideration for those being served play a role in both leadership approaches?

6

EFFECTIVENESS REQUIRES MORE THAN ACTION

Unfortunately, not very many people want theory. And not very many want philosophy. They just want a plan. Above all, they want action and results. This reality presents a problem when it comes to developing effective leaders. If we want to be successful in a leadership position, we would be wise to embrace a positive and proactive attitude toward theory and philosophy—and to do so promptly. Because of our "conditioning," however, this may not be an easy achievement. After all, we are all products of our environment and our experiences.

We live in an "instant" world. Today, things are fast and quick and, most of all, easy. That's the way we want it. We have instant availability of all kinds of food in the grocery store. We have fast food places to eat. We have instant replay, instant credit, and daily interest on our money. We have cleaners that dissolve dirt instantly, cameras that develop pictures in seconds, and express mail that will deliver mail anywhere by 10:30 a.m. the day after we send it. Indeed, we are people who have been "programmed" to want and expect instant service, instant gratification, and immediate success. In other words, we want it now, not tomorrow or next week or next year. We want to go directly to the bottom line.

PLANS AND ACTIONS ARE A PROCESS

When it comes to leadership and management, instant wants can mean big trouble because we can want to make plans quickly and easily. We can want those being led to accept and take action on our plans instantly. And we may get darned impatient if we don't get plans, implementation, action, and successful results in a short period of time. What we need to know, however, is how to get acceptance, action, and achievement as teachers and administrators in the classroom, the school, and the district.

Implementation of plans and progress toward results in leadership and management come via a process. And this process begins with sound objectives and a solid foundation of professional theories and philosophical beliefs which both the leader and those being led can accept, believe in, and take action to achieve. And these theories and philosophical beliefs must fulfill the responsibility and mission of meeting the needs of students and the work of the school. Our beginning, therefore, always starts with our philosophical foundation, not just with a plan of action.

Without question, we need a professional philosophy. We must have the leadership theory and professional beliefs. And we need these foundations more than the average person thinks. Our philosophical beliefs are the vital core values the leader, those being led, and those being served must hold before we begin our plan. Yet, too many people discount or avoid theory and the philosophical foundations which facilitate success. It is a mistake.

That's precisely why foundations are featured heavily in this book. That's why professional and ethical foundations are being combined with methods, techniques, and skills. Over the years, your plans will change as the needs of students and society change. They must. But your professional foundations will remain. In truth, your foundations must become more and more embedded in your being. And you will find that you must live by your foundations. In addition, the ingenuity, ability, competency, character, credibility, creativity, and insight of your plans must result from an agreement between your foundations and the tenets of education and sound leadership and management practices necessary to be highly successful. It is out of these foundations that you begin "causing others to want your leadership."

All leadership and management studies should contain both the philosophical and the practical—and for very good reason. The philosophical is the foundation. The practical is the applied. One without the other renders the other less valuable. With only the philosophical, you have the foundation, but you still don't have the ways and means regarding what to do and how to do it for the right reason and in the right way. With just the practical, you may simply have the easiest way or a bag of tricks. This may seem valuable, but it's not. Without being backed by foundations, techniques can be gimmicks or manipulations. People don't like to be manipulated. Most won't be—and few people can be manipulated by a leader over the long term.

NO PHILOSOPHY MEANS NO PLAN OR ACHIEVEMENT

Remember, without both the philosophy and the theory, you really don't have any meaningful professional stance for functioning, much less a defensible position when you are challenged, questioned, or attacked—or when you make a mistake. And without a good stance or position, you can't have a good plan. It's impossible. And having no plan means having no purposeful direction or meaningful achievement—all of which makes following you as a leader very difficult, if not impossible, for intelligent and competent people. After all, without a philosophical and theoretical foundation, you have no basis for your plan, your proclaimed goals and objectives, or your proposed action.

Without a strong philosophical base, the truth of the matter is that you're likely to go where the events of the day point you. You'll hang your hat on many popular ideas and goals that have little substance. You'll wander—usually toward more failures than toward success. In the process, you are apt to blame others for not following your lead. Yet, if you don't have philosophical and theoretical foundations, people have no reason to follow you because they don't have the core values to share with you and your objectives. And not many intelligent people are prone to follow blindly.

Without a leadership and management philosophy, you'll never develop a passion for your work or your mission or help others do the same. You may love math, but not get many students to love it with you. You may develop a pet project, but teachers will seldom share your affection. Without philosophy, you may not develop a passion for either the excellence or achievement which leads to success and happiness for yourself and those you lead. And this is what leadership is all about.

It is your philosophical beliefs about education which are the foundations that allow you to think, create, and carry out your hopes, dreams, and plans—and help others do the same. It is also your philosophical foundations or beliefs which allow you to know when to reject plans for the right reasons.

Skills are important. Methods, techniques, approaches, tactics, and wits are vital. Yet, your professional foundations precede the development of these necessary leadership characteristics. Without foundations, you can't even defend what you have done or want to do. Without foundations, you won't hold up in difficult times—and we all have difficult times. Without foundations, you will inevitably make big mistakes—and you'll be without a meaningful defense with each error.

It Begins with Our Beliefs

OUR BELIEFS ARE THE INTELLECT
UPON WHICH WE THINK AND ACT

Foundations are our beliefs. They are the intellect upon which we think, choose, decide, and stand. They are the basis upon which we act. The foundations include the tenets of education, the purpose and objectives of education and schools, being student-centered always, what we know about teaching and learning, what we know about human behavior, and the laws and principles of leadership and management in relation to getting the work and mission of the school accomplished. Once we understand and accept the foundations of leadership and management and they become a functional part of us, we are prepared to make plans and lead in agreement with sound educational and management practices which meet the needs of students. When this occurs, we have a much greater probability for success and we lessen our chances of failure.

Most of the failures I see in schools, as well as in business and industry, are not ability problems. They are foundation problems. Foundations prepare us to do the right thing, for the right reason, in the right way. We actually need foundation programming for a very valid reason: We are bombarded from every direction to act wisely, make good decisions, and lead people every minute of the day. And the bombardment comes from students, teachers, parents, staff members, boards of education, interest groups, citizens, and even the government. That's why we are always looking for quick answers and fast solutions. We are continually searching for the best "cookbook." And we should. After all, we have to make plans. We have to take action. We have to get results. In the process, however, we need to know whether or not our plans and actions are based on the right footings so that we can make the right choices and get the best outcomes. We need to know immediately if our plans and actions have any substance. We need to know just as quickly if our plans are in agreement with the reason we have schools in the first place.

FOUNDATIONS AND BELIEFS
COME FIRST

If our theory and philosophical foundations and beliefs aren't developed first, we can't think properly, much less make good plans or take appropriate action. And this applies to teachers, principals, superintendents, cooks, custodians, aides, librarians, board members,

33

and everyone else involved in the process of educating students. Therefore, we can never let ourselves say, "Don't tell me why; just tell me what." We can never allow ourselves to say, "I don't want the theory; just give me the application." We need to get to the point, but for the right reasons. That's why our philosophical base comes first. Our philosophical base is what gives plans and actions the best chance of success in both the short and long term. And it is our philosophical foundation which allows people to provide input as well as to buy in to and follow our plans. Without a philosophical foundation, our leadership effort is not likely to be very successful. We need to ask ourselves at least six questions:

1. What do I believe?
2. What do I, or can I, stand for?
3. What do I believe a teacher and administrator should be?
4. What do I expect from my leadership?
5. What can others expect from my leadership?
6. What needs should I be meeting for those being led?

Without question, we must know the answers to these questions—and continue developing as a leader so that we can continue to give better answers. To put it bluntly, when people lack foundations, they flounder and fail. They can't lead themselves, much less anyone else. And they usually think that they have all the right answers. In truth, however, they have all the wrong questions. They almost always put the cart before the horse. They do the wrong things, for the wrong reasons, in the wrong way—and they don't even know it. But everyone else does.

WHAT DO YOU BELIEVE?

The question remains: What do you believe? I probably believe in the same things you do. And so do the vast majority of the personnel in your school. And it is out of these beliefs that we acquire the foundations to lead—and cause others to want our leadership.

For instance, I believe it takes a quality teacher to give students a quality education. I also believe that it takes a good principal to have a good school—and a good superintendent to have a good district. I don't think you can have a good school without a good principal—or a good district without a good superintendent.

And I believe all kids can learn. I believe people can change and that all people have a gift. I believe professional growth is a necessity—and that we must all grow at least 15 percent each year to stay even with last year. I think that, without continuous professional growth over the years, the master teacher of ten years ago would not do very well in today's classroom.

I believe that, as teachers and administrators, we are managers. We are also leaders. It is important that, as managers and leaders, we know what we believe—and then lead in agreement with those beliefs. And we must never lead in contradiction to those beliefs. If we do, we should expect failure. We shouldn't expect others to follow us. Our professionals beliefs are where our management and leadership begin. This is our starting point. I believe we would be wise not to listen to anyone who says it isn't.

What do you believe? If you want results to come from your leadership, you need to know.

A CHECKLIST FOR UNDERSTANDING
AND APPLICATION

1. What do I believe?
2. What do I, or can I, stand for?
3. What do I believe a teacher and administrator should be?
4. What do I expect from my leadership?
5. What can others expect from my leadership?
6. Discuss why everything we do should be student-centered.

*It Begins
with Our
Beliefs*

ONLY WHEN OTHERS ARE SUCCESSFUL CAN WE COUNT OURSELVES AS SUCCESSFUL

To be a successful leader, one must produce successful outcomes or results, of course. After all, the only meaningful measurement of leadership is effectiveness. Therefore, we cannot say we are successful if we aren't producing results. This may seem obvious, but many teachers regard themselves as good teachers even though many of their students aren't doing well. And many administrators think they are doing a fine job even though there aren't significant results to support this belief.

If a teacher or administrator intends to lead for results, one of the first realities that must be accepted is that those being led may or may not know how to be successful. Adopting this belief and proceeding accordingly is the only practical approach a leader can take to lead successfully. Therefore, if you want results, it's best to approach any task by saying, "If those being led knew how to be successful, they would be—and it's my job to teach them how."

To understand the necessity for this leadership approach, all you need to do is look around. You'll arrive at some simple, but absolute, conclusions if you do. You'll see that some people, including students and educators alike, are already very successful—but some aren't. And because of their attitudes, beliefs, and lack of skills—some never will be. Rather, their present condition will continue unless you teach them precisely how to achieve and be successful. In the process, you must also teach those who are successful how to be more successful. You have to raise the level of success experienced by all because you can't be successful unless those being led are successful. And the measure of your success *is* determined by the level of success of those you lead. Unfortunately, leaders don't always take such a course for a wide variety of reasons, including overestimating the ability of those being led.

A LEADER CANNOT MAKE ANY ASSUMPTIONS ABOUT COMPETENCY

As the appointed leaders, teachers and administrators often make assumptions based on what they believe ought to be so rather than what is so. For instance, we assume that a student knows how to be successful because his or her parents are successful. We assume that because a student has intelligent and highly motivated parents, the child is intelligent and should be highly motivated too. Maybe yes, maybe no. Or a teacher believes that because a student comes from a wealthy family, he or she is, therefore, very happy and has had many advantages. Again, this is not necessarily so.

*Only When
Others Are
Successful
Can We Count
Ourselves as
Successful*

Likewise, we assume that because a teacher or administrator has a bachelor's degree, a master's degree, or a Ph.D., he or she is highly skilled and professionally competent. Not necessarily so. We may assume that because a teacher has ten years of classroom experience, he or she knows how to relate to and teach students. Maybe yes, maybe no.

Administrators often believe teachers know *how* to be successful—and will be successful if they so choose. Teachers may believe the same about students. Likewise, we assume that because those being led have years of experience in a job, whether it's cleaning rooms, preparing meals, counseling parents, teaching students, or administering a school, they know how to be successful even when they are not experiencing success. Yet, these are all leadership assumptions—many of which are without substance.

What we need to remember is this: If the vast majority of people really knew how to be successful, the vast majority would be. But most people don't know how to achieve. That's why teaching those being led how to be successful is a prerequisite when it comes to leading for results in the classroom and from the office. Remember, included in the definition of *leadership* is "showing the way."

Rather than concern ourselves with whether someone is or is not motivated to do a job, we must first keep in mind that being successful requires two foundations of expertise: the knowledge to do a job and the attitudes necessary for doing it successfully. One without the other does not qualify anyone for knowing how to be successful—and it's a leadership error to believe otherwise. Therefore, when we observe or hear about someone not being successful, we can only arrive at one viable assumption: He or she doesn't know how. The second assumption we must make is: He or she must be taught. The third assumption: Reteaching foundations, information, values, attitudes, and skills is necessary.

Teachers are more apt to understand and practice this leadership necessity with students than principals and superintendents are to practice it with the staff. After all, *teach*, *test*, *reteach*, and *retest* have long been leadership responsibilities of classroom teachers with students, but they have not been common practices of administrators with teachers.

THREE MOTIVATIONAL REALITIES
FOR BEING UNSUCCESSFUL

As the appointed leader, you'll also find big contradictions between what those being led have learned about being successful and what they will actually do to find and experience success. Too, you'll find huge variances between what people would like very much to have—and what they'll do to get it. Mostly, though, you'll find that there are three common motivational realities that prevent those being led from being successful.

The first consists of past negative experiences that actually control people's attitudes and behaviors. Because of the heavy influence of a negative past which governs their thinking and action in the present, these people are programmed to fail. The second reality is a lack of training. Third, misconceptions, misjudgments, and ill-advised beliefs get in the way and prevent people from adopting beliefs and practices which facilitate success. A leader must always take all three of these realities into account in order to lead for results.

For instance, a person may have volunteered in the past, experienced a big failure or been made fun of and, therefore, made up his or her mind never to volunteer again. Others may have had a teacher or boss who was unfair or who mistreated them, so they have vowed never to trust any boss again. Others may have extended themselves with a classmate or colleague and got burned, so they won't do it again. The point is this: People bring negative experiences to a job as a student or a worker—or even as a leader. These experiences are their ever-present ghosts. And these ghosts not only determine and control their beliefs, but their actions as well. And these ghosts continually get in the way of their success.

To lead for results, you must teach people how to get by their ghosts. If you can't help them learn to get beyond their negative past, many people will hold on to their ghosts for as long as they live. They'll operate out of these negative and ill-advised foundations which will prevent them from being successful.

WITHOUT TRAINING, OTHERS WILL GIVE THE WRONG ADVICE

You can go to the cafeteria, halls, playgrounds, or the rest room and find negative students giving other students negative advice which is counterproductive to success. You'll even see negative students urging classmates to break a rule, misbehave, skip school, or not study. Likewise, you can go into a teachers' lounge and listen to negative teachers advising other teachers on what to think and what to do. And the advice they are giving often includes what these fellow teachers *ought not to do* for students, administrators, and the work of the school.

Teachers delivering this negative advice really believe what they're telling other teachers to think and do. They truly believe they are offering sound advice. So do the negative students. Yet, these students or educators are seldom those who are highly productive or finding very much satisfaction in their work. And if others listen to them, accept what they say, and function accordingly, they, too, will be guaranteed low productivity and dissatisfaction. Indeed, the listeners will learn precisely how *not* to be successful in school, whether they are students or educators.

When it comes to achieving goals and getting effective results, leaders must be aware that there is a constant need to teach those being led how to be successful. And all of these teachings need continuous reinforcement. It is a never-ending task. In the process, a leader must know that his or her lessons may be contradicted or pooh-poohed by co-workers, family, and friends.

To be successful, appointed leaders must not stop leading and teaching. And they must not make any assumptions about what those being led know and don't know. They must not arrive at any conclusions about what those being led will or won't do to be successful. Rather, appointed leaders should adopt a tenet of leading for results: They must continually show the way by teaching people how to be successful—and continually reinforce and reteach these messages. This teaching must, without exception, include professional foundations. It must include both the theory and the practice that facilitates success. It must include both attitudes and skills needed for success and satisfaction as a student or as a professional educator. This is the best approach for making stars out of those being led—and being effective as a leader.

A CHECKLIST FOR UNDERSTANDING AND APPLICATION

1. What assumptions should be avoided by a leader?
2. What assumptions should we make as a leader?
3. What bad experiences of the past are adversely affecting your future?
4. What ghosts affect (students) (teachers) (administrators)?
5. What must those being led be taught in order for them to be successful in the (classroom) (school) (district)?

6. How do you intend to teach them?
7. How can you make this teaching continuous and ongoing?

*Only When
Others Are
Successful
Can We Count
Ourselves as
Successful*

FOUR COMPETENCIES NEEDED TO BE EFFECTIVE LEADERS

There are four areas of knowledge you must have to even begin to be a successful leader. First, you must know yourself—intimately. Second, you must know your people—inside and out. Third, you must know your job completely. Fourth, you must know the laws and principles as they relate to leading yourself, leading others, and causing them to want your leadership. Extensive knowledge in these four areas is the best preparation one can have to become and remain a successful leader.

FIRST, WE MUST KNOW OURSELVES

Leadership competency begins with knowing ourselves very, very well. What we know about ourselves, coupled with how we feel about ourselves as human beings, as professional educators, and as leaders, is of paramount importance to our effectiveness. Many of us learned the teaching "love thy neighbor as thyself." In truth, however, we may have learned the "love thy neighbor" part the best—and overlooked or even shied away from the "as thyself" part. Yet, it is the whole teaching of these words that has worth and meaning to us and those we lead—and for good reason. We can't and probably won't do much for others unless we feel pretty good about ourselves. Love, like charity, begins at home.

Knowing ourselves includes recognizing that all of us are actually three people in one: what we *are*, what we *think* we are, and what *others think* we are. What we think of ourselves is very important, but not more important than what we really are, of course. And a close look will reveal that, as leaders in the classroom or school, we often try to operate out of what *we are* or what *we think we are*. In leadership and management situations, however, the *truth* is what others think we are. That's right, truth in a leadership situation is *whatever* those being led believe to be so. This is the *truth* we have to concern ourselves with—and deal with—as we lead people. We must feel very good about ourselves to be able to make adjustments and handle and deal with this reality of leadership and management.

Therefore, *what others think we are* is the most important factor we must deal with in leading others. If our students or staff think we are unfair or that we're incompetent, arrogant, or a poor communicator, it doesn't really make any difference whether we are or not. We must deal with—and trust as reality—the perception of those being led. Remember, right and wrong and good and bad are immaterial. What those being led *think* is the primary issue when it comes to functioning successfully as a leader. And we can't say, "They're wrong" and forget the issue—even if they are wrong in their perception. Neither can we make long lists which prove them wrong and then discount what they think. Rather, we must accept student or staff perceptions as the *truths which count*—and take action to change these perceptions of us. We must know ourselves and feel good about ourselves to operate from this platform.

As leaders, we must also know ourselves well because we are all the result of our experiences—past, present, and anticipated. Whether we were a poor child or a wealthy one, our past experiences as human beings can dictate that we bring our *past* to our jobs in some way. Whether we love our work or hate our work, we bring the *present* to our job. And if we are looking forward to retirement, the *future* and the experiences we anticipate may prevent us from doing the job today. And we must recognize that we all have expectations, prejudices, idiosyncrasies, and hang-ups as the result of our experiences. That's why we must know ourselves intimately. If we don't, we may impose our weak side or dark side on those we lead. If we don't know ourselves, we may abuse our positional power and victimize rather than lead those in our charge in the right ways for the right reasons. If we don't know ourselves, we may not know what changes or adjustments we need to make to cause others to want our leadership. That's why knowing ourselves is a prerequisite for becoming and remaining an effective leader.

SECOND, WE MUST KNOW OUR PEOPLE

To lead effectively, we must also know our people—thoroughly. We may not be psychiatrists or psychologists, but we must be behaviorists and know human behavior. We must know what makes our people "tick." We must know their strengths and weaknesses. We must know what turns them on and what turns them off. Without such knowledge, we won't be able to motivate people with the right ideas, the right work, and the right methods or techniques. We won't have the right expectations. Rather, we're apt to try to lead by treating all people the same. Worse, we probably won't make any adjustments to cause others to want our leadership, because we won't know what adjustments to make with each person we are leading.

We need to know human behavior and those we lead because people are our number-one responsibility and our number-one asset in the classroom, the school, and the district. It's hard to help people win if we don't know them or know what motivates them as human beings. And it's hard to get the work of the classroom, school, or district accomplished if we don't know the strengths and weaknesses of the people doing the work.

We must know people because the day of "We'll do it my way because I'm the boss" is over. It's gone—forever. So is the myth that the higher we go in position or title, the more others must adjust to us and follow our commands and demands. It doesn't work that way. In fact, the opposite is really the truth. The higher people go in title, rank, position, or function, the more knowledge of human behavior they must have. The higher they go in position, the more methods, techniques, and skills they must know and be able to employ to get people to do what they want and need them to do.

We must know those being led individually, because we don't lead groups. We lead individuals. And this is done by acquiring a thorough understanding of the primary needs, secondary needs, and people motivators on an individual basis—and for good reason. We need this knowledge to lead people. We need this knowledge to know how to engage people, meet their needs, and cause them to want our leadership.

As leaders, we are in a people profession. We have to lead people to get work accomplished and to experience success. And we have many different kinds of people to lead: students, parents, teachers, principals, superintendents, cooks, custodians, nurses, bus drivers, aides, and many others. If we don't understand human behavior and know those we lead, the chances of our being an exceptional leader in the classroom, the school, or the district are very slim.

THIRD, WE MUST KNOW OUR JOB

As we said earlier, there are two sides to every job in a school—for leaders and followers alike: the technical side and the people side. We must be highly competent on both sides of our job if we intend to be successful. Unfortunately, schools often spend 85 percent or more of their budgets on employee salaries—and less than 1 percent on continuous training to increase the value of the school's most important investment: the faculty and staff. It really doesn't make much sense. After all, it's a fact of life that teachers and administrators must grow continually if they intend to survive, much less find exceptional success.

In any job, we are continually faced with the decision to concentrate our efforts, expertise, and resources on either things or people. We often focus on things because they are tangible. We can see and touch them. And things are so much easier to manage. Yet, the vast majority of the material things we use in schools come and go. They get used up or worn out. But people stay. It may not be the same people—but they're still people. And the new people who come into our classrooms and schools will be more *like* than *unlike* people of the past who worked in our school or studied in our classrooms. We need to ponder this reality if we think getting rid of a couple of people will solve all our problems.

The students who come to our classes next year will be more *like* than *unlike* those we have this year. Why? Because all people have the same primary and secondary needs. All people have the same motivators, even though their motivators vary in degrees of intensity. We need to remember this fact the next time we think our problems would be over if we could get one particular student out of our class. When people leave, they are replaced by other people—and these people will be more like than unlike those who left. We must have equal competency on both sides of our jobs—the technical side and the people side—if we intend to be highly effective leaders.

FOURTH, WE MUST KNOW THE LAWS AND PRINCIPLES

We also must know the laws and principles of leadership and management as they relate to leading ourselves—and leading people. The value of the laws and principles cannot be overstated. If you want to play the game, you've got to know the rules. The laws are the rules of the game. They should be seen as guideposts to use in every leadership situation. They are our leadership predictors or forecasters. They tell us what will usually happen to us as well as those we lead if these laws and principles are violated. They continually give us insight, vision, and direction—even when we are bombarded with a hundred different urgings or requests. The laws help us to act wisely because they apply in every situation—normal or abnormal. They also apply in every instance of decision making and problem solving and helping people move to higher levels of performance. The laws give a leader consistency in thinking and effort. They always agree with sound teaching and management practices. They give constant direction that is in agreement with leading and functioning in agreement with the work and mission of the organization. Better yet, the laws give a conditioned response in the many problem situations we face. The laws give us a support system to follow continually—and a way to take the trial and error out of leading.

The laws are objective, not subjective. They reveal the normalcy of people and their behavior. Therefore, we are less likely to believe those we lead are bad and are more likely to see them as human beings who have limitations and shortcomings—and then have the perspective to respond accordingly. Equally important, these laws govern all of us in leadership positions: students, teachers, staff, and administrators. When these laws are taught to those being led, everyone benefits because we can all operate with the same foundations, values, and opportunities for success.

The laws and principles are the foundation for effective leadership practices. My contribution was simply recognizing, defining, and labeling the laws and principles so that leaders can use them easily and purposefully. Yet, I can't take much credit for them because I honestly believe they are natural laws. Therefore, I don't feel as though I created them. Rather, I just brought them into an identifiable form with a practical application in the classroom, school, and district.

In truth, these laws and principles of leadership and management are just like economic laws. Nobody created the economic laws. It's just the way things work. And so it is with the laws and principles written in this book. However, in successful schools, teachers, principals, and superintendents are applying these laws whether they know it or not—naturally. In places that are failing, leaders are almost always doing exactly the opposite of what these laws teach.

These are the benefits of the laws to every teacher, principal, and superintendent. This is why every leader ought to know these laws and principles as they relate to leading themselves and leading others. When they do, leading is made easier, and following a leader becomes a more productive and satisfying experience as well.

A CHECKLIST FOR UNDERSTANDING AND APPLICATION

1. How does the past, present, and future affect you as a leader?
2. How does the past, present, and future affect those you lead?
3. What adjustments have you had to make because of past or present life experience?
4. Share examples of why "truth" in a leadership position is what those being led perceive.
5. Discuss the statement: You don't lead groups; you lead individuals.

THE VITAL THREE FOR UNDERSTANDING HUMAN BEHAVIOR

Just as we are unique and different as human beings, we are amazingly alike. As educators, we should know this reality better than most. As classroom teachers, we understand individual differences better than most people because we deal with differences in students every day. We've studied and practiced individualized instruction. We've been trained to be sensitive and knowledgeable about the *whole* student. We have been and are committed to meeting the needs of every student in the classroom.

When we leave the classroom to become administrators, stepping into an administrative position should only broaden our scope, because we are now dealing with more people—and different kinds of people. In many ways, we only need to apply what we learned and practiced in the classroom with students to the task of working with students, teachers, parents, citizens, fellow administrators, staff, and others.

After all, specific needs are the foundation of our similarities and dictate human behavior. For a teacher or administrator, knowing these needs is imperative to effective leadership. They make human behavior both understandable and predictable. To write an entire book on the laws and principles of leadership and management as related to the task of being a teacher or administrator without devoting time to this vital aspect of human behavior would be like going fishing without a hook. We would, in truth, neither hear the right questions nor find the right answers when it comes to causing others to want what we are doing as a leader.

While studying the laws and principles, you will see a linkage with human behavior. Inherent in the laws are all the human needs. That's why the laws and principles work.

THE PRIMARY AND SECONDARY NEEDS... AND THE INDIVIDUAL MOTIVATORS

Psychology has traditionally classified human behavior into two major categories: primary and secondary needs. I have added a third group: the individual motivators. A clear understanding of the identification, meaning, and implication of these needs is vital for any teacher or administrator who truly wants to motivate and lead people effectively and make both leading and being led a productive and rewarding experience.

Many leaders will confess that motivating people is not an easy task—and add that motivating some people is extremely difficult. And many have asked, "How do we motivate all of our people?" The answer: Via the primary and secondary needs. We also need to know that everyone we lead *has* the ability to motivate as well as to be motivated. That's why we should never say that certain students or some educators aren't motivated. All our people are motivated. Some people just aren't motivated to do what we want them to do.

For instance, some students are motivated to watch TV, drive cars, comb their hair, or play games—but not to study. Some educators are motivated more by Saturdays and Sundays—as well as by June, July, and August than by the school day. They are motivated, however, and our task is to lead them in the direction we want them to go. That's why we should never say those being led are not motivated or do not have the ability to be motivated. They do. Accepting this belief is important because some educators do not believe that one can motivate another human being. They believe a person can motivate only himself or herself. However, this is simply not true. If it were, none of us would ever be influenced or inspired by anyone else. Without question, finding the individual need and meeting it in each individual will get the results we want as leaders.

Remember, all of these needs are part of and within us all. It is only their arrangement in terms of individual intensities and priorities that varies in each of us. Some of these wants and needs are more significant in some people than others. And some of these needs are the driving forces in our lives. As leaders, we have the tasks of knowing our people and finding the wants and needs within them—and making sure we do not miss the meaning of a need. Then, we must use these needs to get high levels of effort and achievement. Before looking at these needs individually, let's look at them collectively to aid understanding.

PRIMARY NEEDS
(Physiological and Unlearned)

1.	Hunger	5.	Rest
2.	Thirst	6.	Escape From Pain
3.	Sex/Sexuality	7.	Eliminate Waste
4.	Air		

SECONDARY NEEDS
(Psychological and Learned)

1.	Gregariousness	5.	Achievement
2.	Aggression	6.	Power
3.	Affiliation	7.	Status
4.	Inquisitiveness	8.	Autonomy

PEOPLE MOTIVATORS

1.	Personal Gain	6.	Convenience
2.	Prestige	7.	The Desire to Avoid Fear
3.	Pleasure	8.	New Experiences
4.	Imitation	9.	Love/Caring
5.	Security		

I suspect that you can think of a student, parent, teacher, secretary, counselor, cook, custodian, nurse, and administrator and see which needs are more intensely revealed in some than in others. You might realize that if you had tried to address and fulfill these needs in order to get work accomplished, you might have been more successful in any effort to influence these people. Too, you might realize that by recognizing and meeting these needs for someone, you could have changed a negative attitude or situation into a positive one—and caused someone to follow your leadership. You are probably right in your assumption. That's how vital these motives are to leadership efforts.

These needs should be your first consideration in leading people. Ignoring or fighting these needs as a leader will almost always result in degrees of difficulty and ineffectiveness—or failure. Remember, people do not give up the needs they hold simply because you disapprove or think their needs aren't important—or because you try to prevent them from meeting the needs. Rather, when needs cannot be met with you, those being led will look elsewhere for satisfaction. In the process, they are likely to ignore and reject you—and your leadership.

PARAMOUNT TO ALL RELATIONSHIPS

An awareness of these needs is paramount to all leadership motivation and human relationships efforts. This principle applies to every person—those we reach as well as those we do not. That's important because even if we are successful with the majority of those being led, it is our failure with a few that can cause us much frustration and disappointment. In truth, however, overlooking needs is the reason behind many of our leadership difficulties. Too often, we think our leadership failures have nothing to do with us and everything to do with the other person. Yet, our failure usually comes from our inability to recognize a need and adjust our attitude and behavior as well as our methods, techniques, and procedures. Rather, we plow ahead, aware of our own needs or the needs of the classroom, school, or district—oblivious to the individual needs of those being led. The result usually is failure to get those being led to do what we want them to do.

As we all know well, any failure to lead can result in many negative emotions. We can get angry, frustrated, and discouraged. We can think those being led are bad or wrong—or are the source of all our problems. We may, on the other hand, start believing that we alone are the entire problem. Often we are, but just as often we are not. That's why we must make sure making an effort to meet the primary and secondary needs is a part of every student and staff relationship—and every leadership action.

There's absolutely no way to know people, including ourselves, without studying the needs of human beings. There's no way to learn how to lead people without seeing how their needs are reflected in the way they think and act. The more we know about these factors and the more we can link their force to the group as well as to each individual student or educator we lead, the more effective we will be. It is not a difficult task. But it does take time. It does take effort. It does take insight, skill, and application. And it does take a sincere desire to know people, including ourselves, so that we can lead toward maximum productivity and satisfaction.

NEEDS—A
STRONG FORCE

The Vital
Three for
Understanding
Human
Behavior

As you lead, be constantly aware of the power of needs. Within these needs lie the interests, desires, and drives of those being led. Within these needs lie the force and stimulation which will give each person what means the most to him or her. Within these needs are also our own. That's why we are likely to try to motivate those we lead out of our own needs. It won't work. That is, it won't work with people different from us. It will only work with people just like us who have the same intensity of the same needs that we have.

Remember, while we all share these vital needs, we don't all share the same intensity and drive from the same needs. It's good that we don't. Otherwise, we would have a school full of the same kind of people. We would all be clones of each other. We would all have the same interests and drives. We would all like the same things and dislike the same things. We would have the same strengths and the same weaknesses. We would all want to do the same things—and not want to do the same things. When it comes to getting *all* the work of the school accomplished, we wouldn't have the people with the needs and desires to do many of the jobs that need to be done.

Unfortunately, many in leadership positions don't understand the various wants and needs inherent in the human condition. They may know math like the back of their hand. They may know the budget blindfolded. But they don't know people. Administrators who don't have many people skills tend to hire "like" people—people "exactly like" them. Teachers who lack people skills only want certain kinds of students in their classes. When this is the condition, appointed leaders can lead those like themselves, but they can't lead everyone else equally well. And they have tremendous difficulty understanding and relating to the many different kinds of people they must lead.

A KEY TO
UNDERSTANDING PEOPLE

Yet, a big problem remains: Many people in leadership positions don't want to study people. Some don't think they should have to acquire such knowledge. They say, "Problems today would be solved quickly if those being led would just do as they are told." These are the leaders who will skim or skip this section of this book. These are the leaders who will *not* study this material with the same intensity as they do the laws and principles. It's a mistake.

Remember, to be effective, you must know yourself. You must know your people. You must master this material and spend the rest of your career learning and applying knowledge about the wants, needs, motives, and motivators of human beings if you intend to motivate and lead people.

So often, the behavior of those being led bewilders us. We can't understand what makes them think the way they do—or say and do the things they do. Yet, the needs of human beings can answer many of our questions. There are only seven primary needs. There are only eight secondary needs. There are only nine people motivators. Within these needs and motivators lies the knowledge you need and must have to know yourself, know those you lead, and discover the keys to causing others to *want* your leadership.

THE PRIMARY NEEDS

The seven primary needs are physiological, unlearned, and within us all. The vast majority of the problems people experience in life pertain to a primary need. Many leaders have numerous problems with those being led due to their failure to see that some are hurting because at least one of these needs is not being met—or that one or more of these needs is getting in the way of everything else at the moment.

This is extremely important to us as teachers and administrators because these primary needs almost always have to be met before interest and motivation in the secondary needs become dominant. For instance, if we are hungry or urgently need to go to the rest room, little else is on our minds. Yet, it's through the secondary needs that we turn people on to work, achievement, and satisfaction in the classroom, school, or district.

MISS THE NEED AND
YOU'LL MISS THE TARGET

It's easy to see why ignoring these needs or not even seeing them in those being led can cause us to miss the target when we're trying to lead people. If we don't understand these needs, we may not be able to respond professionally to what those being led do or say. Rather, we may take every act of resistance personally—and react personally in ways that lessen our chances of being effective. It's also easy to see why those being led may think that we don't really know who they are, that we don't care about them, or that we are only using them if we are oblivious to these needs. Failure to recognize a primary need void in a student or staff member causes a wide range of human emotions and responses—and none of them are usually good. Certainly, being oblivious to a primary need can cause resentment. Hopefully, we can see that if anyone—student and educator alike—comes to school with a primary need void, he or she will have problems that make learning or helping others more difficult.

For instance, if a teacher comes to school distracted by the countless problems that can exist at home, working hard to help students be successful can rank low on his or her list of priorities. Problems at home are distracting for students as well. In fact, holding high expectations for students with primary need voids can foster strong and negative resentments. The lack of fulfillment of a primary need can cause hate for a teacher, administrator, academic work, or the work of the school. It can cause jealousy and bitterness toward happy and successful students and colleagues who are perceived to be more fortunate. Remember, primary need fulfillment comes first for all of us.

PROBLEMS ARE INEVITABLE
WHEN NEEDS AREN'T MET

Indeed, an unfulfilled primary need can breed antisocial and unprofessional attitudes and behaviors. Then, having a leader who seems oblivious to this personal void and is urging some to "study harder," "meet the needs of the students," or "accomplish the work of the school" can produce a wide variety of hostile feelings. It's not difficult to see why.

For instance, a teacher who is having a marital problem at home may bring that burden to school. Or a student who is being abused at home may do the same. Sometimes we forget the strength of these primary needs when we're trying to relate to and motivate those we lead. We might even believe the primary needs of those being led aren't our problem. They are. We may think there is nothing we can do about such voids, but there are many things we can do. In the beginning, we can care. We can be empathetic. We can give comfort, extend friendship, and "see" what we can do. We may be able to give direct help—or give help simply by demonstrating an awareness of and an interest in their situation.

Whenever we experience any kind of problem leading, we must first look for a primary need void. In the process, we need to remember that we all need a leader who knows us, understands us, is concerned about our welfare, and is willing to help us. We all need a leader who cares enough to treat us as a person and tries to help us meet our needs. Remember, until the primary needs are met, nothing else may matter to the person we're trying to lead.

Why are some students always angry? Why is a colleague hostile toward students? Why is an administrator always unavailable? More often than not, we need to look no further than a primary need. Furthermore, I believe that 75 to 85 percent of the discipline problems we have in schools are the result of primary needs. There are seven primary needs. Remember, they are *physiological* and *unlearned*. They are:

1. Hunger
2. Thirst
3. Sex/Sexuality
4. Air

5. Rest
6. Escape From Pain
7. Eliminate Waste

1. & 2.   THE NEED OF HUNGER AND THE NEED OF THIRST

When people are hungry, eating is their first and only priority. And until the need is satisfied, little else can capture their interest. Some students come to school without eating. So do some teachers and administrators. Make no mistake: When such is the case, problems can result. Working, learning, and performing are made more difficult. For instance, some students are "starving" and just waiting for the lunch bell to ring. The teacher who tries to hold the class a few minutes for more learning, rather than allowing them to go to lunch, can expect trouble from some—and maybe all—students. So can the administrator who lets the school faculty meeting extend into the dinner hour.

Remember, human beings need to eat to work—and usually don't work very well on an empty stomach. And human beings need to eat at regular intervals—whether they choose to or not. And empty stomachs are often the cause of poor performance as well as conflicts between people whether we are students, teachers, staff, or administrators.

In addition, different ethnic groups prefer eating different kinds of food. And different socioeconomic groups prefer eating different kinds of food. Remember, too, that some people don't eat because they don't want to, and others don't eat because they don't have money to eat—today or every day. Many families are on welfare. A record 23.1 million people are receiving food stamps. And one in six households gets some form of public assistance. This includes welfare, Medicare, and free school lunches. There is, indeed, a lot of hunger pain out there. And what do you think teaching would be like without a free lunch program?

Understanding Human Behavior—

- *Hunger*
- *Thirst*
- *Sex/Sexuality*
- *Air*
- *Rest*
- *Escape From Pain*
- *Eliminate Waste*

Always keep in mind that young people come to school hungry for a wide variety of reasons. Some students have no choice in the matter. Others do. Just because a student lives in an expensive home doesn't mean he or she gets to have breakfast. Too, a student may spend lunch money on something else or choose not to eat or to maintain a proper diet. Teachers and administrators do the same thing. We may not want to eat breakfast, get up too late for breakfast, or we may grab a soft drink and doughnut in the lounge before school and call it breakfast. The point is this: If we haven't eaten breakfast or if we miss lunch, we may be irritable, reveal a wide range of negative attitudes, and demonstrate many negative behaviors.

And most of us are on countless diets each year. If we think that being on a diet doesn't alter our behavior and effectiveness, we are mistaken. We simply need to ask ourselves, "What is the *only* thing we think about when we are on a diet?" The answer: food. Every diet is accompanied by one focus: the constant thought of food.

As we all know, family financial problems may lie at the root of this problem. And these financial problems may be temporary or permanent. A husband or wife may not be working and not have money to eat. Or the problems may involve overspending, cutting food costs, or being broke until payday. Eating problems may also be caused by punishments imposed by the parents—including withholding lunch money from the child.

Regardless of the circumstances, we need to be aware that hunger is a primary need. It must be filled. And when we cannot get those being led to do what it is we want them to do, we cannot overlook the role this need plays for or against our leadership. Silly? Think again. A leader who is oblivious to this need and condition can make people feel very unkindly toward him or her.

The need of thirst is similar to hunger. However, this need can include drinking problems, medical problems such as diabetes, or a wide variety of illnesses. It could be a need to get a drink between classes because a person ate something distasteful or salty.

We may be more aware of the need of hunger and thirst if we know what it's like to be hungry or thirsty. Too, we need to watch what we say—or we may have students who can't possibly relate to us. For instance, calling the cafeteria food *bad*, *horrible*, or *garbage*—or saying anything negative about cafeteria food is a mistake. After all, to some of our students this may be the best meal of the day—and it may be the only full meal for some. If our words or actions make students pretend it's *garbage* when it's their best meal, the resentments caused can be unbelievable.

When it comes to hunger and thirst, we need to watch and react. Our awareness is important. That's why we must observe. Who sits alone? Who never talks to anyone during lunch? Who seems to be hurting? Which students don't have lunch money? Which students don't eat a bite? Which give their food away? Who is eating off others' trays or stealing food? Who is on a diet? Do we have any students who are exceptionally thin and are still dieting? Which students seem ineffective, lethargic, or listless in the morning or after lunch or at the end of the day? Which students may have a health problem? Which may have a drug problem?

A CHECKLIST FOR UNDERSTANDING AND APPLICATION

1. What evidence of the need of hunger and the need of thirst do you see in students, teachers, staff members, and administrators?
2. How can you recognize, meet, or adjust to this need in the classroom? How can you meet this need in the school? In the district?
3. Discuss various (student) (educator) behaviors that have not been discussed which you see manifested by these needs.

3. THE NEED OF SEX/SEXUALITY

Psychologists call this primary motive a need for sex/sexuality. We can call it many different names: sexuality, relationships, personhood, gender identity, or whatever makes us comfortable. I say this because whenever I address this need in *The MASTER Teacher*, I get letters from teachers who deny the existence of this need. I've had parents insist their teenage children have no such need for sex, sexuality, or relationships. These parents resent anyone implying they do. Regardless, the primary need of sexuality does exist. And it causes many people a great deal of trouble. This reality is evident in many areas of our lives as children and adults. Research shows that the majority of people, young and old alike, are very interested in how they look. Worse, the majority aren't satisfied with the way they look. This affects how people view their personhood and sexuality. No matter what we claim, beauty is a huge value in our society. As leaders, we also need to be aware that research indicates different nationalities and races may view beauty differently.

The need of sex/sexuality is revealed by many attitudes and behaviors as well as life experiences. For instance, some men can't work well with other men, and some can't work well with women. Some women can't work with men, and some can't work with other women. This need involves male-male relationships, female-female relationships, and male-female relationships.

People's interest in sex is obvious to us all. We know it can result in teenage pregnancy. We also need to know that 56 girls get pregnant every hour in this country, 450,000 abortions are performed each year, and 100,000 babies are placed for adoption each year. There are also homosexuality and AIDS, which cause stress and anguish. The latter can cause death.

Remember, students and educators alike may have problems related to this need. Divorce and single-parent homes take their toll on schoolwork for a student and for an educator. The problem may be temporary. But the fear may be permanent and revealed in feelings, such as "I don't fit in," "I hate my dad," "I can't stand my brother," "My sister gets everything," or "Life always hands me a loss."

Relationships present us all with problems. A person may have many friends—or may not have any friends. We can have problems related to dating—or not dating. People have a fear of not fulfilling the proper or accepted male or female roles. Students may feel too fat, too tall, too short, ugly, or hairy. They may have all kinds of negative emotions because they have big ears or a big nose—or because they wear glasses or braces. They may be made fun of by other students or other adults, including their loved ones. A student may not be big enough or tall enough to make the team—or pretty or popular enough to be chosen. A student may not have the right clothes, may have been kicked out of the group, or may want to be part of a group that doesn't know he or she exists. These all are problems related to the need of sex or sexuality experienced by the people you are trying to lead. And you wonder why you are having difficulty leading them? And that's not all.

Understanding Human Behavior—
• Hunger
• Thirst
• Sex/Sexuality
• Air
• Rest
• Escape From Pain
• Eliminate Waste

There also are potential career problems, such as the pressure of advancement or experiencing put-downs from superiors. Women may be seen as a threat to men. Women may be oppressed professionally by men. Men can be oppressed professionally by other men—or by women who can't handle the physical aspects of the job. Of course, some men think certain responsibilities are "women's work" or fear male and female interactions. Just look at how many special interest groups have been formed around the primary need of sex or sexuality. The list is extensive—but it is real.

We need to watch and react. For instance, we have to observe who has problems with the same sex? Who gets along better with boys or girls? Who seems fearful or talks negatively about the opposite sex? Who has a problem with sexual identity? Who are the loners? And who lacks meaningful relationships?

We can begin by accepting each student or colleague as a person and human being. We can help those being led accept each other, fit in, and belong. We can help those we lead get attention and self-affirm. We can keep classrooms and offices inclusive and friendly. In the process, we can check ourselves regarding this primary need. If it affects us in one way or another, we need to recognize that fact and make some adjustments—or get some help.

We need to see that this primary need lies at center court—and is the focus for many people much of the time. For teenagers, it can be the complete focus of their lives. This primary need calls for your attention continually as you work with people.

A CHECKLIST FOR UNDERSTANDING
AND APPLICATION

1. What evidence of the need for sex/sexuality do you see in students, teachers, staff members, or administrators? How can you be sensitive to this need in the classroom?
2. How can you be sensitive to this need in the school? In the district?
3. Discuss various (student) (educator) behaviors that have not been discussed which you see manifested by this need.

4. THE NEED FOR AIR

The need for air includes the need for space. We need air to breathe, but we also need "a little breathing space." We have a need for distance between us and other people. We have a need to avoid crowded conditions, to get away from people occasionally, and to enjoy the safety of solitude.

Business people will say that the density of their workplace population is the highest per square foot of any place in town. This is not true. Teachers and students work all day long in the place with the highest density per square foot—a classroom and school. Both teachers and students are confined to the classroom most of the day.

Students sit in desks that are within the 18-inch personal zone. They can be touched by other people whether they want to be touched or not. But that's not all. Teachers and students may not even be able to retreat or to escape after a bad experience. Rather, they must go through experiences while in close contact with other people.

In addition, body odors, claustrophobia, or being close to someone with a cold as well as other physical, mental, and medical problems have a bearing on this need. So does the weather. We know how we and those being led react to snow, rain and, of course, the first day of warm sunshine in the spring. The temperature is also a factor. Is it too hot or too cold in the room? What are the air quality and ventilation conditions in the room?

Working conditions are a big factor in the need for air. Students may ask themselves questions, such as "Who do I sit next to?" "Who do I want to be with?" "Do I participate—or do I simply sit in class and listen?" The lack of space caused by overcrowding affects this need. We can see the effects on everyone. Students may not be fighting us or our teaching—they may be fighting to meet the need for air. Our colleagues might appear to be obstinate in a meeting but, in reality, they may be experiencing the primary need for air.

That's why we should ask those we lead about their comfort. We should check temperatures and ventilation. We must consider the possibility that people's health problems are affecting their behavior and keeping us from leading. Above all, we should allow appropriate movement and avoid restrictive rules, regulations, and procedures. Too, we should vary seating, activities, room arrangement, groupings, and interaction.

If possible, we need to provide a private place for students to go to meet this need. Educators have a similar need. It may not be character or personality that is making a teacher act badly in the classroom, lounge, or at the faculty meeting—it's being cooped up all day in a classroom with people so close he or she feels that he or she can't breathe at times.

This primary need demands your attention.

A CHECKLIST FOR UNDERSTANDING
AND APPLICATION

1. What evidence of the need for air do you see in students, teachers, staff members, and administrators?
2. How can you meet this need in the classroom? How can you meet this need in the school? In the district?
3. Discuss various (student) (educator) behaviors that have not been discussed which you see manifested by this need.

5. THE NEED FOR REST

We all need to meet the primary need for rest. But we also need rest from work, rest from pressure, and rest from an activity-packed hour, day, or week. Students do. Teachers do. Administrators do. We even need rest when we play too hard. And if this need is not met, students may not do very well in the classroom and we may not do a very good job as teachers or administrators. Worse, none of us may be cooperative and easy to lead if we are not getting enough rest.

There are countless reasons people may not have met this need on any given day. Being sick last night can affect any of us. Maybe we had worries and couldn't sleep last night—or we have insomnia frequently. Whatever the case may be, our reasons for not getting rest may be temporary or permanent. In addition, there are many other reasons people don't get enough rest to function successfully during a school day.

For instance, families may be fighting. And when parents fight, no one in the family may be resting or sleeping because of tension in their house. And young people may have night jobs, including taking care of brothers and sisters while a parent works. Sixty-one percent of U.S. high school students work after school. Fifteen percent work 1 to 10 hours, 22 percent work 11 to 19 hours, and 18 percent work 20 to 30 hours per week. Six percent work more than 30 hours, which is about the percent of average daily absence in schools.

The need for rest extends beyond the need for sleep. We need rest from planning. We need rest from teaching. We need rest from changes—and rest from problems. We need rest from after-school and night meetings. We need rest from being with the same people every day. Too, some people work well in the morning and have greater needs for rest in the afternoon and evening. Others need more rest in the morning and have more energy in the afternoon and evening. Research indicates schools may be structured wrong when it comes to meeting this need because teenagers need more sleep than young children—and should come to school later—while young children should come to school earlier in the morning. The cause is biological and must be considered. That's why we need to watch out for and react to this primary need. Who seems tired or burned out? Who burns out by 2:00 p.m.? Who is irritable in the morning, and who doesn't do well in late afternoon? Who has physical problems or can't cope? What is the reason?

We must be aware of those students who have part-time jobs. As we all know well, many teachers or administrators work two jobs. We must observe those who have problems at home or keep late hours. Make no mistake: Neither student nor educator can watch TV until midnight and do a great job in school the next day. Therefore, we must discuss with students problems related to rest. We must be careful about the amount of homework we assign. And we shouldn't be afraid to allow breaks in class if we see a problem developing.

It may not come as a surprise, but we need to recognize that when young people do not perform, they usually are given *more work* as a punishment. In fact, assigning more work is the most common punishment adults give to young people. Such action can be a big mistake, especially if the problem is a lack of rest.

There are many actions we can take. We can be flexible. We can be concerned and caring. We can counsel and use different techniques with different people at different times. We can vary tasks and alternate hard and easy assignments. And, of course, we can visit with parents and offer assistance without judging their character as we do.

The need for rest is a physical problem. And when problems are being experienced, this primary need calls for your attention.

A CHECKLIST FOR UNDERSTANDING AND APPLICATION

Understanding Human Behavior—

- *Hunger*
- *Thirst*
- *Sex/Sexuality*
- *Air*
- *Rest*
- *Escape From Pain*
- *Eliminate Waste*

1. What evidence of the need for rest do you see in students, teachers, staff members, and administrators?
2. How can you meet this need in the classroom? How can you meet this need in the school? In the district?
3. Discuss various (student) (educator) behaviors that have not been discussed which you see manifested by this need.

6. THE NEED TO ESCAPE PAIN

How many teachers and administrators reject all the new information about effective teaching and learning, not because they really think this new information is wrong or won't work, but because they don't think they can do it? How many teachers and administrators don't want to learn how to be better educators to avoid the possible pain of not being successful? This is the primary need to escape pain.

I think the vast majority of all discipline problems are a result of trying to avoid pain of some kind. It may get a student in trouble to knock a book on the floor or talk back to the teacher, but it won't cause the student nearly as much pain as math, English, or science is causing him or her. Getting kicked out of math class may cause a student pain, but it won't cause him or her nearly as much pain as having classmates find out he or she can't do math problems or is failing math because of a lack of ability. What behaviors are manifested in those being led who can't achieve? How do people try to escape the pain of failure? The answer: Many reject and refuse. Many question and challenge. Many act as if they aren't interested or don't care. Many are passive. And many run—and just as many fight.

Many attitudes and behaviors can be caused by the desire to escape pain. Most of these behaviors do not help make those being led more successful. And all these behaviors make leading more difficult. The behaviors include apathy, absenteeism, nonperformance, procrastination, complaining, and the creating of emergencies. They all include a continuous preoccupation with possible failure.

Personal problems, including alcoholism and drug addiction, are two classic examples. Attempted suicide and mental illness are others. The boss who has to go to every meeting in town may be doing so to escape the job he or she is supposed to be doing in school. We need to watch and take action when it comes to the need to escape pain. Who is always running away? Who fears change? Who talks down anything new? Who says "I can't" or "I won't" before he or she even tries? Who always responds, "We shouldn't have to do that"?

Look closely: Who is always embarrassed? Who is shy, fearful, introverted, or ill a lot? This primary need may be the cause of such behavior. As leaders, we must focus on strengths. We must help those being led find a measure of success before we can lead them to bigger successes. We must be able to see the pain caused by feeling stupid, as well as the pain of failure—and take action to change this condition. If we don't, our leadership efforts will be rejected more often than they are accepted.

We can examine whether this need is a factor every time we offer an idea or suggestion—or initiate any plan or change in the classroom or school. And we can make it a point never to minimize, ridicule, or abandon those in pain. And we can recognize that those in pain usually focus all their attention on themselves.

Make no mistake: We all fear the pain of failure. We just all take different actions to escape the pain a possible failure will bring. If we think not, we need only to think of all the things we purchase to escape pain. We buy insurance. We have police and fire departments. We have locks on our doors. We have umbrellas, raincoats, safety belts, smoke detectors, and fire alarms. We buy vitamins and have dental checkups and physical examinations. The list is endless—and so is the need to escape pain.

This primary need demands your attention if you want to lead people.

Understanding Human Behavior—

• *Hunger*
• *Thirst*
• *Sex/Sexuality*
• *Air*
• *Rest*
• *Escape From Pain*
• *Eliminate Waste*

A CHECKLIST FOR UNDERSTANDING AND APPLICATION

1. What evidence of the need to escape pain do you see in students, teachers, staff members, parents, and administrators?
2. How can you meet this need in the classroom? How can you meet this need in the school? In the district?
3. Discuss various (student) (educator) behaviors that have not been discussed which you see manifested by this need.

7. THE NEED TO ELIMINATE WASTE

The physical aspect of this need is obvious to all of us. Yet, we may not understand how it can cause us problems in a classroom. For instance, we may say to a student, "Why didn't you go to the rest room during the passing period or recess?" Yet, the real question may be: What's keeping students from using the rest room during the passing period or recess? If the rest room is not supervised, is it an "office" or "hangout" for some students? Make no mistake: Some students are afraid to go into the rest rooms. The shy ones don't want to. How many of us would use rest rooms in the teachers' lounge if the stalls didn't have doors? Not many. And, of course, we should recognize that the older a person becomes, the more concern he or she has for regular bowel movements.

We would all know more about the problems students experience regarding this need if we could hear and see what goes on in some school rest rooms. We might be shocked. Too, we might be very upset if we knew what a personally degrading experience a rest room stop is for some of our students. The language, the behavior, and the degrading activities might help us know immediately which of our students would avoid a rest room at any cost during recess or passing period—or anytime that it was being used by other students.

Of course, there can be medical problems attached to this need. They are seen daily in a school and can indicate illnesses such as flu, stomach upset, and a wide variety of other problems. We must watch and respond to people regarding this need. In addition, we need to remember that every individual is different. Therefore, our rules must be clear—and flexible. Rest rooms must be checked for safety, and we must recognize embarrassment when it exists. And, of course, we must look at our own uniqueness and be more sensitive. This primary need calls for your attention.

A CHECKLIST FOR UNDERSTANDING AND APPLICATION

1. What evidence of the need to eliminate waste do you see in students, teachers, staff members, and administrators?
2. How can you be sensitive to this need in the classroom? How can you be sensitive to this need in the school? In the district?
3. Discuss various (student) (educator) behaviors that have not been discussed which you see manifested by this need.

THE PRIMARY NEEDS
ARE FIRST—ALWAYS

The primary needs account for many of our leadership problems in the classroom and school. That's why we can expect to experience more problems in leading when we don't consider these needs first. These needs are probably overlooked because most leadership efforts focus on using the secondary needs to motivate people. And this is fine—except for the fact that a primary need will cause a blockage that prevents those being led from even being interested in the benefits gained in the secondary needs.

More often than not, unfortunately, it is a primary need that prevents a person from functioning on a secondary need level. We may not think we can do anything about a primary need—or we may not know what we can do. And herein lies a huge problem because, sometimes, we *can't* satisfy a primary need in the classroom or school—but we can meet a secondary need. Yet, we can be aware. We can be sympathetic and empathetic. We can be considerate and caring. We can counsel. And we can attempt to meet these needs in creative or innovative ways because of their overwhelming importance to an individual.

Leaders in all positions, as well as organizations of all kinds, must do everything they can to meet these primary needs for the people being led. It is easy to see why. In our efforts to lead, our first consideration is these primary needs. Without fulfillment of these needs, moving to a higher level of functioning—which is made possible through the secondary needs—is almost impossible. Rather, we are consumed by our primary needs.

It's easy to see how we go to great lengths to meet these needs at home. Before anything else, we all have to feed our families. We have to make sure each member of the family fits in, belongs, and has a good relationship with the others. We have to try to make sure the need for air is met by furnaces, fans, air conditioners, and windows. We try to make sure a family member has a place to sleep to ensure he or she rests—and may even have a room for each member to get rest. We try to make our family feel secure from intruders as well as safe from pain inflicted on each other from within the family. If family members are constantly inflicting pain on one another, very little else is likely to matter. And, of course, we have bathrooms that enable our bodily functions to be performed conveniently and privately. We may even have one rest room for parents and another for children. And many of us know the problems that result when one rest room is shared by the entire family.

Making sure these primary needs are met is the first consideration of creating a family unit and making a home. When these needs aren't met, trying to motivate people through the secondary needs of gregariousness, aggression, affiliation, inquisitiveness, achievement, power, status, and autonomy is difficult. This is true for students. It is true for teachers. It is true for administrators. A test on Friday, getting an A for the nine weeks, or going to college is meaningless to a student who is hungry, abused, or experiencing problems meeting any of the primary needs. And a close look will reveal that families who are failing to meet primary needs are called dysfunctional.

GOOD LEADERS AND GOOD ORGANIZATIONS
FOCUS ON PRIMARY NEEDS

Understanding Human Behavior—

• Hunger
• Thirst
• Sex/Sexuality
• Air
• Rest
• Escape From Pain
• Eliminate Waste

If you'll look closely, you will see that the good organizations are doing everything possible to meet the primary needs of their employees so that employees can be motivated to become totally immersed in the work of the organization. Labor unions place a vast majority of their emphasis on taking care of the primary needs of their members. For instance, unions place big emphasis on demanding a living wage for members so that a higher quality of life can be experienced—from food on the table to a roof over their heads. And a big emphasis is also placed on sexual equality and opportunity for their members in the workplace. Unions promote tenure and seniority to reduce fears. And many of the labor union demands in regard to working conditions have to do with air, space, and physical well-being. Unions focus on rest in the form of breaks, lunch hours, sick leave, holidays, overtime, and vacations. And, of course, unions demand escape from pain in the form of everything from job security to insurance programs to employee rights to retirement programs.

In truth, while employers pay for these benefits, the union receives the credit for them. As we all know well, many employees are more loyal to the union that is getting these benefits for them than they are to the organization which is paying for these benefits. School districts are no exception to this reality. Why? Leaders and organizations tend to focus on meeting the needs of the organization, rather than on meeting the needs of the employee. Yet, if the needs of the employee aren't taken care of, the employee may be hard to motivate without force, fear, and pressure to get the needs of the organization met.

The point is this: Within the primary needs lie the problems faced by everyone. That's why a leader, whether dealing with a child or an adult, must know and strive to be aware of, understand, and meet these needs for those being led to the best of his or her ability. And we can't act as if these needs don't count. Because of the overwhelming significance these needs hold, if a child or an adult has a leader who is not concerned about these needs or is unaware of their existence, he or she may choose not to follow that appointed leader and to look elsewhere for fulfillment of these needs.

OVERLOOKING PRIMARY NEEDS
CAN LEAD US ASTRAY

As the leader in the school or district or the learning leader in the classroom, we can be led in the wrong direction by our failure to look at these needs. As we try to motivate people to do what it is we want them to do, we often can't understand why someone is acting badly, obstructing our plans, or is totally disinterested in learning in our classroom or in being a more successful educator. We may be doing everything we know how to do to motivate via the secondary needs, but discover that this is not the issue at all. And as a leader, we've got to know what the problem is. Once we know what the problem is, we will automatically be in a better position to do something about it. Too, once we know what the real problem is, we won't knock our head against a wall or, equally important, spend time and energy working on the wrong problem.

For instance, when we are aware that an unmet primary need is causing a person to think or act inappropriately, we won't assume that he or she doesn't like us. Neither will we conclude that the person is not interested in doing a better job as a student, teacher, or administrator. Rather, we will see what we can do to help. One thing is certain: Being aware of and meeting the primary needs of those we lead can make the task a whole lot easier. And if we aren't aware of the needs in those being led, we don't know our people. And knowing those being led is a prerequisite for successful leadership.

APPLICATION: PROFILE YOURSELF FIRST

1. To lead others, you must use the primary needs. However, this is often easier if we profile our own needs first. Otherwise, we may not understand or accept how an individual need can be such a strong force in someone's life. Profiling ourselves can be a valuable exercise. It shows us our needs. It tells us the areas in which we may have trouble leading.

2. Use this same form to uncover an unmet primary need that may be hindering the performance of a (colleague) (student).

PRIMARY NEEDS
(Physiological and Unlearned)

Primary Needs	Circle the degree to which each primary need affects attitude/behavior.
Hunger	1 2 3 4 5 6 7 8 9 10
Thirst	1 2 3 4 5 6 7 8 9 10
Sex/Sexuality	1 2 3 4 5 6 7 8 9 10
Air	1 2 3 4 5 6 7 8 9 10
Rest	1 2 3 4 5 6 7 8 9 10
Escape From Pain	1 2 3 4 5 6 7 8 9 10
Eliminate Waste	1 2 3 4 5 6 7 8 9 10

Very little effect ◄————————► Very strong effect

THE SECONDARY NEEDS

Leading people can be very frustrating. It can be very perplexing. Trying to get a student to be interested in classwork, act responsibly, and participate in class can be nerve-racking. Trying to get a teacher to stop being so negative or to quit criticizing everything and everyone can cause emotions ranging from anger to pity. Attempting to get an administrator to see teachers' concerns and take positive corrective action can be maddening. Yet, what we need to understand is that all behavior has a purpose and a reason. And all behavior has a driving force. Make no mistake: All behavior is an effort by an individual to meet his or her needs—especially those which are very important to him or her. And until we understand the reason for the behavior in terms of needs, we will continue to be stymied by the behavior of those being led.

There is simply no way a teacher or administrator can lead without a thorough knowledge of the secondary needs. They are the foundation of human motivation—and getting those being led to do what we want them to do. The secondary needs lie at the root of causing others to want our leadership. Called *derived needs*, they are psychological and learned. Never forget this fact: *They are learned. They can be changed.* Although the degree of intensity and priority of each need can and does vary from person to person, all these needs are within us all.

It is through the secondary needs that people self-actualize. It is via the secondary needs that a leader individualizes and personalizes leadership. The secondary needs allow each person being led to answer the primary question: What's in it for me? It is through these needs that we show the way and guide those being led to want to learn, to want to try to reach goals, and to want to enhance their standard and level of living. It is within these needs that we influence those being led to self-actualize and want to find high productivity and high satisfaction. It is also through these needs that students and educators alike improve their self-worth and maximize their potential.

A leader must be fully aware that people will seldom give up their wants, needs, and motivations. Indeed, people will usually fight hard to meet and fulfill their needs. If they can't meet them with us, they will try to meet them elsewhere in other arenas of their lives. For instance, students who can't meet their needs in the classroom and school will try to meet those needs outside the classroom and school. So it is with educators. Some experts believe that so many people have so much difficulty fulfilling their needs in the workplace, they have given up trying. As a result, their needs are being met by hobbies, clubs, sports, and other activities away from work.

There are eight secondary needs or motivators. Remember, we *acquire* these needs as well as an intense desire to meet them. As a leader, we must know the need, how it is manifested by behavior, and how we can use the need to motivate those being led to do what we want them to do. The behavior gives us the real clues we need to cause those being led to want our leadership.

THE SECONDARY NEEDS
(PSYCHOLOGICAL AND LEARNED)

1. Gregariousness
2. Aggression
3. Affiliation
4. Inquisitiveness

5. Achievement
6. Power
7. Status
8. Autonomy

Like the primary needs, all eight of the secondary needs are possessed by all people of all ages. Even the intellectually impaired or the slow learner has these eight needs. And slow learners meet these needs in their own unique and individual ways. However, we must understand that, until the primary needs are met, the force of the secondary needs will be weakened. Obviously, if a student is hungry, he or she may find it very difficult to be interested in achieving in math class. Yet, this is not always the case.

For instance, we've all known people who work through lunch and dinner. In fact, we know people who will forgo meals and rest on a long-term basis to achieve or gain status. We've also known people whose work constitutes 90 percent of their life—at the expense of family, friends, and relationships. We've seen people work at the computer or in their office for an entire day, seemingly without the need for many basic human necessities. Even though this behavior can be fairly common, it's not the rule. And while these kinds of behaviors can't really be called *abnormal*, they can't be called *normal* either. But such behaviors could be called unhealthy. And it can be said that if a leader discounts the primary needs while continuing to hold the usual expectations for those being led, he or she won't last too long as the leader.

LINKING THE NEED
TO THE PERSON

When you're trying to lead people, you must look at them individually to see which of the secondary needs is most important to them. A particular need may be the strongest force in a person's life. For instance, some people are totally driven by status. Others are actually driven by affiliation. Others are driven primarily by achievement. The key is to link the need with the individual. And, of course, because we all have these needs, we can use them all when leading a group or an individual. Don't think for a moment that there is anyone who is not trying to meet all these needs to a certain degree. There isn't. Therefore, don't be fooled by the person who says, "I'm not influenced by status at all." The fact that he or she makes such a statement should tell you that such a proclamation is a form of status.

Through our leadership, we, as leaders, want to use the work of the classroom and school to actually promote meeting the needs of those being led. After all, the classroom and school can meet these needs extremely well. And every time we fulfill a secondary need, it becomes easier to cause others to want our leadership. It is via the secondary needs that we, those being led, and the school achieve goals and objectives. To be a dynamic and positive leader, one must not only appeal to those needs of the high performers, but also set a course of action which will stimulate those needs in others as well. When we do, we will achieve the maximum utilization of personnel and effort per task.

These eight needs are the foundation of motivation for us and those being led. And they are also the foundation for motivating cooks, custodians, parents, secretaries, aides, and everyone else. Unless we lead to meet these needs, we'll find ourselves having to give those we lead bribes, incentives, rewards—and threats, commands, and ultimatums to get them to work.

We make a mistake if we try to fight these needs or try to deny those being led fulfillment of these needs. If we want those we lead to follow us, we must work hard to find their needs and fill them. One thing is certain: When we fill needs, we will find leading and being led a very rewarding experience. And remember, within these needs lie our own. And knowing our own drives is important. It allows us to be able to adjust our methods and techniques when leading others.

*Understanding
Human
Behavior—*

• Gregariousness
• Aggression
• Affiliation
• Inquisitiveness
• Achievement
• Power
• Status
• Autonomy

1. THE NEED FOR GREGARIOUSNESS

The need for gregariousness is the need to associate with a group, to work with others, and to avoid working alone. This is the force that makes some people avoid solitude at all costs. It also drives people to be a vital or intimate part of something—a class, club, school, department, team, or district. This need is clearly evidenced by those who have strong desires to socialize and to be included in the "inner circle"—especially with those who are in authority. This is also the motive that causes some individuals to be upset if left off a committee, not asked to attend a meeting, not invited to a party, or not told about a decision.

People who have a strong need for gregariousness are easy to identify. They like being with people and will always flock to the crowd. They are outgoing—and don't know "a stranger." They enjoy organizing things. They often come to see you to tell you what they are thinking or doing. They like to share and keep people informed. Because they would rather work with others than work alone, they often invite others to join them—or ask to join others.

In leading, we must recognize that making people who have a strong need for gregariousness feel that they are on the outside looking in kills their motivation. On the other hand, visiting with them frequently, forming partnerships, sharing responsibilities, and making these people feel included will increase their motivation. If we fight this need by excluding rather than including these people, we actually force them away from us—and maybe even out of the classroom or school. If their need cannot be met, they will form their own structures, such as clubs, gangs, or cliques.

In the classroom, we can help fill the need for gregariousness by making those being led feel included. We can show appreciation—and let them know they are missed whenever they aren't there. We can use them as aides or helpers. We can utilize groupings and cooperative learning. We can ensure that students are involved in opportunities to review and study with classmates for daily work, projects, and tests.

With the staff, we can emphasize *the team* and utilize a team approach to getting work accomplished. And we can use these people to plan and organize socials. We can put them on committees. And we can celebrate the efforts and success of students and staff alike. Remember: Students function as a group in a classroom. A faculty operates as a team in a school. Therefore, teachers and administrators must meet and nurture this need.

A CHECKLIST FOR UNDERSTANDING
AND APPLICATION

Relative to knowing yourself and knowing those being led, some of the questions you need to answer are:

1. How strong is your need for gregariousness? How do you see this need manifested in yourself?
2. How do you meet this need?
3. How do you see this need manifested in those being led?
4. How can the need for gregariousness be met in your (classroom) (school) (district)?
5. How is the need for gregariousness being denied to those in your (classroom) (school) (district)?

2. THE NEED FOR AGGRESSION

The need for aggression is the need to assert oneself, express oneself, be counted, and have one's say. It's a need to take initiative—and even be bold and pushy. People who have a strong need for aggression are easy to identify. They are often very assertive. They fight for what they want. They will not take no for an answer. They are usually achievement-oriented. They are ready and willing to take issue or engage in direct action. They can be militant. They will start quarrels and fights. In addition, they pester others to listen to their ideas, usually tell people directly how they feel about everything, and would rather not do things "by the book." They fight authority if they feel suppressed. In a school, they are often anti-other departments—because they see no one else's priorities as being as important as the ones they hold.

Be aware that all people need an environment in which they can self-actualize, experience ownership, and express themselves. Some *must* have it. And those who have strong aggression needs are a prime example. Therefore, putting people down, putting people "in their place," or getting in the last word doesn't make leaders winners with highly assertive people. And people who feel this need strongly will fight or flee. If we fight this need by not letting aggressive people assert themselves, they'll find their own ways to do it.

We can help those being led fill this need by letting them seek input, letting them express themselves, and giving them authority and a sense of ownership. We can allow them to express opinions, share power, give responsibility, and plan involvement in problem-solving activities. Inclusion in certain decisions, involvement in planning activities, and responsibility for choosing specific courses of action are good techniques that can be employed to help meet this need. We can be sure to ask open-ended questions and use advisory committees of all kinds for students and staff alike. In the process, we can check our own aggressive mannerisms. After all, if we have a strong need for aggression and try to "play over" those we lead to get our way, we're in for a lot of fights—especially with our students or teachers who have the same driving force.

As leaders, we must remember that we should always give those being led assertive allowances. An "open door" policy always helps. Delegating responsibilities to people with this need will also aid them in meeting the need. Above all, we must always teach these people the difference between *assertion* and *aggression*. The lesson: Aggressive people will walk over people to get what they want. They may not even see the damage they do. On the other hand, assertive people take care *not* to hurt others in their quest to meet this need. Therefore, we need to say, "We will promote and help the assertive. We will not take the same stand with the *aggressive*." Therefore, we must remind those with strong aggression needs to go for what they want, but to be careful to make sure nobody gets hurt in the process. We must help people become *assertive*, rather than *aggressive*, so we can give them a skill which will help them be successful, rather than experience the failure that aggression usually causes.

Understanding Human Behavior—

- *Gregariousness*
- *Aggression*
- *Affiliation*
- *Inquisitiveness*
- *Achievement*
- *Power*
- *Status*
- *Autonomy*

A CHECKLIST FOR UNDERSTANDING AND APPLICATION

1. Relative to knowing yourself and knowing those being led, some of the questions you need to answer are:
2. How strong is your need for aggression? How do you see this need manifested in yourself?
3. How do you meet this need?
4. How do you see this need manifested in those being led?
5. How can the need for aggression be met in your (classroom) (school) (district)?
6. How is the need for aggression being denied to those in your (classroom) (school) (district)? What problems have resulted from this denial?

3. THE NEED FOR AFFILIATION

The need for affiliation is the need for friendly unions, connections, and relationships. It's a drive to be close to others, including peers and the boss. It is a need to be liked by others, wanted by others, and needed by others. It is the desire to work in conjunction with others. Therefore, it includes a need to belong—and a need to be sought out by subordinates, peers, and superiors alike. Unfortunately, it can also be the need to possess a person or a place—as well as to have a positive and constructive sense of place and a feeling of personal ownership.

People who have a strong need for affiliation are easy to identify. They like belonging to clubs—and especially like holding offices. They like to be in charge. They volunteer to work on committees—and love to plan social activities. People with strong affiliation needs usually have a wide range of friends and acquaintances. Yet, they often exclude those who don't like them—or those who prevent them from being part of the inner circle.

We must be aware that none of these people are loners. People who feel this need strongly desire *close*, intimate, and integrated relationships—accompanied by a personal sense of power and control. If we fight their need to be with people, they will be very unhappy. They need to feel close to others. Therefore, we must never be aloof with these people.

We can fill their need by the structure we use in a class or meeting, the assignments we make, and the specific responsibilities we give them. We can also help fill this need by using first names and personal examples in our lessons. We can use caring words and phrases when we talk to them. Too, we can change groups and seating arrangements and recognize friendships—as well as help them establish relationships. Remember, if these people do not fit in, they don't cooperate. They don't participate. When lonely, they are not happy, productive, or satisfied people.

Developing, maintaining, and strengthening associations with other individuals is a strong human need. This need is often accented on the professional level. Teachers need to be close to each other, but they also often have an intense need and desire to be close to students, parents, and administrators. We would be wise to never forget this truth.

A wide range of class and extra-class activities helps meet this need for students. Interschool and intersystem activities are always a good leadership practice. Activities ranging from socials to curriculum planning should be a part of the leadership plan, or many may not have the need met. Union leaders are masters at developing ways to meet this secondary need. Simple observation will reveal that union management has perfected the "all for one, one for all" procedure in effecting leadership on a real-life level. As leaders, we need to do the same in the classroom, school, and district.

A CHECKLIST FOR UNDERSTANDING
AND APPLICATION

Relative to knowing yourself and knowing those being led, some of the questions you need to answer are:

1. How strong is your need for affiliation? How do you see this need manifested in yourself?
2. How do you meet this need?
3. How do you see this need manifested in those being led?
4. How can the need for affiliation be met in your (classroom) (school) (district)?
5. How is the need for affiliation being denied to those in your (classroom) (school) (district)?

4. THE NEED FOR INQUISITIVENESS

The need for inquisitiveness is the need to know, to seek information, to question, to doubt, to wonder, to inquire, to investigate, and to be curious. It is also the force which causes people to pry. People with this need are eager to discover, to learn, and to be gratified by the pursuit of knowledge. To be a good student or a good educator, we must have this need. A close look will reveal that this need is often the driving force in the life of a scholar, scientist, or researcher.

People who have a strong need for inquisitiveness are easy to identify. They ask questions and question everything. They want to know the innerworkings of everything. They can stay on the details of any subject for hours. They are intrigued by anything they don't know—and will delve deeper for more information. They also shoot holes in plans and play devil's advocate to the ideas and suggestions of others. And they like adding to other people's ideas and plans. In fact, they can drive others crazy with all their suggestions. In addition, they want others to look at, review, and test everything they do—or what others do.

As leaders, we need to be aware that we all have a need to know. Yet, inquisitive people are curious people who either "make things go" or "get in the way of things going."

We need to let those being led know what we're thinking and the "whys" of what we are doing—if we want to motivate or lead them more easily and successfully. If we fight this need by stifling their inquisitiveness, we demotivate them. They need opportunities to be involved—and they need to know the "whys," "hows," "whats," and "whens" if we expect them to want our leadership. Remember: Inquisitiveness is not a negative. Curious people want to know what is going on. They have to know. It drives them crazy not to know—or to be in the dark.

Understanding Human Behavior—

• *Gregariousness*
• *Aggression*
• *Affiliation*
• *Inquisitiveness*
• *Achievement*
• *Power*
• *Status*
• *Autonomy*

We can help fulfill this need by keeping those being led informed. In the classroom and the faculty meeting, we can relate new experiences or ideas to familiar ones and ask questions without knowing the answers. We can use unfinished projects or challenges to motivate them. And whenever possible, we can relate activities to their experiences as well as involve them in planning and decision making.

This need has been expressed more forcefully in recent years because people want to fulfill the need to control their own lives. The leader who fights the fulfillment of this need may encounter unlimited difficulty. And, sometimes, when we think someone is being nosy, we turn him or her off. That's a leadership mistake.

People also have a drive to know how we feel about them as people—as well as how we feel about them as students or professional educators. This is one reason we need to communicate continuously with those we lead. Educators need weekly bulletins, briefings, and regular department and faculty meetings in order to meet this need of inquisitiveness. However, in addition to revealing plans for work, we must also communicate to those we lead that we are concerned for them personally as well as professionally.

This need is easily met by teachers and administrators. There is simply no excuse for not filling it. Those leaders who are secretive, withhold basic information, and don't have a viable way to help each person being led find success are acting contrary to a human motive—and this action will prove detrimental to both the leader and the leadership practice. You can count on it.

A CHECKLIST FOR UNDERSTANDING AND APPLICATION

Relative to knowing yourself and knowing those being led, some of the questions you need to answer are:
1. How strong is your need for inquisitiveness? How do you see this need manifested in yourself?
2. How do you meet this need?
3. How do you see this need manifested in those being led?
4. How can the need for inquisitiveness be met in your (classroom) (school) (district)?
5. How is the need for inquisitiveness being denied to those in your (classroom) (school) (district)?

5. THE NEED FOR ACHIEVEMENT

The need for achievement is the need to succeed and, equally important, to be recognized for effort and success. This is the need to get better, progress, and grow. It is the need to try. Achievement can be related to many accomplishments: attitude, effort, persistence, skill, courage, and other traits. It is the need to do, to gain, to attain, and to achieve a goal. As leaders, we have a fundamental responsibility to see that those being led achieve. If we can't fulfill this responsibility, we really shouldn't be leaders.

People who have a strong need for achievement are easy to identify. They plan. They organize. They work hard to achieve goals. In fact, they will continue to work hard and try even when others won't. They like showing others their plans, their work, and their achievements. Therefore, they often resort to "tooting their own horns." They love to talk about what they're doing—and often love to talk about anyone who is achieving. People with high-achievement needs are usually very successful. On the other hand, they are often feared and disliked by those who feel put down, diminished, or inferior because of their enthusiasm and success. People with this need *should* be high achievers. If they aren't, something is wrong with their planning or with their leader.

We need to remember that all people need to succeed—and some actually *can't stand* to fail. In addition, people also need to be recognized for their achievements. Therefore, we must be aware of these needs and notice achievements, offer praise, and give rewards. We must magnify, glorify, and perpetuate success in every way possible. And we must never forget that we all need recognition. We must show those being led that we cherish learning and excellence, and we must remove the bureaucratic obstacles and give people the opportunities needed to achieve and meet their goals. We must also know that people with high achievement needs *must have* meaningful responsibilities.

We can always help fill the need for achievement by becoming an advocate of those we lead. We can also challenge them, involve them, and be sure to recognize their effort, commitment, and excitement. As leaders, we must be aware that success without recognition weakens the motivation. Recognizing student and staff achievements is one of the most important things that we do. Certainly, parents and students don't give teachers enough appreciation and recognition for their efforts in the classroom. And teachers may not give administrators much appreciation and recognition either. This is dangerous because no recognition can lead to no motivation—and people with high achievement needs are not motivated by a lack of appreciation or recognition. They are motivated by their successes and the recognition for those successes. That's why a leader must never forget that people don't like to do what they do not do well. Sometimes, people won't even try what they can't do well.

We need to remember this secondary need the next time we are trying to move those being led toward working harder, spending more time on the task at hand, and accepting a new procedure or increasing their productivity. And if we expect those being led to want our leadership, we must always be instrumental in showing them how to be successful. Unfortunately, leaders often miss seeing a strong achievement need in those being led if it is not related to school tasks. For instance, does the student who diligently saves money to buy a car have strong achievement needs? Yes. Does the student who brags about a job after school have strong achievement needs? Absolutely.

A CHECKLIST FOR UNDERSTANDING
AND APPLICATION

Relative to knowing yourself and knowing those being led, some of the questions you need to answer are:

1. How strong is your need for achievement? How do you see this need manifested in yourself?

2. How do you meet this need?
3. How do you see this need manifested in those being led?
4. How can the need for achievement be met in your (classroom) (school) (district)?
5. How is the need for achievement being denied to those in your (classroom) (school) (district)?

Understanding
Human
Behavior—

• *Gregariousness*
• *Aggression*
• *Affiliation*
• *Inquisitiveness*
• *Achievement*
• *Power*
• *Status*
• *Autonomy*

6. THE NEED FOR POWER

The need for power is a tremendous force in the lives of many people. It is the need to choose, do, act, or produce. It is the need to have control over our lives—as well as the lives of others—to gain authority, to be given responsibility, and to receive the cooperation of others. This is the need to have rights and privileges and to use individual prerogatives.

The need for power has a wide range—from the ability to actually dominate to the power to sway and influence. The need for power can even be physical. We need to remember that teachers want power, students want power, parents want power, and administrators want power. And everyone wants the rights that go with the power. Too, it can be wise to remember that every social movement—women's, labor, civil rights, and all the others—began as an attempt to meet this need, which was being denied by someone in a power or leadership position.

People who have a strong need for power often want a title. They also want both authority and responsibility—and the rewards that go with them. They are the people who speak up and out in the classroom or staff meeting. They fight decisions, especially if they feel "the powers that be" are deciding arbitrarily—because this cancels their rights and denies them power. Those with strong power needs like to have the final say. Often, unfortunately, they must have their way. And they often think they "know it all." We need to be aware that if we use our positional leadership power and fight this need by denying those being led power, they will fight us—forever. If we share power with them, they will want our leadership.

Make no mistake: Those being led want some measure of jurisdiction in the way things are done. Some *must* have it. We must give them responsibilities along with guidelines so they can learn to manage power and have others want to follow them. We must remember—and help those being led to remember—that with power comes responsibility.

These people need a role in plans, ideas, and work. They must be allowed to participate. Never forget, the need for power can be a strong positive or negative—and we must make sure it is positive and constructive.

What a leader should recognize is that those being led need to know that they count. This is a form of power. Making those being led feel significant is an absolute in meeting this human need. Equally important, a leader ought to be very careful taking away power or trying to eliminate power from the base of people's needs. We do this every time we tell those being led that we are the boss. We do this every time we give those being led responsibility without granting them the degree of authority required for them to be successful. We do it every time we take away a privilege or refuse to listen to them—and especially when we penalize the entire group for the actions of a few.

We can't forget, titles are important in filling the power need, but the authority and responsibility that go with the title are equally important. When we give both while assigning tasks, even if it's just the title of "leader" or the option of choosing how to do the work, we provide those being led with both the motivation and the satisfaction needed to get the job done.

A CHECKLIST FOR UNDERSTANDING AND APPLICATION

1. Relative to knowing yourself and knowing those being led, some of the questions you need to answer are:
2. How strong is your need for power? How do you see this need manifested in yourself?
3. How do you meet this need?
4. How do you see this need manifested in those being led?
5. How can the need for power be met in your (classroom) (school) (district)?
6. How is the need for power being denied to those in your (classroom) (school) (district)?

7. THE NEED FOR STATUS

The need for status is the need to be special or significant. It is the need to be "somebody" or to have special privileges. It is the need for position, rank, and standing within the group. Some students have a burning desire to be regarded as number one—and to be a vital part of what is happening in the classroom and school. So do some teachers and administrators. Unfortunately, however, we all know we can be replaced. This knowledge hurts. Yet, this reality can make people with strong status needs "fight for their lives" in ways that are both acceptable and unacceptable to others. If we, as leaders, remind those being led that they are replaceable too often, we may turn them away from us permanently.

People who have a strong need for status are easy to identify. However, sometimes we don't see the *real needs* being revealed by the behavior. For instance, people who are easily insulted or think other people look down on them are often revealing a status need. So are those who want information before others get it, who go "crazy" if we make decisions without consulting or considering them, or who try to make themselves appear superior by making others appear inferior. This is the need for status being acted out.

People who have a strong need for status often try to deny status to others. For instance, they put people down, try to "put people in their places," label, and prejudge people. They also form cliques or exclusive groups. Those with strong status needs are joiners. And they often take on more work than they can handle. The volunteer who is up to his or her ears in work, but who continues to volunteer for the next task, is often motivated by status.

We need to be aware that status gives us a sense of well-being, position, and feeling of high worth. It justifies a person's value. And everybody wants to be somebody. Those with strong status needs are *driven* to be somebody. Therefore, any de-identification action is a mistake with everyone, especially these people. It makes them feel less significant. It denies the status need. We need to make those being led feel important—because they are. We need to give them credit when it is deserved. We need to give those being led work, positions, and activities that will help them feel important. Taking action that makes them feel like a *number* rather than a *person* will almost always make them angry.

Nothing should ever be done that detracts from the identity, individuality, or worth of the individual. Nothing should ever be done that detracts from the work people do. We must never think individual needs can't be met in group work. They can. In fact, it's the different kinds of individual skills and strengths within a group that bring forth individual strengths and make group endeavors successful—and give both the individual and the group status. One of the basic rewards of teamwork is status.

The challenge of leadership is to combine the needs of the individual with the needs of the classroom, school, and district. Some might say this is "picking the right people for the right job." This is true, but it's only one aspect of successful leadership. The effective leader can help the majority of people be suited for the task that needs to be accomplished by fulfilling the needs of people in the process of completing required tasks.

Understanding
Human
Behavior—
• *Gregariousness*
• *Aggression*
• *Affiliation*
• *Inquisitiveness*
• *Achievement*
• *Power*
• *Status*
• *Autonomy*

A CHECKLIST FOR UNDERSTANDING
AND APPLICATION

1. Relative to knowing yourself and knowing those being led, some of the questions you need to answer are:
2. How strong is your need for status? How do you see this need manifested in yourself?
3. How do you meet this need?
4. How do you see this need manifested in those being led?
5. How can the need for status be met in your (classroom) (school) (district)?
6. How is the need for status being denied to those in your (classroom) (school) (district)?

8. THE NEED FOR AUTONOMY

The need for autonomy is the need for independence and self-governance. It is the need to be free, call the shots, set our own guidelines, and be our own boss. This is one reason we wanted to be a teacher. It's one of the reasons we wanted to be an administrator. Too, self-governance is a way of life in a democratic society. We are taught from the time we are little children to take charge and be the masters of our own lives. Why are we surprised when people of all ages reveal this need? Why are we offended if those we lead want more autonomy?

We should neither be surprised nor offended. Some people want freedom and independence more than anything else—and it's a normal desire. They want to do *what* they want to do, *when* they want to do it, and *how* they want to do it. They want to be a leader. They have a need to control that which concerns them.

People who have a strong need for autonomy are easy to identify. They are independent. They are self-centered. They like to make their own rules. They want a say in matters pertaining to things that govern their lives—and things they fear may affect their independence at some point in time. They want to come and go as they please and would prefer two sets of rules: one for them and one for others. They are often idealistic and very aware of "fairness." They will work hard to reach goals. And they usually have potential for individual achievement.

People with strong autonomy needs fight for room to operate. Standard operating procedures kill motivation for people who strongly feel this need. Yet, they will readily follow leadership that allows them to meet the need for a degree of autonomy. They will follow leadership that allows their input or shares decision making with them. But we must stress standards, goals, common rules, the value of teamwork, and cooperation when we give them autonomy.

Make no mistake: With good leadership, those being led who have a strong need for autonomy have a high probability of being creative achievers and team players. Yet, we must not believe that they do not need the authority to perform well. They do. However, we may be holding these people back—if we fail to realize the capabilities of those being lead—or reject them because they always want and ask for more autonomy. This need can be among a leader's greatest assets in achieving the work of the classroom, school, and district.

A CHECKLIST FOR UNDERSTANDING
AND APPLICATION

1. Relative to knowing yourself and knowing those being led, some of the questions you need to answer are:
2. How strong is your need for autonomy? How do you see this need manifested in yourself?
3. How do you meet this need?
4. How do you see this need manifested in those being led?
5. How can the need for autonomy be met in your (classroom) (school) (district)?
6. How is the need for autonomy being denied to those in your (classroom) (school) (district)?

CONTINUOUS STUDY IS NECESSARY
TO UNDERSTAND PEOPLE AND THEIR BEHAVIOR

The primary and secondary needs provide a teacher, principal, and superintendent with valuable leadership insights and constructive functional powers in getting work done. They are the clues to all human behavior. They tell us why people think and act the way they do. We could spend a lifetime studying each of the primary and secondary needs and applying them to all within the school orbit—from student to teacher to parent to ourselves. The primary and secondary needs make an excellent topic for a seminar or workshop.

These learned and unlearned needs must never be ignored or overlooked by any leader in either individual or group endeavors. They are the key that unlocks the door to individual and group motivation, including positive actions and reactions. Without giving attention to primary and secondary needs, we may find that leading drives us crazy. We may find the behavior of those being led bewildering. Worse, we may find that orders, commands, and directives are an absolute necessity in our every leadership action. We may find causing others to want our leadership to be an impossibility. If, by chance, we treat these primary and secondary needs as unimportant, we may find mass dissent and even insubordination at our door. We should also remember that dissent and insubordination need not be out in the open to be in existence. Fear may keep them hidden. Yet, at the first sign of opportunity or weakness, we may find an explosion we cannot control.

A lack of leadership awareness of the primary and secondary needs is likely to lead to a great management misconception: All those we lead are alike. We are apt to stereotype all students, teachers, administrators, cooks, custodians, counselors, and others into neat little packages. We are also prone to believe, for instance, that all people are equal. They are not. People are not equal in their experience, ability, or motivation. They are all different. Their priorities, wants, and needs vary in intensity. What is extremely important to one is not to another. All of those being led are products of their personhood, environment, and their experiences—past, present, and anticipated. That's why these motives are the first place a leader must look when leadership efforts are being accepted and followed—or ignored and rejected.

Remember, rejection of leadership may be for professional reasons. However, more often than not, it is personal—absolutely and totally personal. That's why so many rejections of our leadership seem irrational and without solution. And they will continue to be if we're looking in the wrong places for the answers. That's what makes leading difficult and frustrating. That's what also makes it interesting, fascinating, challenging, and tremendously rewarding.

It is your ability to cause others to want your leadership that has allowed you the opportunity to lead in your classroom, school, or district. Your actions must be rational and objective. Your actions must also rest on a base of leadership knowledge and skill. If you don't make the primary and secondary needs a part of your leadership knowledge and skills, you won't be using the best information or good judgment in many leadership situations.

Understanding Human Behavior—

- *Gregariousness*
- *Aggression*
- *Affiliation*
- *Inquisitiveness*
- *Achievement*
- *Power*
- *Status*
- *Autonomy*

APPLICATION: PROFILE YOURSELF FIRST

1. To lead others, you must use the secondary needs. However, this is often easier if we profile our own needs first. Otherwise, we may not understand or accept how an individual need can be such a strong force in someone's life. Profiling ourselves can be a valuable exercise. It shows us our needs. It tells us the areas in which we may have trouble leading.

2. Use this same form to uncover an unmet secondary need that may be hindering the performance of a (colleague) (student).

SECONDARY NEEDS
(PSYCHOLOGICAL AND LEARNED)

Secondary Needs	Circle the degree to which each secondary need affects attitude/behavior.
Gregariousness	1 2 3 4 5 6 7 8 9 10
Aggression	1 2 3 4 5 6 7 8 9 10
Affiliation	1 2 3 4 5 6 7 8 9 10
Inquisitiveness	1 2 3 4 5 6 7 8 9 10
Achievement	1 2 3 4 5 6 7 8 9 10
Power	1 2 3 4 5 6 7 8 9 10
Status	1 2 3 4 5 6 7 8 9 10
Autonomy	1 2 3 4 5 6 7 8 9 10

Very little effect ←――――→ Very strong effect

A study of human behavior should not stop here. There is a need to delve into the implications of the primary and secondary needs, specifically as they relate to classroom teaching and school administration. Why? Because the majority of positive and negative as well as constructive and destructive situations that you will experience with those being led—and even with your best friend—are rooted in these needs. Therefore, I have developed what I call the people motivators. They can serve you well in the classroom, school, and district.

THE
PEOPLE MOTIVATORS

These motivators are my creation. I've used them for the past 35 years. They were created out of personal and professional experiences in business as well as in education. Let me explain.

I was employed by a CBS AM/FM and TV affiliate for over 13 years. I worked for this company while I was a student, a classroom teacher, and an administrator. As a result of this employment, I received extensive media training. In addition, I was exposed to comprehensive training and experience in the areas of advertising, programming, and public relations.

During this time, I worked on, created, and evaluated many different advertising messages used on radio and television, and in the newspaper, including the advertising used to introduce the Polaroid camera and the Ford Mustang. I was also on the fringes of many political campaigns, including the campaigns of presidential candidates. Over a period of time, I began to notice that almost everything advertised in the world was sold through appealing to what I classified as the seven motivators. I later added two more—for a total of nine motivators. These nine motivators are:

1.	Personal Gain	6.	Convenience
2.	Prestige	7.	The Desire to Avoid Fear
3.	Pleasure	8.	New Experiences
4.	Imitation	9.	Love/Caring
5.	Security		

Whenever we were designing any kind of advertising message, I noticed that the values, benefits, or advantages of the products and services were associated with one or more of these motivators. I came to the conclusion that whenever we used a combination of the motivators to persuade the public to buy something, the effort was much more successful. And whenever three of the motivators could be used, success was almost certain. However, getting these motivators into a one-minute radio or television commercial was not an easy task.

To test the validity of these motivators, all you need to do is read a newspaper tonight or listen to a radio commercial on your way to work. Or closely observe an advertisement on television. You'll see these motivators at work. And they work well. Indeed, everything you have ever purchased in your life, from a loaf of bread to a car, was probably advertised to appeal to at least one of these motivators.

You may say, "Nonsense, *I'm* not influenced by advertising." Yes, you are—both consciously and subconsciously. Even if you don't buy name brands, it is advertising that has played a role in your attitudes, thinking, and action. Examination will reveal that these nine motivators are an extension of both the primary and secondary needs. In many ways, these motivators serve as a "bridge" from both the psychological and unlearned primary needs and the psychological, learned secondary needs to specific, practical, and workable ways to motivate those being led.

APPLIED TO
CLASSROOMS AND SCHOOLS

As a classroom teacher and administrator, I became interested in these motivators because I was certain that if these motivators were so effective in the media as a distant third-person motivator, they would be much more powerful if used one on one in the classroom. It was my belief that with direct usage in the classroom, school, and district by a teacher or administrator, these motivators could have a startling impact. My assumptions have been confirmed by years of practice.

By using the primary and secondary needs individually—and using the appeals offered by the "bridge" of the nine people motivators with individuals as well as with groups—you'll find it easier to cause others to want what you're doing. It's easy to see why. These motivators are totally geared to meeting needs and offering a benefit or advantage to those you are leading. These motivators enable you to show the values, advantages, and benefits of what you're teaching to those you're teaching it to. These motivators make it personally advantageous and rewarding to the individual to do what you want him or her to do.

Let's discuss each motivator and its application. Please note that the motivators are written in a combination of paragraph and outline form. Each has the following four sections for each motivator:

1. The motivator itself and what it means.
2. What people want from the motivator—or the behaviors that tell us this is the motivator.
3. Questions you need to ask yourself to make sure you're using this appeal.
4. The conclusions.

This format was used for some very simple reasons. It is easy to read. It facilitates study and quick review. At the same time, this format offers an in-depth explanation of the motivators so that you can master learning—and also makes it easier for you to write in more material. After all, examples of each of the nine motivators are endless.

1. PERSONAL GAIN:
THE MOTIVATOR AND ITS MEANING

Personal Gain. *This is the strongest of all motivators. Consciously or subconsciously, the need for personal gain is inherent in all decisions to do anything—and is expressed by* *what is called the primary question: "What's in it for me?"* And if the answer is "Nothing," we are in trouble as a leader.

The primary question, "What's in it for me?" is asked by every human being at every level. Teachers are asking it on a daily basis. "What's in it for me to work on this committee or take on this extra duty?" "What's in it for me to attend staff meetings, work with slow students, do as my principal asks, or be evaluated by my administrator?"

Students are asking, "What's in it for me to be taught by this teacher, to do my homework, or to show up for class every day?" Principals, superintendents, and boards of education ask their own primary questions too. And in each case, we are searching for one thing: benefits—personal ones. If we can't provide a positive answer, we shouldn't be surprised when those we lead don't want to follow us.

When a teacher or administrator is having difficulty getting along with those being led, knowledge of this motivator will reveal immediately that it would be wise to ask these questions: "What's in it for this student/teacher/administrator to work with me?" "What's in it for him or her to trust me?" "What's in it for him or her to believe in my ideas and put them into practice?"

Once we apply these questions about where our difficulties lie—we will see where our opportunities and advantages lie as well. We should also be aware that it's an error to assume that each person being led always knows the answers to these questions—or that each will always comply with our requests simply because we're the leader. The answers to the primary question, What's in it for me? must often be taught to those being led.

Understanding Human Behavior—
• Personal Gain
• Prestige
• Pleasure
• Imitation
• Security
• Convenience
• The Desire to Avoid Fear
• New Experiences
• Love/Caring

WHAT PEOPLE WANT FROM THE MOTIVATOR

1. More of—or better than—what I have now.
2. Examples: More...

a. Success	h. Leisure	o. Privileges
b. Satisfaction	i. Trust	p. Advantages
c. Respect	j. Opportunity	q. Money
d. Say	k. Choices	r. Rights
e. Responsibility	l. Intelligence	s. Authority
f. Recognition	m. Influence	t. Time
g. Freedom	n. Power	u. Improvement

QUESTIONS TO ASK YOURSELF

1. What's the personal gain for the students in my class or teachers in my school or district to do as I ask?
2. I may know how those being led can be good for me. The question is: How am I good for them?
3. What is special about this grade, class, task, school, district?
4. Do I focus on rules and regulations or opportunities and benefits?
5. Do I provide those being led with immediate feedback—or do they have to wait for my response?

6. Do I assign those being led work according to their ability?
7. Do I promise those being led extra help if they need it?
8. I have ideas about what (teachers) (administrators) should do for the school. The question is: What should the school do for (teachers) (administrators)?
9. What individual benefits do I offer those being led?
10. What advantages do I give those being led to fulfill the need for personal gain?

SOME CONCLUSIONS

1. The answers we give to these kinds of questions are important. They tell us if the person gains by following us.
2. Our answers tell us if we are student-centered, teacher-centered, or administrator-centered.
3. They tell us precisely how we use this strongest of all motivators with those we lead.
4. When leading, we are wise to use determiners, the personal gain people want and can expect by following us.
5. We would be wise to point out the benefits and advantages of following us when planning our messages or appeals to get others to do as we ask and follow our lead.
6. The biggest mistake we can make as a leader is to believe that those being led do not have any expectations of us.
7. A leader must know what those being led want.

2. PRESTIGE: THE MOTIVATOR AND ITS MEANING

Prestige. *Everyone has the desire to feel important. There are no exceptions to this reality. As people, we are motivated by what helps us win approval, by what makes us feel powerful, and by what gives us recognition and a good reputation.* Students are not an exception to this reality. Neither are teachers, principals, superintendents, cooks, custodians, secretaries, or anyone else. In fact, prestige may be a powerful individual motivator.

Many people win prestige by proclaiming all the good things they are doing and by revealing which clubs they are asked to join, by bragging about how much money they make, how smart they are, the important telephone calls they have received, the important people whom they have assisted, or how influential or successful they are. Prestige is a strong motivator. The way we dress, the car we drive, and the neighborhood we live in, all contain a prestige factor. Likewise, whether or not a person graduated from high school or college or what college or university his or her degree came from contains prestigious elements.

In school, students work to earn good grades. They also wear certain shoes, belong to certain groups, and run for certain offices to gain prestige. Athletes have letter jackets with medals pinned on them to make sure that everyone knows who they are. So it is with teachers. Some want you to know they are coaches, so they never appear out of uniform. This is the prestige motivator at work. The leadership rule of thumb is this: If you can make people feel important, successful, and necessary, they will think you are intelligent and perceptive. This includes all the people you come in contact with daily — children, teachers, support staff, and community members.

We all know that people respond in more positive ways when we address them by name, ask for their input, return their telephone calls quickly, answer their correspondence immediately, take time to brief them on what we are doing, and hear out their questions, concerns, and suggestions. School employees and the public alike respond to all of the above considerations in similar ways. We can very quickly improve our leadership skills by going out of our way to have meaningful interactions with as many individuals as possible—with the intent of making people feel important—and by never doing anything which makes people feel insignificant. On the other hand, anything done to make people—individually or as a group—feel like second-class citizens is counterproductive to meeting the need for prestige.

Understanding Human Behavior—

* *Personal Gain*
* *Prestige*
* *Pleasure*
* *Imitation*
* *Security*
* *Convenience*
* *The Desire to Avoid Fear*
* *New Experiences*
* *Love/Caring*

In a bureaucracy of the classroom, school, or district, it is easy to make rules, procedures, and requirements which are void of personal prestige. Rather than treating people as unique and important individuals, we may have a tendency to make sweeping generalizations and rules that penalize the majority for the actions of the minority. This will always work against our ability to use the prestige motivator to its full potential.

In most schools, educators have been successful in awarding prestige to high-profile students—scholars, monitors, cheerleaders, student council members, and athletes. The question remains: What have we done for students who haven't attained this status? The lack of prestige is one of the chief reasons we are failing to reach some students. Some of our students are saying to themselves, "I don't count," "I don't belong," or "I don't fit in or have any ability." Remember, it's hard to be a good student if you don't seem to count. It's hard to be a good citizen if you don't seem to count. It's difficult to believe that the opportunities available at school are for you—if you don't seem to count.

In all kinds of ways, students tell us, "If you make me feel important, I will think you are important too. But every time I'm in your class you make me feel dumb. I don't like this feeling and, therefore, I don't like you or what you are teaching." Teachers can make the same statements about administrators. It should be increasingly clear that we have to be able to find more and better ways to make those being led feel important, not only for their achievements, but for just being. We can't reserve prestige just for those who have managed to achieve something significant. Why? Because if we wait for achievement before giving prestige, some of those we lead may go their whole lives feeling very unimportant indeed.

BEHAVIORS THAT TELL US PRESTIGE IS THE MOTIVATOR

1. Telling us the good things they are doing, then waiting for us to respond.
2. Openly and freely revealing awards and honors they've received.
3. Telling us the good things said about them.
4. Telling us about all the clubs they've been asked to join.
5. Informing us about all the important telephone calls they've received and the important people they know.
6. Talking about how others want and need them.
7. Saving and displaying all evidence of their successes.
8. Wearing clothing that is unique, popular, name-brand, or in style.

QUESTIONS TO ASK YOURSELF

1. Is there any prestige in following me?
2. Is there any prestige in being in my class? In my school? In my district?

3. Is there any prestige in "buying" what I say?
4. How do I make it prestigious to be in my (class) (school) (district)?
5. Can I follow as well as lead?
6. How can I give prestige to each student? To each teacher? To each administrator?
7. What am I doing to make those being led feel special?
8. What am I doing for the slow learner? Average learner? Fast learner?
9. What am I doing for those being led who haven't attained a feeling of prestige for anything?
10. How do I use information, including academic knowledge, to meet the need for prestige?

SOME CONCLUSIONS

1. Giving people authority and responsibility is prestigious.
2. Recognition is prestige. Appreciation is prestige. Reward is prestige.
3. It is prestigious to those being led when we seek them out and when we listen to them.
4. Treating people as subordinates takes away prestige.
5. People see some classes, activities, duties, achievements, and groups as being more prestigious than others. Why?
6. Prestige is created by the leader who teaches values and benefits.
7. Once created by the leader, prestige is perpetuated by the group being led.
8. Drawing attention to success in any way generates prestige.
9. Giving people meaningful responsibilities and relying upon them to perform these tasks is rewarding to those being led.
10. Denying people's needs is a mistake. And if you don't think prestige should be a motivator and you have a hard time with people who need it, you may not lead a lot of people very well.

3. PLEASURE: THE MOTIVATOR AND ITS MEANING

Pleasure. *This is the need for joy, enjoyment, happiness, fun, gratification, amusement, and satisfaction. When the need for pleasure is combined with the need for prestige, motivation to follow leadership is enhanced.* There is a need in everyone to have pleasurable experiences rather than unpleasant, difficult, or nondescript ones. The more pleasant and pleasurable the experience, the greater the chances are that those being led will want to repeat it. Therefore, to motivate others, we must ask ourselves these questions:

• How can I make it more pleasurable for those being led to interact with me?
• How can I, as a professional educator, make it more pleasurable for my colleagues to interact with me?
• How can I make it more pleasurable for students/teachers/administrators/parents to attend this school?
• How can I combine pleasure and prestige in my leadership efforts?

As we consider these questions, we shouldn't overlook the aspect of *fun*. And we should never, under any circumstances, go out of our way to take the joy and fun out of the work of the classroom, school, or district. Unfortunately, sometimes we do, and when this is the case, being out of school becomes more pleasurable than being in it. Remember, one of the reasons people put off going to the doctor or the dentist is that they believe it's going to be an unpleasant experience. It may not be—but they think it will be. The same is true of getting a loan at a bank, buying insurance, and attending some meetings. Children cut class and skip school for similar reasons. Educators use a "personal day" or a "sick day" to do the same. Being out of school is more pleasurable that being in it.

Certainly, classrooms and schools cannot and should not be all fun and games. Yet, there's no reason that classrooms and schools have to be void of pleasure in order to have much learning and achievement going on within them. Therefore, we would do well to think of ways that pleasure can be incorporated into the existing climate and services we provide—and not take the pleasure out of schools. In fact, research indicates that learning is often retained longer through the use of pleasurable activities and exercises that heighten interest.

Does this mean that it's our function to entertain those being led day in and day out? No, of course not. But, we need only to be aware of how we respond to things that are pleasurable to know that pleasure is a very successful motivator. Whether passing a bond issue or adding a new rule or requirement, we must make the task more pleasant than unpleasant, or it may not be accepted by the people we are trying to influence. Sometimes, all leaders need to do is state a rule or procedure as a positive instead of a negative to insert pleasure. In addition, all a leader may need to do to get the desired results is reveal the benefits of following the rule, rather than focusing on and proclaiming only the punishment for breaking the rule.

In incorporating pleasure into school life, you should not let sophistication fool you. Some years back, Bernard Neary, an enthusiastic elementary principal who is now retired, shared with us some of the things he and his staff were doing in their school in Iowa. Without reservation, this school was an exciting place to visit—and to have a child attend. They had Dress-Up and Dress-Down Days, Teacher Appreciation Days, Reading Days, and Pride Days. In fact, they had special days for all conceivable occasions. They also had notes, badges, signs, and bulletin boards to insert pleasure into every possible learning situation, recognize children's achievements, and motivate both staff and students.

However, while sharing these ideas with fellow administrators at The Master Teacher Leadership Conference, Principal Neary almost apologized for the fact that both the events and the tools used were not very sophisticated. And he noted that other elementary educators—and, most certainly, junior high, middle, and high school colleagues—might be turned off by many of the ideas the faculty members were using to make their school a productive and satisfying place for students and educators.

Certainly, the ideas and tools he had developed didn't look sophisticated—because they weren't. And yet, pleasure, fun, and excitement, not sophistication, were the aims. The ideas of this staff worked. As educators, we would all be wise to think very hard before we reject something just because it appears unsophisticated—and for good reasons. Simply looking around the town where you live might show precisely why.

Sometimes we forget that when merchants want to increase traffic and sales, they stage a special, unsophisticated, and pleasurable event. They have a Whale of a Sale, Dog Days Sale, Crazy Days Sale, Two for One Sale, Moonlight Madness Sale, or One Cent Sale. These kinds of unsophisticated events excite people, draw the big crowds, gain participation, and motivate people into a desired action because they give pleasure. They're fun. They're enjoyable. They meet a big need that we all have as human beings.

Understanding Human Behavior—

• *Personal Gain*
• *Prestige*
• *Pleasure*
• *Imitation*
• *Security*
• *Convenience*
• *The Desire to Avoid Fear*
• *New Experiences*
• *Love/Caring*

Some of the best devices for motivating students, creating a positive classroom climate, and making the school exciting for students and staff are used primarily in elementary schools. In middle schools, the use of such special events decreases. In high school, such events may be limited even more. Too often, in our search for sophistication, we become quite dull—and our classrooms or schools become places filled with routine rather than places filled with pleasure and excitement. In an effort to create more order or be more adult-like, we lose our creative imaginations. Yet, if we turn class or school motivational plans over to student or parent committees, they often come up with the kinds of suggestions we regard as "hokey." They suggest Speak-Up Days, Reading Marathons, Note Days, Praise Days, No-Fail Assignments, and Double-or-Nothing Days. They suggest ideas which involve everyone and which jolt people out of their indifference and make them notice that something is going on which will benefit them and be pleasurable at the same time.

The goal of such activities is not just fun and games. Rather, it's to create a pleasurable climate conducive to more work, more study, more learning, and more achievement. After all, the two goals of climate—productivity and satisfaction—don't apply just to students. They apply to teachers, cooks, custodians, media specialists, nurses, secretaries, and administrators too.

BEHAVIORS THAT TELL US PLEASURE IS THE MOTIVATOR

1. Arriving at school early and/or staying late.
2. Stopping by to see and visit with us.
3. Volunteering readily.
4. Participating easily.
5. Demonstrating an obvious enjoyment for people and school.
6. Telling jokes.
7. Smiling continually and seldom being angry.
8. Being positive and trying to see the good in people and situations.
9. Wanting to serve on committees.
10. Asking to give reports.
11. Wanting their name on reports and in the paper.
12. Requesting hard or important jobs.

QUESTIONS TO ASK YOURSELF

1. What can I do to make my classroom/school one of the best places in which students/staff members spend their time?
2. What joy or fun is it to be with me? To follow me?
3. Am I a happy person?
4. Does my demeanor mirror pleasure—and seem to be contagious?
5. Do I take myself too seriously?
6. Do I make work pleasant or unpleasant?
7. Do I find pleasure in being a teacher? An administrator?
8. How pleasurable is it to come to my class? To come to a faculty meeting?
9. Do I like those I am leading? What is the condition of my relationships with those being led?

10. If I were a student, would I want to be a student in my classroom? Would I want to be a teacher in my (school) (district)?
11. Is there anything I am doing that makes class/school less pleasurable than it could be for students/staff?
12. What rules and procedures are unpleasant?

Understanding Human Behavior—

• *Personal Gain*
• *Prestige*
• *Pleasure*
• *Imitation*
• *Security*
• *Convenience*
• *The Desire to Avoid Fear*
• *New Experiences*
• *Love/Caring*

SOME CONCLUSIONS

1. School can't be all fun and games. However, work does not have to be unpleasant.
2. Learning is enjoyable.
3. Good relationships are enjoyable.
4. Achieving is joyous.
5. Working with others is enjoyable.
6. Growing/learning is fulfilling.
7. People look forward to—and like repeating—pleasurable experiences.
8. People tend to avoid the unpleasant—and people who are unpleasant.
9. Helping people achieve and reach goals is pleasurable.
10. Expressing enthusiasm enhances pleasure.
11. It's a mistake to take pleasure away from people. If we want school to be hard or if we are a "pay the price" kind of leader, we may actually take the motivation out of the classroom, school, and district.
12. Success gives pleasure, and people are motivated by pleasure and success.

4. IMITATION: THE MOTIVATOR AND ITS MEANING

Imitation. *This is the need to follow a crowd. It's the need to do what the majority or minority is doing—as well as the need to model successful attitudes and behaviors.* This is a need or desire to model the attitudes, thinking, beliefs, actions, and mannerisms of others. People have a need to associate themselves with those they admire and want to emulate. Little polo players and alligators have been responsible for selling millions of dollars in sportswear—just out of this need. Likewise, leaders who understand the vital link between modeling and imitation are better equipped to develop strong students in the classroom—and strong teacher, administrator, and staff models in the school and district as well. Leaders who strive to show those being led the values of hard work, enthusiasm, achievement, and curiosity tend to develop students and staff who try to imitate these same behaviors. In truth, imitation is one of the ways we teach core values to those being led.

The imitation motivator should show us how important it is for us to look and act successful inside as well as outside the school. For those being led to admire and respect us—as well as want to be like us—we must be admirable. This trait has many dimensions—and just as many advantages for leading people.

Remember, imitation can be a positive or a negative because it is also the need to model different, oppositional, and inappropriate behavior. Some students are following a street gang, or those who drink, or those who use drugs, or those who do not study. Likewise, some adults are following negative leadership as well. The question is why? One reason is that they identify more readily and can find acceptance and success much easier

83

with these groups. They do not identify with good students or with good educators. This condition will never change until we take specific leadership actions to influence values.

Most certainly, we must make the values we cherish clear and admirable to those being led—as an aid and not as a "club." Then, we should do everything possible to perpetuate these values and the benefits from adopting them as well as recognize and acclaim those being led who uphold them. For instance, if we say that we cherish scholarship, we must ask ourselves, "What are we doing to model scholarship and to recognize good students—or those students who are showing academic improvement? Do we honor student athletes more than student scholars?" If we aren't giving more recognition for academic achievement or improvement, we should not be surprised if the majority of students imitate our apparent lack of enthusiasm for scholarship.

A similar case should be made for the superb teachers, administrators, cooks, custodians, nurses, secretaries, and others in our school. In our leadership action, we must be good models. We must also "hold up" the good models for others to imitate. If not, we aren't using imitation as a leadership motivator. If one student is doing something well, encourage other students to use the same technique. If a teacher is employing a successful teaching technique, utilizing equipment in a unique way, or handling learning or discipline problems effectively—we must capitalize on his or her success and stimulate others via the imitation motivator. It's called *third-person support*.

The use of third-person support is a valuable instrument to reinforce leadership decisions, urgings, and teachings. The leaders in industry use the third-person support of "what the competition is doing" at every opportunity. In many ways, third-person support says, "I'm not the only one who thinks this way. Look at what other successful people are doing." It also allows a teacher or administrator to open doors to new ideas as well as to say things *through others* that might otherwise go unsaid. In the marketplace, a lot of products are sold by means of the imitation motivator. Companies use movie stars and athletes to sell everything from toothpaste to automobiles. And we all know students are motivated to imitate peers in what they do, say, think, and wear.

From a leadership viewpoint, we should use imitation to stress the positive, reinforce good work, gain acceptance of a new idea, motivate those being led, or get people to change their behavior. Third-person support is vital to allowing us to consistently lead by modeling and reinforcing what others are doing successfully.

BEHAVIORS THAT TELL US IMITATION IS THE MOTIVATOR

1. Trying to fit in.
2. Trying to be like others in the group.
3. Dressing similarly to others.
4. Talking the way others do.
5. Believing the way others do.
6. Modeling the style of someone else.
7. Perpetuating what others are doing.
8. Working whether others do or not and following advice, even when others don't.
9. Saying, "I don't know if I agree, but if Mr. Smith said it's okay, then it is okay with me too."
10. Seeking the opinion of others before making a decision.
11. Looking around the room to see what others are going to do before taking action.

QUESTIONS TO ASK YOURSELF

1. Do I see myself as a model for students? For teachers? For administrators?
2. What can I do to make those being led want to imitate excellence?
3. Do I take people into my orbit?
4. Are my standards worthwhile?
5. Why should students follow me?
6. Why should teachers/principals/boards of education follow me?
7. What do I do to get people to look up to me?
8. Am I regarded as honest? Competent? Trustworthy? Ethical? Admirable?
9. Do people "quote" me? Why? Why not?
10. How can I make those being led imitate those who work hard, achieve, and are involved in the (classroom) (school) (district)?

Understanding Human Behavior—

- *Personal Gain*
- *Prestige*
- *Pleasure*
- *Imitation*
- *Security*
- *Convenience*
- *The Desire to Avoid Fear*
- *New Experiences*
- *Love/Caring*

SOME CONCLUSIONS

1. To use imitation effectively, we must model the attitude, behavior, and performance we want. We should also group people with those we want them to emulate.
2. If we want respect, we should give it.
3. If we want people to accept responsibility, we should accept responsibility—and give it to those being led.
4. If we want people to work hard, we should work hard.
5. If we do not instill values, those being led will develop their own—positive or negative.
6. Everything a teacher is asking students to be to each other, a teacher must be to students.
7. Everything a principal is asking teachers to be to students, a principal must be to teachers.
8. Everything a superintendent is asking principals to be to teachers, a superintendent must be to principals.
9. To further positive imitation, we must display good work.
10. It's a mistake to believe that until those we lead show us that they are responsible, we should not give them something big and responsible to do. Likewise, it's a leadership error to expect anything and refuse to give anything until those we lead demonstrate the trait we desire. We must model it first. If we don't, this motivator will not be available to us.

5. SECURITY: THE MOTIVATOR AND ITS MEANING

Security. *This is a desire for safety. It's a need to feel secure from anxiety, danger, uncertainty, attack, and making mistakes. It includes comfort as well as a concern for being both physically and psychologically safe.* This need is revealed in many ways by all people. It's one of the reasons people are concerned with rules and always want to make sure they are doing the right thing. It's also the reason some people fight change or never offer an idea or endorse one—and won't even offer opinions when asked. They want to be safe, and they fear the insecurity of change.

This need appears on every list as both a primary and a secondary human need. Therefore, a leader should be very careful about purposely arousing the insecurities of those being led. Neither should we force the insecure individual to "take a stand" publicly. The individual will, without reservation, withdraw from that leader, maybe permanently. The individual simply cannot and will not allow himself or herself to be placed in such an insecure position. Therefore, when we point out a mistake or present a difficult task, we must relate how we will help to enhance the security factor.

Millions of dollars worth of life, automobile, mortgage, and fire insurance is bought each year as a result of this need. People also have regular physical examinations, purchase countless burglar alarm systems, contribute to pension plans, and buy credit card protection services—all because of the need for security. The whole tenure system in education is built on this need. When we accept how important the need for security is to people, we will begin asking ourselves how we can give those being led a greater security and peace of mind in trusting us, listening to us, or following our leadership.

I will never forget my first day in college. I attended an orientation session. The speaker said, "Look to your left. Now look to your right. Two of you won't be here on graduation day." What a terrible thing to say. I thought he was talking only to me—and so did many others in that room. He didn't help me get off to a good start.

As administrators and teachers, we should always be asking ourselves what we are doing to make those being led secure in being with us. Too often, we *create* fears and insecurity. When we say, "This is going to be a hard course—many will fail," we arouse fears in all. Sometimes we do so in order to gain interest. We may even do so in order to get control. Regardless of *why* the fears exist, it is a reality that many factors in a school make students insecure. After all, students can't choose teachers, bring forth complaints, automatically make A's, or always get on the teams for which they try out. All of these realities point out the need to work at ways to offer students physical and psychological safeguards which reduce fears.

BEHAVIORS THAT TELL US SECURITY IS THE MOTIVATOR

1. Being constantly concerned about standards and requirements.
2. Wanting to do the right thing.
3. Worrying about everything and everyone.
4. Pointing out risks.
5. Worrying about dangers.
6. Never offering an idea or endorsing another's idea because of fear.
7. Hedging—or refusing to offer an opinion when asked.
8. Fearing the possibilities—and continually pointing out the pitfalls.
9. Asking for permission before doing anything—and asking every time.
10. Asking for some kind of protection or guarantee before doing as we request.
11. Never volunteering.
12. Asking others to speak for them.

QUESTIONS TO ASK YOURSELF

1. How can I make my (classroom) (school) (district) physically and psychologically safe

for students?

2. How can I make a (classroom) (school) (district) physically and psychologically safe for teachers? Administrators?
3. Do I motivate with pressure? Fear? Force?
4. Do I feel any sense of obligation/commitment to all students?
5. Do I feel any sense of obligation/commitment to all teachers?
6. Do students work for me, or do I work with students?
7. Do I work with the staff, or does the staff work for me?
8. What forms of security or protection do I offer students?
9. What forms of security or protection do I offer teachers?
10. What role does punishment play in my leadership style for people who do something wrong or make a mistake?
11. Is my word good?
12. Can those being led count on me? Do they think so?

Understanding
Human
Behavior—

- *Personal Gain*
- *Prestige*
- *Pleasure*
- *Imitation*
- *Security*
- *Convenience*
- *The Desire to Avoid Fear*
- *New Experiences*
- *Love/Caring*

SOME CONCLUSIONS

1. A leader can make people feel either secure or insecure—as well as dumb or smart.
2. A leader can feel more control when people feel insecure, but a leader is secure only when those being led are secure.
3. Insecurity separates a leader from those being led.
4. Many things create security: fairness, information, flexibility, and plans, to name a few. What else creates security?
5. Insecurity can cancel good judgment.
6. People who are fearful are seldom progressive.
7. Leaders who are secure and offer security to those being led are on a solid footing.
8. Fear can consume people and dictate everything they do.
9. Fearful people may have a roadblock to success.
10. Fear can cancel intellect.
11. It's a mistake not to try to make those being led feel secure being with us and being influenced by us.
12. A leader can create security.
13. Security can be rational or irrational.

6. CONVENIENCE: THE MOTIVATOR AND ITS MEANING

Convenience. *This is the need to make things handy, useful, easy, quick, and trouble-free. This is the need to add ease and comfort, save effort, and have access. It is the need to enhance personal well-being and comfort.* People are always looking for a better way or the easy way. This is not abnormal. Neither is it wrong. In addition, people are more likely to approve anything that does not involve more trouble, more inconvenience, more difficulty, or more work for them. They may even vote for anything that relieves them of some duty. And they will usually accept any easy task before they accept a difficult one.

Drive-up windows for banking, convenience stores, and fast food restaurants all meet this convenience need. So do catalog shopping, toll-free numbers, and credit cards. The

Book of the Month Club wasn't successful until it added the convenience factor and made buying easy. In the beginning, when you joined the club, you received a description of the selection of the month. If you wanted the book, you had to make out an order form and mail in your request. As a consequence, the club didn't sell many books. Then the club changed the procedure. Members were required to mail back their response cards *only* if they *did not* want the book. And if they failed to do so, they received a book. In essence, the club made it easier and more convenient to accept the monthly selection than to reject it. The club became an instant success.

The need for convenience is a strong one indeed. That's why we need to ask ourselves continually whether we are making it convenient for students to learn, participate in extracurricular activities, and function on a day-to-day basis in our classroom and school—and we need to be honest with ourselves about the ways in which we make these things convenient. We need to ask the same questions regarding how convenience is used to get teachers to follow administrative leadership.

When a leader can combine the need for convenience with the need for personal gain, leadership acceptance and motivation are enhanced dramatically. Remember, we all want things to be convenient. We all want life to be a little easier. The knowledgeable leader never reacts negatively to this need. Neither does he or she "explode" or express disappointment when those being led reveal the need for convenience. Rather, he or she realizes that leaders must adjust both their thinking and action to make the hardest task as easy and trouble-free as possible. If we *can* make something easier, we must never complicate it with an order, policy, rule, regulation, or procedure which makes it more difficult—or appear difficult.

BEHAVIORS THAT TELL US CONVENIENCE IS THE MOTIVATOR

1. Looking for the easy, simplest way.
2. Taking every shortcut.
3. Approving anything—if it does not involve their doing anything.
4. Voting for anything that relieves them of some duty.
5. Accepting an easy task and rejecting difficult and complicated ones.
6. Seeing only work—and never benefits.
7. Always voting against change.
8. Refusing to participate.
9. Being lazy.
10. Saying "I can't" or "I won't" even before thinking or trying.

QUESTIONS TO ASK YOURSELF

1. Do I make jobs hard?
2. Are my instructions clear?
3. Is it easy to follow me?
4. How convenient is it for those being led to learn in my (classroom) (school) (district)?
5. Do I think it's good for people to learn the hard way?
6. Am I approachable?
7. How do I handle (appointments) (meetings) (explanations) with others?
8. Do I make it easy to "buy" what I have to say?

9. How many rules do I have in my (classroom) (school) (district)?
10. Do I pace my teaching so every student can learn at an equitable rate?
11. Do I review frequently?
12. Do I make it convenient for those being led to have access to resources and get help?
13. How can I combine the need for personal gain and the convenience motivator?
14. If others follow my leadership, how many of their peers will be upset with them?

Understanding
Human
Behavior—

• *Personal Gain*
• *Prestige*
• *Pleasure*
• *Imitation*
• *Security*
• *Convenience*
• *The Desire to*
Avoid Fear
• *New Experiences*
• *Love/Caring*

SOME CONCLUSIONS

1. Rules and procedures can make things convenient or inconvenient for people.
2. The "way we have always done it" can increase or decrease inconvenience.
3. Standard operating procedure can facilitate convenience or curtail it.
4. People will almost always choose the convenient.
5. People will almost always avoid the inconvenient.
6. The more power we have, the more self-serving we may be.
7. Convenience is a form of power.
8. Convenience can increase productivity.
9. Convenience can increase satisfaction.
10. Convenience can improve the quality of life.

7. THE DESIRE TO AVOID FEAR: THE MOTIVATOR AND ITS MEANING

The Desire to Avoid Fear. *This is the desire to avoid or escape any kind of fear, threat of fear, and the person who creates fear, as well as the consequences that accompany it. It's the desire to avoid being behind or losing or failing. This need also includes the need to avoid fear of attack, ambush, danger, and being "trapped."* This need stops people from even trying. A leader can never forget this reality.

This is a much stronger need that we may suspect. Fear dominates the lives of many, many people. It controls their every move and keeps them from making changes, considering options, and developing. Many people are afraid and will refuse to be involved in anything beyond the scope of what they know. They worry about everything, and they often reject new concepts or anything that is not accompanied by leadership promises and guarantees, including the pledge to "bail them out" if they get in over their heads. This is one of the reasons so many products and services carry warranties and guarantees. And many carry unconditional guarantees. If you don't like the product or service, you can take it back and get your money back with no questions asked. Why? To stop customer fear and enable you to take buying action.

Another fear people have is the fear of not knowing the right thing to do. Many students don't do what's right because they are afraid of peer and adult rejection. People lie to protect themselves. People refuse to participate to protect themselves. People avoid some academic subjects to protect themselves. And many are reluctant to serve in leadership capacities—because of fear.

People also fear being intimidated, being forced to reveal their intelligence or judgment, or having to reveal their lack of knowledge about a particular subject. Many of these fears are irrational. But the truth is that for many people, school is a fearful place. For students, the fears include fear of other classmates, of the opposite sex, of students who are older and physically dominating, and of adults. In today's school climate, many educators avoid fear by avoiding people and situations.

Parents often have a multitude of fears about school, many of which are carried over from the days when they were in school. That's why identifying these fears and the times of year they are apt to surface—as well as finding ways to help those being led overcome fears—is a leadership must. And a leader should be careful about making those being led fearful. Remember, fear can cancel intellect. And when aroused by fear, kittens can become tigers.

BEHAVIORS THAT TELL US A DESIRE TO AVOID FEAR IS THE MOTIVATOR

1. Refusing to be involved.
2. Worrying about everything.
3. Rejecting new concepts.
4. Serving reluctantly in leadership capacities.
5. Asking "What if?" Example: "What if this happens, or what if that happens?"
6. Saying "I could have." Example: "I could have been successful if this or that hadn't happened."
7. Opposing new ideas.
8. Worrying about the future.
9. Wanting a rule for everything.
10. Requesting safeguards or assurances before saying anything.
11. Wanting promises and guarantees.

QUESTIONS TO ASK YOURSELF

1. What can I do to reduce or eliminate fears in the (classroom) (school) (district)?
2. What times of the year create fear—and for whom?
3. Do I avoid motivating with guilt?
4. Am I tough/hard-nosed?
5. Do I believe that I can't be nice to people and still be an effective leader?
6. Am I intimidating?
7. Is it safe to make a mistake in my classroom?
8. Is it safe to make a mistake in my school?
9. Is my word good?
10. Is it safe to talk to me, or do people say I use what they say against them?
11. Do I motivate people with fear?
12. Am I a "pay the price" teacher/administrator?
13. Do I "keep my thumb" on people?
14. What do I do to make my (school) (classroom) (district) as risk-free as possible?
15. How do I make the (classroom) (school) (district) a friendly place where fewer people are motivated by fear?
16. What fears are rational/irrational in my (classroom) (school) (district)? How do I attack those fears?

SOME CONCLUSIONS

1. Fear is a very effective motivator. It works.
2. What it does for control, however, it does against creativity, ingenuity, and intellect.
3. Fear can increase or decrease effort and productivity, but it seldom increases satisfaction in normal situations. It is true however, that some people are stimulated by fear.
4. If a leader uses fear, subordinates are likely to use fear against others as well.
5. Fear makes people run, hide, or fight.
6. No teacher can use fear to "beat," control, or dominate a roomful of students and expect to find a high level of success.
7. No principal can use fear to "beat," control, or dominate teachers and students and expect to experience a high level of success.
8. No superintendent can use fear to "beat" principals.
9. People who lead via fear are not likely to survive over the long term.
10. Fear makes leading and being led unrewarding experiences.
11. If a leader enjoys using fear to lead people, he or she should not be the appointed leader.
12. The less skill a leader possesses, the more he or she is likely to rely upon fear as a motivator.
13. It's better to think in terms of motivation rather than reprimand.
14. Maintaining interaction with those being led can help people be less fearful.
15. When people reveal fear, let them know you are going to handle their fear together.
16. Some fears are rational. Some fears are irrational. But both affect the fearful.

Understanding Human Behavior—

- *Personal Gain*
- *Prestige*
- *Pleasure*
- *Imitation*
- *Security*
- *Convenience*
- *The Desire to Avoid Fear*
- *New Experiences*
- *Love/Caring*

8. NEW EXPERIENCES: THE MOTIVATOR AND ITS MEANING

New Experiences. *This is the need felt by many people to do, see, or participate in something new, different, unique, or varied.* This includes a change of pace, working with new people, a new procedure, a new schedule, a new approach, a new technique or skill, or any kind of change. This is the need many people have to try, attempt, risk, and venture into new domains.

Doing the same thing in the same old way often becomes boring and demotivating to us and those being led. We find it dull and void of personal motivation. New experiences are the prerequisites of personal and professional growth. They create excitement. They are challenging. They are progressive. To some people, new means "good," "progressive," "growth-producing," "modern," and "up to date." Doing things the same way all the time is regressive to many people.

Every year the fashion and automobile industries capitalize on the overwhelming need people have for new experiences. It has been the trademark of the travel industry. We can use it too. New courses can be studied each year on a new level. New opportunities abound in a school—and we can create many of them. Experiences that are slightly different from the regular routine can enhance motivation and stimulate those being led to become involved. Rearranging the furniture in the room, holding an unscheduled assembly, inviting a surprise speaker, or planning exciting activities, tours, and field trips are all ideas that offer chances for new experiences—for us and students. New ideas, new objectives, new practices, new activities, and new services give students a reason to continue their interest in the classroom and school.

New experiences can keep school employees stimulated, interested, and growing. When teachers and administrators are open to new ideas and ways—and aren't stubbornly tied to old ones—we can earn a reputation for being forward-looking, stimulating to work with, and invigorating to be around.

BEHAVIORS THAT TELL US NEW EXPERIENCES ARE THE MOTIVATOR

1. Asking for "dress up" or "dress down" days.
2. Requesting carnivals, fairs, or parties.
3. Requesting tours or trips.
4. Wanting to meet new people.
5. Asking to change the room or to do tasks in a different order.
6. Requesting to visit another school.
7. Wanting to change the schedule or vary an activity.
8. Getting overly excited about anything new.
9. Wanting to do things "not in the book."

QUESTIONS TO ASK YOURSELF

1. What new experiences do I give teachers?
2. What new experiences do students have from grade to grade?
3. How would I describe the average (day) (month) for students?
4. How would I describe the average (day) (month) for teachers and administrators?
5. How would I describe my average day?
6. What is "new" in my classroom? School? District?
7. Do I always teach and test in the same way?
8. What is my attitude toward change?
9. Am I comfortable with routine?
10. What kind of new experiences would students/parents/citizens be interested in to help them learn, get involved, or support schools?
11. Do I have a routine that never varies?
12. Do I have parent-teacher committees? Inservice committees?
13. Do I have assemblies that parents can attend? Lunches? Visitations?
14. Do I have explanation "coffees" or tours for parents or civic groups?

SOME CONCLUSIONS

1. Always doing things the same way can be dull and boring. And few are bored into following your leadership.
2. Attention can be created with new experiences.
3. Interest and success can be created with new experiences.
4. Involvement and achievement can be created with new experiences.
5. Variation can be motivating.
6. New experiences can be learning experiences.
7. New experiences can be beneficial for leader and follower alike.

9. LOVE/CARING: THE MOTIVATOR AND ITS MEANING

Love/Caring. *This is an extremely effective motivator—and a necessary one. Why? Because the reality is that love is the only human emotion that human beings cannot live without.* Therefore, love is more than important to all of us: It is vital to us all. The presence of love, however, means caring, concern, and wanting to please.

To be meaningful to those being led, love and caring must be without condition, without strings, and without contingencies. Love is inherent in friendship. And compassion is impossible without love and caring. So are devotion and attraction. It is with love and caring that relationships and loyalties are built. If we leave these motivators out of leadership, we leave out what leading and living are really all about. There is also no doubt that this is the motivator upon which connections and steadfast followings are built.

The truth of the matter is that you can make a lot of mistakes as a leader, but if those being led believe that you really like them, love them, and care about them, you can weather most storms. On the other hand, if those being led don't think that you love or care about them, they will try to "hang you from the nearest tree" every time you make a mistake.

When we accept people for just being, we do care and we do give them love. When we give respect, show consideration, help those being led find success, and honor achievement, we reveal caring and give love. When we remember and take the time to recognize the birthdays of those being led, we show our caring and love. When we acknowledge that a tragedy has befallen a student or a student's family, we teach the meaning of love and caring. This is a most important teaching, because many of our leadership actions can be seen as self-serving and manipulative—if we leave love and caring out of our leadership actions. When those being led see our leadership efforts as manipulations, they will think that they are being used and abused. Then, building a solid relationship for achieving meaningful work and relationships is impossible.

As teachers and administrators, we are in the business of teaching those we lead "how to walk" via the curriculum we teach. But we are also in the business of teaching those we lead "where to walk" as well. And if all of our love and caring is for academics, books, buildings, and budgets—we have shown that we don't love people, we love "things." A good rule to follow is this: Put love and caring into everything you do—and take any hate and rejection out, or everyone loses. After all, these two powerful motivators—love and caring—create passion for work, achievement, and people.

Understanding Human Behavior—

- *Personal Gain*
- *Prestige*
- *Pleasure*
- *Imitation*
- *Security*
- *Convenience*
- *The Desire to Avoid Fear*
- *New Experiences*
- *Love/Caring*

BEHAVIORS THAT TELL US LOVE/CARING IS THE MOTIVATOR

1. (Students) (teachers) (staff) trying to please us—and doing anything we request.
2. Running to the aid of anyone with a problem.
3. Being emotional about students, colleagues, school, or district.
4. (Teachers) doing anything to help students individually and collectively.
5. (Students) volunteering to help teachers.
6. (Teachers) volunteering to help administrators.
7. Giving home phone numbers to students needing help with homework.
8. Providing socials for the staff.
9. Meeting with students individually concerning wants, needs, problems, and performance.

10. Bringing us gifts, giving us information, and asking us "how we feel."
11. Telling us how they feel about us.
12. Wanting to be with us.
13. Volunteering to help us.
14. Doing what we ask without question or hesitation.
15. Noticing what we wear.
16. Revealing concern when we are upset or hurt.
17. Telling us we can count on them.
18. Openly telling us they love us—and care about us.

QUESTIONS TO ASK YOURSELF

1. What special concerns are shown to parents? Students? Faculty?
2. What special services do I offer those being led?
3. What am I doing that is above and beyond the call of duty?
4. What evidence exists to show that love is a dominant factor in my classroom? School? District?
5. Do I fear making myself vulnerable?
6. Am I kind?
7. Am I gentle?
8. Am I nurturing?
9. Am I a lover or a hater?
10. Am I a giver or a taker?
11. What tangible evidence do those being led have that I care about them as persons?

SOME CONCLUSIONS

1. Love is vital to relationships.
2. Love and caring are vital elements in the leader-follower relationship.
3. Love cannot exist unless we accept people for "just being."
4. If love is giving only on the condition that people prove themselves to us before we give love to them, we do not love.
5. People will follow a leader who makes many mistakes if they feel loved. Few will follow if they don't.
6. Followers who don't feel loved, feel used.
7. Love and caring are motivating to human beings.
8. Love and caring are recognition.
9. Love and caring are appreciation.
10. Love and caring show that the leader values those being led as individual persons of worth.
11. Love and caring provide special emotions.
12. Hate nurtures hate.

THE CORE
OF MOTIVATION

These are the nine individual motivators of perception and action which can be used to induce people to follow a leader. It's funny that we can put a man on the moon, but we often can't understand why close friends, loved ones, colleagues, or those being led think and act the way they do. Maybe it's because we haven't taken the time and given the effort and thought to find out. Certainly, the seven primary and the eight secondary needs plus the nine individual motivators contain the objective rationale for teachers and administrators to begin leading with understanding and direction.

The needs show us how we are alike and how we are unique. They reveal the areas of our individual motivation. They point out a fact which every leader must remember: The priorities of people vary. What may be a strong priority to one individual may not be as intense to another. But most of all, these needs should tell us that if we are going to lead and get all the work of the classroom, school, and district accomplished, we must relate to many different wants and needs in many different ways.

It is hoped that every leader will be quick to realize that identifying and making use of the wants and needs of those being led is not manipulation. Make no mistake: Meeting our wants and needs as individuals is what we want out of life. It is what we want out of work. It is what those we lead want from their leaders as well. Therefore, if we help those we lead meet their needs, they will follow us for a very practical reason: There aren't many people in any of our lives trying to help us get what we want. We do not fight such leaders. We follow them—and cherish them.

I'd venture to say that every leader could sit down right now with a list of those he or she leads and identify the needs that would characterize each individual. And we should all do exactly that. I suggest making out a personality guide for each person in our charge. Then, to get to know those we lead, there are some things we should observe, identify, and watch:

1.   With whom will they associate, and with whom will they not?
2.   What do they talk about?
3.   What do they avoid talking about?
4.   What are they confident about, and with what are they insecure?
5.   What drives them?

As a leader, you must also remember that within these needs lie your own needs. Make sure you are not victimizing others or trying to satisfy your wants and needs at the expense of those you lead. A teacher or administrator can victimize those being led in countless ways. The shy always present an opportunity to show power. Staff and student accomplishments may be your source of stolen personal status. Agreeing with a teacher, administrator, parent, or student may be your way of avoiding fear. A bad decision may be the need for security revealed in an unhealthy manner. A new rule may make an organizational need take precedence over student needs. That need within yourself may deny the delegation of authority and responsibility. A new procedure may be initiated to gain approval rather than to further the best interest of students—or it may be made simply to make your tasks more pleasurable or convenient.

Never forget, you, as well as those you lead, are governed by the same wants and needs. The only difference is the intensity of each need and the fact that the weight of authority lies with the appointed leader. In addition, remember that we, as leaders, are also asking, "What's

Understanding
Human
Behavior—

• *Personal Gain*
• *Prestige*
• *Pleasure*
• *Imitation*
• *Security*
• *Convenience*
• *The Desire to*
Avoid Fear
• *New Experiences*
• *Love/Caring*

in it for me?" These facts add a special responsibility to being a leader if being a teacher or administrator is a function rather than a position for you.

APPLICATION: PROFILE YOURSELF FIRST

1. To lead others, you must use the people motivators. However, this is often easier if we profile our own motivators first. Otherwise, we may not understand or accept how an individual motivator can be such a strong force in someone's life. Profiling ourselves can be a valuable exercise. It shows us our motivators. It tells us the areas in which we may have trouble leading.
2. Fill out this form for individuals you are having a difficult time leading.
3. List the people motivator voids you see in the those you lead.

PEOPLE MOTIVATORS

People Motivators	Circle the degree to which each people motivator affects attitude/behavior.
Personal Gain	1 2 3 4 5 6 7 8 9 10
Prestige	1 2 3 4 5 6 7 8 9 10
Pleasure	1 2 3 4 5 6 7 8 9 10
Imitation	1 2 3 4 5 6 7 8 9 10
Security	1 2 3 4 5 6 7 8 9 10
Convenience	1 2 3 4 5 6 7 8 9 10
The Desire to Avoid Fear	1 2 3 4 5 6 7 8 9 10
New Experiences	1 2 3 4 5 6 7 8 9 10
Love/Caring	1 2 3 4 5 6 7 8 9 10

Very little effect ◄————► Very strong effect

THE FOUNDATION LAWS

These five laws stand alone—and, at the same time, they embrace all the laws and principles of leading people. These laws must be embraced and employed as an integral part of all the other laws. To be highly effective in the classroom, the school, and the district in the 21st century, proactive leadership is a must—and all leadership must adhere to the Law of Origin.

The Law of Proactive Leadership
The Law of Origin
The Law of Total Responsibility
The Law of Top-Down Leadership
The Law of Ever Present Leadership

A REFERENCE FOR
STUDYING THE LAWS

I call the laws and principles the *foundation* of leadership and management. Why? It is because they give us a set of rules to learn and follow which provides our leadership the highest probability of success—and the least possibility of failure. These are guidelines people need to know before they begin to lead—and which they must continually remember to apply while they are leading—because they are predictors of how those being led will respond and what will happen in most leadership situations. This fills a huge need for teachers and administrators alike. We are bombarded continually to react in problem situations. We are expected to make wise decisions on the spot. Using these laws can help us get the job done.

By studying these laws, we can acquire vast amounts of knowledge and information. We can stay on course. We are most apt to make the right decision for the right reasons in the right ways. Once we commit them to memory, the laws and principles serve as part of our professional being and a guidepost in any normal, decision-making, or problem situation we face. Without understanding the laws, we can be pulled in countless directions while trying to decide what to do. The stress and pressure of continually sorting out and making the right decisions can affect us adversely in many ways.

Again, that's why I call these laws and principles the leadership and management *foundation*. They are designed to become a part of you as you function as the leader in the classroom, school, or district. I wrote these laws not only to help a leader be more successful—but to help leaders put more substance, confidence, security, and satisfaction into leading as well.

Please note, I wrote these laws, but I did not create or manufacture them. To me, they are just natural laws pertaining to the way things work. In this book, I refer to these guidelines as laws, principles, theories, and hypotheses of the social science of leadership and management. As we know, a *science* is concerned with the relationship between cause and effect. By this definition, teaching and administrating can each be considered a science because both functions use:

1. Logical reasoning.
2. Observation.
3. Research and experiments to solve problems and reach conclusions.

In the classroom, school, and district, we deal with facts, hypotheses, theories, laws, and principles. In order to understand fully the meaning and implications of these laws and principles, we must first define the terms that make up these concepts in this book.

1. **Hypotheses**. A *hypothesis* is a logical formulation which attempts to establish one fact, or series of facts, as the cause of another fact, or series of facts. In practical terms, a hypothesis is really an *educated guess* at a causal relationship.
   a. We should realize that a hypothesis may or may not be true.
   b. The correctness of a hypothesis can only be established when it has proved to be successful through the tests of time and experience.

2. **Theories**. A *theory* is a hypothesis which has proved to be true through tests under various conditions.
   a. Remember, a theory is more than just a "shot in the dark." Experience has proved it to be consistently true. A satisfactory cause-effect relationship has already been established.
   b. Often, a number of theories will satisfy the same condition equally well. The truth of this fact encourages constant reexamination in order to find a better alternative.

3. **Laws and Principles**. A theory becomes a *law* or *principle* after leading authorities and practitioners have widely accepted the truth and inevitability of the idea. Common examples are the "Law of Gravity" and the "Law of Supply and Demand."
   a. There is a significant difference between tacitly agreeing with the truth of a law and truly understanding how the law works.
   b. Because the word *law* has the connotation of "being fixed," many people prefer to use the word "principle," recognizing that our world continually changes and that new, more encompassing principles may be discovered. Yet, we should all be aware that regardless of all the changes being experienced today, the Law of Gravity remains fixed.

4. **Facts**. A *fact* is a physical happening which our experience has consistently proven to be true. For example, it is a fact that if we do not replenish our bodies with food, we will eventually starve to death. Likewise, it is a fact that fire burns or that we need a medium of

exchange to pay our bills. However, at one time, it was also a *fact* that the world was flat and that space travel was only possible in science fiction novels.

a. Therefore, as teachers and administrators, it is essential to realize that what is an absolute fact to one person may not be to another. Often, therefore, facts are only relatively true.

b. This does not mean that facts are worthless or of uncertain value. Every field of learning is based upon a series of interrelated facts which form the foundation of that field. This is true in chemistry, physics, and in the social science of human leadership and management.

When everyone, or almost everyone, accepts a law or principle for a long time, it may become a fact.

5. **Myths.** A *myth* is an unproved or false collective belief that is used to justify a social institution. A *myth* is a traditional or legendary story, usually concerning some practice, beliefs, being, hero, or event—with or without a determinable basis of fact or a natural explanation.

a. A myth may be widely believed.

b. A myth may be practiced.

6. **Fallacies**. A *fallacy* is a deceptive, misleading, or false notion or belief.

a. A fallacy may be believed.

b. A fallacy may be the foundation for decision making.

c. A fallacy may be practiced.

If we are to profit from our study of the human side of leadership, we must approach it with an open, accepting, and objective mind. At times, we must form evaluations and judgments and arrive at conclusions. However, our decisions should be based on an objective analysis of the facts, not our subjective, personal opinions of people or situations. The laws and principles will help guide our thinking and facilitate making the right decisions when we are leading people. One thing is certain: If you learn and use these laws and principles faithfully, you won't make very many mistakes. And when you do make mistakes, you'll know exactly what you need to do.

THE
LAW OF
PROACTIVE LEADERSHIP

Rationale: The primary function of a leader is to continually acquire and teach the attitudes, beliefs, core values, knowledge, and skills which facilitate success and move the leader and those being led to higher levels of performance.

While I will not define all the words in this book, I must give the definition to *proactive* in the full context of my intended usage because it is linked to all the laws, principles, theories, and myths. As you read this book alone or study it in a group, we need to be on the same page when it comes to understanding, accepting, and using the proactive stance.

For functional purposes, let's divide the word *proactive*, and define its parts, and the whole word. There are three words within the word *proactive*: *I, pro*, and *act*.

I means "each of us."

Pro means "progressive; forward; to the front of; before; in advance; professional."

Act means "to put in motion; to exert power; to do; to lead; to perform; to play a part of; to behave a certain way; to intervene effectively; to produce an effect."

When I use the term *proactive leadership*, I am referring to all the dimensions indicated in the individual words. In addition, I also use *proactive leadership* as meaning:

"serving to prepare, to intervene in or control an expected or unexpected occurrence or situation, including a negative or difficult one—in an anticipatory manner to cause others to want your leadership."

As you ponder being proactive, keep in mind that choosing to be passive is in direct opposition to this stance. Passive means not active. It means inert and not acting. Passive means receiving, enduring, or submitting without resistance. Passive means not reacting visibly to something that might be expected. It means not participating—readily or actively. Therefore, passive is the opposite of proactive in every way.

In addition, know that being proactive does not mean just being reactive. *React* means "to act in return to an agent or influence; to act in a reverse direction or manner; to act in opposition, as against some force; and to respond to a stimulus in a particular manner." There are many times when a leader must react, of course. In fact, if you can't react you can't be successful. However, if your predominant leadership stance is reacting, you are not going to find leading very productive or satisfying. And herein lies the problem of many leaders: They find themselves simply reacting rather than being proactive leaders. As a result, they don't feel like a leader. They don't feel a sense of influence. To them, it seems as though all they do is wait for what and who is going to come at them next. In the process, they feel like someone who has the responsibility to lead, but hasn't been given the authority to think, decide, and take action. The less a teacher, principal, or superintendent understands leadership, the more he or she will find himself or herself only reacting.

I apologize for being so academic, but because proactive leadership is so vital to success, taking this step to create understanding is absolutely necessary. You may add to the definition, of course. However, please do not delete from it.

A LEARNER
AND TEACHER—FIRST

Those of you who have read *Causing Others To Want Your Leadership* are aware that I called the Law of Origin the Law of Laws. Therefore, please note that the Law of Proactive Leadership has joined The Foundation Laws—and for good reason. The 21st century leader must primarily be an action-oriented learner and mentor. Without continuous and comprehensive learning, mentoring, and action, a leader cannot and will not draw others into the orbit of work, facilitate change, create a positive and productive climate and culture, enable those being led to experience success, and cause others to want his or her leadership.

The Law of Proactive Leadership embraces all the laws of leadership and management. It is only after we have made a strong commitment to accept the necessity of proactive leadership that we can adhere to all the laws. Only after we accept the Law of Proactive Leadership will we be able to activate the Law of Origin. Only when we adhere to the Law of Proactive Leadership will we know adherence to all the other laws is a continuous, comprehensive, and proactive leadership activity.

The adage "You can lead a horse to water, but you can't make him drink" is true. Leading people would be a lot easier if it weren't true, and those being led would be a lot more successful as well. The truth is: We can't make a person work or learn. We can't demand that those being led study or grow. We can't force anyone to believe or act a certain way. And we can count on the fact that we will experience obstacles and resistance in our efforts to help those being led to learn, grow, and accept the attitudes, beliefs, and practices which move them to higher levels of performance. However, to be a successful leader in the 21st century, continually striving to meet this leadership responsibility in a proactive manner is mandatory.

This law teaches us that, as teachers or administrators, we can't sit on our hands and lead effectively. We can't hide on the sidelines. We can't be afraid to lead. Neither can we be hesitant or reluctant to lead. What we need to know is that people want competent leadership. They know that they need competent leadership. They are very much aware that good leadership is vital to their success. And to be a good leader, you must be proactive and follow the laws and principles which are in agreement with good leadership and management.

Unfortunately, too many teachers and administrators abandon this right and responsibility to lead through proactive modeling, teaching, mentoring, and acting—which always makes leading more difficult. Yet, passive leadership does not work well in the short or long term. A hands-off approach ensures that leadership can be held by anyone who grabs it. With passive leadership, the leader can only let the organization run itself. Passive leadership makes achievement, as well as moving to higher levels of performance, difficult. And, of course, passive leadership makes initiating change painful and extremely difficult.

It's also true that 21st century leaders will find themselves in circumstances and situations where they are followers. We may be asked to observe an activity. We may be on a committee as a member rather than the leader. Regardless of the situation, however, we must always take a proactive stance within our role in the situation. If we choose to be passive, we make no difference when we observe anyone—or when we are a member of a committee or work in any situation as a follower.

A LEADER MUST CONTINUALLY LEARN AND TEACH ATTRIBUTES WHICH FACILITATE SUCCESS

To be successful in the 21st century, a leader must be proactive by continually functioning as a learner, coach, mentor, and teacher by showing the way. He or she must think continually in terms of arousing, persuading, sharing, contributing, and convincing those he or she leads.

Proactive leaders know it is their responsibility to "blanket" the entire organization—whether it is a classroom, school, or district—with the attitudes, beliefs, core values, and skills necessary for everyone being led to be successful—and for the organization itself to be successful. They must create the climate and culture which encourages those being led to think constantly and creatively regarding how to function in better ways. They must know that this teaching must come from the "top," wherever the top is—the teacher, department head, principal, or superintendent.

Without such proactive leadership action, there may be as many attitudes, beliefs, practices, and core values as there are people in the classroom, school, or district. And many of these attitudes, beliefs, practices, and core values will be superb—but many will be misguided and counter to productivity, the work and mission of the school—and success. Worse, many practices may be more self-serving than serving to those being led or to the work and mission of the classroom, school, or district.

In the classroom, the teacher must learn—as well as teach—attitudes, core values, and skills to each student and the entire class. Remember, you teach core values by what you value. And what you value is communicated to those being led whether you think so or not. Principals and superintendents must do the same with the faculty and staff. This task is not easy. It requires diligence and commitment. Too, there will be resistance and rejection. This reality, unfortunately, is why many leaders decide to stop their proactive efforts. A leader can almost always find proof or a rationale that seems to make giving up or quitting the right and sensible choice. After all, we can find confirmation and logic for our "backing away" in the old saying "You can lead a horse to water, but you can't make him drink."

However, only with continuous proactive leadership can we help those being led *want* to "drink." And as some begin to drink and find success, only a leader's continuous and unfaltering efforts will ensure that more and more people will follow. As the circle of those who want our leadership grows, fulfilling the responsibility of leadership is easier and more effective. But being proactive means you have to act and participate all the time. You can't lead one month and hide the next. You can't decide that you have learned all you need to learn about leading and stop. You must not fail to practice what you preach. It won't work. And you can't follow what you preach without adhering to the laws and principles of leadership and management revealed in this book.

PROACTIVE LEADERSHIP HAS EIGHT PRONGS

Proactive leadership encompasses eight prongs: *passion, positioning, planning, preparing, promoting, practicing, protecting,* and *providing*. Without faithful attention to the eight dimensions of this law, a high level of success is not likely to be experienced—and career-long success is unlikely. In addition, without attention to these eight prongs, facilitating continuous individual and group improvement is almost impossible. In fact, trying to initiate progress and change is likely to drive a leader crazy and make him or her begin to believe that "the job is impossible" or "just isn't worth it."

PASSION

The first prong of proactive leadership is *passion*. A passion is a deep feeling. It is a strong emotion by which the mind is swayed. It is a pursuit to which one is devoted. To lead effectively, we must have a passion for leading work and people.

In 1746, Denis Diderot said, "Only passions, great passions, can elevate the soul to great things." Without question, a leader must love the work and mission of the classroom, school, and district if a high level of success is expected. And a leader must also have a passion for the people he or she works with as well as those being led. This passion for what we are doing as well as what we need to do must be within our very being.

Without such passion, we are only a submerged force. We are an authority figure without enthusiasm and zeal. We will never see or experience the real possibilities—and neither will those we lead. The passion for being an educator lies in the heart. And a proactive leader can put passion for work and achievement in the heart of those being led.

It is the passion for the work and mission of the schools which will help you identify and tackle needs. It will help you keep your focus and vision sharp. It is passion which will help you make the right decisions, in the right ways, for the right reasons. It is heart-felt passion that will keep you holding to your values and caring about people through hard times—and keep you from giving up. And it is passion for the work and mission of education that will allow you to trust others and surround yourself with those who hold the same passion.

If one doesn't hold such passion, being a proactive leader is not possible over the long term. After all, passion is vital because we are in an emotional profession. We're in a people profession. We're not manufacturers, making refrigerators or automobiles. What we do with students, teachers, and administrators can affect the whole of their life. That's why, if leaders do not have a strong passion for the work they are doing, it will adversely affect them and those being led.

It's very difficult to be a good leader if you don't have the desire for it. Are there any of us who believe we can be good at what we do if we do it half-heartedly? And if we have the power in the classroom, school, or district, but don't have the passion to use that power in appropriate ways, the responsibility of leading is likely to make us use our power in self-directed ways or ways that abuse the power we hold. Make no mistake: Passion comes in many forms: love, hate, joy, anger, affection, and dislike. And when we don't hold passion in the positive and productive sense, we are likely to find the negative forms dominating our mind-set. When this happens, causing others to want our leadership becomes impossible. Therefore, because we are all the chief executive officer in the classroom or school or district, we all need the strong desire to lead in order to fulfill the whole of our responsibilities.

The *passion* prong of proactive leadership is revealed in:
The Law of Origin
The Law of Total Responsibility
The Law of Ever-Present Leadership
The Law of Top-Down Leadership

POSITIONING

The second prong of proactive leadership is *positioning*. How you decide to position yourself with those being led is one of the most important decisions you will ever make. A leader's positioning must be in relation to the work and mission of the organization, the people in and served by the organization, and the constituency of the organization. The organization may be a classroom, a school, or a district. It may be a club or a team. It may be a committee or a task force.

Proactive leadership mandates that you continually position yourself to act and lead. If you are not positioned to lead by learning, modeling, acting, and teaching, you cannot lead. Positioning to mentor and lead is vital because it determines the perception others have of you—and the perception you have of yourself and your function. It gives you the leverage to influence. It is the stance that affects your ability to see what is needed for those being led to be successful and to respond appropriately and effectively. Positioning declares your intent and conveys to your constituency your willingness to accept the leadership role.

Positioning is not a stance you can turn on and off. It is a continuous proactive process. Without it, those being led will never come to the point of depending upon you as a point of reference. Positioning is linked with those being led expecting and accepting your leadership. Remember, you can't drive a car from the back seat.

Using the sport of baseball as a parallel offers an excellent example. If you play your position, your chances of success are enhanced. If you do not, you aren't likely to do well. And when you are out of position, you can be assured that someone will hit the ball through the hole you haven't covered.

The *positioning* prong of proactive leadership is revealed in:

The Law of Origin
The Law of Total Responsibility
The Law of Ever-Present Leadership
The Law of Top-Down Leadership
The Law of Adjustment
The Law of Survival
The Law of Longevity
The Law of Leaving
The Law of Real Value
The Law of Action and Reaction
The Law of Trust
The Law of Transference
The Law of Timing
The Law of Right/Wrong Conflict
The Law of Conflict
The Law of Dominance
The Law of Power
The Principle of Sharing Power
The Theory of Power and Responsibility
The Law of Control
The Law of Leader-Follower Relationships

PLANNING

The third prong of proactive leadership is *planning*.

Planning provides the "how to" and the "can do" of proactive leadership. It includes the ideas you have to help individuals and the group be successful as well as achieve goals. Planning gives direction to those being led so that you can cause them to want your leading—and to achieve to your expectations. It also provides reassurance and confidence that what you're proposing can and will be done.

Planning breaks down that which may appear to be overwhelming into identifiable and achievable goals and objectives. Planning fosters thinking and creative thought. It stretches, encourages, and facilitates the continuous growth of those being led by providing structure, purpose, and instruction. Planning is the yardstick that lets those being led know when they are progressing and when they have been successful.

A close look will reveal that planning develops involvement and shows each person how he or she "fits." It also answers the primary question: "What is in it for me?" Planning maximizes the use of time, energy, attention, and resources in the classroom, the school, and the district. It also allows you to seize opportunities, recognize distractions, overcome obstacles, and determine necessities and opportunities.

Many leaders have a singular plan. It may be a very good one. But they try to work their singular plan A throughout a year—and even their entire careers. For instance, many teachers start the year with a great plan A. They put it in motion. They have success. Yet, they fail to see that plan A needs additional plans B, C, and D in order for them to move to new levels of achievement. Likewise, additional plans are needed when a plan hits roadblocks, when resistance surfaces, and when changes need to be made.

To cause others to want your leadership as well as to take a class, a school, or a district to higher levels of achievement, you need to establish precise as well as alternate plans to meet both short- and long-term goals. Some teachers and administrators are employing last year's lessons and tests. Without multiple planning efforts, however, they will find it very difficult to meet needs, adjust, and implement change.

The *planning* prong of proactive leadership is revealed in:

The Law of Origin
The Law of Ever-Present Leadership
The Law of Top-Down Leadership
The Law of Planning
The Law of Collaboration
The Myth of the Perfect Plan
The Fallacy of Standardized Procedure
The Law of Cycles
The Law of Real Truth and Time

PREPARING

The fourth prong of proactive leadership is *preparing*.

Preparing means to fit; to adapt; to put into such a state as to be fit for use or application. It means to make ready for something that is to happen: a day, a lesson, a parent conference—or a schedule, a budget, or a bond issue. Above all, preparing means readying yourself and those being led to the point or degree that all of you are much more likely to find success than experience failure.

This prong includes being physically and mentally ready for each hour, each day, and each task. It also means getting those being led ready for each hour, each day, and each task. This can't be done without teaching ourselves—and those we lead—the attitudes and skills necessary to be prepared.

Therefore, proactive preparing covers three areas: self, others, and the organization. In preparing to lead yourself, others, and the classroom or institution, you must think "active," not "passive." You must say "I must do something," rather than "something must be done." To be prepared, the leader must have a sense of purpose, maintain a proactive attitude, acquire a wide breadth of knowledge and skills, and constantly pursue a high level of learning. Unless we do so, we may be prepared for one day, but not the next. We may be ready for one task, but ill-equipped for another.

Proactive preparation for leading others also requires knowing those being led. This preparation requires thorough study. We can get high levels of performance only by identifying and using the primary needs, secondary needs, and people motivators to help both the individual and the group find success. We must recognize and use the wants, needs, and strengths of those we lead. Remember, we are all driven by the same needs. We are all driven by the same instincts. We can be kind and gentle. We can be considerate and loving. We can be focused and hard-working. We can also be the opposite. If we want to be successful and lead people constructively in the classroom, the school, and the district, we must meet their needs in positive and constructive ways.

Proactive preparing of the classroom, school, and district involves management of the necessary resources coupled with a clarity of organizational purpose. Finally, preparing includes actually creating the conditions to support the climate and culture necessary to meet the needs of the individual and the organization.

The *preparing* prong of proactive leadership is revealed in:

The Primary Needs
The Secondary Needs
The People Motivators
The Law of Origin
The Myth of Quality and Cost
The Law of Measuring of Achievement
The Law of Plateaus
The Law of Substandard Performance
The Law of Persuasive Communication
The Law of Listening
The Law of Proactive Listening
The Law of Leader-Follower Relationships
The Law of Group Communication

PROMOTING

The fifth prong of proactive leadership is *promoting*. This includes continuously promoting the work, the people who do the work, and the people who benefit from the work. It also means promoting via mentoring the attitudes and behaviors which lead to success and progressively higher levels of achievement and satisfaction. In this regard, our work in the classroom, the school, and the district needs to be proactively promoted by the leader as important and necessary as well as rewarding and fulfilling because it is.

This task is twofold. A leader must continually promote the work of the classroom, school, and district—and the people who do that work. In the process, the leader must also continually model and teach the attitudes, beliefs, methods, techniques, skills, and vision which enhance the success of the individual—and the success of the classroom, school, and district.

Make no mistake: Energy follows attention. Recognition and effort are linked. To prevent splintering, diffusing, and diluting the attention and energy that should be devoted to work and achievement, the leader must continually promote what is most important—by the minute, the hour, and the day. Remember, ignorance and distraction result in disorientation and confusion which hinder teamwork, achievement, and moving to higher and higher levels of performance.

The promoting prong of proactive leadership establishes priorities. Promoting focuses constant attention on priorities. Promoting causes others to understand your expectations and your leadership. To initiate growth and change and create the climate and culture vital to success in the classroom, school, and district—the leader must proactively teach those being led.

The *promoting* prong of proactive leadership is revealed in:
>The Law of Origin
>The Law of Ever-Present Leadership
>The Law of Top-Down Leadership
>The Law of Substandard Performance
>The Law of Evaluation
>The Law of Standards for Performance
>The Law of Loyalty
>The Principle of Pride
>The Law of Persuasive Communication
>The Law of Group Communication

PRACTICING

The sixth prong of proactive leadership is *practicing*. This practice must include attention to the core values that are in agreement with the work and mission of the classroom, school, and district. This needs to be a constant task—and for good reason. It is only when we share the same core values that we can all function on the same page—and give our attention and talents to a common focus for maximum results.

Organizational practice takes place within the context of plans. Lesson plans, curriculum plans, discipline plans, budget plans, comprehensive organizational plans, and the plans designed to help those being led grow all require teaching and practice. Practice articulates what we are trying to accomplish, how we intend to achieve our plans, and in what manner we intend to function. Practice of the plan offers opportunities for us to demonstrate what is important to the organization—both to the individuals and the groups within the organization—including how we intend to work together and treat each other in the process.

Practicing is the day-to-day implementation of your words, your plans, and your values. This is a continuous process which demonstrates consistency between what you say and what you do. It includes the promises you make to serve and help individuals and the group be successful. Unless your practicing behavior is consistent with your words, you cannot build the trust and confidence necessary for those being led to follow your leadership. It is also the daily practice that allows individuals in the classroom, school, and district to achieve to the level of their desires and abilities. However, teaching precedes practice. Thus, the process of teaching, practice, reteaching, and more practice is a must in order to be a proactive leader.

Practicing our values is more than consistency of our words and implementing our plans. Practicing our professional values gives long-term direction and growth to individuals and the organization and creates the climate and culture for doing the right thing, for the right reason, and in the right way. It defines lasting standards, values, and modes of operation for everyone in the organization.

The *practicing* prong of proactive leadership is revealed in:

The Law of Origin
The Law of Ever-Present Leadership
The Law of Top-Down Leadership
The Law of Perfectionism
The Law of Whole Truth
The Law of Sharing Truths
The Law of Defensiveness
The Law of Anger
The Law of Third-Personality Emergence
The Law of Varied Thinking
The Myths of the Put-Down, Put-On, and Put-Off
The Principles of Handling Alibis, Objections, and Complaints
The Law of Respect
The Law of Problems
The Law of Self-Control
The Law of Disclosure
The Law of Listening
The Law of Proactive Listening

PROTECTING

The seventh prong of proactive leadership is *protecting*. This leadership element includes providing an environment in which it is physically and psychologically safe for people to think and function. This also includes keeping people focused and protecting them from all kinds of distractions, including protecting them from interruptions, busywork, or getting off task.

It is the protecting dimension which allows us to offer security and become advocates for those being led. This function helps us move to the higher platform of standing out front and assuming the responsibility for the problems as well as the achievement of those being led. It is within the protecting function that we teach those being led by word and deed how to relate to and treat both work and people. We have several vehicles in classrooms, schools, and districts which serve the protecting function of proactive leadership.

The first vehicle of protecting is structure. It includes policy, rules, regulations, and procedures. Structure in the classroom helps students understand what work needs to be done as well as what behaviors are appropriate. The curriculum sorts what is to be taught and in what sequence—including sorting among the choices of the things that could be taught. The existence of an adopted curriculum plan protects students, teachers, and administrators from attacks by special interest groups that seek to have different perspectives given priority. It acts as a protective shield to keep us on course to achieve goals. Therefore, the protecting function also sorts out expectations, standards, and priorities.

The second vehicle of protecting is accepting responsibility. When the leader accepts responsibility for everything that happens within the realm of his or her leadership, the leader automatically protects those being led from a degree of blame, criticism, and undue attack. It moves those we lead and the organization from preoccupation with fear and blame to getting work accomplished, solving problems, and finding solutions.

The third vehicle for protecting is defending core values. When the leader protects key organizational values from attack or compromise, those being led are reassured of what is important to the organization, whether that organization is a classroom, a school, or a school district. They also experience constancy of direction and predictability of organizational behavior. This is the action that allows those being led to acquire perspective. It is the protecting nature of proactive leadership that encourages and allows people to get involved with the least amount of risk—and be committed rather than adopt such stances as "wait and see" or "this, too, will pass."

Protecting leadership behaviors are the object lessons through which those being led can be taught the most important truths held by the leader and the organization—including the work and mission. In many ways, protecting is the test of the strength of the leader. Remember, our richest opportunity to teach and lead occurs when the pressure is on. The leader who avoids or walks away from pressure or problems will seldom cause those being led to want his or her leadership.

The *protecting* prong of proactive leadership is revealed in:

    The Law of Origin
    The Law of Ever-Present Leadership
    The Law of Top-Down Leadership
    The Reality of Problem Existence
    The Reality of Problem Solutions
    Proctor's Spiral of Futility
    The Law of the Grapevine
    The Law of Filtered Information
    The Law of Conflict Resolution
    The Law of Blame
    The Law of Credit
    The Law of Core Values
    The Law of Morale Fluctuations
    The Law of Confronting

PROVIDING

The eighth prong of proactive leadership is *providing*. Not only does this leadership behavior include giving those being led the ways and means to be successful, it means giving them a model that they can and want to follow and emulate. In this regard, we must set the standard if we expect others to follow our leadership.

The proactive leader's role in providing begins with clarity. Providing clarity of vision to those we lead in the classroom, school, and district is paramount. Only when the leader provides clarity of direction and vision are those being led empowered to practice leadership in their own context, including leadership of self.

The leader also fulfills the providing function through encouragement and reinforcement of behaviors and efforts aligned with the goals, work, and mission of the classroom, school, or district. Encouragement and reinforcement are two of the most valuable resources available to a leader to cause others to want and emulate his or her leadership.

Finally, the leader must provide continuous and comprehensive teaching and supervision as well as the tools to get the job done. The leader must literally pick up those being led wherever they are and take them where they should go via mentoring. This action constantly builds and maintains the capacity of the organization and those being led. It enables individuals and the organization to find success and to move to higher levels of performance — and effectiveness.

The *providing* prong of proactive leadership is revealed in:
> The Law of Origin
> The Law of Ever-Present Leadership
> The Law of Top-Down Leadership
> The Law of Positive Reinforcement
> The Law of Cumulative Action
> The Law of Organizational Competency
> The Law of Effectiveness
> The Law of Work Satisfaction

With every success in proactive teaching, our leadership will become more influential and more effective. After all, when people share core values, leaders and those being led are all on the same page. Work is seen in the same light. We have unity. We have agreement. We have bonding. We hold a common purpose. We have safety. We can all become proactive and strive to reach specific and achievable goals. Both leading and being led take on the highest level of meaning and depth.

It all begins when the leader "blankets" the entire group being led with the proactive attitudes, beliefs, core values, and actions which facilitate success and reduce the possibilities of failure. Equally important, this proactive action sets the stage for handling failure, correcting mistakes, and initiating change.

FIVE BELIEFS WE MUST HOLD TO BE PROACTIVE

A leader will never become proactive without at least five fundamental beliefs:

First, we must believe that we must learn and teach in order to lead effectively.

Second, we must believe that those being led can learn, they want and/or need to learn, and they want and/or need to be successful.

Third, we must believe that people have to continually improve their technical/academic knowledge as well as their people skills to experience both success and higher levels of functioning in the classroom, school, and district.

Fourth, we must also believe that those being led have a responsibility to learn — but it's the leader's responsibility to continually teach and reveal those attitudes and skills required to be successful regardless of the attitudes or behaviors of those being led.

Fifth, we must believe people are more motivated by success than by fear or failure. We must believe that improvement will not usually begin without a measure of success, that one success breeds the desire for another success, and that the leader's job is to help those being led be successful.

These are the five proactive beliefs we must hold before we will ever fulfill our responsibility to help those being led grow and move to new levels of performance.

THE LAW:
APPLIED

1. What does the term *proactive leadership* mean to you?
2. If those you lead are to be successful, what areas will require your teaching?
3. In your leadership position, in what ways do you need to be proactive?
4. Discuss the eight prongs of proactive leadership relative to your leadership responsibilities.
   a. Passion
   b. Positioning
   c. Planning
   d. Preparing
   e. Promoting
   f. Practicing
   g. Protecting
   h. Providing
5. What is the evidence that you are continually trying to help those you lead find success?
6. Discuss how the Law of Proactive Leadership precedes all other laws.
7. Share the need for multiple plans—and how change is difficult without them.
8. Discuss the five proactive beliefs. What would you add to the list?

THE
LAW OF
ORIGIN

Rationale: Institutions, and the people who work in them, must operate in agreement with the reason for their origin and existence, or failure rather than success becomes the probability.

This law applies to business, industry, governments, families, churches, and schools. Without doubt, it is a leadership absolute in education—in the classroom, school, and district. Failure to adhere to this law will get teachers or administrators in trouble with more people, more quickly, than any other thing they can do. And a leader is always without defense when he or she violates this law. In fact, one can be made to look like a fool if he or she tries taking a proactive or defensive stance after violating this law. Violating this law can result in the failure of the individual as well as the demise of the institution.

In truth, educator action which violates this law reflects an incompetency and an obvious professional misdirection that is, indeed, reason for termination. Little can or will be achieved by a teacher or administrator in the presence of such inconsistency of direction, purpose, and action. Constant personal and professional conflicts and a division of staff as well as student, staff, and public unrest will be the ever-present classroom, school, or district condition. That's the reality produced by repeated violations of the Law of Origin.

Make no mistake: Compliance with this law not only ensures leadership direction, it also provides educators with the foundation and skills to make and defend decisions that are consistent with good educational, management, and leadership practices. Even when we are wrong, if we can show that we believed what we did was in the best interest of students, we are on more solid footing—and can at least professionally defend our mistakes. This law must be entrenched like a rock and practiced faithfully—for it is the foundation of our appointment to the professional position we hold as teachers and administrators.

A CLASSROOM, SCHOOL, AND DISTRICT MUST BE STUDENT-CENTERED

A school must be student-centered. This is a simple, yet all-encompassing fact inherent in the reason for the creation and existence of schools and, therefore, inherent in the work of the school. Everything we do in a school must be in the best interest of students. Schools were not created—nor are they maintained—to employ teachers, psychologists, cooks, secretaries, nurses, media specialists, custodians, counselors, administrators, or anyone else. Schools were created to meet the needs—academic, social, and in the case of parochial schools, the spiritual needs—of students.

Recent years have brought forth a new feeling among some educators. The school, they say, is doing too much. And the school can't do everything. That may be true in a sense, but the school must be very careful in placing limits on what it will or will not do to meet the needs of students. When the school places limits on what it will do, it places limits on its usefulness, effectiveness, and security as well.

The school was created to perform a broad-based mission. It serves the whole of society. It is a large part of every community. It is a focal point in the lives of parents as well as students. Therefore, the school must be careful in making proclamations about what it will not do for those it was created to serve. Such action by any institution is the first step in bringing people to decide the organization isn't very competent or there is no need to support it. And remember, in our free-market society, competition is an ever-present condition. Someone is always waiting to fill a gap left by others.

Because we are workers of the school, our reputation, our competency, and our employment security are totally and directly linked to how effectively the school can meet the needs of students. And that means the needs of *all* students. Therefore, any time we become teacher-centered, administrator-centered, or centered in any direction other than the welfare of the student, we have lost sight of the reason for our existence. That is a violation of the Law of Origin—and it's dangerous.

WE ARE EITHER STUDENT-CENTERED, OR WE ARE NOT

The Law of Origin operates on every level for every worker of the school—from custodians to teachers to administrators to members of the board of education. There are many ways we can violate the Law of Origin. For instance, we can do what is best for us, rather than what is best for students. Likewise, deciding not to teach a specific unit because we don't want to or deciding that some students don't *deserve* an education can be a violation of the Law of Origin. If we clean classrooms at times convenient for custodians rather than students, we are being custodian-centered, not student-centered. Unfortunately, these kinds of decisions are not uncommon.

True, it is harder to handle and teach some students. And it may be inconvenient and difficult to arrange cleaning schedules to get custodians to work at certain times in order to meet the needs of students. Yet, a school is either student-centered, or it is not. Other examples of violations of this law can be seen when a film is not shown in a classroom because a projector would be difficult to locate and would have to be transported from another place, when activities are eliminated because a faculty sponsor cannot be found, when flexible scheduling is disallowed because teachers don't want it, or when an assembly is not scheduled for fear teachers would be angered by the interruption. In all these instances, students' best interests have been overlooked or avoided for one reason or another. In each case, students' best interests have been placed in a position secondary to the wants and needs of someone else. That's a dangerous position for either a teacher or an administrator to be in. These kinds of deviations can develop into big contradictions when one does not understand the full meaning of the Law of Origin.

When teachers violate this law in the classroom, failure rather than success becomes the probability. When administrators violate this law by leaning in various directions—for any reason—the institution is jeopardized. When the Law of Origin is violated, everything from the ability to the judgment to the credibility of the leader is subject to question and criticism. In truth, it should be. However, in whatever we do, if we truly believe our actions to be in the best interest of students, our actions are at least defensible from a strong professional platform. In most cases, a close look will reveal that our problems come when we do what may have been best for someone else—but wasn't in the best interest of students.

REFLECTED IN EVERY DECISION WE MAKE—
IF WE WANT TO BE SUCCESSFUL

Every educator's leadership must be in agreement with the reason for the existence and origin of the institution. When it is not, the failing process begins. And it has been started by our hand.

We must establish rules and regulations for the day-to-day operation of the classroom, school, or district that coincide with the professional attitudes, philosophies, and methods needed to fulfill the work and mission of the institution. After all, rules and regulations must serve students, rather than have students serve rules and regulations. Whatever action we take must be preceded by the question: Is it good for students? And when the day comes that we start asking, "Is it good for teachers or good for administrators?" we have made ourselves vulnerable.

It's not uncommon for leaders to talk one direction and act another. Of course, this is easily detected by students, parents, and everyone else. Teachers may tell students to work hard, then refuse a student's request with the excuse that it's too much trouble. Administrators may tell teachers to be student-centered when they ask them to do something—regardless of the extra work involved—then refuse a teacher request which would facilitate learning because it would require an administrative effort or adjustment. They may even eliminate a student-centered service because it takes too much administrative time and involves too much work or red tape.

These types of contradictions may begin causing doubts and spread to a general feeling of discontent. Such violations of the Law of Origin may culminate in leadership problems that move beyond solution. Remember, all leadership efforts must support and promote the fulfillment of the Law of Origin. Any deviation is a leadership mistake—one serious enough to bring about our destruction as well as the failure of an institution.

We might say, "We will always have schools." This is probably true. Yet, there is a difference between schools that are *allowed to exist* and ones which are encouraged by public or private support to flourish and grow. Remember, people may tolerate an institution when it loses sight of its purpose, but they will not support it to the degree that is required for it to prosper and thrive. Maybe this is one of the reasons schools always seem to face a public outcry or a financial dilemma. Never forget, the public cares not that the institution satisfies the wants and needs of the workers of that institution—unless the workers of the institution are fulfilling the needs of the people. That's a fact.

ASSURING THAT TEACHING AND ADMINISTRATION
ARE FUNCTIONS RATHER THAN POSITIONS

Practicing the Law of Origin allows us to meet the objectives of the school. It ensures that teaching and administration are *functions* rather than *positions*. It allows us to put in perspective our roles as leaders. It helps us sort out the right from the wrong, the good choice from the poor one. It keeps the direction of our leadership efforts clear—not only to us, but to those we lead. The Law of Origin facilitates the acceptance of the decisions, plans, and actions of a leader more than any other management law does.

On the other hand, if a leader is teacher-centered or administrator-centered, nothing the institution does seems to make any sense. That's why every decision a teacher or administrator makes must be preceded by the question: Is it good for students? When all our decisions answer this question in agreement with the Law of Origin, everything from new programs to rules and regulations have purpose, direction, reason, and a meaningful as well as common-sense foundation. Too, it is the Law of Origin that gives educators, individually and collectively, a common foundation. It gives us and those being led common values. It gives us a common objective. It gives us all a base for attitude and decision making—be it disciplining a student or failing a student. It also gives us a system of checks and balances.

When we follow this law, the orders, directives, and decisions we make as educators are seen as facilitating the work of students and of the school rather than hindering both. Those being led can follow us because our leadership efforts make sense. In truth, it is when we attempt to lead in contradiction to the Law of Origin that the majority of our problems begin. That's why the acceptance of this law is the first requirement of those who intend to lead. It must be accepted by teachers, administrators, and everyone connected with the schools—or we will not be seen as serving. Rather, we will be seen as self-serving.

THE LAW:
APPLIED

1. Discuss rules, regulations, and procedures in your (classroom) (school) (district) which are:
    a. Student-centered
    b. Teacher-centered
    c. Administrator-centered
    d. Staff-centered
    e. Special interest-centered
2. Discuss the various checks and balances we have in our society to make sure institutions meet the needs of those they are supposed to serve.
3. Discuss (institutions) (businesses) (governments) which were toppled because they violated the Law of Origin.
4. Discuss individuals who lost their jobs because they violated this law.
5. What individual needs are met by the Law of Origin?

THE
LAW OF
TOTAL RESPONSIBILITY

Rationale: The superintendent is responsible for everything that happens within the district. The principal is responsible for everything that happens within the school. The teacher is responsible for everything that happens within the classroom. This responsibility includes the attitudes, skills, and success of those being led and applies to every level of appointed leadership.

It's a fact: The leader is responsible for everyone and everything within the realm of his or her appointed leadership. It may not seem fair for a simple reason: It isn't. But that's how things work. The leader is held responsible. If, for any reason, we can't hold the leader responsible, we usually get rid of the leader.

Like it or not, a principal or superintendent is responsible for everything that happens as well as what doesn't happen in a school or school system. A teacher is responsible for everything that happens or doesn't happen in the classroom. Whether it is an individual classroom, a school, or the entire system, leaders are the ones held accountable and responsible for all. This includes the attitudes, skills, and achievements of those being led— and for good reasons. First, if the leader doesn't accept this responsibility, who should? Who will? Who can? Second, how can a leader be effective if he or she doesn't assume the responsibility for the attitudes, skills, and success experienced by those being led? The answer: He or she can't.

If we doubt the truth of this law, we need only recall what happens when something goes wrong. If students can't read, do we blame them? No, we blame the teacher. And whether a boiler blows up, a teacher mistreats a student, or a student throws an egg at a passing automobile—the principal or superintendent will be the one who gets the call. Worse, if the situation cannot be corrected or mended, the administration will receive the blame and be regarded as ineffective.

THE LEADER IS TOTALLY
RESPONSIBLE...FOR EVERYTHING

Right or wrong, good or bad, fair or unfair—that's the way it is, and that's the way it will always be. In truth, however, it can be no other way. The important thing is for every teacher and administrator to accept the reality of this responsibility from a positive, professional, and proactive point of view. This is the challenge and excitement inherent in leadership. It is also the burden and the opportunity of appointed leadership.

Education is not a place for the weak or for those who cannot accept the authority that goes with total responsibility. A problem results for the individual teacher or administrator as well as for the institution when the appointed leader cannot or will not accept this management law. It is the failure to accept this principle that causes both a responsibility and performance breakdown within an organization. This is because the organization has a leader in charge who cannot or will not accept some of the responsibility inherent in the leadership function. Therefore, incompetency reigns. A void of both performance and accountability always exists.

A failure to accept this law can produce stagnation. Regression and lack of action along with a failure to know and accept who is responsible is common. The ultimate result, of course, is the destruction of the leader or the institution itself. This is not an uncommon occurrence. Experience has revealed that entire organizations have self-destructed because their leaders did not accept *total responsibility* for everything from performance to finances to policy. However, once the Law of Total Responsibility is accepted, it changes a leader's entire perspective, approach, and action.

A REQUIREMENT FOR PROBLEM SOLVING

This law encourages and facilitates the identification of needs. It also facilitates problem solving. When teachers and administrators do not accept and adhere to this law, problems may be identified, but they usually are allowed to lie in their place. This is true because nobody feels responsible for—or is willing to accept responsibility for—the problem or situation. Too often, we tend to identify problems, blame others, and absolve ourselves of all guilt and responsibility for any situation. As a result, we voluntarily remove ourselves intellectually, emotionally, and physically from the leadership position to which we were appointed. We don't deal with the work and mission of the classroom, school, or district for which we have leadership responsibility. We say "Don't look at me—that's the students' fault, the math department's fault, or the coach's fault," or "The English Committee was supposed to get that done." The problem with taking this stance is that a negative situation remains.

When we practice this law, and the person of lesser authority does not perform, responsibility for that failure *always* reverts upward. It never remains static. If a student is not doing the job in the classroom, the responsibility for performance automatically reverts upward to the teacher. If a teacher isn't doing the job, it automatically becomes the responsibility of the principal. If a principal isn't handling the problem successfully, the responsibility goes to the superintendent—automatically.

Leaders who fail to assume a personal and professional attitude of responsibility for everything that happens within the realm of their leadership will never be totally accepted or effective leaders. Such leaders may be able to develop the skills which enable them to identify problems accurately, but they will never be problem solvers. They will never be able to make hard decisions. Remember, final responsibility always rests at the highest point in any organization, and unless this management philosophy is accepted, the Law of Total Responsibility cannot be effected.

ON EVERY LEVEL...
A SYSTEM OF CHECKS AND BALANCES

Remember, the Law of Total Responsibility operates on every level. For example, students are responsible for their actions. Teachers are responsible for all the things students do well or do not do well. And administrators are responsible as well. This law is simply our check and balance for performance. The law makes sure a higher authority is always in place to pick up the responsibility to meet the needs of those being led as well as to take action when faltering occurs.

The Law of Total Responsibility does not imply that responsibility and authority cannot and should not be delegated. Quite the contrary. It simply means that when anyone in a position of delegated responsibility fails to perform, the responsibility for that failure automatically reverts upward. That's why the functions of teaching and administering require an appointed leader to accept and practice the Law of Total Responsibility. When a leader fails to accept this principle, problems and failures tend to become permanent and nobody ever corrects the situation. A department head doesn't call meetings—so there is never a meeting. A teacher is failing too many students—and continues the practice. A principal has poor relationships with teachers, but nobody does anything about it. In every case, however, everyone may talk about the problem. Indeed, everyone may know what to do to solve the problem. But nobody does it. Consequently, everyone feels helpless and participates in the failure.

AN ALL-ENCOMPASSING
LAW OF LEADERSHIP

The total responsibility concept is an extremely simple, yet all-encompassing law of leadership and management. When it is absent from leadership action, a close look will reveal that the person at the lowest responsibility level is usually blamed first and may be even blamed totally for any failure. Worse, both the blame and the problem are allowed to lie there because nobody at the higher level is willing to assume responsibility for the state of existing conditions. When this is the case, there is no leadership. This is the real problem. It is not uncommon.

However, when a teacher or administrator accepts and practices the Law of Total Responsibility, control and a sense of responsibility are always maintained within an institution. Most important, control and responsibility can never be lost because responsibility always continues to flow upward. Loose ends are eliminated. Feelings of helplessness are reduced. True, students must be helped and encouraged to solve their own problems, for they, too, must understand and accept total responsibility. So must teachers. Yet, if a teacher becomes stymied or falters for any reason, the responsibility for help or correction lies with the department head—then the principal. The problem is never left to exist or to be perpetuated. The same applies to administrators. Whether it be a teacher having a problem with a specific student or a committee that has failed to report, the administrator must assume the management position of total responsibility. That is, he or she must if success is to be achieved. When this law is not accepted by the leader, unfinished business and unsolved problems become the rule of the day. When this happens, guess who receives the blame? You're right—the leader. And that's exactly where the blame should lie—with the one responsible for everything that happens within the organization. That's a law of leadership that applies to all leaders.

THE LAWS MUST BE TAKEN OFF
THE DRAWING BOARD AND APPLIED

I must emphasize that the laws and principles of leadership and management will be of no value to any of us as teachers or administrators unless we are willing to actively incorporate and practice them in our leadership plan. These principles need to be applied consistently day in and day out before positive and dramatic effects will take place in the classroom or institution where we have the delegated responsibility for leadership and the success of those being led.

Once we have committed ourselves to the fact that leadership means "total responsibility for everything"—and see both our position and function relative to this commitment—we can cause ourselves to become real leaders in the full sense of the word. Then we can make it possible for those being led to follow in the fulfillment of goals. Once we accept this law, we will seldom feel helpless. Indeed, we will feel the control we need to manage both work and the people who do that work.

THE LAW: APPLIED

1. Discuss how all of us in the school, including students, are responsible for everything. Be specific.
2. How does this law make sure problems are tackled?
3. Share the ways this law serves as a vital check and balance.
4. Reveal violations of this law—and the consequences.
5. How does this law complement the Law of Origin?
6. What individual needs are met by the Law of Total Responsibility?

THE
LAW OF
TOP-DOWN LEADERSHIP

Rationale: Leadership may come from those being led, but it must come from the
appointed leader in the classroom, the school, and the district. Therefore,
grass roots is not good leadership, but the result of good leadership.

We're in a era when anything that says *top-down* draws suspicion. Yet, too many leaders are prone to expect too much from those being led—and not enough from themselves. This law holds that leadership is a responsibility that must come from the leader to those being led. Unfortunately, many leaders do not have a full grasp of this responsibility. Therefore, this is one of the biggest problems in many classrooms, schools, and districts today.

Many teachers and administrators experience continuous misery, frustration, and failure because they neither understand nor practice this law. Frankly, some fail because they are confused by this law. They believe that it conflicts with their beliefs regarding the necessity of gaining the involvement of those being led. They believe it conflicts with the need to generate participation and share power. They believe it cancels efforts to instill ownership. It does not.

But the law does remind the leader and those being led that it's a mistake to do anything to negate or diminish the leadership at the top. In the same vein, it's also a mistake not to use the talent that exists throughout the organization. In both instances, the focus should be on responsibility, not power. Unfortunately, in the new trends toward empowerment, shared decision making, and site-based management, we have erred both ways because the focus has been on power and position instead of responsibility. The Law of Top-Down Leadership does not discourage the involvement of those being led. However, it does assign responsibility for leadership rather than allow responsibility to be discarded or pawned off on others.

GRASS ROOTS IS NOT GOOD LEADERSHIP—
IT'S THE RESULT OF GOOD LEADERSHIP

Many appointed leaders fail because they can't or don't take responsibility or action. In fact, some don't think they should. They wait and watch as well as confer continually on everything and with everyone before initiating or offering leadership thought or direction—not to mention action—and can't understand why nothing happens or ever gets done within the organization. Some leaders actually always expect ideas, plans, and decisions to come from those being led. In many ways, they demand both ideas and plans from those being led before they will act. They mistakenly believe that group suggestion from those being led is a prerequisite for acceptance and success. As hard as it is to convince some leaders otherwise, this is a management misconception.

Yet, common sense should tell us we were not hired as teachers and administrators to be *monitors* or *pollsters*. We were not made the appointed leader in order that we might take a vote before we think, make decisions, and initiate action. We were hired to influence and lead. That's why we need to take a close look at the grass roots approach to leadership. Many good things come from within a classroom or school and work their way to the leader—as they should. Those being led are a great source of input, ideas, opinions, and responsibility. However, while a leader should promote and encourage involvement and participation, he or she must never expect or demand leadership to come from within the organization. Leadership is a management responsibility. It is not the duty or responsibility of students in the classroom or the teaching staff in a school.

When leadership comes from students within a classroom, it is wonderful. When it comes from the staff in a school, it is marvelous. Remember, leadership *may* come from within the various places in the organization—but it *must* come from the top of the various places in the organization. It must come from the appointed leader in that place. In every institution—be it a business, industry, school, or church—leadership must come from where the authority is. With appointed authority and title comes responsibility to lead. This is the function of appointed leadership.

When "grass roots" is the expected way of functioning, leadership becomes merely a position rather than a function. In organizations where leadership is effected only through grass root efforts, those being led know it. Some love it. Many resent it. All too often, however, those being led regard such leaders as weak—or as obstacles to meaningful achievement. From the viewpoint of those being led, the leadership position is primarily one of noninvolvement, noncommitment, and nonaction.

A close look will reveal that these kinds of leaders are unknowledgeable, misguided, or fear the leadership role they hold. They also fear those they lead and fail to understand the work and mission of the organization. Amazingly, teachers and administrators who do not lead are usually bewildered, hurt, and disappointed because others—subordinates and superiors alike—are critical of their leadership and reluctant to follow them.

LEADERSHIP IS NOT TRULY DEMOCRATIC

The input and involvement of those being led must be nurtured and sought out. Although student and staff involvement is the desired condition, we must remember that those being led are not responsible for leadership of the group. We are. They are responsible for leading and managing themselves. Regardless of what we may think, running a classroom, school, or district is not a democratic process. Let's not think or pretend that those being led have more responsibility and authority than leaders do, or we'll find ourselves in more trouble than any leader can handle.

A teacher or administrator cannot delegate responsibility and authority where it cannot be granted. That's where many leaders get in a bind. They put themselves in a precarious position by pretending to be democratic when they can't be—by reality as well as by law. Then, they can't get out of situations when those being led want to make the decision they were told they could make.

It is simply impossible to be completely democratic and lead effectively. Common sense should reveal that no one expects us to be. In truth, neither do they want us to be. Remember, our asking for input in making a decision is not a request for another to actually make the decision. That is, it isn't unless the leader has indicated by word, action, or lack of action that the final decision would result from the input of those being led. Remember, democracy ends the first time a teacher or administrator must say no to students or staff.

ONE CANNOT DELEGATE RESPONSIBILITY INHERENT IN THE LEADERSHIP POSITION

A teacher can and should delegate responsibility to students. Administrators can and should delegate responsibility to the staff. But neither teacher nor administrator can delegate responsibility that was meant solely for the leader. For instance, some rules in a classroom can be negotiable. Others can't. Likewise, we can't let students evaluate or grade other students. Too, an administrator cannot delegate the leadership responsibility that is inherent in a principalship or superintendency to teachers. This is no more possible than it is for teachers to delegate the responsibilities inherent in teaching to students. It won't work. If a teacher puts a student "in charge" and goes to the lounge for coffee and something bad happens while he or she is absent from the room, who is at fault? The student? I think not. Likewise, if administrators pass their authority or responsibility to teachers and something goes wrong, who is responsible?

The teacher or administrator who does not recognize his or her top-down leadership function and responsibility is in trouble. An individual simply cannot fail to provide leadership in a classroom, school, or district and then rationalize away this void as the fault of those being led. This is exactly what happens when the Law of Top-Down Leadership is ignored, forgotten, or rationalized away. We become passive leaders. We become seekers of approval rather than decision makers. We become followers rather than proactive leaders. We expect every new idea, plan, or innovation to come from those being led rather than from the top—where the authority and responsibility are.

Site-based management and shared decision making do not negate this law. The law says that the site-based leader *must* lead. So must department heads and anyone else in a leadership position. In truth, if this law is not practiced, site-based management and shared decision making will not work. Why? Because the only concerns will be for who has what power. We will try to get more power, but be reluctant to give any power away—and for good reason. We wouldn't be able to do our jobs without the power inherent in our leadership position.

THE LAW:
APPLIED

1. Could the Law of Top-Down Leadership imply dominance?
2. What kinds of actions do you expect a leader to take?
3. What responsibilities (can) (cannot) be delegated by a teacher?
4. What responsibilities (can) (cannot) be delegated by a principal?
5. What responsibilities (can) (cannot) be delegated by a superintendent?

THE
LAW OF
EVER-PRESENT LEADERSHIP

Rationale: Whenever two or more people gather, leadership is automatically present. This resulting leadership may be a positive or negative force in the lives of individuals as well as the work of the classroom, school, or district.

Some leaders feel that their position or title alone denotes to everyone that they are in charge and they are the source of leadership within a classroom, school, or district. In many ways, this kind of thinking results in some vital misconceptions, especially if the appointed leader assumes there is no need to take action to establish his or her position or to maintain it within the group being led. Such leaders are likely to believe that issues will get decided—when they are ready to make a decision. They are also prone to believe that when all else fails, an order or directive will cause others to follow their leadership or correct any negative situation. If these leaders would look more closely, they might see that titles which denote positions of leadership, such as *teacher*, *department head*, t*eam leader*, *principal*, *curriculum director*, or *superintendent* can sometimes be secondary and even insignificant to the actual leadership that is occurring in a classroom, school, or district.

TWO KINDS
OF LEADERSHIP

Basically, there are only two kinds of leadership: *appointed* and *emerging*. The *appointed* leader is the individual who has the legal title, authority, and responsibility to effectively carry out the work of the place or institution he or she is serving. However, in any situation where two or more people are present, when appointed leaders do not take charge of the responsibilities inherent in their granted positions, leadership will always emerge from the group that the appointed leader should be directing. This is the Law of Ever-Present Leadership. Therefore, leadership is always present—whether we are leading or not.

The basic truth of this law is one that every leader would be wise to remember when dealing with people. Failure to comply with the Law of Ever-Present Leadership can result in a loss of appointed leadership—either temporary or permanent. In truth, whether the loss is permanent or not is determined to a great extent by the attitudes, desires, and actions of the emerging leader and others in the group being led. If the emerging leader wants to take over permanent leadership of the appointed leader—it is his or hers for the taking.

Fortunately, the emerging leader may take leadership for one task or on one issue and then refuse the leadership imposed upon him or her by the group. On the other hand, he or she may become the classroom or staff leader, not in title, but in reality. We've all seen administrators lose their leadership to a member or members of the teaching staff operating out of the teachers' lounge. We've all seen students take over a classroom. That's the Law of Ever-Present Leadership at work.

NEGATIVE ATTITUDES AND ACTIONS
ARE THE PROBABILITY

Emerging leadership may be either positive or negative. Sometimes emerging

123

leadership is good. Unfortunately, most often it is not. There are reasons that negative rather than positive leadership most often results from an emerging leader.

First, negative leadership emerges most often because the people who gain authority within a group—without being given a corresponding degree of accountability—are most likely to act and react out of self-interest rather than in the best interest of those the institution serves. This is exactly what happens in many teachers' lounge discussions where teachers teeter on the edge of insubordination as they attack and criticize administrators. Examples of emerging leadership in schools are countless: an emerging leader simply *takes* or is *given* leadership by peers. Sometimes an emerging leader is sought out and encouraged by the group to take over the lead. After gaining the authority and power granted by the group, the emerging leader usually proceeds in the misguided direction of self-interest, rather than student- and school-interest.

Second, people of equal rank are very unlikely to speak out against each other to defend an appointed leader who is absent or nonacting. This is not abnormal. Neither is it disloyal. It is simply the common way people react in the presence of their peers regarding a nonacting or ineffective appointed leader.

For instance, if one teacher is telling colleagues about all the mistakes and wrongs that exist in a particular situation, what teachers shouldn't have to do, or how incompetent the superintendent is, it is very unlikely that the vast majority of teachers who usually support the administrator will say anything. They may not join the negative discussion, and they may not participate in the negative claims, but neither are they likely to disagree or correct the thinking of a colleague and defend the administrator. Once in a while someone may speak up. Generally, however, silence is the norm. Some may even get very angry. But to speak out in support of the administration and against a colleague in the presence of peers is the exception rather than the rule. An administrator should not be angered or disappointed when such events take place. This is simply people reacting in a human way. Students would respond the same way.

In many instances, it is through the influence of negative emerging leadership that teachers begin to acquire teacher-centered rather than student-centered attitudes and practices. A negative leader simply has emerged from the group and begun feeding colleagues negative thoughts which serve them instead of their work and mission.

NEGATIVE EMERGING LEADERS MAY MEAN WELL

Don't be misled: A negative emerging leader may be well-meaning. He or she truly may not be fully aware of the discord he or she brings. Too, the emerging leader may be "pushed" or "forced" into a leadership role by his or her colleagues or classmates. I have always wondered, if this outspoken and misdirected emerging leader were suddenly made principal, would he or she say those same things in the same way to colleagues in the teacher's lounge tomorrow? I think not. Why? Because once a person is made an appointed leader, formal responsibility and accountability have been added to formal authority. This fact changes the entire situation. And what is the result? The emerging leader will talk out of the other side of his or her mouth. We see negative students do the same. We make them the leader, and they get serious about everything they propose.

Without reservation, the best way to counteract the power and effectiveness of negative emerging leadership is for appointed leaders to meet their leadership responsibilities. Please note that I said "negative emerging leadership," for we are constantly striving to encourage the emergence of positive student and teacher leaders within our classrooms and schools. We could not operate without them. However, the chance of positive emerging leadership developing without the guidance of positive appointed leadership is very slim.

EMERGING LEADERS ARE A POWERFUL FORCE

A leader must never ignore or discount the power of emerging leadership. Its force can be overwhelming. Without reservation, the intention is to have appointed leaders lead. If they do not, those in positions of higher authority must correct the situation quickly or look for new leaders. Otherwise, they, and the entire institution, will always operate at the mercy of various emerging leaders.

When a teacher or administrator accepts the Law of Ever-Present Leadership, he or she immediately realizes that an appointed leader must make decisions. He or she must take action. We can't sit on our hands and be an accepted, respected, or effective appointed leader. We must realize that being granted a position as an appointed leader is no more than being given an open-ended opportunity to prove that the right appointment was made — and no guarantees come with the appointment.

Leadership respect cannot be granted by an appointment or title. Certainly, respect is not something that a leader can demand, force, or insist upon. It must be earned. And once earned, it must be maintained by leading continually, or it will be quickly lost.

None of us were always appointed leaders. Nor are we always the appointed leader in every situation. Our experience should tell us that leadership acceptance and respect can be best achieved by leadership example as well as by providing tangible evidence of help, direction, and assistance to those we lead. That's why teachers must help all students be successful. And that's why administrators must help all teachers be successful. Unless an appointed leader is willing to be an example of good leadership by word as well as deed, leadership acceptance and respect cannot be earned. And if those being led don't have any expectations of the leader, they don't have a leader. For instance, if teachers don't expect a principal or superintendent to be involved in providing staff development or helping them grow professionally, neither administrator is looked upon as a leader in this regard.

Our primary function as teachers is to help all students find success in our classroom. Therefore, we must have a plan that helps everyone succeed. One of the primary functions of being a school administrator is to facilitate the work of the classroom teacher. This is not accomplished by simply providing the physical things teachers need, such as books, paper, chalk, and other materials.

Never forget, we all ask the same question of our leaders: "What are they doing to help me be successful?" If the answer is "Nothing," then those being led will look somewhere else for assistance as well as leadership. And this is when an emerging leader is likely to be born.

A principal looks to the superintendent and says "What is he or she doing for me personally to help me be a better principal and find happiness in the process?" Teachers ask the same question about principals and superintendents. Students ask the same question of their teachers. It's as individualized and personal as that. If the answer is "Nothing," then people look elsewhere for leadership. That's the Law of Ever-Present Leadership revealed. If we forget this law, we can lose the position we hold in the classroom. If we forget the law, we can lose our leadership influence. Worse, everyone will know it—including us. And where emerging leaders dominate, life for the appointed leader is not very good.

**THE LAW:
APPLIED**

1. Can you identify the emerging leaders in the classroom? School? District?
2. Have you ever been an emerging leader? How did you get the position?
3. Discuss the benefits of positive emerging leaders. How do you guide them?
4. Why do many leaders lose their influence completely?
5. Why does an emerging leader have many advantages not held by the appointed leader?
6. How can you help a nonacting leader?
7. How can you help keep the influence of emerging leaders positive rather than negative?
8. What individual needs are met by the Law of Ever-Present Leadership?

THE LAWS AND PRINCIPLES OF SELF-MANAGEMENT

As essential as the fundamental laws of human management are to leadership success, equally important are the laws and principles of self-management. We must realize that it is very important that we begin to look closely and honestly at ourselves as classroom, school, and district leaders. Leadership and management does not pertain just to what we do with others. It begins with the leadership and management of ourselves.

If we can't successfully lead and manage ourselves, it is very unlikely that we will successfully lead others. Surely, no leadership teaching that is intended to be people-focused could ever be effective until we, as the responsible parties, clearly understand our own intentions and motivations.

This chapter considers exclusively the twelve laws and two myths as they relate to teachers and administrators. The function of these guidelines is to help us discover how to understand ourselves and our motivations more clearly in relation to the abilities needed for leading others.

The Law of Adjustment
The Law of Planning
The Law of Perfectionism
The Myth of the Perfect Plan
The Myth of Quality and Cost
The Law of Survival
The Law of Whole Truth
The Law of Sharing Truths
The Law of Defensiveness
The Law of Anger
The Law of Measuring of Achievement
The Law of Plateaus
The Law of Longevity
The Law of Leaving

THE
LAW OF
ADJUSTMENT

Rationale: To effect leadership, one must adjust his or her own behavior in order to get others to change or adjust their behavior. Therefore, the leader, rather than those being led, must be the primary adjustor.

Many times, appointed leaders believe that the higher a person goes in rank, title, salary, and appointed position, the more subordinates must adjust to that individual. With this belief, of course, goes the attitude that the leader can and should be the boss. A person is likely to believe that's the way it is supposed to be and any adjusting done should be done first by those being led—not the boss.

This belief is totally and completely false. Yet, many educators continue to firmly believe that students should adjust to teachers, teachers to principals, principals to superintendents, etc. A close look will reveal that the opposite is true—if one expects to manage oneself in order to lead others. In truth, the higher a person goes in title and position, the more knowledge of human behavior, as well as methods, techniques, and skills, he or she must have—and the more he or she is required to adjust his or her own actions to get others to adjust theirs. That's the lesson taught by the Law of Adjustment. It is also what leadership and management are all about. It is by adjusting our methods, techniques, and skills that we get others to do what we want them to do.

THE LEADER MUST BE
THE PRIMARY ADJUSTOR

The successful leader learns quickly that it is he or she who must make adjustments to compensate for the strengths, weaknesses, beliefs, opinions, and behaviors of those being led. It is only by using our knowledge about human behavior and the individuals being led—then making adjustments—that we are allowed to cause others to want our leadership. That's a fact. Therefore, the leader must always make the first move—and keep making the first move. If we wait for those being led to change an attitude or behavior before we act, "nothing" may be the result.

Every leader must also learn quickly that in problem situations, it is the leader who must stop and evaluate the strengths and weaknesses of self as well as the strengths and weaknesses of those being led—then adjust his or her methods and techniques to cope with the people, their abilities, and the situation. When this is not the leadership practice, problems may get defined, but they don't get solved. In addition, people do not change.

When the leader does not make technical and behavioral adjustments, those being led are seldom motivated to change or achieve. It is the adjustment to the quirks, abilities, attitudes, priorities, and behaviors of those being led that allows the leader to change the attitudes, behaviors, and actions of those being led. The leadership attitude that "I'm the boss, and that's the way it's going to be" only promotes superiority—and resistance. It only makes people fight or pull away. It seldom brings those being led closer to the leader or stimulates or motivates them to follow.

Teachers and administrators are the professional leaders in classrooms and schools. It is a teacher's responsibility to acquire and utilize the methods and techniques which make students go in the desired direction. Administrators have the same responsibility when it comes to teachers and staff. This can only be achieved by adjustment. This is both the challenge and the responsibility of the leader. And it is in adjusting that we become influencers and motivators. If we can't make adjustments in methods, techniques, and behaviors to motivate people—with some measure of success—effective leadership will never be achieved. And if teachers believe they can get high achievement by continually *dominating* or *forcing* students into compliance and submission, they are mistaken. If administrators believe that they can *dominate* the whole staff, they are mistaken.

THE NEED TO ADJUST
IS SIMPLY ENDLESS

When management cannot or will not make adjustments first, any movement toward goals or solutions to problems is temporary—at best. To get people to do what we want them to do requires one prerequisite if we are even to hope for success: We simply must adjust our methods, our attitudes, our techniques, and our actions to get others to adjust theirs. And we can't lump everyone being led into the same group and use the same methods and techniques for all. We do not lead groups; we lead individuals. We'll talk about this reality later.

Remember, the higher we go in rank, the more professional understandings and skills we need for adjusting—and for good reason. If something isn't getting done, we must adjust our methods and techniques to see that it does get done. If someone has a bad attitude, we must adjust our approach to change that negative attitude to a positive one. At times, it may seem that our need to adjust is endless. It is. That's why a school needs both teachers and administrators who are trained to be leaders. We are supposed to have the self-concept, the knowledge, the skill, and the personality to lead. We are supposed to have the ability to adapt to lead others to accomplish the work of the classroom or the work and mission of the entire school.

If we think of ourselves as the primary adjustors in all situations, we have the foundation tools needed for effective leadership. If we don't, those we lead do not have a leader. They only have a boss. There is a significant difference. And if we are only a boss, we'll have to keep our foot on people continually. It's very hard to get any job done effectively if one foot always has to remain in one place to control those being led.

THE LAW:
APPLIED

1. Discuss the kinds of adjustments a (teacher) (principal) (superintendent) has to make continually.
2. If the leader is always adjusting, is the leader weak? Will those being led regard the leader as weak? Why or why not?
3. Discuss the signs which indicate a leader must adjust.
4. Are there any situations in which a leader should never be the first to adjust? Discuss.
5. Share adjustments you have difficulty making.
6. What individual needs are met by the Law of Adjustment?

THE
LAW OF
PLANNING

Rationale: In achieving objectives, the leader's success is dependent upon the means, the tools, and the measurements of the plan which are established and communicated to those being led prior to beginning the task.

In many ways, the less a teacher or administrator publicly reveals and discusses a new idea, concept, or change before thorough planning, the better off everyone would be. Too many good ideas get shot down simply because they step on someone's toes or arouse countless fears on a wide variety of fronts. Remember, those being led don't always get to determine the means, the tools, and the measurements of plans. Leaders do. Therefore, complete management thought and planning are prerequisites and must precede the public offering or announcement of any plan to those being led. In addition, it is a leadership responsibility to decide:

1.   What will be done.
2.   How it will be done.
3.   What resources will be used.
4.   When the task should be finished.
5.   Which people should be involved in the completion of the task.
6.   What extra planning will be necessary when *all* those being led by the leader must be involved in the tasks.
7.   What will be regarded as successful.

MANY STRATEGIES ARE
PROGRAMMED TO FAIL

Much of our leadership strategy fails because we do not complete the leadership responsibilities listed above before discussing or initiating plans with those being led. Stated plainly, we offer too many plans to our students and staff "cold turkey" and proceed with the hope and expectation that all will accept the plan and work hard, and that success will result. Too often, it does not. When we proceed in such a manner, leadership planning has been inadequate.

Planning is the function of management. A teacher must be a master planner in the classroom. An administrator must be the master planner in the school or district. If we do not meet our planning responsibilities, failure on some front is likely to occur. Included in this leadership responsibility are:

1.   Selecting tasks.
2.   Establishing progress timetables.
3.   Identifying and selecting people to be involved in the task.
4.   Establishing completion dates.

Without a doubt, making these decisions and providing guidelines and assistance usually facilitate success. Without leadership help, structure, and guidelines, the chance of plans achieving success is diminished. Without this action, groups may leave an initial class or meeting where ideas are offered not even knowing what the proposal, idea, plan, or problem is—much less the direction they are expected to go. Remember, loose ends worry and scare people. If, for instance, students or staff members ask questions during initial presentations and are told, "That hasn't been worked out yet," they worry even more. More fears are aroused. Worse, faculty members can leave such meetings feeling that they have been asked to accept a challenge—but have not been given enough information, direction, resources, and leadership to even begin.

Management must provide the structure needed to begin. However, when creativity is our desire, we may want to allow an openness within the structure after the guidelines have been established. The easiest-to-understand examples of this practice are revealed in sports. In sports, the rules are firm, but the creativity promoted within the rules is without limits.

Golf has eighteen holes; football has lines and four quarters. Baseball, tennis, and basketball also offer this necessary framework. It is within the structure that creativity reigns supreme. In fact, it is the structure which permits the participants open-endedness and free movement within the framework. It is the framework that allows maximum creativity, achievement, and completion of objectives. Remember, if those being led are not given such guidelines, hours can be spent and people can walk away from meetings saying, "We didn't get one thing decided" or "We spent all our time deciding what needed to be done."

Leaders simply cannot present an idea without a plan. Questions need to be answered before the idea is introduced to the group, or the group is likely to fail before it has accomplished the following goals:

1. Defined the objective.
2. Defined the plan.
3. Agreed on the plan.
4. Decided who will accomplish the plan.
5. Decided what can or will be used to accomplish the plan.
6. Established a time line for plan progress and completion.
7. Predetermined the standards for success.

ESTABLISHING PRIOR MEASUREMENTS OF GOALS IS VITAL TO PLAN SUCCESS

The establishment of goals, as well as how these goals will be measured, is vital. If the leader does not reveal these measurements prior to implementing the plan, anyone can evaluate the success of the plan at his or her own discretion and by his or her own beliefs and standards. This reality is significant to a leader because a successful plan can actually be deemed and proclaimed a failure if the objectives are not shared prior to beginning.

If we don't tell those being led what we expect and intend to achieve, and if we don't state what results we will regard as successful, then students, staff, parents, or superiors can say whether the plan is going well or not. They can say whether the plan was a success or failure. And there is little we can do to change their minds after the fact. In truth, we may look foolish if we try. All this can result because the leader did not reveal the level of expectation of a plan before beginning. Far too often, we spend all our time with our plan— and actually "put off" any attempt to establish how we will evaluate our efforts. This is a huge mistake that sets us up for failure in the eyes of those being led.

Too, if the leader does not outline the expectations of the plan to those being led, he or she cannot provide the incentives during the attainment of the plan or the rewards following attainment. Rather, the leader can only give praise following completion of the task when evaluation is made. And such an evaluation may come a long time after plan completion.

Every legitimate assignment given by a leader must contain a definable purpose and practical measurement of progress that is visible to all. For example:

A. Assignment: To eliminate long cafeteria lines.
   Questions to be answered:

   1. How long are the lunch lines?
   2. How many students are standing in line?
   3. How long does it take to get served?
   4. How many lunch periods are there?
   5. How many students are eating lunch?
   6. What results do we expect?

B. Assignment: To increase math test scores.
   Questions to be answered:

   1. How many students are taking math?
   2. What were previous scores?
   3. How much time will we allocate to meet these new levels of achievement?
   4. What new (methods) (resources) (tools) will we use?
   5. When do we expect results to be revealed?

C. Assignment: To get more parents to attend the next back-to-school night.
   Questions to be answered:

   1. How many parents attended the last meeting?
   2. How many parents attended the meeting at this time last year?
   3. How many parents could come?
   4. What barriers to attendance do parents face?
   5. How many parents regard back-to-school night as important? Not important?
   6. What results do we expect?

The law of planning relates that the success of any plan is dependent upon the means, tools, and measurements that the leader establishes prior to beginning a task. When this law is violated, both the plan and the leader may experience constant criticism. The leader may be criticized for being disorganized, not knowing what he or she is doing, not giving adequate help and direction in achieving the goal, and never being successful. Indeed, those being led can say our plans never work very well. There's an adage in teaching that we should apply in our leadership role: *Tell them what you're going to teach them. Teach them. Tell them what you taught them.* This practice might serve us well in the classroom and the office—if we combine it with prior measurements or expected results.

THE LAW:
APPLIED

1.   Identify your next plan for the (classroom) (school) (district). Answer the following questions:

       a.   What will be done?
       b.   How will it be done?
       c.   What resources will be used?
       d.   When should the task be finished?
       e.   Which people should be involved in the completion of the task?
       f.   What extra planning will be necessary when all those being led by the leader must be involved in the tasks?
       g.   What will be regarded as success?

2.   What individual needs are met by the Law of Planning?

For related information, see the Law of Effectiveness.

THE
LAW OF
PERFECTIONISM

Rationale: Perfectionism is not a desirable leadership trait. It can result in compulsive attitudes and behaviors which curtail starting as well as finishing work and, therefore, work against the perfectionist, his or her peers, and the work and goals of the classroom, school, and district.

Many people who think they are perfectionists wear that label like a badge of honor. No matter what the circumstance, they find a way to make sure everyone knows not only do they regard themselves as perfectionists but others see them in that way too. They will even proudly proclaim that they are perfectionists who must do everything *right* and are unhappy unless everything meets their high standards. Yet, a close look will reveal that such a stance may not be what it appears. In fact, while being a perfectionist can result in lots of work, it often results in a lot of wasted work and little constructive productivity. Perfectionists may start a project, tear it up, and start again many times. Therefore, the quantity of their work is almost always low—and the quality of their work is often not what they profess it to be. Therefore, if you have perfectionist tendencies or have students who do, stop and look closely at this situation. Sir Winston Churchill said it best, "The maxim 'Nothing avails but perfection' may be spelled 'Paralysis.'"

THE BEHAVIOR IS
OFTEN SELF-DEFEATING

Perfectionists are driven by the need to be seen by others as perfect. However, a big difference exists between the act of perfecting something and the concept of perfectionism. Rather than working so things are the best they can be, perfectionists often seek flawless results. They perform primarily to attain high levels of self-worth, not to reach goals. The behavior originates in a fear of failure. They tend to believe that unless they are perfect, they are nothing.

Unfortunately, many people think perfectionism contributes to excellent results. Yet, the behavior is often self-defeating. Perfectionists usually work unceasingly on tasks and set unrealistic standards that almost guarantee failure because nothing is ever good enough for them. There is always a discrepancy between what is needed and available—and what they perceive as perfect. Worse, they are intense people who can't relax, who tend to alienate others, and who often have a distorted view of priorities. The bottom line is that perfectionists do not have the value many think they have. In addition, people often let them off the hook for what they do not achieve. Unlike the nonperformer who is generally confronted, the perfectionist is not. Instead, people say "He just can't get it done to his standards" or "She won't turn in the assignment until it's perfect." Therefore, the perfectionist often achieves status and value without producing.

Fortunately, there are actions you can take to become less of a perfectionist and still be productive. Whether you're dealing with yourself, a colleague, a student, or a parent, you would be wise to use this information.

134

NINE ACTIONS
TO TAKE

First, recognize that your drive to be perfect is self-defeating. It's rooted in your basic values about life. Confronting and understanding the origin of your perfectionism can help you change your behavior.

Second, understand that your work is *not* your worth. While it is *part* of you, it is not *all* of you. Therefore, your feelings of self-worth should not be tied exclusively to how hard you work or how perfect you are.

Third, talk about your behavior with someone who is an achiever and who knows you well. Get this person's input on the potential causes of your perfectionism. Ask him or her to support your efforts to change.

Fourth, alter your standards in some activity—just to see how the results differ. Lowering your expectations might enable you to perform the task more effectively and gain satisfaction from doing so. Reducing unrealistic standards frees you to plunge in and get going.

Fifth, improve your relationships. Your perfectionism may be keeping others away. Work on expressing your positive feelings *first*.

Sixth, try being less hard on yourself. In the process, make sure you are less demanding of others.

Seventh, examine your alternatives. There are more effective ways to approach your life. Search them out, and then take action in this direction.

Eighth, recognize that giving up your perfectionistic behavior will actually improve your ability to accomplish things. It will let you finish work rather than just redo it.

Ninth, arrange for professional help if your stress is excessively high. Unless confronted and changed, perfectionism can lead to obsessive-compulsive behavior. While perfectionism is not an easy problem to solve, sound advice and perseverance can help you conquer it.

NOT A
VALUED CHARACTERISTIC

Although perfectionists tend to see themselves as highly valuable and effective, they are not. In fact, the adopted behavior counters efforts to finish work and, therefore, works against the perfectionists themselves, their peers, and the school. And because they feel nothing is "quite right," they often actually do less. Therefore, the perfectionist stance gives them license not to start unless they have all their "ducks in a row," not to finish, and to criticize what others do—as well as how they do it. And more often than not, perfectionists get hung up in the details and miss the big picture altogether.

We would be wise to eliminate any perfectionist tendencies—and help those being led do the same. Perfectionism is not a behavior which will take people to new heights. Rather, it is one that places excessive demands on the individual and others. It results in impatience, irritability, and dissatisfaction. And these are not the behaviors we need in a school—and a close look will reveal that we often reinforce them when we glorify perfectionism.

THE LAW:
APPLIED

1. Are you a perfectionist?
2. If you have perfectionist tendencies, what steps are you willing to take to eliminate these tendencies?
3. Why is it possible for a perfectionist to lower his or her expectations and, yet, increase performance and satisfaction?
4. How can you help those you lead who are perfectionists overcome this stance?
5. Discuss the effect of stress on a perfectionist whom you know.

THE
MYTH OF
THE PERFECT PLAN

Rationale: No plan, regardless of how simple or complex, is without flaws and imperfections.

There simply isn't any doubt that plans are essential to any achievement. Without plans—whether they are daily lesson plans or guides for curriculum implementation or district budgets, our direction will be scattered, at best. We all realize that the plans of teachers and administrators affect the welfare of students. And we all know that intelligence, thought, and careful preparation are necessities in planning. Yet, it would be unfair to say that educators have never made the mistake of "going off half-cocked." We have. All leaders have.

Regardless, leaders usually expect total success from their plans and are frustrated when they stumble, falter, or fail. We expect our plans to be initiated by those being led. And we expect success to result from our plans. Too, we continually look for plans to be complete, all-inclusive, and foolproof. We want plans with all the "hitches" and "bugs" worked out before we activate them. We want a perfect plan because we think it ensures an ideal beginning, problem-free operation, and total success. This desire gets us in trouble. Why? Because our desires for the perfect plan simply cause us to think, expect, and act beyond reality.

ALL PLANS ALWAYS
HAVE FLAWS

A teacher or administrator must always remember that no plan, regardless of how simple or complex, is perfect. There is no perfect plan in every situation for teaching a lesson or getting the faculty to carry out a new idea. All plans have flaws. In every plan, there are holes. There isn't a plan that could be presented by a teacher or administrator that someone could not rip apart. In fact, every plan could probably be criticized by someone to the point that it looked as if no planning at all had occurred. We can even shoot holes in the people who made the plans. This fact affects the achievements of teacher and administrator alike. It also affects the achievement of those being led. It shouldn't.

Whether we're planning the school calendar or developing a procedure for reporting tardiness, planning flaws can be found. If we're preparing a student handbook, working out class schedules, or developing a procedure for ordering supplies—something will be wrong with the plan and some aspect of the plan can be improved. It has to be—for no plan is totally perfect for everyone. Yet, if we don't plan, we can't lead. And if we reject every plan, we may operate without any. Worse, we may find it safer to refer everything to committees where time is wasted and energy is spent—than to deal with the flaws that will most certainly be exposed. In the meantime, nothing happens. While we wait to act until we create the perfect plan, nothing gets done. We may not even worry about achievement until our perfect plan is complete. When this happens, "doing nothing" becomes our professional reputation as leaders.

OUR BEST EFFORT...
AT THIS TIME

Holding a professional, realistic, and people-wise attitude toward plans is necessary before progress can occur. We must readily acknowledge to those being led that all we can do is plan thoroughly, go with the very best plan we can create at that particular point in time, and make improvements as we initiate our plan. The important thing is that we, as classroom, school, and district leaders, plan to the best of our ability and adopt the attitude that changes and improvements can and will be made in the plan with time and experience. Make no mistake: Being willing to alter and refine plans *after* they have been accepted and while they are being implemented is the best way to reduce fears and keep those being led from being afraid to say yes to our proposals.

A leader must recognize and teach others that a plan is a scheme of action—no more, no less. It is not permanent. It is not carved in stone. It can be changed. It is meant to be improved. It can even be halted. Remember, plans reflect only current ability and reality. As our abilities and the reality changes with time, so do the conditions affecting the plan. Consequently, plans should change. Plans can include only what we know today. As we learn, we must be ready and willing to incorporate new knowledge.

Often, believing the myth that our plan is perfect prevents the adoption of our plan or delays our beginning. It also results in our being unable to distinguish the critical from the trivial. People being led often fear that "something will be accepted as it is" so much that they cannot focus on the larger goals during initial presentations. Indeed, a minor or insignificant flaw in the plan can capture the full attention of those being led. That's why a leader must adopt and teach those being led a professional attitude toward plan objectives, concepts, acceptance, beginnings, modifications, and even terminations. We must also teach people to think *major point* rather than *minor conflict*, and do the same ourselves. After all, some leaders act as if the details and specifics of their plan are bigger than life itself. They think any change or suggestion ruins their entire plan—or reflects negatively upon them. It doesn't. Rather, receiving input and suggestions from others simply means those being led are buying into the plan, taking some ownership of the plan, and beginning to think in terms of making sure the plan works.

THERE ARE PERFECT
WAYS TO PRESENT PLANS

Experience should teach leaders that, without the support of those being led, the critics of any plan will often be proven right. On the other hand, with the support from those being led, a plan seldom fails totally. That's a fact of life in the success of plans. That's why thorough communication with those being led is an absolute in initiating any plan. Part of that communication must include an open admission that the plan may have holes and, therefore, must be alterable. And, of course, if we present our plan to those being led as "the perfect plan," we ought to be prepared for the inevitable. Intelligent people will know it can't be perfect. Many will have instant fears. They should. And some will reject it— openly or behind our backs. That's normal. It's unlikely that very many will respond, "Wonderful. Let's get started." Rather, by word and action, they are likely to say, "Wait," "Stop," "Hold on," or "No." That's why we need to know that while no plan is perfect, our presentation will go better if we realize that it will suffer from at least two deficiencies.

First, only the planning process can benefit from the experiences of the past and the present; the future is only speculation. Conditions that did exist and that exist today are not guaranteed for the future. As conditions change and as new information becomes available, the implementation and the success of the plan are likely to be impacted. Therefore, as time passes and implementation of the plan progresses, we can continue to learn about factors and strategies that are more—as well as less—effective. This knowledge can be crucial to the success of the plan, but was not available when the plan was constructed.

Second, planning requires the selection of one course of action from multiple alternatives. Any time a single course of action is chosen, the possibilities and opportunities unique to other options are eliminated. Therefore, potential flaws and inefficiencies are introduced to the plan and the chosen course of action.

Rather than attempting to build the perfect plan, we should focus our efforts on developing the very best plan we can today while committing to review and adjust the plan at significant implementation stages. This procedure allows the plan to benefit from new information and changing circumstances. This approach to building the best plan we can today allows us to remain focused on our goals while remaining flexible in the strategies and paths we choose to help us reach our goals.

In addition, this approach provides us with the opportunity to gain and utilize experience and to remain on course even as new barriers are encountered and new opportunities are discovered. After all, the purpose of developing a plan is to take us from where we are to where we want to be—not to develop a perfect document that is free of flaws and the need to be adjusted during implementation. If we approach planning from this perspective and choose a course of action that can be revisited or modified, we remain positioned throughout the development and implementation of the plan to listen and incorporate helpful information from people who otherwise could represent strong resistance and be harsh critics.

THE LAW:
APPLIED

1. If you believe you have ever created a perfect plan that needed no changes or modifications, share your experiences.
2. Even though all plans have flaws, discuss why a leader must plan thoroughly and try to work all the bugs out before presenting the plan to those being led.
3. Discuss why the leader should work on problems as they arise and those being led should work on initiating the plan.
4. Relate what you can tell those being led about resolving problems as they occur—in order to reduce fears.
5. What should you do if those being led want to make modifications, but you don't?

THE
MYTH OF
QUALITY AND COST

Myth: There is always a direct correlation between high quality and high cost.

For as long as one can remember, people have had the tendency to link quality with cost. In professions, business, industry, government, and schools we have long held the belief that bigger was better—and high quality automatically meant that we could expect to pay more. In the same vein, if we paid a lot, we believed that we got the best. In the process, we developed an adage, "You get what you pay for."

In retrospect, our beliefs in education probably mirrored the beliefs of American industry—where it has been assumed for a long, long time that quality and cost were in opposition to each other. As a result, if high quality was the desire, it was simply assumed that you would have to spend more and endure higher costs. This, we believed, was the price one had to pay if he or she wanted quality. And we all want to believe that higher cost means higher quality. After all, who wants to say you can have good teachers or administrators, but you don't have to worry about paying them?

Likewise, we have long believed that if you wanted to drive costs down, you simply had to sacrifice quality in the process. Nobody argued these points—until recently. Rather, all the arguments were confined to whether or not the higher price was really worth the money—or if price were the highest and best value. Once we decided, we simply moved with our choice of quality or price. Occasionally, we found a "bargain," but it was a result of someone's misfortune—not by design.

IT TOOK THE JAPANESE
TO TEACH US A NEW LESSON

We gave up the "bigger is better" notion several years ago. We found out by experience that it simply wasn't true. In fact, we actually discovered that small could be very superior to large. In education, we see the truth of this daily. Large salaries don't mean better instruction or happier teachers. Likewise, our biggest problems and failures seem to occur in our largest schools and our biggest school districts. As educators, we know bigger is not better.

However, it took the Japanese to teach us that cost and quality are not at odds with each other. They taught us that if you want high quality and you pursue this goal intelligently and effectively, you will actually save money—for many reasons. If you do a job right the first time, you don't have to do it again. You don't have to spend time, effort, and money fixing it. You also don't have to hire people to monitor the job and inspect it. You don't have to devote time, effort, and money to establishing a multitude of "controls." And from small organizations to large ones, all these actions which focus heavily on quality don't cost money, but save a lot of money—without sacrificing quality.

140

BELIEVING THE MYTH WILL
AFFECT YOUR PERFORMANCE

The lack of direct correlation between high quality and high cost is now an accepted truth. In the 1980s, it was not. As a result, we have programs in schools today such as QPA, restructuring, empowerment, site-based management, and The Master Teacher program of weekly staff development that advocate high productivity, high quality, and high satisfaction rather than just higher costs. Yet, there are many who persist in believing the myth regarding cost and quality. They are mistaken—and believing the myth can adversely affect the quality of their work as administrators and teachers as well as the quality of the work of those they lead.

We now know that quality can soar while costs are actually plunging. Herein lies a tremendous strength and a big pitfall. That is, a pitfall can develop if management does not remember to take care of the people who produced the quality and reduced the cost. If, for instance, our teachers teach all day and also are heavily involved in restructuring, empowerment, attending meetings before and after school, and working on projects during the weekends, we had better take care of them. They should be paid, of course. And administrators should occasionally get substitutes so that meetings can be held and work can be done during the day. Unless this action is taken, administrators may not see the quality last very long.

Likewise, teachers must do the same. If some students are going the extra mile to make things happen, but are never given any leeway or reward for their commitment, they may stop giving the "extra effort" at the height of their achievements. And if administrators must work longer hours and more months during the year, we must pay them an appropriate salary. In either case, when we take care of people we will find the "cost" small in comparison to the "savings" we have experienced in getting high-quality effort, work, and achievement.

Remember, quality need not be costly. Quality need not be sacrificed for any reason. With knowledge, skills, imagination, innovation, and work, people can produce the highest of quality at a lower cost. Look around, you'll see the evidence of this truth every day. The quality of a product or service goes up while the cost goes down.

THE LAW:
APPLIED

1. Discuss the aspects of this law which make it difficult to accept.
2. How can we protect ourselves and accept the teaching of this law?
3. Share why this law is not a cop-out for not spending money.
4. Give examples which prove that quality does not have to be sacrificed due to lower cost.

THE
LAW OF
SURVIVAL

Rationale: The most consistent survivors in leadership positions deal honestly and sincerely with those they lead.

It's a leader's normal, human concern to be focused toward self and survival of self. Survival is an integral part of every person's psyche. Those who become classroom, school, or district leaders are no exception. Yet, the need and drive for self-preservation may cause a leader to act contrary to the teachings of the Law of Survival. And the fewer leadership foundations and skills a teacher or administrator possesses, the more vulnerable he or she is to fall into a trap and to violate this law—and suffer the consequences.

For instance, leaders often tend to avoid the truth or deviate from it in some way in stressful situations. This is especially true when we err and know the fault lies wholly or partially with us. Nobody likes to be wrong, much less admit to the world when he or she is. If the question of individual survival is the issue, whether real or imaginary, a leader can make big mistakes. We can even attempt to serve as judge and jury of our own thinking, behavior, and mistake—then rationalize our error as unimportant. Worse, when we decide to skirt the issue or use the strategy of omission, we often rationalize our actions as "necessary" or "the only thing we could have done" under the circumstances. We may even think our actions were "smart" or "wise."

As we take such a course, we may prejudge what the repercussions or penalty would be if we had to tell "everything." Then, we can permit ourselves to skirt the truth—and live with ourselves in the process. It's called *self-preservation*. It's a common reaction. But it's not a good or healthy one for the short or long term.

THE NEED TO SURVIVE
GROWS WITH AGE

Unfortunately, the older we get, the stronger and more dominant this need for self-preservation and survival can become. It can govern our every communication, decision, and action. In fact, as we get older, the need to survive can be the most powerful and negative force in our professional life.

Often, young teachers and administrators say that they can make their own security. If worst comes to worst, they say, they can and will change jobs. There is no apparent fear or hesitation accompanied by this proclamation. I've had older colleagues tell me, "That's the way I talked twenty years ago too. I'll be anxious to hear you twenty years from now when you have time invested here or are too old to start all over and get another job." Yet, even these proclamations from the young are only rationalizations, and, in truth, fear is being expressed. The older teachers or administrators are simply more honest and too experienced to fool themselves. They realize that they can't change jobs readily. They acknowledge the investment they have made in the present position. They don't want to lose it. These realities, unfortunately, can cause them to violate the law of survival.

As a leader, one must keep in mind that, basically, all people are afraid of failure and negative exposure—regardless of their age. In a leader, this failure may be intensified.

Maybe it's because a leader feels he or she is supposed to be right and has a set of critics standing around waiting to point out his or her failures. This reality has caused many teachers and administrators to think the only way not to fail or reveal failure is to remain totally and obviously in command by being "right" all the time. They run the classroom with an "iron fist." They act as if there were only two ways to do things, their way and the wrong way. They are the purveyors of all right, wrong, good, and bad. They would never admit an error to students, staff members, parents, or colleagues. Maintaining a distinct separation from those they lead will, they believe, prevent others from seeing their faults. Even creating a kind of false superiority helps, they think. Total command is their goal. They may not really believe any means justifies the achievement of this end, but their actions indicate that they do. When this is our thinking as teachers or administrators, fear is our motivator and secrecy is a huge part of our communication practices. Unfortunately, this common response can produce our failure. That's why a teacher or administrator should never forget two important facts.

TWO IMPORTANT FACTS WE MUST REMEMBER

First, security is a basic human motive. Second, people are basically insecure—including us and those we lead. Compound these two facts with the realization that we, as leaders, know we are responsible and in charge of a classroom, school, and district—and with an intellect which tells us that we don't know all the answers, but can never admit it—and trouble can be the result, unless we understand people and the laws and principles of management as they relate to leading ourselves.

As teachers and administrators, no matter how we act, we don't know all the answers—and everyone knows it. We are not faultless—and everyone knows it. The question is: Why does something within us make us believe we should always be right or know the answer? If all teachers and administrators could come to the realization that they don't know everything and nobody expects them to—they might be better able to act honestly and sincerely with themselves as well as those they lead. It's the pure struggle for survival that makes a leader attempt to gain personal security through several self-destructive behaviors such as:

a. Putting others down.
b. Displaying one-upmanship.
c. Attempting to build a private dynasty.
d. Withholding information.
e. Withholding authority when delegating responsibilities.
f. Offering misinformation.
g. Creating a false superiority.
h. Proclaiming not to need anybody.
i. Calling ourselves a perfectionist.
j. Lying.
k. Blaming others.
l. Hedging.

SURVIVAL CAN
GET IN OUR WAY

Make no mistake: Teachers and administrators exhibit these attitudes and behaviors for self-preservation. Yet, each of these actions places our survival in more jeopardy. It is hoped that we will realize that the firmer our professional foundations and the greater our leadership skills and confidence, the less likely we are to violate this law. The greater our understanding is of ourselves and those being led, the less likely we are to violate the Law of Survival and get ourselves in big trouble. We can never forget this management law, for it reminds us that our actions can be self-deceiving—and the survival need can result in our not surviving.

Survival as a leader depends upon our influencing and controlling our environment in an honest, sincere, positive, and constructive way. This control is dependent upon two things: First, it depends upon our image of honesty, competency, sincerity, and effectiveness in the eyes of those we lead. Second, it is dependent upon our success in avoiding self-perpetuated conflict with those we lead by what we say and do.

The Law of Survival relates that the most consistent leadership survivors always deal honestly and sincerely with those they lead. Any action or movement in the opposite direction greatly increases the probability of self-perpetuated conflict and failure. Remember: Truth cannot be continually suppressed. Once revealed, an untruth is both a personal and professional insult to those being led. It results in one of the biggest leadership problems of all—a credibility gap. Credibility gaps spread both internally and externally more quickly than most management diseases. Those being led are apt to believe that if we lie or misrepresent ourselves to one, we will do so with all. They believe if we have been dishonest once, we will be deceitful again. These assumptions usually are correct.

Once established, credibility gaps are one of the most difficult obstacles for a leader to overcome. When those being led believe that your word is not good, you're dead in the water. Unfortunately, without full disclosure of all past actions, plus time for confidence to be reestablished, a negative personal image is formed. Few leaders can survive and lead effectively between the time a credibility gap occurs and the time that confidence is restored. And only time and truth can reestablish credibility and confidence in leadership.

We need to be aware of one more thought as we attempt to lead. If we resist admitting our mistakes to those we lead, we teach them by example that errors are bad and should be avoided rather than used as learning opportunities. These lessons prevent those being led from taking risks and maximizing their own learning. In this sense, not admitting and not learning from mistakes and errors is contrary to our teaching and learning mission. Furthermore, credibility and compassion can be built when we admit our failures and go forward.

THE LAW:
APPLIED

1. Discuss the various behaviors which result from the desire to survive.
2. Share the ways people can respond to a half-truth.
3. Discuss why overcoming a credibility gap is so difficult.
4. Privately, list your (securities) (insecurities).
5. How can your insecurities affect your leadership?
6. What individual needs of those being led are affected by any form of dishonesty?

THE
LAW OF
WHOLE TRUTH

Rationale: Those in leadership positions who have difficulty relating whole or total truths do so out of misjudging those being led or out of unsubstantiated fear. This fear can result in a leadership behavior that causes distrust of all management communication and may result in a loss of the trust and confidence of those being led.

This law is an extension of the Law of Survival. It has some similarities and differences. However, because truth plays such a large role in generating leadership effectiveness, I have chosen to make the Law of Whole Truth separate. In many ways, we humans are afraid of the *whole* truth. This must be so, for so often we get ourselves into a bind and cause ourselves and others considerable turmoil simply because we didn't tell it as it was—exactly and completely. The question is: Why?

Why can't we say that one person told us about something rather than indicate everybody did—or that one or two are unhappy about a situation rather than say everyone is mad? If we make a decision, why can't we offer all the reasons rather than only those we believe others will accept? If we give someone a job to do, why do we downplay the hard or unpleasant part? Whatever we call them, these kinds of distortions breed distrust and cause many anxieties for those being led. And if we gain a reputation for telling half-truths to those being led, they may not believe our whole truths.

It's a fact: Leaders want what they say to count and to be accepted as important. Leaders want people to do as they are asked quickly, eagerly, and with the minimum of problems. Teachers and administrators are not the exception. Maybe that's why we tell half-truths, for half-truths are often omissions or exaggerations in one direction or the other. An exaggeration almost always offers more impact. It can offer the path of least resistance, we think. Yet, the truth of most situations will eventually surface. We know that. If this is so, then it would seem our goal should be to avoid such difficulty. Yet, the need to have our leadership result in action may outweigh our logic or intellect. Most certainly, we must be aware that a need for power, along with our misjudgment of those being led and our fears, may get in the way of our truthful communication with those being led.

PURPOSELY OMITTING
KNOWN FACTS

There is another facet of our failure to tell it straight that deserves consideration. This is when known facts are purposely omitted. Leaders often tell only part of a story—knowing all the time that the whole story provides negative answers to most of the questions which might arise. Yet, we must know that a partial story only creates doubt and often causes disturbing questions to arise about us. What moves leaders to take this course of action? Do we enjoy seeing others upset or fearful, or is this another case of our wanting to say something important and exert our power? Or is it because of real or unsubstantiated fears we have regarding the whole truth?

Then, of course, there are some leaders who don't tell the truth at all in certain situations.

They knowingly change the facts. We may know such leaders. And we may be able to say, "I know someone who doesn't tell the truth, and he or she is very successful." But just wait. He or she won't be successful forever. A close look will reveal that very few such leaders finish a career at the head of the class and without countless career moves.

Without doubt, a half-truth is often used to avoid or absolve ourselves of involvement in mistakes or a situation which has caused problems. Here, we can imply, "He did" rather than "I did," or leave out our participation by inference or actual omission. Also, a half-truth can serve as an opportunity to bestow more credit upon ourselves than is due. We can act as if we were the one who was responsible for a success and simply not mention the roles others played in the success.

Sometimes we tell half-truths to protect others. We are afraid that if we told them the whole story they would get mad or "come unglued." The reason for our action is obvious: we simply don't think others can handle the truth. Although some of this action is pure self-protection on our part, much of it results from a fear that the whole truth may create unnecessary turmoil for us and others. Yet, all are serious mistakes. Worse, all are underestimations of the capabilities and reactions of human beings. Unfortunately, many teachers and administrators are vulnerable to this type of erroneous thinking—and this kind of leadership mistake.

LEADERS USE HALF-TRUTHS TO MOTIVATE

It is not uncommon for leaders to use half-truths as motivational devices. For instance, if a staff needs reprimanding for being lax in hall discipline, greater emphasis may result if teachers are told that other colleagues or parents are complaining. And if teachers tell students that "the office" has mandated a rule, students may respond without blaming us—or complaining to us. This half-truth allows us an excuse to act and criticize as a third person, for we alone have not reprimanded the staff—colleagues and parents have. We have not made a rule for students—the office has. For the same reasons, we may say that it is the board of education or superintendent who has instituted a rule, when, in truth, that is not really the case. People involve higher authorities in half-truths out of the belief that it may prompt immediate action, whereas reluctance might follow their requests. Students do it. Teachers do it. Administrators do it.

Without doubt, sometimes we tell half-truths because we fear that the truth would turn someone against us. Teachers may tell a colleague that he or she acted wisely in a situation— when in fact we believe he or she did not. Administrators may say a supplier has not sent an order—when the purchase order has not yet been sent. When the truth surfaces, however, more anger will follow because of this deception. You can count on it.

All of these failures to tell it straight handicap the individual leader or the person being led. Truth is the foundation of relationship. Truth is the foundation of teamwork. When it is absent, distrust and doubt replace confidence. That's significant. Trust is the cornerstone for people's working and living relationship with each other.

PEOPLE CAN
HANDLE THE TRUTH

Make no mistake: It is not *truth* that people cannot handle. It's deception or a lie or half-truths that present us with human relationship problems that move beyond our control. Even when truth arouses negative emotions in those being led, the best course has been chosen for both the short and the long term. Time after time, this fact is proved as better understandings and working relationships follow a negative initial reaction.

Truth promotes the formation of professional and human relationships which are prepared to meet tests and crises. This is not so with half-truths. Imposing a half-truth says, "I don't think you are worthy, capable, or intelligent enough to be confronted with the whole truth." This leadership action offers those being led nothing—except maybe a choice between ignoring our insult or confronting us with our lie.

It is not easy to confront the boss who leads with half-truths. But it is easy to distrust and resent such a leader. The opposite is the reality of whole truth—for whole truth almost always brings people closer together. Only whole truth presents an opportunity for support, involvement, and meaningful action, which are leadership necessities. That's why it's important that a leader tell it straight—the first time through—and insist that those being led do the same.

A VERY PRACTICAL
AND ETHICAL DECISION

We've been told since we were children that honesty is the best policy. Our parents were our first leaders regarding the absolute necessity for telling the whole truth. Yet, none of us are completely honest all the time. And most of us have been guilty of lying. Regardless, we all need to be very much aware of the necessity to tell the truth, the whole truth, and nothing but the truth—if we expect to find effectiveness in leadership.

There are many reasons related to morality that a leader must tell the whole truth all the time. Each of us could give a thousand reasons that telling the truth is an absolute necessity. We know it will affect our competency and our ability to have control over our jobs. We know it will affect our ability to instill trust and confidence and communicate effectively. We know it will affect our ability to gain cooperation from those we lead. Therefore, we have no valid reason for not embracing whole truth as our leadership tool. It is the only method that will work—even when it causes us pain.

THE LAW:
APPLIED

1. Share some of the fears you experience as you lead.
2. Which fears are real and can be substantiated? Which are unsubstantiated?
3. In negative situations, do people respond differently to the whole truth than they respond to a half-truth? Discuss.
4. Do you feel that there are situations where you cannot tell those being led the truth? Discuss.
5. How can a leader respond successfully if confronted with a half-truth?

THE
LAW OF
SHARING TRUTHS

Rationale: A leader can and should *share* his or her truths openly and freely with those being led—without pressure or demands for acceptance. However, a leader can expect resistance when trying to impose or force his or her truths upon those being led.

It's an impossible task: We simply can't impose or force our truths upon those being led, no matter how right we feel those truths are or how much we believe they will benefit those we lead. It won't work. Without question, leading is much easier if those we lead believe, accept, and follow our truths. But we can only reach this level of influence by sharing our truths, not by imposing them upon others.

In the past, doctors, lawyers, and educators have held the somewhat Olympian position of being the keepers of special knowledge and truth. From time to time, these truths would be dispensed among the masses, who felt privileged and honored to receive them. Superintendents gave their truths to principals. Principals gave their truths to teachers, and teachers gave the ultimate truth to students. All these "truths" had one thing in common: They told those being led how things were—and how they were going to be.

This public view has changed. We no longer feel that only certain people in our society have special access to the truth. We all do. We no longer believe that the expert does the telling and those being led do the accepting. We now believe everyone is a knowledgeable stakeholder. In schools, we are trying to involve everyone. Therefore, one thing which is being learned is that nobody has a right to force or impose his or her truths upon others. This is an improvement over previously held public attitudes and beliefs—and leadership beliefs as well. That's why the teacher or administrator who tries to impose his or her truths on those being led will fail and experience considerable rejection in the process.

THE LEADER'S TRUTH IS
NO LONGER ABSOLUTE

A close look at history will reveal that when one particular group has held the reins of power, there was only one set of truths. Everyone was expected to abide by the beliefs coming from the group leader. Nothing more could be entered or said. The base for having to live by established formats has had several foundations, including familial and political.

For instance, if the head of the house held certain beliefs, there was no question that the whole family would have to adopt and conform to those beliefs. The head of the house could insist that his or her truths were the ones to be believed and followed. The rest of the family might differ and plead that disbelief, dislike, compromise, or even immunity should be allowed. Yet, adherence was usually demanded. Herein lies a big lesson for teachers and administrators. We need to be careful not to confuse truth-giving with a power play. There's a big difference.

We may be able to control students by wielding power, although this is a debatable point. But no one's mind can be "bought" unless he or she allows it to be—not students', parents', teachers', administrators', or board members'. That's because those beliefs which are truths for us may not be truths for other people. And that's why a leader's truths can only be shared, not imposed.

It may come as a surprise to know that we can't even impose truth upon ourselves. We can force ourselves to pretend belief, perhaps out of pressure or fear. However, deep within us, we seldom, if ever, consciously accept what is being imposed upon us as a belief of our own. Until we accept what is being said as "ours," it's not truth to us. The truths of others don't become ours until we find ourselves living out of them. It's important for teachers and administrators to know this reality. Most of us do. The question is: How does all this translate into teaching students in the classroom and serving as the leader of a school or district?

OPINION, NOT TRUTH, IS RIGID

To paraphrase, once we know that we are true to ourselves, we can move to being true to those being led. All of our relationships with those being led are made stronger when we live from the center of our own truths. In turn, all our relationships with those we lead are weakened if we find it necessary to try to live by the truths of people around us. So it is with those we lead.

Many words have been softened and given greater dimension out of what we have been learning about people. *Truth* is one of those words. This is a healthy reality, but we need to take care that these words don't soften down to the point that they have no meaning at all. After all, *truth* is a dangerous word unless it is handled with respect. That's because it can be transposed into raw power in an instant by a teacher, principal, or superintendent. This is especially evident in our relationships with students and parents. We have no right to talk of truth except in our own terms. We can only relate *our* truths—without any strings attached. We cannot *tell*, *demand*, or *force* our truths in absolute ways. Herein lies a key for getting those we lead to accept what we share—and to benefit from our influence.

If we know that truth is something that keeps changing as we and our world shift, then we can be easy about our use of the word. There's one thing truth is not. It's not rigid. When it is, it's just *opinion*. Hopefully, we realize the full weight of this possibility. Truth is driven by what we know today. It is powered by what we know now. As we learn, our "truths" can be transformed and changed.

Therefore, truth is always open to challenge. It can only be improved out of openness. These are the things we should keep in mind as we work as leaders. Both our ethics and our professionalism should help us know how to present our truths to those being led while trying to teach and vie for acceptance of what we are teaching, suggesting, or urging.

SHARING IS SOMETHING WE CAN AND SHOULD DO

We have opportunities in our various leadership positions to share some things that have become truths for us. Sharing is a responsibility we have to exercise if we intend to help and influence those we lead. Therefore, sharing is what we should feel free to do. It is, for example, one of the primary reasons I have written this book. However, we can't demand that others take on our views or values. We can merely express some things that we know to be valid for us. This fine line constitutes the difference between sharing and imposing—and leading and trying to dominate those we lead.

We should always make it clear to others that they have a right to feel however they choose about what we say. In fact, there should be an opportunity in every leadership situation to have good discussion, and we should promote such exchange to improve the learning of those we lead as well as our own learning—if we expect to lead people successfully. We may know some truths, but we don't know everything about them. And, for a leader, it's always impressive and insightful to hear what a thoughtful student, teacher, or administrator has to add to what we already know.

Once we can permit such freedom, everyone will come to understand the merit of sharing truths, rather than imposing them on each other. It's out of this mutual respect for one another's beliefs that we are positioned to begin the process of teaching and learning from each other. Without such a stance, there are no ingredients for a partnership of any kind. Rather, the openness necessary for meaningful study, discovery, learning, and achieving has been diminished—and the raw power of the leader's beliefs has been instilled as a replacement.

Power is a base for wars, not leading. We can eliminate such barriers simply by telling others we are *sharing* rather than *telling*—and that it's their right to do the accepting or rejecting. This law reminds us that this would be a wise course for us to take. This is not idealistic. Indeed, it is the most practical course a leader can take. Why? Because if you try to impose your truths on those being led, you are going to experience a lot of rejection. In the process, leading is going to be a miserable experience marked with conflicts.

THE LAW:
APPLIED

1. Share your truths about teaching and learning. Next, ask for agreement with your truths.
2. Describe the results you would expect if those being led adhered to those truths.
3. Discuss examples where (students) (teachers) (administrators) are forced to accept certain truths.
4. Are these impositions (valid) (invalid)? Discuss.
5. Discuss methods, techniques, and skills which can be employed to share truths.
6. How does imposing truths deny individual needs? Which ones are denied?

THE
LAW OF
DEFENSIVENESS

Rationale: When a leader responds defensively when questioned, challenged,
confronted, or attacked, he or she is apt to lose on all fronts.

You have worked for days on an idea that you want to present at the next faculty meeting. It's an exciting concept that will benefit students in significant ways. You know all will endorse it. No other reaction is possible—for your idea solves a big problem, is all-inclusive, and gives the entire faculty an opportunity for meaningful participation—and will benefit the majority of students in your school. The day comes, the faculty meeting convenes, and you are nervous and eager as you present your thoughts. The first reaction comes from a colleague who always speaks up and out against everything. He bluntly says that it won't work, and he moves that it not be discussed, much less considered. How do you react?

You are having a discussion with colleagues in a department meeting. The subject is controversial. Your colleagues are a core of very intelligent educators. They regard themselves as authorities and, in all honesty, usually reveal their versatility. You are well-prepared for any possible question. But you do not anticipate that, at just the crucial moment in the discussion, a colleague who is the most unyielding and verbal will interrupt the proceedings to ask you if anything is being gained from the discussion and if you honestly believe this subject should be a priority when there are so many other *important* issues that need to be addressed. How do you react?

IS REACTING DEFENSIVELY
REALLY A NATURAL RESPONSE?

These kinds of situations happen to us. Sometimes they come during our most sober moments. We may experience hair rising on the back of our necks and the blood surging to our faces when we even read accounts of such happenings. The lack of consideration on the part of our colleagues seems to support and justify a defensive stand. One might even conclude that for a teacher or administrator to react defensively in such situations is not only *natural*, it is justifiable. But is it?

If, by using the word *natural*, we mean that this reaction would be the accepted and healthy thing for a leader to do, then we have to scratch that usage. Here, the use of *natural* would mean "of being born with us and, therefore, an innate part of us." Yet, being defensive is not a natural human characteristic. It is a learned reaction. It is one we have to consciously choose to make. Therefore, it is not natural.

Too, we must ask: If we react defensively in these kinds of situations—what will the result of our defensiveness be? The answer to this question is obvious. The situation will probably be made worse. A closer look will reveal that to react defensively, we must "take the bait" that the respondent gives us in such situations. If we are inexperienced leaders, this is an easy mistake to make. However, if we are experienced, we recognize immediately that, regardless of the respondent's intentions, to be defensive would be to "bite the wrong hook." This kind of "bait" is often given to us in school situations by students, teachers, administrators, staff, parents, and the public. We would be wise if we not only refused to take it—but gave it back in a professional and dignified way.

FIRST, TRY TO TURN
THE CHALLENGE AROUND

Without doubt, how we react in such situations can improve our position with peers as well as with those being led. Our reaction can also upgrade the tone, climate, and responsibility level of all. For instance, if we meet these kinds of comments by asking the respondents—students and staff alike—why they feel this way, we have immediately made the respondents responsible for what they have said. If we ask others present if they also share this opinion, we have opened responsibility to the group. However, we must also take care not to appear as though we are setting up the objector. After all, such action could turn those being led against us in defense of a peer. Personal and professional maturity should allow us to avoid a defensive course of action.

Experience should tell us that challengers who make a crude or blunt show of confrontation are seldom prepared to discuss the rationality of their position. That's a fact. In pressing them to clarify their reactive reasons, nine out of ten times we will experience the satisfaction of seeing our own ideas look more reasonable as well as more intelligent.

If, on the other hand, the challenger does establish some viable reasons for rejecting our ideas, then we are in a position to consider and respond to his or her thoughts. By simply asking questions of the respondent, we have put ourselves in a position to accept as well as respond. And this all happened because we refused to take a defensive stand.

BE CAREFUL WHEN
CONFRONTED OR ATTACKED

Learning not to be defensive is one of the hardest of all leadership and management lessons. It's easy to respond defensively when we feel attacked or confronted. Yet, it is far better to understand that most harsh responses to what we say or do have little or nothing to do with us personally. More often than not, the person doing the attacking is doing it for his or her own reasons. Therefore, it's *always* very important to realize that someone's poor treatment of us or our leadership often says more about that person's poor feelings about himself or herself than about us. This realization can help us resist feeling victimized. If we take the bait and react defensively, we provide him or her with a convenient vehicle in which to ride over us like a bulldozer.

As leaders, we will be challenged. We will be confronted. We will be questioned. And from time to time, we may even be attacked. In every instance, however, our response is very important because our response makes it possible for us to maintain our power. This law teaches us that if we respond defensively, we are apt to lose on all fronts.

Are there times we must respond defensively? Of course. But we need to be aware that how we treat those being led and how we use our defense does not minimize the danger—or change the law.

THE LAW:
APPLIED

1. Discuss questions you can throw back to the person questioning, challenging, confronting, or attacking.
2. Share what you might do with their (good) (inappropriate) replies.
3. Discuss why the power is always in your hands if you respond appropriately.
4. Discuss how those being led may react if you respond defensively.
5. If you were giving a presentation tomorrow to the faculty, could you identify possible objectors? What can you do before the meeting to be more prepared to face those who may object?
6. Which individual needs are denied when a leader is defensive?

THE
LAW OF
ANGER

Rationale: The anger of those being led is both a state of mind and a behavior which cannot go unconfronted and unresolved without adversely affecting the productivity and satisfaction of the leader and those being led—and the work of the classroom, school, and district.

Almost everyone gets angry from time to time. Students do. Teachers do. Administrators do. Whatever our leadership position, we are likely to get angry ourselves and be involved with angry people. Most of us in teaching and administration have experienced this reality. Whether we can manage a workable relationship with those being led depends not only on how we come to understand and deal with their needs, but also on how much we are aware of our own. Being able to identify anger in those being led is the first step toward this understanding. Unfortunately, leaders do not always know when those being led are angry.

Those being led who are open with their anger are easy to identify. They present us with the opportunity to approach them because their anger is on the surface. We can rationally identify the source of their anger, and maybe even find the point at which the anger took form. But there are other kinds of anger besides overt anger. These additional types all have a similarity—the anger is concealed.

Few of us would deny that we know people who mask their anger behind other behaviors. As we know well, however, being able to identify concealed anger can be a vital key to understanding the real motivations of some people. Such identification is also necessary in resolving problems and leading effectively. Let's look closely at two of the most common types of concealed anger.

HIT AND RUN
IS OBSTRUCTED ANGER

Those being led who always say "no" are prime examples of people who conceal their anger. These individuals always know why what we're asking them to do is wrong or won't work. They know why a new program or change won't work—and why it's not even worth trying. They say their piece in absolute terms—usually very forcefully—and then retire into silence. They refuse to give any such matters further consideration and will avoid others' points of view completely after they have given their first and final word.

Those being led who react this way really are angry. When we are on the receiving end of such concealed anger, we may, unfortunately, back off with irritated frustration to avoid further engagement. This is a mistake. This is exactly what these angry people want us to do, because their behavior keeps us from leading.

They have found that strong disagreement followed by silence will usually cause others to withdraw. But if we begin acting as though the issue is not closed, quite often these people can be drawn back into the discussion and may be willing, eventually, to shift positions entirely. Remember, the effectiveness of their anger depends on their being able to hit and run without being held accountable for things they said. They feel they can attack and victimize

154

others. They plan on it—unless the leader takes a more active and assertive stance with them. This law says that anger must be resolved, or productivity and satisfaction will be curtailed.

SILENT ANGER
IS ALSO CONCEALED ANGER

On the opposite side of the scale are the people who greet everything with silence. They never contribute. They play off their silence. They may even say things, such as "I don't care what you do" or "Whatever you decide is all right with me," without ever offering a token opinion, idea, or assistance. They are different from cooperative people because they don't go along with the majority. Rather, they refuse to give any input and simply go their own way—always. As a result, they negate leaders and leadership.

Make no mistake: This kind of silence also reveals anger and needs to be treated rather than ignored. The best course is to persist until you gain their involvement. You must pull them from their silence. If these are students, teachers, or administrators who happen to be on committees, a good leader might be able to draw them out by insisting privately that they undoubtedly have some worthwhile thoughts to offer the group. If all efforts to draw them out fail, then the leader must go on. One thing is certain: A leader cannot quit or drop ideas simply because he or she can't gain the cooperation or involvement of these people.

Most certainly, there are other forms of anger. But of the three types of anger discussed here, open anger is the easiest to handle. It's also the healthiest. Silent anger is the most difficult and the most unhealthy, for it buries an emotion. Those who exhibit silent anger must be confronted with this reality. And they must never, under any circumstances, be rewarded for their actions. Too, we cannot quit trying to change their behavior.

ANOTHER BIG ISSUE:
OUR ANGER

We should also realize that when evaluating various angry people, we might be wise to pause at our own doorstep. Where do our own angers lie? We all have them. Only some of us solve them completely. Most of us shade them out of our consciousness or bury them under whatever disguise effectively conceals them. We need to look carefully to see how we react when challenged by others. Do we personalize the matter immediately, or are we able to discuss issues professionally? If we are angered by the words or actions of those being led, do we reject, slam doors, and refuse to speak further about the problem, or can we stand still and accept the confrontation with an investigatory interest?

Anger is an obstacle to getting the work of the classroom, school, and district accomplished. It always affects satisfaction. It goes beyond obstructing progress. It is a destructive kind of victimizing which damages all within its orbit. Anger is an emotion within us all. It is normal. However, how we handle it may produce an abnormality for us and those being led. That's why it needs to be dealt with continuously, seriously, and effectively. This law reminds us that if we don't resolve anger, our success will be limited.

Leaders must be problem solvers. Our interest and involvement must exceed our anger. We must know what fairness is—and practice it by being willing to explore situations with an aim toward resolution rather than obstruction. That's the difference in dealing positively with anger as opposed to being defeated by it. And, unfortunately, the anger of someone will always be present in our lives trying to defeat us and our leadership.

**THE LAW:
APPLIED**

1. How much do you fear angry people?
2. Discuss how often you are really an angry person.
3. Discuss the importance of confronting anger—then casting away your anger when an issue is resolved. What steps can you take to achieve this objective?
4. How is anger getting in the way of productivity and achievement in your (classroom) (school) (district)? What are people angry about?
5. Share ways to approach an angry person (publicly) (privately).
6. Identify individual needs which are affected by angry (colleagues) (leaders).

THE
LAW OF
MEASURING ACHIEVEMENT

Rationale: The primary goal of a leader must be improvement, for it is the only reasonable and practical goal.

So often, people in leadership positions program themselves for leadership failure through the establishment of unrealistic goals. Leaders also have a tendency to target one or two major areas and channel all their time, effort, and resources toward attaining these so-called priority objectives. In fact, we're apt to have a "theme for the year," such as "The Year of Science" or "The Year of Math." When this is the case, a leader may allocate the majority of financial and/or human resources to achieve excellence in these areas. Likewise, a leader is likely to communicate these priority objectives with broad, sweeping statements.

OUR GOAL MUST
BE IMPROVEMENT

Too often, we expect to go from one point to the highest point quickly. But life simply doesn't work that way. Rather, we get better in steps. The idea is to move to higher and higher levels of performance by continually improving. Each day, each month, each year, we get better at what we do. As leaders, it is our task to move students, teachers, principals, and superintendents toward continuous improvement. Remember, the only practical and realistic management goal is improvement. However, the improvement goal must include progress in every facet of the classroom and school system operation. If progress in *all* areas is not the goal which teachers and administrators communicate to the students and staff, then we may be promoting the status quo or regression in some areas.

Without question, special areas of emphasis may be included in our goals. However, care must be taken in both the effort extended and communication rendered to those being led when such is the case. If certain areas receive the majority of the financial and human effort extended in a given year, a leader may find many unhappy students, teachers, and parents. We may also find that we are actively promoting standing still in the majority of other areas. That's a leadership mistake. It is vital that a teacher or administrator look at everything within the realm of classroom, school, and system responsibility in terms of improvement.

A VOID PRODUCES
COMMON PROBLEMS

When the Law of Measuring Achievement is violated, it is inevitable that we will experience success in some areas and failure in others. In the process, we put pressure on parts of the organization and take off expectations in other parts. Therefore, spotty leadership results. "Brush fires" seem to flare up continually from many different areas that we had forgotten about. Putting out these fires seems to take all our time—even the time we had planned to devote to the one or two major objectives for the year.

Not knowing this management law causes many leaders to move with great determination in the wrong direction. A leader may waste countless hours looking for one or two major objectives to present to students or staff as challenges each year.

And often, if a teacher, principal, or superintendent can't find a "theme for the year" or one or two major objectives, a sense of leadership failure is experienced. In many ways, such a failure may be the best thing that could have happened—for the leader, the institution, and those being led—because these objectives may cause us to forget that the primary goal of management is improvement in every area within our leadership arena. As we all know well, it's very easy to gain in one area and slip in many others. And, of course, it is impossible to be a successful and respected leader when this happens.

THE LAW:
APPLIED

1. What would be included in comprehensive improvement for a (student) (teacher) (principal) (superintendent)?
2. What would be included in comprehensive improvement for a (classroom) (school) (district)?
3. Discuss the (attitudes) (behaviors) that can be expected when one area is named the "priority of the year" in a (classroom) (school) (district).

The Laws and Principles of Self-Management

THE
LAW OF
PLATEAUS

Rationale: Most careers are marked by periods of growth followed by leveling-off periods where refinement occurs. Within each of those leveling-off periods, however, lies a plateau trap which can result in stagnation and failure.

Plateaus are as common and normal as the automatic blinking of our eyes. It's true, some careers reveal a steady and continuous climb. In the vast majority of cases, however, we move forward and upward—then we level off. As we level off, we refine and hone the skills discovered during our last professional climb. After a period of time, most of us surge forward and upward again with higher goals and expectations. Then, another plateau follows. This process can continue throughout our career.

The danger, of course, is obvious. We have seen it, and we may have experienced it ourselves: We get stuck on a plateau. We can't get off—and may not even have a desire to do so. And if we want to, our effort is weak. Because the trap can get us all, let's discuss ways to avoid it as well as get out of it. After all, the leader who "levels off" for an extended time is in trouble.

WITHIN EVERY PLATEAU TRAP
IS A COMFORT ZONE

First, understand that careers marked by rises and periods of leveling off are not bad. Many experts believe that periods of accelerated growth along with the work and effort that go with it need leveling periods. However, also be aware that refinement occurs during the plateaus, but our comfort level comes into play at this point as well. Within the plateau trap is the personal comfort zone trap. It's easy to succumb to the temptation to avoid moving beyond our emotional comfort zone. After all, our comfort zone was created by growth and refinement. It resulted in more success. It's normal to rest on our laurels. It's also common to believe that we have "paid our dues" and decide to stop growing—especially toward the end of our careers. Be aware, however, that successful comfort zones don't last forever. The time span is limited. The best of today can be the mediocre of tomorrow.

Second, to overcome the plateau trap, it's necessary to be very clear about what you want to achieve in your personal and professional life. This involves setting new goals, of course. Before you set goals to move ahead, ask yourself: Are you satisfied with your progress? Are you as excited and as enthusiastic about goals as you were? What's your plan to get inspired about reaching new goals? It can be motivational to look back at your career and examine where you started, measure how far you have come, and decide how far you want to go.

Third, to overcome the plateau trap, you must have or develop a firm philosophical belief regarding ongoing improvement. You must believe lifelong learning is a prerequisite for lifelong success. It helps if you think professional growth is a personal opportunity to live life more fully, rather than a professional obstacle to be overcome. It also helps to believe that your greatest achievements are ahead of you—and to have the desire for living up to the best that is within you. The questions are these: Can you challenge yourself to reach higher? Will you devote the time and effort to get better? As you answer these questions, be aware that the success you are having now may not last much longer.

THE PLATEAU TRAP CAN PERTAIN TO
BOTH OUR PERSONAL AND PROFESSIONAL LIFE

Fourth, recognize that when we get stalled on a plateau trap, our priorities are usually out of balance—especially between our personal and professional life. For instance, traps usually remain because we are giving more and more to the personal side of our life and less and less to the professional side. Or we start putting limits, including time limits, on what we will do at work. We can't seem to organize and prioritize our life to get maximum growth and achievement in both areas. The need, of course, is to achieve balance. This may require discussing career challenges and family needs with our spouse. Regardless, if we intend to overcome the plateau, we must balance both priorities—home and school.

Fifth, we must be willing to create new opportunities by taking risks outside our personal comfort zone. In the process, we must trust in our abilities. Make no mistake: Many teachers and administrators remain stagnant because of fear. It's not that they don't want to grow or that they really believe the old way is better than any new way. Rather, it's that they fear they can't achieve at a higher level or master the new way. Until they can believe in themselves enough to overcome their fears and take the risks, they will remain in place.

Finally, to overcome the plateau, we must still have the ability to dream. Then of course, we must have the motivation to turn dreams into reality. Most of us would agree that we aren't using our talents and ambitions fully. We know we haven't reached our potential. We know it would be great to experience our hopes and dreams more fully. Yet, until we identify what we really want out of life, our minds and bodies will not produce the energy required to achieve to our full potential. Without question, just as all children can learn and grow, all teachers and administrators can learn and grow. Yet some leaders have been conditioned to never dare to dream big. And, of course, it's also possible to honestly believe that we've already achieved more that we thought was possible. When such is the case, the plateau we are on will probably last the rest of our career. Unfortunately, the success we are enjoying today won't last until we retire. It is true that many educators retire bitter because the last years were not good ones.

OVERCOMING A PLATEAU TRAP INVOLVES
BOTH OUR MIND AND OUR ACTION

When we feel that we've reached a plateau, we must begin to fight our way back to further achievement. We must get more creative. We must get more determined. We must get more industrious. And when we get stuck, we must get competent help to get ourselves unstuck. After all, overcoming the plateau trap involves both a state of mind and professional action designed to perform on high levels.

Becoming good and staying good is not an overnight happening. It's a result of a lifetime of hard work. It requires the ability to lead oneself, including leading ourselves to get tough regarding moving to higher levels of performance when the situation warrants it—

and for good reason. The classroom teacher is the single most important factor in giving students a quality education. It takes a quality teacher to give students a quality education. And it's hard to believe that we can give students a quality teacher or a quality education with a professional educator who is stuck in place. Likewise, we know it's possible to have good teachers in a school without good administrators. But we also know it's impossible to have a good school or school district without good administrators. Therefore, if principals and superintendents are stuck on a plateau, the results are obvious.

THE LAW:
APPLIED

1. Identify the greatest periods of professional growth in your career.
2. What did you do to get this growth?
3. Share any difficulties you have experienced in career growth—both personal and professional.
4. Discuss the risks one must take to move off a plateau.
5. What is your plan to keep growing until you retire?

THE
LAW OF
LONGEVITY

Rationale: All employees, including teachers and administrators, increase in value
               with time and experience on the job if they are good at what they do.
               They decrease in value with time and experience if they are not good at
               what they do.

This may not be a law that we like to talk about, especially if we are veteran teachers and administrators. But this is a law we would all be wise to know very well if we want our organizations as well as the people we work with to want us around until we retire. After all, we start our careers at the bottom of the salary schedule. All things being equal, we will probably earn more money almost every year simply because we have another year of service in the job we hold.

If we're good at what we do, we become more valuable as an employee each year. And if we're really good at what we do, we probably have more responsibility than others—and we are probably more productive and have more accomplishments than others as well. Indeed, if we get better every year, our experience works for us, for students, for those we work with, and for our school and district.

EXPERIENCE DOESN'T NECESSARILY
MAKE US MORE VALUABLE

Unfortunately, experience doesn't always result in a teacher or administrator being the most responsible, most productive, and most successful person in the school. In fact, some of the most experienced teachers and administrators in our school may not be the most valuable or successful, and some may not even be doing as much as they did in the early years of their career. For instance, they may not head committees anymore—they may not even serve on committees anymore. And some may no longer serve as a faculty sponsor for student activities or pick up the slack for anything.

In the beginning of our careers, we may have been eager beavers and wanted to be involved in everything. Indeed, we may have had hall duty and playground duty, served as faculty sponsor of a club or class, and worked at athletic events. We may have even had more students in our classes then. All this, of course, was a factor in being good at what we did—and being considered a value to students, colleagues, and the school. It also affected the feelings others held about having us around. From time to time, we would all be wise to assess our current value. After all, the *only* security any of us really have is to serve and be good at what we do.

The point is this: As experience lengthens and wages increase, if productivity does not show a corresponding increase, we lose our relative value in the eyes of colleagues and those being led. Too, our fifties and sixties should be our most productive years. Our age and experience should make us extremely valuable educators in our schools and districts. When this is not the case, this law tells us that somebody would probably like us out of the organization. Why? We are simply making more money than we are worth—even if we honestly feel that we are not making as much money as we should be. This law applies to teachers. It applies to administrators. It applies to all workers in any job and in any place.

EVENTUALLY, PRODUCTIVITY
AND SUCCESS WILL MATTER

This law tells us that the more dependent people are on us and the quality of our services rendered, the better off we are. It tells us that if we don't perform vital functions and perform them well, we're not as valuable as we need to be. And if we're making more money than others, these realities should tell us that someone may not be happy we're on the payroll.

This law should also tell us the dangers inherent in the "good old boys syndrome." Even if we are a member of a clique of teachers or administrators that goes back a long way, being a vital key in the productivity and achievement of our students, school, and district will eventually matter. At some point, someone may have to say, "We cannot have the luxury of having them in the organization simply because of longevity or friendship." And we can count on the fact that colleagues who make less than we do will have such feelings—even if they can't do anything to get rid of us. What's more, they may not respect us or support us.

We would all be wise to remember this law. And the longer we work and the more money we earn, the more aware we should be of this law. Our professional goals should be simple. We should make sure our experience and seniority work for us and everyone else so that we become more valuable to students, colleagues, and our school. Too, as we make more money, we should aim to increase our productivity as well. And, of course, we should remember that nobody likes deadwood—especially high-priced deadwood.

This is true no matter how nice a person we are or how many friends we have in the school, district, or community. And, in truth, whether we feel we are underpaid or not, it does not alter this fact. Unfortunately, there are a lot of people who are not performing on a wide range of fronts because they believe they are being underpaid, but this excuse is simply unacceptable. When it comes to our being effective, after all, such a stance will not work for us because it does not work for those we work with or those we are leading.

THE LAW:
APPLIED

1. When you need someone to do a job, do you always pick the most experienced or the highest paid to do the job? Why or why not?
2. In your school, are (those who are the highest paid) (those with the most seniority) the best?
3. In regard to this law, how would you rank yourself?
4. How would your (students) (colleagues) (superiors) rank you?
5. What factors get in the way of your being regarded as one of the best?

THE
LAW OF
LEAVING

Rationale: Once those being led know a leader has an interest in another job, is
looking for another job, or has decided to take another job, they will begin
to separate themselves from the leader and his or her leadership.

Many people no longer take jobs with the intent of staying in them for a lifetime.
Indeed, we are a very mobile population today. This reality can and does, without question,
prevent long tenures in one leadership position or place. If we check, we might be surprised
how few teachers, principals, or superintendents have stayed in the same job in the same
district over 25 years.

For a wide assortment of reasons, both personal and professional, many educators
continually look for other jobs. In the same vein, we are often sought out to take other jobs.
Certainly, we may leave a school or district because we are unhappy, because we are feeling
pressure to move on, or because we think moving is necessary to make a career
advancement. There are over three million jobs in education, and we should seek a new one
if we aren't happy where we are. It's hard to believe that any of us can be very effective if
we are unhappy in our job, whether we are a teacher, a principal, or a superintendent. If we
are sought out to take a job someplace else, the temptation can be great to move on. Yet,
whether we are interested in another job, looking for a job, interviewing with another district,
or have taken a job elsewhere, how we handle leaving is vitally important.

NEVER SAY ANYTHING TO ANYONE
ABOUT ANOTHER JOB

The rule of thumb is this: Don't tell anyone you're interested in another job, looking
for another job, or interviewing for another job. Outside your immediate family, tell no
one—and make sure your family vows to do the same. This includes your best friend or
your most cherished colleague, because once others know you are entertaining such
thoughts, conditions will never be the same again.

"Sunshine laws" in many states make it public information when you accept an initial
interview. Where this law does not apply, those you are interviewing with must be told to
honor your wishes of confidentiality. Your interview with another district need not be the
topic of teachers' lounge conversation the next day nor the basis for an article in the evening
newspaper.

Many administrators may claim that this can't be avoided because the press will find
out and call for a story. Yet, we all know that when there is a leak, we were often the one
who leaked the news. Ninety-nine times out of one hundred such matters can be kept
private—if we wish. If you are asked about a job by the press, you must be truthful, of
course. Never, never, never lie to the press. For instance, never tell the press that you know
nothing about a job one week—and then go for an interview the next week. If you do, you
have just announced to the world—via the press—that you are not truthful. Now you have
another problem: You have created a credibility gap with everyone.

Too often, unfortunately, our ego gets in the way when we are offered another job. We have to tell the news to somebody inside or outside the school. We have to tell how someone else wants us—and especially how much they will pay to get us. This is a mistake.

We all like to be wooed. We enjoy being wined and dined. And we also enjoy telling someone—maybe everyone—about the experience. The stronger our ego needs are, the bigger problem we can expect if we talk to others about another job. For instance, after looking at another job, you may think everybody will be thrilled that someone else wants you. You may think everyone will rally toward you—and even urge or beg you to stay. And they may. But remember what people say and what they really feel are two different issues. And it will be assumed that you think you are going to a "better place." If the place you are going is "better," how do you think the people you are leaving feel? And if your looking for other jobs becomes an annual affair, your supporters and detractors alike may actually want you to go. They'll come to the point of wanting you to make a decision, settle the issue, and move on. They will dislike the instability or the limbo condition you have created. This is a normal human response to a normal human condition.

PEOPLE WILL BEGIN TO PULL AWAY ALMOST IMMEDIATELY

From a leadership point of view, people you work with as well as those you lead will begin to distance themselves from you the minute they know the possibility of your leaving exists. Emotionally, they will begin to move away. Your influence will wane. You will become a *lame duck*. Even within the community, your strongest supporters in the past will begin to move away from you—and don't believe for a moment that this reality doesn't apply to you. Rather, be aware that this reality is just part of the normal human condition. And the more people are tied to you, the more they will be disappointed, distraught, hurt, and even angry that you have chosen to leave them and the work you are doing together. They may even feel misled. After all, you have been working together and making plans together—maybe just days before they discovered you were leaving. As a result, students can feel abandoned. Likewise, teachers, staff, administrators, parents, and community leaders can have the same feelings.

The fact that somebody else in another place wants you does not increase your value to those you are working with now. It's true, the discovery of your leaving may cause people to line up at your door begging you to stay. If you get tremendous ego satisfaction out of seeing those you are leading in a state of agony, this reality should tell you something about yourself. Too, the prospect of your leaving may bring forth an offer of a promotion or more money.

If you decide to stay, many people will be very happy, but some will have mixed emotions. But *all* will be unhappy if they find you looking again in a short period of time. At this point, people say to themselves as well as to each other, "Go," "Go now," "Go quickly," "Go quietly."

Make no mistake: While looking for another job may be stimulating to you—and while all job offers may be good for your ego and give you strong feelings of being wanted and needed, the "searching" does little for anybody else. From the minute people think you will be leaving, those being led won't buy in to you or your leadership like they did before. They won't see you as a vital member of the team like they did before. Worse, many find that unless they move away from you emotionally and professionally, they can't handle the uncertainty you put into their lives.

There have been many able leaders who have done an outstanding job in the classroom or the office. People loved them. People depended on them—and wanted them to stay forever. They may have been the most popular and effective teachers or administrators the school had known in a long, long time. Then they started to look for another job—and the word got out. They interviewed for a job, but didn't take the job. They returned home thinking things would be like they had always been. After all, had they not chosen to stay? But things changed. People treated them differently. And they couldn't understand why.

Yet, the reason was quite simple: The handwriting was on the wall. Those being led came to the conclusion that the leader's primary interest had changed—and it was only a matter of time until the leader would leave. These perceptions are usually more often correct than not—and these responses from those being led are predictable. After all, past experience has taught people to arrive at such conclusions. If the teacher or administrator has a history of job jumping, people will pull away even faster.

A DAY YOUR DETRACTORS
HAVE WAITED FOR...

As a leader, we need to know that those we lead stand up with us. They follow us. They support us. They count on us. We have become a part of their security system. In many instances, they have probably come to our defense and put their necks on the line for us. Once we start looking for another job, they can have many emotions. They can feel deceived. They can feel let down. They can feel foolish. They can feel abandoned. They can begin to feel that they must begin to separate from us for countless reasons—including self-protection.

None of us enjoy 100 percent support from those we lead. Very few leaders can claim they do not have detractors, if not open critics or enemies. Quite the contrary, all of us—no matter how good we are—have people who are jealous of us, don't like us, or simply think we're not very good at all. Some don't think we deserve the position we hold, aren't smart enough to have the position we have, or aren't taking the actions that need to be taken.

Once we make known our interest in or desire about the possibility of leaving, those who are not our supporters will come out of the woodwork. This is the hour they have waited for. And when they act negatively, they may not find the resistance that was offered by our supporters in the past. And once our support base becomes neutralized or silent, the negative voice of our detractors sounds louder. It can even get stronger and the number of our detractors can get larger. Again, this has all been set in motion by our talking to someone about our interest in taking another job. And our telling may be the reason we can't operate effectively until we do leave—or the reason our staying proves to be an uncomfortable experience.

THE LAW:
APPLIED

1. Share examples you have witnessed of this law at work.
2. Discuss how leaving is seen by some as an opportunity for them.
3. How should you handle job interviews elsewhere?
4. Discuss do's and don'ts for leaving.
5. What individual needs of those being led are affected by violating this law?
6. If you want to find out your "worth" in other districts, how can you use professional publications and government statistics to uncover your possible earning power?

CHAPTER
15

THE LAWS AND PRINCIPLES OF PEOPLE MANAGEMENT

In this chapter are the laws and principles that pertain to the leadership and management of other people. The 30 laws, principles, myths, and fallacies of people management provide us, as teachers and administrators, with a practical basis for motivating all of our students. They give us the practical, workable, and professional basis for motivating all of our peers and staff to function cooperatively and harmoniously out of sound educational practices which hold the well-being of students as the fundamental value in accomplishing the work of the school. Consider them relative to your own classroom or school environment. They are predictors. They tell you what to expect as well as what to do—and offer what the *predictable* responses of the people you lead will be if you follow these guidelines—and what those responses will be if you don't.

The Law of Positive Reinforcement
The Law of Real Value
The Law of Third-Personality Emergence
The Law of Cumulative Action
The Law of Action and Reaction
The Law of Trust
The Law of Organizational Competency
The Law of Substandard Performance
The Law of Effectiveness
The Law of Evaluation
The Law of Standards for Performance
The Fallacy of Standard Procedure
Proctor's Spiral of Futility
The Law of Loyalty
The Principle of Pride
The Law of Varied Thinking
The Law of Transference
The Law of the Grapevine
The Law of Timing
The Law of Cycles
The Law of Filtered Information
The Law of Right/Wrong Conflict

The Laws
and Principles
of People
Management

The Law of Conflict
The Law of Conflict Resolution
The Law of Real Truth and Time
The Law of Blame
The Law of Credit
The Law of Work Satisfaction
The Myths of the Put-Down, Put-On, and Put-Off
The Principles of Handling Alibis, Objections, and Complaints

THE
LAW OF
POSITIVE REINFORCEMENT

Rationale: In the absence of continuous positive reinforcement from appointed
             leaders, negative attitudes and behaviors are most likely to emerge from
             individuals and the entire group being led.

This is not only a management law. It's also a law of human behavior. People gravitate toward the problem side of life. They see what's missing as well as what's wrong or bad, rather than what's right. They get discouraged. Unfortunately, the truth of this law is revealed often in both our personal and professional lives. In a school, negative students can cause others to become negative too. And negative staff members are overwhelmingly frustrating and depressing for those who are not. Yet, if these negative attitudes cannot be changed—or at least neutralized by those who are positive—the negative may emerge as the strongest force within the institution. That's the Law of Positive Reinforcement.

THE NEGATIVE
DOMINATES

Sometimes, I am amazed that competent, intelligent, and positive teachers will sit in the teachers' lounge or a faculty meeting and listen while a negative colleague offers every possible "I can't," "What's wrong," or "How terrible teaching is"—without even offering token resistance. Sometimes superb teachers will even pretend agreement with a negative colleague rather than risk disagreement. This is a good example of the power of peer pressure revealed. Certainly, we often see this behavior in the student body as well.

Regardless of how common this acceptance of the negative stance is, we need to recognize that negative attitudes can be overwhelmingly stifling and destructive in meeting the needs of students, accomplishing the work of the school, finding satisfaction, and effecting positive leadership in the process. A leader must continually counter negativism with concrete help and positive reinforcement. Allowing the continuation and perpetuation of negative attitudes to remain unchecked has an influence on the entire student body, as well as the entire staff.

Yet, a teacher or administrator needs to understand both the reason behind negativism and the people who have a tendency to be negative. Make no mistake: Being negative is not easy. It is not satisfying or rewarding. It is difficult and unrewarding to always operate out of the negative. It is difficult to operate negatively because being negative is self-defeating and self-degrading. It is a horrible experience. All negative people realize this truth. They are not happy people. Worse, they don't know what to do about it. It is much easier to function out of the positive.

As leaders, we need to realize that being positive is vitally important to us and those we lead. We simply can't be effective while being negative—and our negativity impacts the effectiveness of those we lead as well. We need to realize that being negative is against everything education stands for. For every negative we offer, we give absolutely nothing to those we lead. On the other hand, out of every positive we offer or propose, we have at least suggested a constructive course of action. This is a practical as well as a professional need for students and educators alike.

The motivation, stimulation, and confidence needed to begin with a high probability for success are impaired—if not eliminated—by the negative. People need positives—if for no other reason than to avoid being consumed by the certain depression, demotivation, and failure inherent in the negative. That's why a teacher or administrator must always be concerned about positives—and understand that they are tremendous forces in our lives as well as the lives of those being led.

A VITAL
NEED

The need for positives as teachers and administrators is a practical part of our existence. For those we lead, positives play a vital role in the development of their mental health. Without positives, hopelessness replaces hope. An obstacle replaces opportunity. If hope and opportunity are denied, none of us can experience happiness, satisfaction, and peace of mind. Rather, we live oppressed by what we have not done or failed to try.

As leaders, we must recognize that when we offer those being led a negative, we have imposed an added burden or inserted an obstacle they must overcome. That's why our lives as leaders have a practical need for positives—and those being led have that same need. That's why the Law of Positive Reinforcement should receive our constant attention—and our continuous application.

Alfred P. Wilson is a professor who serves as the liaison between The MASTER Teacher and Kansas State University. In this role, he participates in MASTER Teacher seminars for which the university grants graduate credit. Dr. Wilson is nationally known for his work pertaining to the relationship between climate and effective leadership in the classroom. He has been called on many times to rectify situations in which relationships have deteriorated. His concern deals with restoring an environment in which teachers and students can function successfully. His conclusions can prove highly beneficial to all of us who work in schools.

WE MUST CREATE POSITIVES BECAUSE
NEGATIVES WILL ALWAYS BE PRESENT

Dr. Wilson firmly believes that unless there is a ratio of six positives to every negative, the environment will fall apart. This is true for a friendship, a marriage, a business, a classroom, or a school. Therefore, when positives aren't dominant, we can control the situation only via two extremes—*force* or *permissiveness*—depending upon who is involved. Neither choice is a good one for a leader to make.

Unfortunately, negatives will always exist in any place. In a school, however, where adherence to rules is absolutely necessary, where students are being taught and evaluated constantly, and where performance standards must be met in order for achievement to occur, the task of decreasing negatives is made more difficult. And reducing negatives for students and staff who are failing is doubly difficult. Yet, the problem remains: if there aren't six positives for every negative, the environment may disintegrate.

As leaders, the only way we're ever going to have a six-to-one ratio, however, is to create positives. If we don't create or manufacture positives, we have little chance of getting the ratio needed to function successfully. This task may be difficult for a very natural reason: most people, including us, seem to see what's wrong first, rather than what's right. For instance, we may function from a negative base because our task is to look for what's wrong and correct it quickly. Yet, if the six-to-one ratio is dominant, resolving problems is made easier. Therefore, the ratio is vital to our corrective efforts. Fortunately, there are some understandings and actions which can put the six-to-one ratio into our classrooms quickly.

POSITIVES AND NEGATIVES COME IN MANY FORMS

First, we need to realize that just as negatives come in many forms, so do positives. Neither is confined to what we say or do. They can be found in the whole of the classroom, school, or district. Our task is to identify positives, point them out, and build up a reservoir to counter the negatives—and for good reason. The negatives will always exist. Yet, positives can be found in everything from temperature, lighting, and resources to procedures, activities, and available opportunities. Therefore, we can begin by making a list of every positive in our room, school, or district.

Second, we can check ourselves. We need to know whether we tend to be positive, negative, or neutral relative to the various conditions which exist in class or school. Then, we need to know that being habitually neutral or negative can hinder our ability to build a reservoir of positives. For instance, do we begin test days or faculty meetings on a negative note? Likewise, do we state rules in terms of telling students and staff alike what they can't do—or what they can do? Before a class or a conference with a teacher, do we convey a neutral stance by sifting through papers and ignoring the person entering the room? Do we leave students at the end of the hour or day by bidding them well—or by inserting a final negative thought?

Third, we can begin pointing out the positives, including the opportunities which exist in our class, school, and district. We can't just hope these opportunities are seen and appreciated. We can also urge those being led to look for the positives. After all, it takes no special talent to see the negative. But it takes intelligence to see strengths and capitalize upon them.

Fourth, we can try to run a positive-dominated operation. We can start by being ready for class, planning positive activities, and seeking out and proclaiming the positive talents and strengths of each child or staff member. We can make good questions out of poor ones and respond in caring ways—even when we say no. And, of course, we can hold our tongue and eliminate some of our criticism. All these acts will help us create a strong foundation of positives.

THE POSITIVES ALREADY EXIST— WE NEED ONLY TO IDENTIFY THEM

We can clearly see the value of the six-to-one ratio. It's easy to become consumed by the negatives in our lives. And when someone presents us with yet another negative, we just turn off—or focus our efforts where the possibilities for success and satisfaction are higher. So it is with those being led. That's why we must build a reservoir of positives. They already exist in our classroom and school. They need only to be identified and taught. And if we work toward the goal of offering six positives for every negative—even if we can't always succeed—we will begin balancing the scales and improving the climate in our classroom, school, or district.

We need to remember that being positive doesn't mean hiding our head in the sand. We are not promoting the ostrich syndrome. We know our leading is positive if we praise rather than condemn, suggest rather than tell, help rather than impose, and share rather than force. We are positive leaders if the glass is not always half empty, but half full. We are positive if we don't exaggerate problems, but focus on strengths. And we offer the greatest positive of all when we continually act as an advocate in helping those we lead find success.

We must never forget, even for a moment, that we should be the positive element in the school scene. We must know that, unless we give positive reinforcement, we will send out a negative attitude that can flourish and may consume all in the school—including students.

Establishing a positive climate is an administrative responsibility in the school and district and a teacher's responsibility in the classroom. We are the climate leaders in the classroom, the school, or the system. The Law of Positive Reinforcement is a constant reminder that the negative will rule unless we provide the impetus for the growth and domination of the positive.

THE LAW:
APPLIED

1. List the positives in your (classroom) (school) (district).
2. Identify the negative perceptions you have heard from (students) (teachers) (administrators) (parents).
3. Share ways to reveal the positives in your (classroom) (school) (district).
4. How can your leadership be positive-dominated?
5. What individual needs are met by adhering to this law?

THE
LAW OF
REAL VALUE

Rationale: People are more important than things in all situations and in all achievements.

In meeting the responsibilities of teaching and administration and accomplishing the work of any classroom or institution, we must recognize that people are always the vital element in the leadership plan and the scheme of things. Because it's a materialistic world, the desire and need for material things as expressed to us by those we lead can easily point us in the wrong direction as leaders. However, a close look will prove to every teacher and administrator that *things* don't cause problems—*people* do. *Things* are not difficult to manage and lead—people are. And things by themselves can rarely cause a teacher or administrator leadership problems. Material things do not have the ability to get angry, criticize, divide, hate, plot, scheme, cheat, or act. But people do—and people will.

A teacher or administrator must never forget that material things come and go. They get used up or worn out. People stay. The vast majority of the things we use in schools today did not exist in the year 1900. We did not have workbooks for each student. We did not have overhead film projectors or computers in the classroom. Neither did we have vast libraries, multipurpose classrooms, gyms, cafeterias, and auditoriums in schools. But people, with their primary and secondary needs, have remained by comparison relatively unchanged.

When one student leaves the classroom, he or she is replaced by another student. Teachers are replaced by other teachers. They are not the same people—but they *are* people. All teachers and administrators should remember this fact the next time they think their problems would be over if they could get rid of one or two students or teachers. People who leave will be replaced by other people—and these people will be more like than unlike the people who have left the classroom or the school. That's why a teacher or administrator must never forget that people are always more significant than things in the leadership plan when it comes to learning and accomplishing the work of the classroom and school. Therefore, people are the real value in a classroom, school, or district. As leaders, we would be wise to act in ways which indicated this belief.

You can have all the things in the world and not have high productivity or satisfaction in the classroom. You can have the largest and most complete physical plant—and not have a good school. This is not a criticism of spending money for the things we use in teaching and learning. It is simply a statement of leadership fact that people are the real value. Books don't learn; students do. Desks don't teach; teachers do. Computers don't create a school environment that enhances productivity and satisfaction; teachers, administrators, and the staff do.

TECHNICAL
VS. HUMAN HELP

In leadership and management situations, we are continually faced with having to decide whether to concentrate our efforts on things or people. Sometimes the simple fact that things are much easier to manage dictates our direction and effort as leaders. After all, things aren't disrespectful or unappreciative. We put our chairs in rows and our books neatly on shelves, and they stay in place. They don't balk, reject, or talk back. We can love our football fields and auditoriums, because they are easier to manage than the student who won't read, the teacher who is an obstructionist, or the parent who is our constant critic. Yet, a teacher or administrator needs to remember that, although things do not cause us as much difficulty or as many problems as people, neither do they accomplish the work of the school. People do.

A classroom, school, or system can be wealthy or poor, but the quality of education that occurs for students will always be determined by people. The quality of education, as well as the quality of relationships which exist in your classroom, school, or system, is not determined by the quantity or quality of physical objects. It is determined by the attitudes and talents of people who make up the school team. The task and the reward in teaching and administration are to be found where the people are—not where things are.

REMEMBER THE
ECONOMIC LAW

To keep things in perspective, it's wise to remember the economic law that human wants are without limit, but that the resources to satisfy human wants are limited. That means a teacher or administrator can never totally satisfy the material wants and needs of those being led.

For instance, the law tells us that as soon as one of a person's needs is met, another need arises. A teacher gets new books. Then he or she wants new desks. The room gets painted—and new tables are requested. If students get ten minutes of free time, they want fifteen minutes. This perplexes us. We say, "You just can't make people happy." No, you can't satisfy people completely with material things. But by giving of yourself to those you lead and by creating relationships, you can get people to want to follow your leadership—and you can elevate their state of happiness in the process.

Make no mistake: By improving the quality and quantity of your human relationships, you can give satisfaction to those you lead. And isn't this commitment what we all want from our leaders? As educators, we ought to learn from the parents who give their children all the material things they want. They give their children money, clothes, and cars—but they won't give them an evening of their time. We all know the results of such parenting—and how bewildered parents are when their children don't think they are great parents.

And, of course, we all know parents who don't have very much when it comes to material things. But they give of themselves to their children and have appreciative and achieving children along with a great relationship with them. As educators, we need only to apply to those we lead what we see in these situations. The human side of leadership will determine our success or failure—both in our eyes and the eyes of those we lead. The Law of Real Value proves this to be a leadership and management truth.

THE LAW:
APPLIED

1. What is the evidence in your (classroom) (school) (district) that people are more significant than things?
2. What is the state of relationships in your school? Discuss.
3. Discuss the statement, "Some teachers live the academics they teach, but don't live people."
4. Do you know as much about the behavior of students as you do about academics?
5. What individual needs are met by adhering to this law?

THE
LAW OF
THIRD-PERSONALITY EMERGENCE

Rationale: A union of leaders and those being led automatically brings forth the emergence of a third personality which may be a plus or minus in accomplishing the work of the classroom, school, or district.

There is a tremendous responsibility in being a teacher or administrator—more so, I think, than many of us realize. The influence and power a teacher has with students—and an administrator holds in the lives of teachers—are immeasurable. They should never, even for a moment, be minimized. The vast majority of this influence and power is reflected in what I call the development of a third personality. Whenever leaders and those being led meet, this personality is developed—in one way or another. The result of this formulation is the very essence of constructive or destructive leadership.

EITHER GOOD
OR BAD

The third personality is that growth which results from the teacher-student or administrator-teacher union. The outcome of this union is either good or bad. There is never any in-between. I say this because, if the relationship with a leader produces nothing for those being led, certainly that result would have to be regarded as bad too. This is a reality that must never leave the mind of a leader.

Of course, third-personality development extends beyond leaders. There is a third-personality development that is the result of the child-parent relationship. Too, we are all aware of the effect one student can have on another. A particular student may be strengthened or weakened by a friend. We all know students who think differently, act differently, and perform on a different level when they are with certain friends.

The same is true in adulthood. We have seen a person "come into his or her own" after marriage. We have seen the opposite effect too. This is what makes the development of the third personality through the administrator-teacher relationship and teacher-student relationship so vitally important. As leaders, we must assume that our association with those being led will always promote the positive, productive, and the strength side of the third personality. We must always opt for unions that bring out the best in both parties. Likewise, we must recognize that what an individual cannot or may not be able to do alone, he or she can do when joined with a teacher or with an administrator. It is this union that makes each leader as well as each of those being led able to realize his or her potential. That's why every leader must look upon his or her position as a privileged function. The creation of a positive third personality in a classroom or school is the primary function of teaching and administration.

Fortunately, we have all seen the good that can come from positive unions. We have seen students join with a teacher to increase productivity. We have seen two teachers join forces and create exciting places out of classrooms that had not reached such levels before. Our goal is to create positive and productive unions with each other and those being led because we can't be highly successful unless we do.

175

A DRASTIC
EXAMPLE

Probably one of the most drastic examples of this electric eruption of a third personality can be found in what others have recorded about such feelings. For instance, while writing *In Cold Blood*, Truman Capote lived in Kansas for a considerable time, getting to know two young men who slaughtered an entire family. He, and many others, worked hard and long trying to understand what went into the men's joint decision to commit such a shatteringly bizarre crime. Psychiatrists concluded that "Neither would have done it alone." Together, however, they created a third personality—and it was *impossible* for them not to commit the crime while with one another. There it is. Weakness met weakness and had its moment of violent spin-off through this third personality.

It happens all the time. Only the degrees vary. Either weakness meets weakness or hidden strength emerges to mold with another strength. In either case, there is an explosion for good or bad, and educators see living examples of this every day throughout their career. Yet, both teachers and administrators need to understand that they have a role in and do cause a third personality—for good or bad. It is inherent in the teacher-student relationship. It is inherent in the administrator-teacher relationship. And it is inherent in the teacher-teacher relationship and administrator-administrator relationship.

If we come to understand that such connections result in forming a third personality and that these are quite real—then we can have some control over their development. We can make a positive, proactive choice—always. This is leading through awareness and understanding. This is leading with intelligence rather than emotion. And this law again points out the value of a principle we addressed earlier: the Principle of Adjustment.

THERE ARE REASONS
LEADERS FALTER

This means a leader must help put this third personality to work constructively and direct its energies into useful channels. However, there are many reasons a leader may fail to help those being led develop a positive third personality. One of the most common reasons is that we reverse the responsibilities of leader-follower because we do not understand leadership. That is, we focus on the followers' responsibility to us rather than ours to them. If those being led are accepting, for instance, we are too. However, if those being led are anything different from what we think they should be, we don't lead until we think they are ready to follow. In the meantime, we think this stance is right—and believe any problems resulting from the union are the followers' fault. When this happens, the follower is the leader and the leader is the follower. The results are almost always negative.

Likewise, for too long there was an intentional, overt separation of administrators and teachers in schools. We even formed separate professional associations. In the process, many administrators moved away from classroom instruction and being teachers of teachers. They did not visit classrooms. Their attitude was, "You teach, I'll administer." It was the operational code. Many teachers began to view administrators only as authoritarians. Unfortunately, in many cases, that's how administrators viewed themselves—and administrators held no sense of responsibility for the development of a third personality.

Another reason this separation occurred was the role many administrators felt they should play with teachers—and teachers thought they must play with students. Many leaders came to feel that they always had to be right. Regardless of the situation, they believed they had to have both the questions and the answers. In essence, they assumed the role of sole purveyor of knowledge and truth while claiming to know the best way to do things.

Leaders in classrooms and schools and districts must never forget that together the team can do almost anything. Alone, little or nothing is likely to be achieved. The third personality that results from the leader's relationship with others—whether good or bad—is the measure of effective management. If it is good, great things can happen. Almost anything is within the realm of possibility because both leader and those being led can and do influence each other continually. Both can use the strengths of people, rather than capitulating to weakness. This, of course, maximizes the potential of individuals and groups.

THE LAW: APPLIED

1. Discuss the Law of Ever-Present Leadership relative to the Law of Third-Personality Emergence.
2. What is the third personality of each of your classes?
3. What is the third personality of each school in your district?
4. Why do some schools have a (positive) (negative) (neutral) third personality?
5. How can action be taken to create constructive third personalities with students who are not achievers?
6. What individual needs adhere to this law?

THE
LAW OF
CUMULATIVE ACTION

Rationale: There is a cumulative effect of every leadership action—and it all adds up for good and bad, positive and negative outcomes.

Everything a leader does counts. All that we do is significant. In fact, some of the small and seemingly little things we do seem to have the biggest impact and mean the most to those being led. Maybe it's because those being led don't expect responsible leadership. Maybe they don't expect small kindnesses. After all, leaders are expected to be around to help with the big issues and big jobs—not the little ones. And when leaders do help with the small things, the perceptions others have of them are enhanced in positive ways.

It's amazing how much small and cumulative actions influence our lives and the lives of those being led. In truth, big problems don't bring our houses down as often as the little ones do. A friendship, a marriage, and a seemingly strong relationship are often terminated because of a continuous series of small incidents or actions, rather than a big one. As the saying goes, "It was the straw that broke the camel's back."

The same is true in a school. A teacher is more likely to "give up" on a discipline problem because of a series of little incidents rather than a big one. In fact, we're apt to provide strong support if a student makes one big mistake. And colleagues' feelings often get hurt as a result of small incidents where they thought they were ignored or treated inconsiderately. That's our humanness.

As leaders, we must recognize how important our every action is, big and small alike. We also need to be aware how vital every contact is, and how much those being led are like us in appreciating small acts of assistance, kindness, concern, and consideration. Someone may think we are the best teacher or administrator in the world simply because we say hello in the hall every day—or think we are the worst because we never offer a greeting.

THE DIRECTIONAL
INFLUENCE IS OURS...

The cumulative effect of leadership action is directional. We alone hold the power to move in consistent, dependable, and considerate ways. We often decide not to make a particular gesture or not to offer a small courtesy because we convince ourselves that it doesn't make that much difference. It does. We need to remember this truth the next time we choose not to "see" a student we pass in the halls, not to take the time to ask a student if he is feeling better following an illness, or not to console a student who has failed a test or is having a bad day.

We might even think about going further and making gestures which aren't expected by those being led. For instance, if we find ourselves between two students or colleagues who are friends in the cafeteria line, we might step behind them and allow them to be together. Such an unexpected surprise can't help but generate good feelings in others. Too, we might show honest empathy and concern for the person who has not done well this year. And because these gestures are unexpected and demonstrate our caring, they prove effective and beneficial—and more motivating than "I told you so's" and reprimands. The unexpected gesture is effective simply because it is not expected.

A CHANCE TO
TEACH POSITIVE LESSONS

Real lessons are taught in schools by the cumulative effect of leadership action. So often we teach those being led only half of every lesson. We drum into them over and over the need to show consideration, then overlook our responsibility to extend ourselves to them. There is a dimension to the second part of this lesson which teaches those being led to be considerate through experiencing our consideration.

Remember, everything we do multiplies. Those being led are altered in some way by every leader contact and action. No matter how big or small the experience may seem, the alteration has occurred. We must recognize that one small action which is good can lead to another which is equally good. The more good things that happen to us, the more likely we are to return the kindness.

The opposite is also true. The more unpleasantness we experience, the less we feel inclined to think about and do nice things for others. The directional choice in a classroom or school is ours. If we, as leaders, expect to live satisfying lives, we must recognize that there is a positive or negative effect of our cumulative action.

And, of course, there is a cumulative effect to all our big actions as well. If we continually respond to the big challenge or big problem in successful ways, our reputation will reflect it. And if most of our handling of big challenges and problems results in failure, our reputation will suffer. Therefore, the cumulative effect of big and small is with us—continually.

THE LAW:
APPLIED

1. Share a series of (positive) (negative) actions you have taken and the outcomes which resulted.
2. What do those you lead appreciate the most?
3. What do those you lead appreciate the least?
4. Discuss the evidence which indicates that everything a leader does counts.

THE
LAW OF
ACTION AND REACTION

Rationale: Every leadership action results in a reaction—and the action and reaction may be a continuous chain.

As leaders, we spend a great deal of time planning what we will say or do. In fact, planning our action takes the bulk of our brain power. And if we are trying to influence, persuade, convince, correct, or motivate, we may think long and hard about what we will say to those being led. Likewise, if we are disturbed or upset with those being led, we may know exactly what we want to say and how to say it. And we may have no hesitation in taking immediate action. That's why understanding this law can help us so much.

THERE WILL BE
A REACTION

This law teaches us that there will always be a reaction to whatever action we take. We hope the reaction is positive. However, the reaction may be negative. It depends upon how we handle the situation. Remember, the only viable measure of leadership is effectiveness. If our action was effective, the reactions will be desirable. If not, the reactions, our next action, and the reaction that follows can cause a whole series of problems.

For instance, we may harshly chastise those being led for something they did wrong. It may be deserved. And they may be fully aware of their wrongdoing. What we need to realize is that there will be a reaction to our action. In this case, their reaction might be not to focus on their wrongdoing at all—but to get angry or hostile because we chastised them. Then, we may get more upset and carry our action even further. Rather than capitulate, the staff may get more angry and bring up more hostilities that have nothing to do with the original issue.

LEADERSHIP THOUGHT MUST
EXTEND BEYOND THE ORIGINAL ACTION

The task of a leader remains: to plan actions. In addition, we must also plan what the reaction to our action will be. And at the same time, we must do our very best to extend the possible scenarios which might result from the continuous action-reaction chain. As we take this action, we are more likely to alter our original action. Most certainly, we probably will alter the way we deliver our action. But that's not all.

When we practice this law, we will see immediately that different people will react to our action in different ways. We will also probably see that too often we speak to everyone rather than the few whom our message was meant to reach. Regardless, we will see that different approaches and appeals work differently with different people. Equally important, when we follow this law we are likely to deliver the right message, for the right reasons, in the right way. And of course, we are likely to be effective and resolve an issue rather than make a situation worse.

THE LAW:
APPLIED

1.   If a teacher tells a student to "shut up," what are the possible reactions to that action?
2.   If a teacher punishes an entire class, what are the possible reactions from (students) (parents) (administrators)?
3.   If an administrator scolds the staff for being disloyal, what are the possible reactions to that action?
4.   If a principal tells teachers that next year's assignments will not be announced until August, what are the possible reactions to that action?

THE
LAW OF
TRUST

Rationale: Trust is a necessary ingredient in the leader-follower relationship which emerges from positive leadership input—not from special privileges, favors, titles, advantages, or appointments—and requires a mutuality of interdependence between a leader and those being led.

Most certainly, if there is one ingredient that facilitates the work of the leader and those being led, it is trust. Trust knocks down walls between the leader and those being led. When those being led give complete and total trust to leaders, doors swing wide open. Reluctance and caution are replaced by confidence, eagerness, and involvement. When trust is absent, this may never occur.

Leaders often make the mistake of thinking that trust is something automatic that those being led should give their leaders. If we believe this to be true, we may be counting on our separate and unique status as the appointed leader in the classroom, school, and district to work to our benefit when it will not. If we insist on leaning on this as a foundation, it will surely collapse. Never forget, trust is built out of positive leadership input—not out of special privilege or position held by the person in charge.

Too, we can't show distrust to those we lead by the negative rules we make and the advice we give—and expect this distrust to stop at our door. It will not. Our leadership teachings, by word and deed, apply to us as well as those being led. We need to think seriously about this fact as leaders. If ever a time existed to renew the moral characteristics of establishing and gaining the trust of those we lead, it is now.

We must know that trust is not automatic. Neither is it always earned quickly. Yet, it is worth nurturing as well as waiting for—because a carefully structured foundation of trust is not easily moved from its moorings. Throughout the entire process of nurturing, a leader must never forget that trust requires interdependence between the leader and those being led. In truth, this condition is trust.

AN ABSOLUTE NECESSITY
FOR LEADING EFFECTIVELY

A leader must fully realize the need those being led have to trust—and to be trusted. That's why we need to give special attention to trust and all of its ramifications in the lives of those we lead. Its revitalization can begin with us, for trust must be shared between a leader and follower. If it isn't, a form of disintegration results. Nothing positive can result when there is distrust on either side. As leaders, the initiative for beginning this teaching lies with us.

The basic ingredient of trust is personal integrity. The teacher or administrator who cannot trust himself or herself will never trust those being led. The foundation of all integrity and trust is the faith we have in our own integrity. Surely, we can openly pass trust to those being led—even if we fear violations of that trust in the beginning. If we can't, then trust will never be on either side of the teacher-administrator or teacher-student relationships, and a leadership necessity will always be missing.

Often, we underestimate the importance of being trusting and having confidence in one another. Rather than trust, we choose to suspect. Rather than have confidence, we choose to doubt or second-guess. Indeed, a close look will reveal that one of the great leadership weaknesses is a reluctance to trust and have confidence in one another and those we lead. As a result, we don't project trust and confidence in ourselves, others, or the educational process itself.

Many experienced educators are experiencing tremendous difficulties today. They say parents and the public don't trust them. They are perplexed and can't understand why. Yet, only when we decide to trust do we allow people to show that they are trustworthy—and vice versa. Only when we trust do we allow those being led to understand and accept the importance of our experience, expertise, actions, and challenges—and perform accordingly. Until we move to this point, nobody will ever have the opportunity to earn our trust and confidence—because we won't let them. Fortunately, this is a pattern we can break. The choice is ours.

LEADING EFFECTIVELY WITHOUT TRUST IS IMPOSSIBLE

We cannot lead effectively without trust. And we may not accept or follow unless we trust our leader—and are trusted by our leader. Unfortunately, in today's world, a word like *trust* can have more meaning in the dictionary than in real life—or so it seems. As much as we may hate to admit it, placing trust in others is not always regarded as the wise thing to do. In fact, it may even be considered dumb. The lessons we are teaching each other as adults—as well as the instruction we are giving students in our schools today—indicate that this is the accepted and practiced truth. This reality does not make the task of leading any easier. Yet, looking at the messages people are sending each other regarding trust can give us some clues regarding things we must never do—and things we should do.

"Trust nobody," we say, "maybe not even yourself." We teach students this every day. "Write your name in your clothes; mark your books; label your gym clothes—not for easy recognition and convenience—but to protect against the untrustworthy. You can't even trust your neighbors. Everybody knows that."

PAST THE POINT OF DISTRUST

We have moved past the point of distrust and suspicion. This move has clouded our perspective. It is not uncommon for people to label the victim of violated trust as "dumb," "careless," or "stupid" after the attack. How many times have we heard parents and even educators condemn the victim for being so foolish as to leave a locker unlocked or leave books in a classroom or cafeteria unattended? How many times have we seen understanding and assistance withdrawn or denied to a student because he or she was so "careless" or "irresponsible"? We even indicated that someone deserved to have something stolen because of his or her carelessness.

As leaders, we need to take a close look at these attitudes which have emerged in our society. After all, we may hold these beliefs too. Worse, we may perpetuate these beliefs by our actions, including the advice we give to those being led. We need to talk about these attitudes with those being led. Trust is a necessary ingredient in the leader-follower relationship. It's almost impossible for anyone in an organization to sustain a high level of productivity and satisfaction without trust and confidence. Administrators, teachers, and students are not exceptions to this reality. As we all know well, trust and confidence are two of the vital factors in creating a productive and satisfying school climate.

TRUST CANNOT BE GRANTED
BY THE TITLE OR POSITION

A close look will reveal that it's difficult to get high productivity without high satisfaction—and vice versa. Therefore, if we think those being led will achieve to high levels without satisfaction, we are mistaken. Yet, we may see the need for—and value of—high productivity and high satisfaction for the educational team. Unfortunately, we may not see that same need for students. And even if we do, we may be more interested in getting high productivity from those being led than we are in ensuring high satisfaction for them. Likewise, we may see more of a need for those being led to trust us than we do for us to trust them. Here again, we need to focus on both ourselves and those being led, rather than one or the other.

Without a doubt, a leader must earn the trust and confidence of others. Then, of course, the leader must work continually to keep that trust and confidence. Trust and confidence do not come automatically with a title. Neither can they be granted by virtue of the position we hold as professional educators or the responsibility we have in our schools—no matter how long we have held the position.

Trust and confidence are achieved by how we go about doing our work with people. These qualities are often the result of how we respond and perform when we communicate plans or are questioned or challenged by others. It's at this point that a breakdown in trust and confidence often occurs. And if an authority figure is arrogant or "attacks" or "pulls back" when questioned or challenged, a breakdown is almost certain. Therefore, we must use the following strategies for earning and keeping the trust and confidence of those being led when we are questioned or challenged.

TO MAINTAIN TRUST, THREE
ACTIONS ARE NECESSARY

First—and this is the most difficult and objectionable for some people—you must accept the right of those being led to question or challenge you. This is a *must* for creating and maintaining trust and confidence. Second, you must have the professional ability to understand the question or challenge given to you. This doesn't mean you have to have all the answers. It does mean you can get the answer or serve as the point of reference for finding it. The same is true regarding a challenge. If you refuse to be challenged or questioned, those being led won't trust you or have confidence in you. In truth, there are many good people who do not receive the trust of those they work with—and it's usually not an integrity problem. Rather, it is a skill problem. These leaders do not have the skill to understand the questions or challenges given to them by those being led, much less know how to give needed help or assistance.

Third, you must appreciate the full importance of the questions or challenges you receive. If you do, you'll be inclined to find answers to the questions you are asked—and respond constructively to the challenges brought to you. If you don't, you'll do neither. As a result, you won't be trusted or instill confidence. This is why you can never discount the importance of the ideas, beliefs, and feelings which those being led present to you.

Once you accept and understand the question or challenge and appreciate its importance to others, it is imperative that you find an answer—either by yourself or by using your resources. Make no mistake: Those being led will judge you on your ability to find an answer. Remember, you don't always need to have the skill or expertise to handle a situation alone. Trust is based on the results of your interventions—not on the method used to get those results as long as they are ethical and not hurtful.

It is via these kinds of responsive actions that you can cause people to begin to have trust and confidence in you. You don't get trust and confidence without taking these three actions—and both your ability and integrity are likely to be questioned in the process.

THE LAW:
APPLIED

1. Examine the rules in your classroom and school. How do they convey trust and confidence?
2. Who in your school has the right to question and challenge?
3. What positive input is necessary to create trust?
4. What positive input is necessary to create confidence?
5. How do special favors and advantages breed distrust and destroy confidence?
6. Identify the individual needs which are met by adhering to this law.

THE
LAW OF
ORGANIZATIONAL COMPETENCY

Rationale: The leader who fails to continually improve each individual in the group being led puts undue pressure on everyone and will not be viewed as a competent leader.

This law can be applied to teachers, committee chairpersons, department heads, team leaders, principals, and superintendents. All schools and districts have personnel who are not performing satisfactorily. They do not do their share of the work. We know it—and everyone else does too. In such cases, we might say to those being led, "I know Jim is weak. I know he isn't carrying his load—but I want you to be very tolerant of the situation. Therefore, until his performance is up to par, I'm going to come to your (meeting) (department) (school) and fill in the void he is creating by doing only a portion of his work." After hearing this comment, those being led should not have a gripe. But that isn't what normally happens.

In reality, while we have five people on the job, four are really doing the majority of the work. Worse, by word or deed, leaders usually expect others to pick up the slack created by such a student or employee. In reality, leaders expect four people to do the work that was intended for five people. And when we say, "There's nothing we can do about it," we make a bad situation worse.

THREE ACTIONS TO TAKE WITH
THE POOR PERFORMER

Make no mistake: An organization can only achieve to the degree those in the organization are able to lead. People who work in the organization are its greatest resource. Therefore, when only 95 percent of the staff is functioning, the competency of the organization is jeopardized. A primary function of leadership on every level is to strengthen the team. And when we don't, we are not fair either to those we are leading or to the organization. We would be wise to remember this reality—and we would be wise to know that three actions are necessary.

First, we must choose people carefully to work on committees—and hire people very carefully. Second, we must conscientiously examine situations and counsel, train, and evaluate people in an effort to make sure they are carrying their share of the load. We must also make sure seasoned veterans are still doing the job. Because of government regulations and all the difficulties associated with both hiring and terminating, leaders must act quickly when the employment of a new person is not progressing as it should—or the veteran is faltering. Third, we must move in to help and guide when any employee is having trouble. And leaders must not "hold on to" employees who aren't measuring up.

Remember, one of the major jobs of a leader is to strengthen the team. When leaders ask four people to do the job of five, the leaders are not doing their job. Worse, they are taking advantage of employees—and becoming a negative factor in the success of employees and the school.

THE POOR PERFORMER
AFFECTS EVERYONE

Without question, weak staff members have an effect on the attitudes as well as the work of others. In fact, poor workers cause problems on many fronts. They create inequity. They add to the work of others. They put their colleagues on overload. What is more, they may not be concerned about the conditions they create.

In addition, the nonperformers take time away from the leader. They keep the leader from having high expectations and functioning on a higher level. They also take time away from their colleagues—and keep them from functioning on a higher level as well.

A close look will reveal that weak employees cause stress and frustration on many fronts. In the process, they automatically become the measuring rod of performance—whether we intend for this to happen or not. And they also become the built-in creator of excuses for the lack of work accomplished, effort exerted, and performance achieved.

A leader needs to be continually aware of these realities in leading people. And anytime we neglect to strengthen the team—for any reason—we should know the first priority for higher performance and job satisfaction has been omitted. As a result, we have created another problem that is revealed in the Law of Substandard Performance, which is discussed next.

THE LAW:
APPLIED

1. Discuss the Law of Organizational Competency relative to the Law of Total Responsibility.
2. Discuss the Law of Organizational Competency relative to the Law of Origin.
3. Beyond selecting people to serve on committees or hiring competent people, what is a leader's responsibility relative to strengthening the team?
4. Share ways to counsel nonproductive (students) (educators).
5. What individual needs are met for those being led if we follow the Law of Organizational Competency?

THE
LAW OF
SUBSTANDARD PERFORMANCE

Rationale: Consciously or subconsciously, almost everybody knows that the most incompetent co-worker actually protects others and serves them in a nonproductive and unhealthy way.

This law applies to students. It applies to teachers. It applies to support staff. It applies to administrators and the board of education. In fact, it applies to peers in any situation and in any organization, even our own families.

We may complain about the poor performers. We may gripe about those who never do anything right or those who get into more trouble in a week than others get into in a year. And we may be disgusted with the colleague who is always thinking-saying-doing the wrong things at the wrong time and in the wrong place—sometimes purposely.

Sometimes these colleagues are affectionately called the incompetents or mavericks. They don't *intend* to measure up or do as others do. But in our own strange way, we often love having them around. We may count on them. That is, we love having them around and count on them if they are a peer. We don't love them very much or count on them at all if we have to lead them.

THIS PERSON TAKES PRESSURE
OFF EVERYONE ELSE

Make no mistake: The poorest student or the most incompetent educator actually takes pressure *off* everyone else—and almost everyone is very much aware of this reality. As long as these people are around, the pressure from leaders is usually on them. As long as they are around, we have a strange kind of protection and security. After all, leaders don't have time to think about us and what we're doing wrong.

As long as the poor performer is around, the standards and expectations for everyone—including us—is likely to get lowered. In addition, he or she serves as our safety net. It's very hard for the leader to do any correcting or criticizing when this totally incompetent person is allowed to remain part of the group.

For instance, how can a teacher compare any other student to this one? He or she can't. How can any student look bad when this student is present? Impossible. And a principal is always thinking about this teacher more than he or she thinks about the rest of the staff combined. He or she has to. Whatever someone else might do or does has a very good chance of being ignored, overlooked, or minimized when comparisons are made. Certainly, whatever someone else is doing will appear *insignificant* in comparison to what this person always does. Teachers have had such a student. Principals have had such a teacher. Superintendents have had such a principal.

THESE PEOPLE HAVE A
NEGATIVE EFFECT ON EVERYONE

Never allow yourself to get accustomed to the poor performance of these people. And never believe for a moment that they are harmless. They are not. Indeed, they affect everyone in a negative way even though their peers may actually "shelter" or "protect" them when the "heat is really on."

Remember, these people impact negatively upon everyone—even the entire organization. If these people are within the ranks of the faculty or staff, they must be neutralized. If such action is impossible, they must be terminated. If they aren't, leadership attention to all being led will become narrow, rather than broad-based. Standards will always be lowered for everyone whether we think so or not. Above all, the leadership responsibility to strengthen the team will not be fulfilled. And if we try to maintain high standards and expectations for everyone else, those we lead will see the unfairness of such an effort.

With students, we can't always take such corrective action. Sometimes, mandates and the law prevent such action. But we must take every action possible, including recommending private professional help for the purpose of turning the behavior of the student from a negative to a neutral or positive force—while adhering to tenets of education, the purpose of education, and the policies of our school district. The key, of course, is whether the student is behaving with all teachers in this manner—or with just one or a few. If it's only with a few, the real problem may lie with us, not the student.

THE LAW:
APPLIED

1. How are low performers rewarded in the (classroom) (school)? Discuss.
2. Share ways to counsel these (students) (colleagues).
3. Relate examples of instances in which standards have been lowered for these people.
4. Is it possible to operate with these people without having double standards? Discuss.
5. Share ways to keep leading poor performers while the rest of the group moves beyond them.

THE
LAW OF
EFFECTIVENESS

Rationale: The success of any job, project, or task is dependent upon the quality of participation delegated by the leader *prior* to beginning a task.

The academic work which teachers could have students do in a course or subject is endless. And certainly the work of the school and district is limitless. Sometimes it seems as if there is more to do in a year than we can get done in a lifetime. Every teacher and administrator should realize that both responsibility and authority must be delegated to those being led if tasks are to be completed. Yet, *what, how much,* and *who* have always been difficult classroom or school management questions for teachers and administrators. Too, because teachers and administrators are ultimately responsible for all within their leadership orbit, delegating both authority and responsibility can be seen as a special problem. And because a teacher operates much of the time as a separate entity in the classroom within the whole of the school, he or she may not think there is much that can be delegated in the classroom. Yet, a close look will reveal that there is.

A LEADER MUST STOP THINKING, "NOBODY CAN DO IT LIKE ME"

Without a doubt, we all know that the leader who tries to "do it all" will achieve less than is required for high levels of success. But the real truth is that unless authority and responsibility are delegated, many of the priorities in a classroom, school, or district which determine our effectiveness will not be started—much less accomplished. To fear delegating is unhealthy on the part of the leader. In many ways, a failure to delegate authority and responsibility is the result of a classroom, school, or district which is teacher-centered or administration-centered.

The personal belief that "I must do it" or "Nobody else can do it" must be discarded if greater effectiveness is to be achieved as a leader. Success in leadership and management is only achieved by getting others to share in the work—and by helping them enjoy every minute of it and find success in the process. The primary tasks of a leader are to:

1.   Involve as many students, teachers, staff members, administrators, and parents as possible in various duties, tasks, routines, and projects.
2.   Assess the proper number of those being led necessary to facilitate success of the job—rather than understaff or overstaff—so that everyone can participate in a meaningful way.
3.   Involve as many students, teachers, or administrators as possible in significant work—including extra work.
4.   Pick the right people to serve in the right places for the right role—and allocate the time and resources to get the job done.
5.   Continually motivate and stimulate people in the direction they need to go—or you want them to go—to achieve meaningful results.
6.   Provide people with the three necessities required for completing a task: responsibility, authority, and tools—*before* they begin.

7. Create an accountability expectation for any delegated job, no matter how large or small, before beginning.

ONE OF OUR
BIGGEST RESPONSIBILITIES

The ability to delegate wisely is one of a leader's biggest assets. Its potential is limitless. Remember, the achievement of the work of the classroom and school and the maximum utilization of personnel prove the competency and effectiveness of leadership—always. That's why personnel in the classroom, school, and district cannot be wasted.

Many leaders don't want to delegate. Others are not able to delegate. Some can't even force themselves to think about delegating, much less move in this direction. Others can delegate only token authority and minor responsibilities, especially if the situation pertains to students. There are at least nine reasons some leaders cannot and will not delegate responsibilities. They do not delegate because it requires:

1. Sharing.
2. Teaching and instructing.
3. Giving up responsibility.
4. Giving up authority and power.
5. Changing attitudes and feelings toward control.
6. Depending on others.
7. Believing in the abilities of others. For instance, teachers may not delegate because they believe students do not have maturity. Administrators may not delegate because they may not believe teachers have the necessary skills.
8. Trusting others.
9. Giving time to those being led.

Yet, the Law of Effectiveness relates that the success of any project is dependent upon the quality of participation which is delegated by leaders—prior to beginning the task. In every classroom, we have students capable of performing countless tasks which must be done. In every school and district, we have teachers, staff, and administrators capable of performing tasks and getting work done. And parents and volunteers comprise a whole host of support personnel. Common sense should tell us that as school resources shrink, the people in or connected to our schools become more and more important to our effectiveness and success. This law reminds us that our objective should be to utilize people in the right way. And much of the right way involves what those being led must do before they begin a task.

THE LAW:
APPLIED

1. Identify work that (can) (cannot) be delegated. Discuss your list.
2. For each task, discuss what needs to be included when you delegate.
3. Identify work that cannot be done because of available personnel.
4. To what degree can this work be delegated? Discuss.
5. Discuss the nine reasons leaders do not delegate. How can these obstacles be overcome?
6. What individual needs are met if we comply with this law?

For related information, see the Law of Planning.

THE
LAW OF
EVALUATION

Rationale: A leader does not have the right to evaluate, criticize, judge, or reprimand those being led until the leader has first fulfilled the function of instruction.

In the classroom, we practice this law faithfully in regard to academics because that's the way we were taught to teach. We were taught the proper function was to teach, test, reteach, and retest until students learn. Therefore, we always teach before we evaluate. We may not, however, use this practice with students in other areas. For instance, we may expect students to take notes in class, but never teach them how to take notes. We may ask them to behave, but never teach them appropriate behavior. And administrators may not practice the law at all. Administrators may simply tell people to do something without any teaching at all—then judge them regarding how well they did the job. Needless to say, this is a mistake. Worse, it is having expectations of others without meeting the expectations those being led have a right to have of us.

TEACHING MUST
COME FIRST

This law teaches us that whatever a leader wants those being led to do, he or she must first teach them. It also tells us that those being led have a "right" to this expectation. Most important, this law reminds us that leadership is showing the way—and if we don't show the way before we criticize, judge, evaluate, correct, or reprimand, we have "the cart before the horse." In addition, if the leader doesn't provide help first, the leader can be the loser.

When leaders evaluate those being led without first providing tangible help and assistance for the standards being evaluated, leaders are likely to be regarded as enemies or critics by those they lead. It's not difficult to see and understand why. This is probably the most common mistake made by administrators in schools today. For instance, every year administrators evaluate teachers. They fill out official forms. Yet, many fail to provide concrete help and guidance to teachers before they evaluate. This is a violation of leadership responsibility. This failure creates negative attitudes toward administrators and lies at the core of many problems between administrators and teachers.

Remember, with the authority of leadership comes the responsibility to evaluate. However, the responsibility to help those being led *always* comes first. Whether we are teachers or administrators, we are the professional partners of those we lead—not just their judges. Our task is to develop to the fullest the talents of those being led. Therefore, the *process* of evaluation is twofold: first, to give help; second, to evaluate. And the *purpose* of evaluation is twofold: first, to find out how well those being led have learned; and second, to find out how well the leader has taught.

DECIDE WHAT YOU
WANT, THEN TEACH

Whatever we want those being led to think, we must first teach them. Whatever standards we want them to hold, we must teach them—before we judge. Whatever we want those being led to do, we must teach them—first. And we must also give them the means, the time, and the tools necessary to do a job before any evaluation or correction takes place. And we should never evaluate them before we teach them.

The primary role of the leader is to teach. It is not to boss. Unfortunately, many leaders want to evaluate, but they fail to teach first. Such action violates the Law of Evaluation.

*The
Law of
Evaluation*

THE LAW:
APPLIED

1. What do you want those you lead to do?
2. Share what you need to do before this is possible.
3. What expectations do you hold which you do not teach?
4. Discuss the (attitudes) (skills) which are always connected to success.
5. How can you teach these (attitudes) (skills) in a (classroom) (school) (district)?

THE
LAW OF
STANDARDS FOR PERFORMANCE

Rationale: Setting standards for performance is often misleading and may not result in reaching the levels of performance those being led are capable of achieving—especially if the guidelines are specific and reflect minimum expectations.

We've all had the student in class who persisted in wanting to know exactly what he or she "had to do to get an A." Our sidestepping or simple answer would not suffice. And at the time he or she asked, we knew that the student would hold us to our answers. We also know that this student is apt to methodically go about meeting the requirements we revealed and expect an A.

One thing always disturbed me about some of these students. It was amazing to me how little many of them would do after their A was assured. At the point they earned an A, many stopped working very hard. As teachers, we're not always sure they are superior students—regardless of the A grade. In truth, they are not. And many of these students do not move to a higher level of achievement not experienced before—or achieve to their potential. But they do make an A, unless we break our promise.

COMMON TO ALL
ORGANIZATIONS

This type of person is not uncommon in a classroom, school, or district. In fact, he or she is not uncommon anywhere. Many people want to know exactly what they have to do to be OK. Business has these people—so does industry, medicine, and law. When it comes to developing a great class or professional team—or a great school—these people present big problems for leaders.

We need to examine this behavior, for these people truly believe they are doing a superior job. In some ways, they are. In other ways, they are not. What they really do most efficiently is limit their output and the achievement of the organization.

Without doubt, there are certain basic requirements in any job. These basics are usually offered as standards for acceptable performance. So it is with teaching a class or administrating a school or district. There are some things everyone who desires to be a professional must recognize about the basics. First, unless we master them, we shall never be successful. Second, the basics are only meant to be minimum requirements. This reality is something people in all walks of life seem to forget. Yet, those who function from this platform often operate with a secure aloofness and an air of superiority, accomplishment, and self-confidence because they are able to meet the necessary requirements of their job. They continually ignore the fact, however, that these are only minimum standards and do not measure what they could do—or what the organization really needs in order to excel. With continued effort, these students could push themselves and their classmates to higher levels of performance. Likewise, these teachers and administrators could do the same for colleagues.

Meeting minimums does not qualify anyone for a title of excellence—student, teacher, counselor, nurse, administrator, or anyone else. And meeting minimum standards—no matter how religiously they are met—never maximizes the potential of the individual, the group, or the organization.

Unfortunately, it's possible for students, teachers, and administrators to work for an entire lifetime adhering strictly to the necessities while ignoring the extended possibilities inherent in their work. And there isn't much anyone can say to them about it. After all, they do meet the standards. Yet, we must address this issue if we want to lead students and educators to higher levels of performance.

There can be no road map of basic requirements if excellence is to be achieved. Our schools don't have colored lines on the floor like hospitals do to guide us to our destination. Schools aren't made that way. Student needs keep shifting and changing. The demands of society change. The amount of available knowledge increases. And we're learning more and more continually regarding how to be more effective in carrying out the work and mission of the school.

STANDARDS MUST NOT BE RIGID OR FIXED

There are some vital aspects connected with being a professional that employment handbooks don't—and can't—tell us. The same is true of student handbooks. For instance, employment guidelines and student handbooks seldom say anything about extending ourselves by doing more than others—and being involved to our fullest. Neither do many employee guides or student handbooks say anything regarding the extent to which one should go to help a student learn—or to learn and perform optimally ourselves. In truth, a teacher who functions from the minimum can "draw the line" anywhere he or she wishes. Some people draw the line at the first hint of difficulty. Some do it if they believe a student doesn't have the background, the right attitudes, or the signs of intellect necessary to be in a specific class.

A teacher or administrator will eventually be paralyzed if he or she stays on the "minimum line" of doing average work. Too many events and circumstances happen daily in a classroom and school which require all of us to use all of our abilities. Perhaps a student can't read, a parent died, a student got hurt on the playground, or a substitute teacher didn't show up. All are examples of times we have to do more than the minimum.

Whatever basic guidelines we establish for those being led, we must first make sure those being led know that these guidelines are not *fixed*. They are alterable. As goals are met, we must move the standards higher. For instance, the time we must arrive at school and the time we can leave are stated in our handbook. But what do we do if a need arises that says we need to be in school early and can't leave until late? These decisions always require that we extend ourselves. In education, as in all other jobs, we simply must move beyond the stated standard for performance if we intend to lead people effectively. There is no other way to be highly successful. If we don't or won't do what it takes to get the job done, we limit what those we lead can achieve.

Certainly, a school may always have a number of students and educators who "follow the book" and never extend themselves and reach for their potential. Although we can never become complacent about this reality, we can live with it as long as their number is very, very small. We will not be highly successful, however, if their numbers grow. As leaders, we can never promote the minimum by the standards of performance we set. Neither can we acclaim those who go by the book and strive only to meet minimum requirements. Rather, we must always recognize, encourage, promote, and glorify those who function beyond the minimum.

Make no mistake: Sometimes we mislead those we lead. The standards we set are not really our expectations. In fact, our expectations are often far greater than those we communicate to those being led. Then, those we are leading think they are doing fine when we, in fact, don't think they are performing in superior ways at all. Therefore, be careful about how you go about setting and proclaiming a standard for performance. Otherwise, you will have a difficult time leading some people after they have met the minimum standards of performance. This is the lesson taught by the Law of Standards for Performance.

A WAY TO HELP
THOSE BEING LED ACHIEVE

At The MASTER Teacher, we use a procedure we call Maximum Performance. The purpose of this procedure is to have everyone improve performance continually. Every year, each person in the entire organization writes an essay. This includes officers, department heads, authors, editors, administrative assistants, artists, and typesetters as well as personnel in the printing, order processing, school services, and distribution departments. In each essay, three questions are addressed.

1. What does maximum performance mean to me?
2. How do I intend to achieve my maximum performance?
3. What action, if I fail to take it, will cost me the success I wish to achieve?

The person reads his or her paper to his or her department head. Then a dialogue is started that can last as long as both parties desire. The sole purpose is to help the individual achieve the maximum performance he or she desires. To achieve this goal, the department head listens as well as responds to the presentation. He or she can help the employee set standards of performance which are in line with personal goals and the needs of the organization. Equally important, the department head can ask, "What do you need?" "What roadblocks are in your way?" and "What obstacles can I help you with?" Both organizational and personal standards can be discussed along with broad guidelines. It is important to note that this is not an evaluation session or a forum to be used for criticism. It is simply a method to help employees achieve maximum performance.

We have used this exercise for years. It is a very friendly, supportive, and professional way to communicate standards and help those being led find more and more success working in the organization. It carries no "club" or demands. Everyone in the organization likes it—and we have never had a problem or complaint come from anyone during a maximum performance conference.

THE LAW:
APPLIED

1. Identify the standards of performance for (students) (teachers) (support staff) (administrators) that you believe are necessary for exceptional functioning. Discuss.
2. As you lead, should standards be individual? Discuss.
3. Share examples of specific expectations which allow for maximum performance.
4. Personally, what are your standards for performance? Can you share them with colleagues?
5. Which individual needs are denied if we violate this law?

THE
FALLACY OF
STANDARD PROCEDURE

Fallacy: When the leader establishes standard operating procedures for all tasks and assignments, success is facilitated. Therefore, standard operating procedures should be established for all projects and responsibilities for those being led.

Not true. I just wanted to insert this fallacy into the laws and principles of management because many teachers and administrators hold this belief. In fact, many actually strive to create a standard procedure for everything and everyone as often as they can. Many students and parents push teachers to have such guidelines. And many teachers push administrators to have such guidelines. There are many reasons people—leaders and followers alike—erroneously push for standard procedures.

Teachers and administrators are usually good organizers. Both are planners. We have a strong need for security and achievement. Like it or not, however, the vast majority of educators are not risktakers. We like specific guidelines because we are leaders of large groups of people doing a wide variety of tasks. As a result, we are prone to favor standard operating procedures and apply them whenever possible to the work of the classroom, school, and district.

THE PRO'S OF
STANDARD PROCEDURE

Standard operating procedures do promote understanding. Standard operating procedures do facilitate job control, completion, and reporting. However, all leadership and management procedures and guidelines should promote critical thinking and achievement in addition to facilitating the decision-making process. That's why the Fallacy of Standard Procedure should be understood by all leaders. In truth, the lower the need to comply with standard operating procedures while making major decisions is, the greater the number of creative and sound decisions that will be made.

There are many different kinds of individuals with a wide variety of talents in education. The profession is made up of many dedicated, bright, strong-willed, and highly educated people in specific interest and learning areas. These people know their area of professional discipline and many have a strong need for involvement within their area of concentration. These kinds of people have good ideas and usually rise to challenges—if leaders permit them to do so. Unfortunately, standard operating procedures can limit high productivity, curtail motivation, lessen higher-level thinking skills, and hinder the decision-making process. Every classroom teacher and administrator must be aware of this reality.

THE CON'S OF
STANDARD PROCEDURE

When standard operating procedures are a must, freedom is prohibited. Never forget, standard operating procedures force leaders to lower their standards to those of the group.

Why? This is the only way everyone in the group can be successful. Unfortunately, standard procedure is often established for the ease, protection, and control of the leader.

What standard procedure does *for* leadership control, it does *against* initiative and creative thinking. Sometimes, when beginning a project, it is better to begin with an open-endedness because of the limits inherent in standard procedure. It should be explained to those being led in this light. Then, at a certain point in the project when the plan becomes operational, some standard operational procedures can be established.

The Fallacy of Standard Procedure teaches us that specific guidelines should not always be employed by leaders to achieve maximum results. Rather, it implies that, in many instances, freedom should be encouraged—especially in the beginning or creative stages of a project. Standard operating procedures are best for routine tasks—not creative ones. They are great tools for handling the mundane. They are wonderful for low-level and repetitive tasks. But they are not good for high-level thinking and creative work.

A leader must never forget that operational guidelines can be established at any time. However, this fact should be communicated to those being led prior to their beginning a task or project. Then, at the time when standard operating procedures will best serve functioning, they can be put into place.

**THE LAW:
APPLIED**

1. Identify all areas in the classroom and school which carry standard operating procedures.
2. Which areas lend themselves well to this practice?
3. Plan a party. Begin without any guidelines. At the point you think it is necessary, establish some standard operating procedures.
4. Identify tasks, jobs, and projects which require creativity in order to develop options fully.
5. How will you approach these projects in the future? Discuss.
6. Which individual needs are met when creativity is promoted?

PROCTOR'S
SPIRAL
OF FUTILITY

Rationale: Beginning with real or imaginary *rejection*, people can pass downward in a spiral of futility culminating in crime or violence. But this process is reversible with one major intervention by one person.

The "Spiral of Futility" theory was developed by Samuel D. Proctor of Rutgers University. It is a marvelous piece of work. Knowing it thoroughly will help anyone in a leadership position more than he or she can imagine. I have used it for a long time, and have never known a student, teacher, or administrator who was faltering who could not be identified in the spiral—then helped with a high rate of success.

We've all seen some of our students go from being pretty good to being bad, and we've seen some go from bad to worse. We've watched in despair as they seemed to give up even though we tried to help. If we thought there was anything we could have done that would work, we would have. Fortunately, there is. That's why being aware of Proctor's Spiral of Futility is vitally important to all of us. It reveals the stages some young people and adults go through—beginning with rejection and ending with crime and violence. Of paramount significance, however, is the fact that the spiral can be reversed for a person with one major intervention by one other person. The first thing we need to do is determine where people are in the spiral—for a very practical reason: we have to know where to start, and a look at the spiral will reveal that without such knowledge, we may be getting improvement, but not think that we are. That's because people start at the top of the spiral with real or imagined rejection, and go down step by step. They come out of it the same way. Note: There are no jumps in the downward or the reversal process. Rather, a person comes out of it the same way he or she went into it.

Without question, Proctor's Spiral can be a great leadership tool. It can give us remarkable success when we thought none was possible.

FEELINGS OF
REJECTION

The Spiral of Futility begins with a person's awareness or feelings of rejection. The rejection may be real. The rejection may be imaginary. It may occur at home, with peers, with parents, or with teachers and administrators. The point is that the rejection may come from many sources.

The downward spiral begins in students, teachers, and administrators when they are rejected—or feel rejected. The feelings can begin when people don't like them or when they sense that people don't like them—or when they believe others doubt their worth. Feelings of rejection can also occur when they feel they can't do certain tasks satisfactorily, when they aren't chosen or considered for committees, when they don't make teams, or when they experience low expectations from the people around them. Regardless of how it manifests itself, a feeling of rejection is the beginning. Therefore, rejection is the beginning of trouble. This reality is of monumental proportions: Acceptance is always the best leadership course. Once we reject people for any reason, we almost always convert possibilities to problems.

When feelings of rejection cannot be overcome, a person may move to voluntary or involuntary isolation.

VOLUNTARY OR INVOLUNTARY ISOLATION

Therefore, real or imagined rejection is followed by voluntary or involuntary isolation. These people move away from others—students, teachers, staff, and administrators. They may not have friends at school. They may spend a lot of time alone, seldom going anywhere or doing anything with anyone. If they appear to have a friend, both may be in the same stage of the spiral and both may be experiencing isolation and feeling alone—even when they're together.

If we move in to help—and the person starts talking about rejection or feeling left out or alone, we are not losing. We are being successful.

NEXT IS INSULARITY

Next, these students or colleagues move from isolation to the position of insularity. This is the condition of being an island. They become narrow-minded. They become prejudiced, especially against popular classmates or colleagues. They also oppose accepted beliefs and authority. They begin to feel that nobody cares—and they say so. As a result, they withdraw even further.

Without intervention, even by one person, these people may move down the spiral—and we will see hostility surface. With intervention, however, these people can move upward. When they do, however, we will see them express feelings and behaviors associated with voluntary or involuntary isolation. And we will have to deal with these feelings, real or imaginary. However, we should know that when voluntary or involuntary isolation reappears, we are winning, not losing.

HOSTILITY SURFACES

At this point, *hostility* surfaces. These students become unfriendly. These teachers become unfriendly. These administrators become unfriendly. Remember, none of us are immune to the spiral.

When hostility surfaces, people are openly disagreeable. In many ways, they act as if they are at war with everyone—students, parents, colleagues, administrators, and the world. They become fighters. They take on hateful characteristics and will fight anyone—just to hurt him or her.

Students may use fists; adults may use words and deeds. The things they say about others are not very nice. They hurt people by word and deed. Suddenly, they find they actually feel good only when they hurt someone or talk badly about him or her. It doesn't bother them a bit to beat up a classmate or tell a nasty rumor about a colleague. In fact, students may drive to another town or across town and beat someone up. They may even brag to others about their negative deeds.

Without intervention, they fall to the next level. With intervention, they will move upward, and we'll know we are getting improvement when insularity is again the issue.

WITHDRAWAL FROM SUCCESS SYMBOLS

Hostility is followed by a withdrawal from success symbols. These people will openly refuse to do some schoolwork. They won't follow rules. They have no interest in doing what anyone in authority thinks is good. They create their own standards and values—and reject all others.

They become purposefully disruptive. They start talking back to people in authority positions. In fact, the attitudes and behaviors they choose are those that represent everything disapproved of by the vast majority of us. They will reject any idea, belief, or institution which represents success by accepted standards, including the values of successful peers.

Without intervention, they move downward to an acceptance of failure. With intervention, they move toward hostility. As leaders, we should recognize that we would seldom consider hostility as a sign of success. In this case, however, it is. Yet, if we see hostility surface while working with a student in this stage of the spiral, we might think the student was getting worse. We might think we were failing rather than succeeding. That's the value of the spiral to our leadership.

ACCEPTANCE OF FAILURE

Without intervention by one person, students actually move to an acceptance of failure. They believe that they're really unable to do or become what's expected of them at school—or at home with their families or in the world they live in. By giving up, getting reprimanded, dropping out of activities, getting put on probation, or getting kicked out of class—they find confirmation of their beliefs.

When this happens, people actually begin trying to live up to all the low expectations leaders and others have for them. A feeling of "I can't win; I will do what I want—to heck with what everyone else thinks," dominates their every move. A belief that "I'll get what I want, regardless of whom I hurt along the way," becomes their functional condition.

Without intervention, these people move to the last step in the spiral: crime and violence. With intervention, they will move back to the previous level, and we'll know we are making progress when they withdraw from success symbols.

CRIME AND VIOLENCE

As we all know well, many young people are at the bottom of the spiral: crime and violence. And many of them get there very quickly. And some of these students are very young. Again, however, we need to know the spiral can be reversed by one teacher or one administrator. That's the power we hold. What we may not know is that some of our colleagues are in a similar spiral—and need the same help.

The spiral is almost a natural evolution. However, the Spiral of Futility continues downward only if there's no intervention in any one of the various steps. Fortunately, the process can be reversed at any point. But there are no jumps in the reversal process. The process of traveling upward on the spiral occurs step by step. Understanding this reality is paramount. Without this understanding, we will not know when our efforts are being successful—and we are likely to give up rather than continue our constructive actions.

INTERVENING IS
A MANDATORY STEP

When the various signs appear, leaders cannot pull away. We must move in. We must intervene. Our job is to reverse the spiral, knowing that we cannot skip steps in the reversal process.

This is the place where leaders often make the biggest mistake—with children and adults alike. When we try to help and don't see total success, we think the person is neither listening nor learning from us. So we quit. How many times have we said, "I've talked to him twice, and it hasn't done any good," or "He was better—but only for a couple of days"? Actually, he is better. Hostility gave way to insularity, but we didn't see it. Too, we may recognize a stage and erroneously think people will work themselves out of it—so we do nothing. They won't.

Sometimes, we also make the mistake of evaluating the situation from our view, not the other person's view. For instance, students tell us how they feel, and we ignore them. Our colleagues tell us how they feel or think, and we ignore them. And ignoring is rejection. Remember, truth in a leadership and management situation is truth as the people we are leading see it. It's what their minds perceive as truth that counts. If they feel rejected—then they are rejected whether we think so or not. That's why we must always listen to what those we lead tell us—and act accordingly. If we don't, the force of the spiral will certainly keep pulling them downward.

As leaders, it's our job to help those we lead be successful. Sometimes insisting on professional help is a must. However, responding to the first sign of rejection is a big step. Countering these feelings of rejection at this first stage can save much despair down the destructive road of futility. That's why we would be wise to keep *rejection* out of the classroom, school, and district. After all, rejection is where it all begins. And from this initial point, it's all downhill.

THE LAW:
APPLIED

1. Identify those being led who are not doing well.
2. Where are they in the spiral?
3. What can you do to intervene?
4. How will you know your efforts are successful?
5. What must be the focus of your intervention when success is experienced?

PROCTOR'S SPIRAL OF FUTILITY

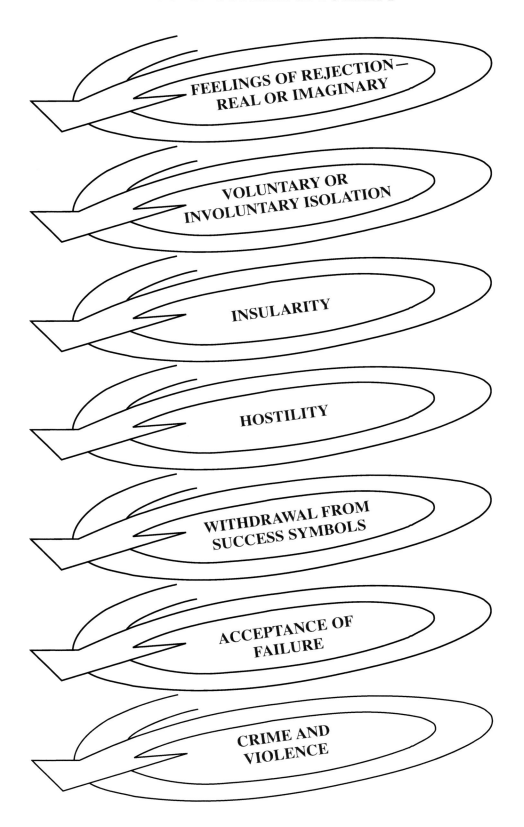

FEELINGS OF REJECTION—
REAL OR IMAGINARY

VOLUNTARY OR
INVOLUNTARY ISOLATION

INSULARITY

HOSTILITY

WITHDRAWAL FROM
SUCCESS SYMBOLS

ACCEPTANCE OF
FAILURE

CRIME AND
VIOLENCE

THE
LAW OF
LOYALTY

Rationale: There is a direct relationship between a person's loyalty to a leader and the degree to which that person sincerely believes he or she is appreciated by a leader.

The management beliefs that some administrators and teachers hold regarding individual student and staff loyalty are among the biggest management misconceptions of our time. Loyalty is not "bought" when leaders give the staff more money or students a better grade. Neither is it achieved when leaders decrease the work or lower the standards for one or all. It is not derived from special privilege or granted favors. Contrary to popular belief, it is not the result of personal friendships. Loyalty is a benefit that is derived from recognition and appreciation. That's why gaining the loyalty of every student, teacher, administrator, custodian, cook, secretary, and others being led is within the realm of possibility for every teacher and every administrator.

MONEY, FAVORS,
AND BENEFITS

Many leaders continue to believe that money, favors, superior working conditions, fringe benefits, gifts, privileges and other advantages, gains, and benefits are the things they must provide for individuals to create and generate loyalty. Many leaders think that a void in these areas will cause those being led to be disloyal and dissatisfied with their leadership.

Some administrators believe these are the things which will keep those being led loyal, supportive, and appreciative. They also believe these benefits will prevent their teachers and staff members from leaving to take positions elsewhere. Not true. In fact, nothing could be further from the truth. Because leaders want so much for those being led to be loyal, and because loyalty is a big source of security for leaders, no misconception could possibly have done more to move leaders in the wrong direction than these widely held myths.

Leaders who believe these falsehoods have never looked inward. If they had, they would have realized that they are not motivated solely by these benefits. Therefore, they must think that everyone is different from them—because they believe loyalty or job reward and satisfaction come from such advantages. This may come as a shock—but people don't work just for money. They work to be regarded as needed and useful. They work for appreciation. All research and employee polls support this statement.

The economic law tells us people are very interested in money, yes. And people always want more money. But money has nothing to do with their loyalty. In addition, money has absolutely nothing to do with the amount of work an individual undertakes. Money and perks have nothing to do with the amount of work one accomplishes. But appreciation does. Think about that for a moment.

Once a living wage is achieved and a person has gained some practical security which he or she can see, financial matters and perks are often cast aside and become secondary to job satisfaction. That is, financial consideration and perks can become a secondary priority if personal growth, appreciation, and recognition are being experienced. Only when appreciation is lacking or void do money, benefits, privileges, and other such tangible things become the primary interest and a sought-after substitute.

In fact, when appreciation is lacking, money and other benefits become the employees' *proof* of importance, status, worth, and appreciation. In truth, the mistaken leadership belief that loyalty comes only from benefits has supported and promoted the teacher movement to gain these benefits. Lack of expressed appreciation by society and educational leadership has caused much of the gap that exists between teacher and administrator today. Make no mistake: Appreciation is the primary factor that creates an educator's loyalty to students, colleagues, community, school, and profession.

For instance, studies indicate that even a more attractive job offer may be cast aside when one feels sincerely appreciated. The difference between being paid $40,000 a year and $42,000 a year will be rationalized away by the appreciated employee as a gain that would be lost in the cost of moving. In this regard, pensions and insurance programs fulfill the security need, but we might gain new insight by knowing that few people actually believe they will ever use such benefits. These benefits often have more of a prestige and family responsibility factor than a security benefit. If we look closely, we will see that these benefits often serve as a substitute for appreciation.

MONEY IS THE LEAST SIGNIFICANT
WAY TO SHOW APPRECIATION

Strangely enough, the least significant way of showing appreciation to anyone is via money. Of all things money is, it is not personal. It is not necessarily appreciation. And when money is given, loyalty is not necessarily achieved.

We humans are strange creatures. When we are given more money for the work we are doing, we are more likely to regard the increased wage as something we were *owed* and should have had a long time ago. We may be happy, but we are not always overjoyed. We still may not feel appreciated. Yet, we often persist in pushing for the wrong things as leaders and ignore or deny the leadership action which would make loyalty a reality. We may violate the Law of Loyalty continually. Then, we can't understand why we do not achieve our desires—such as gaining the loyalty of those we lead.

As teachers, we all know children who have received all the money a parent could give them—but no personal attention or appreciation. As educators, we all know and fully understand the results of such parent action too. We can't understand how parents could be so dumb. Yet, we can't transfer this personal knowledge to our profession when we work as leaders of students. We make the same mistakes over and over again in our attempts to gain loyalty. If we think we can avoid our responsibility to help students fit in, belong, and learn and they will be loyal to us—we are mistaken. And if we think being permissive will help us now, we ought to wait a few years. Our ears will burn from the criticism of former students.

A COMMON
BASE

Appreciation is love—and love is appreciation. Love is recognition—and recognition is love. Lack of appreciation and recognition can destroy love and loyalty. Don't fool yourself for a moment by thinking that love is only personal. It is professional too. It belongs in the classroom. It belongs in the office. The real problems people face in their professional lives are the same ones they face in their personal lives. These problems are loneliness, neglect, mistreatment, lack of touch, lack of communication, not feeling needed, not feeling wanted, and not getting any recognition. All result in a loyalty void—both as givers and receivers. All are the result of leadership neglect. In many ways, they are unforgivable failures for leaders and followers alike.

Revealing appreciation to people is not only a leadership responsibility. It is also a leadership opportunity. It is the opportunity to give recognition and bestow gratitude for work, effort, and contribution as well as the acceptance of an individual's contribution as a student or school worker. It creates loyalty to the leader and vice versa. Remember, loyalty is a two-way street.

Surely, every teacher and administrator can realize that this is the primary reason behind promoting professionalism. Professionalism gives us *instant respect and status*. Professionalism puts a name and label on respect and status. That's a fact. This is also the reason for the value and importance of granting titles. Yet, neither will give loyalty. Loyalty can be achieved only through the demonstration of sincere appreciation for who a person is and what he or she is doing and has accomplished while working.

In truth, this law is as important to a leader both personally and professionally as it is to those being led. Here, both leader and follower win, or they both lose. It's unfortunate that those we lead often don't know that some appreciation needs to be headed our way too—if it is going to be easier for teachers and administrators to be loyal to those they lead. And if we don't get it, guess what we will ask for first? That's right, we'll ask for more money.

THE LAW:
APPLIED

1. Share why money (is) (is not) a form of appreciation.
2. As wages are increased, why don't educators feel appreciated? Discuss.
3. Discuss what loyalty is to you.
4. Discuss what appreciation is to you. As a leader, how can you give appreciation?
5. What individual needs are met with appreciation?
6. Whenever the word *money* is presented to educators, the walls of resistance go up. Why?

THE
PRINCIPLE OF
PRIDE

Rationale: Once pride is established by the leader, it will result in greater individual and group effort and achievement through self and peer pressure—without additional pressures or incentives from the leader.

When people have pride in their work, in achievement, in their class, and in their school, everyone is the beneficiary. When people have pride in themselves, both motivation and the possibilities of exceptional success are enhanced. That's why every leader should want the existence of pride.

What we may not realize is that pride is the creation of the leader. It is, without reservation, the result of proactive leadership. Once established, however, pride is perpetuated by those being led out of self and peer pressure—not leadership and management pressure. Once established, it only needs to be reinforced by leadership challenge, praise, encouragement, appreciation, and acknowledgment. The leader simply continues to provide the environment and set the tone which creates the probability of self and group pressure development. And the leader needs to be aware that the presence of pride is one of the most enjoyable and satisfying experiences for both leader and those being led. Those being led love it—and so does the leader. It creates a spirit. It creates a special climate and culture. It generates motivation. It creates relationships between people, including between the leader and those being led.

Ask yourself these questions to discover the truth inherent in this leadership and management principle:

1. Why do some staff members suggest having more programs or activities for students?
2. Why do many students join clubs and participate in activities?
3. Why do some teachers work at night, planning and preparing for the next day?
4. Why do students have rivals in other schools?
5. Why do teachers "fix up" their room or the teachers' lounge?
6. Why do some teachers volunteer for every group?
7. Why do some students/teachers/classes/faculties/districts move relentlessly toward excellence?
8. Why are some teachers always the first to school in the morning—and the last to leave?
9. Why do students wear school T-shirts and letter jackets?

Because of pride. A leader must recognize pride for what it is: ownership. Pride is a form of positive power. It is affiliation, achievement, and status. Once established, pride is among a leader's best motivational tools. It operates when things are going well, and it operates when things are going poorly. It is an effective rallying tool. It promotes cooperation and teamwork. It gets things done regardless of the odds, and it always unites for good. That's why every leader needs to establish pride in the classroom and school—then let it develop to its fullest.

ESTABLISHING A CLIMATE
OF PRIDE

Unfortunately, in our society we have different rules and regulations that people think they must follow concerning pride. For instance, we are taught that we should not be motivated by pride in self—that such a behavior is too self-directed or conceited. We may go to great lengths to hide our personal pride because we feel it is a sign of arrogance or vanity. We may even think certain kinds of pride are unmanly, unfashionable, or a sign of weakness. For instance, boys shouldn't cry. Boys shouldn't appear hurt either. As leaders, we're supposed to endure cuts, put-downs, and attacks without saying a word or showing any emotion.

Failure to understand pride is a foolish leadership error. Pride has deep and far-reaching implications for everyone because the need for pride is within us all. It governs our moods, our thinking, and our behavior. As leaders, we can never deny an individual's pride if we expect that person to perform to his or her potential.

For instance, our failure to allow those being led to "save face" and keep their dignity in certain situations can cause us many problems. Remember, a leader can't ever put people in a box in any way and expect to be accepted or effective as the leader. To do so diminishes them and elevates the leader. A person with a good self-concept usually finds this difficult to do. So does the person who places a heavy value on the worth of others. Therefore, we can't embarrass those being led by word, action, rule, or regulation—and expect to instill pride. Such teacher or administrative action insults people, denies them their dignity, and pushes them away from us. To be oblivious to the fact that, as leaders, we often deny pride is an error of significant proportion.

How many times have we seen those being led seethe on the inside but say nothing—and then explode later over "nothing"? In truth, we often fail to see that the real cause of these explosions was a combination of pride-denying incidents. And when the explosion occurs, we try problem solving on the second issue and can't understand why our efforts are not successful. Pride is often the issue. And denying a person pride can make a tiger out of a kitten. It can create an enemy. Worse, it can create an enemy with vengeance in mind.

PRIDE CAN CAUSE US
TO LOSE THE WAR

Every leader must be cognizant of the need everyone has for pride—from student to custodian to the board of education. As leaders, we have pride too. We also have power. That's why our pride can cause us to deny those being led their pride. We must make sure that we don't try to "win the battle" by denying pride, but "lose the war," because our treatment of those being led directly or indirectly denies them the pride they need to function in unity and with a sense of security and ownership. Pride is something we must promote— not deny. It is one of our most positive, constructive, and self-perpetuating motivational tools for accomplishing the work of the classroom, school, and district.

Pride can't be achieved with leadership demands, pressure, orders, or directives. It can't be created by fear or guilt either. It is derived from having worth, value, merit, and success in the eyes of those leading us. It is derived from developing a cooperative sense of mission, high expectations, and a firm belief in the capabilities of those being led—even when they are not performing well. It is the criterion which makes us all feel bigger, stronger, and more successful because we are part of the whole, rather than alone. That's why a leader must be very careful not to deny people pride. Sometimes, we deny pride by:

1. Withholding information.
2. Telling rather than asking.
3. Belittling any kind of idea or achievement.
4. Giving instructions in a dictatorial way.
5.   Poking fun at the weak.
6.   Saying some courses or student activities are more important than others.
7. Imposing our truths upon others. When we try to impose our truths upon others, we are telling those we lead that we think we are smarter than we are.
8. Getting involved in the rights and prerogatives of others without invitation.
9.   Embarrassing those being led.
10. Looking down on any job. Remember, when we look down on any job, we automatically look down on the person who does it.

MATURITY HAS NOTHING TO DO WITH PRIDE

A leader must recognize that many pride motivators are hard to detect because people have been taught to hide pride. Some people will even tell us they feel pride is shallow. Others will say it is wrong or unimportant in their lives. We tend to believe them, and this leads us astray.

It's also a mistake for a leader to think these people are more mature and possess more self-confidence when they tell us pride is not a factor in their lives. Consciously or subconsciously, it is a factor. We all know the behaviors which reveal pride. Unfortunately, we may not recognize the behaviors which reveal a need for pride. These behaviors may include:

1. Requesting consideration.
2. Acting hurt over being left out.
3. Revealing fear of rejection.
4.   Displaying inadequacy.
5. Requesting recognition, authority, and power.

Individual pride is within us all. If it is not openly valued and promoted by the leader, however, proud people will not reveal pride—and they won't participate in order to avoid facing the consequences of revealing their true feelings. Remember that people do strange things when their pride is attacked, when pride must be concealed, and when trying to resolve any problem situation in which pride is the issue. And, of course, a leader must make sure pride doesn't get in the way of leadership attitudes, behaviors, and actions.

Students, teachers, and administrators should be fiercely proud of themselves, each other, those being led, their work, their school, and their organization. If they are, motivating those being led to accomplish the work of the classroom, school, and district in a cooperative manner is made much easier. It is also made more enjoyable. If those being led are not feeling pride, we need look only as far as their leader for the reason. After all, the proactive creation begins with them. And those being led can't take over until the leader initiates the creation of pride.

THE LAW:
APPLIED

1. If one does not have pride, what are the possible results?
2. Share ways to allow those being led to have pride.
3. Discuss what you consider to be (good pride) (bad pride).
4. What are the sources of pride in your (classroom) (school) (district)?
5. Identify those you lead who have no pride. Why? What can you do to instill it as a leader?
6. What individual needs are met by pride?

THE
LAW OF
VARIED THINKING

Rationale: By necessity, administrators think predominantly in terms of the whole and the future while teachers, by necessity, think predominantly in terms of specifics and immediate needs.

This is a law all who work in a school and district need to understand and accept. While teachers and administrators may have the same mission, they do different work. Likewise, teachers and administrators do not think the same way, nor do they have the same daily priorities. Without the awareness and action necessary to meet the daily working needs of the teachers, an administrator can lose sight of his or her role and responsibility—and get into a lot of trouble. That's because the nature of administrators' work and their state of mind can get in the way. And if teachers don't understand the work of administrators, they may experience considerable frustration—and arrive at the wrong conclusions.

Specifically, administrators think predominantly in terms of the whole and the future, while teachers think predominantly in terms of specifics. They think about immediate and daily needs. Administrators work on the whole because they must. Administrators work in the future. They must. If an administrator isn't working at least six months ahead, he or she is behind in his or her work. It doesn't take an experienced administrator or teacher to see why. On the other hand, while teachers plan for the future too, they are in the classroom each hour taking care of immediate and daily needs. If they weren't, the work of the school would come to a standstill very quickly.

EACH HAS
A DIFFICULT ROLE

Administrators are trained to think in terms of the whole school. Teachers are trained to think in terms of the whole student and whole class. An administrator's concern is with how the whole is running. A teacher's concern is how the whole student and whole class are performing now. An administrator is concerned about discipline throughout the whole school and the state of total deportment in the cafeteria, in the halls, on the playground, and in the classroom. A teacher's concern is primarily with discipline in his or her classroom—or the state of discipline in the school that affects his or her classroom. An administrator is concerned with the needs of the entire student body and with how well students are doing as a whole academically. The teacher is concerned about how *every* student in class is doing. A superintendent is concerned about the entire district.

Therefore, administrative concern is for the overall state of productivity and satisfaction. An administrator expects a degree of problems everywhere—but doesn't press a panic button until the number of problems exceed the proportion he or she regards as normal. For instance, in the spring of the year, administrators are working on budgets, purchasing, and schedules for next year. They are concerned about closing the school this year—and next year's ordering and class schedules. This reality can be dangerous—and for good reason.

The function of teachers is just the opposite. Teachers are concerned with using each hour of the day. They want and expect help with specific problems—today. It's the one student who is continually late to class, can't read, is failing, disruptive, or won't stay in his or her seat that ruins teachers' total effectiveness. Therefore, as administrators are thinking and working on the whole picture or working in the spring to be ready for next year, teachers are focused on needs that have immediate urgency to them—and to students. And teachers may be in the hardest and most stressful part of *their* year at the time administrators are working on next year.

AWARENESS AND ACTION
AFFECT EFFECTIVENESS

These different perspectives and priorities of teachers as leaders and administrators as leaders are what make schools work—today and tomorrow. However, these different perspectives and priorities can prevent an administrator from seeing the real value and absolute necessity of helping an individual teacher with the smallest of problems— immediately. After all, both roles, teacher and administrator, are proper. Both stances are needed in each of the leadership roles to make a school effective. Both teachers and administrators need to be aware of this reality. Yet, if an administrator doesn't meet the immediate and specific needs of the staff, some teachers may not be able to function because of the one student they can't motivate, keep seated, or get to class. If administrators don't give teachers direct help or specific suggestions for handling these classroom problems, only trouble lies ahead. In fact, teachers may think their administrator isn't able to help or doesn't care—or is not a good leader. And this assumption is true.

As a result, teachers may even believe that what administrators are doing is not important. In reality, it is only because teachers are focused on today and handling the hour-by-hour and day-by-day jobs of the classroom that administrators can work on the whole and the future. If teachers stop worrying about handling the present, administrators won't be free to work on the whole. Neither will they be able to work on the future. Rather, administrators will be tied down to a daily schedule that makes it impossible for them to lead the whole school or do any of the planning or work necessary for the future.

Administrators can't let the nature of their work keep them from seeing the real needs of teachers—and they must never ignore, downplay, or fight these needs. If administrators don't deal with the immediate needs of teachers each hour, day, and week, they are not student-centered. They are administrator-centered. Administrators must constantly help teachers—and show teachers that they know what classroom teaching is all about. In the process, administrators must do something positive and constructive on a daily basis to help teachers do their job in the classroom.

With the Law of Varied Thinking as our constant guide, both teachers and administrators can keep proactive attitudes and actions in good working order. However, the law also teaches us that everyone needs to be aware of the "varied thinking" that occurs in a school as a result of our different leadership roles and functions. When this awareness is present, all will see the value and contribution of the other. All will recognize the normalcy and necessity of varied thinking. And all will see the need to lead in our respective roles. Without this understanding, we may engage in a lot of unnecessary criticism, frustration, disappointment, and failure.

THE LAW:
APPLIED

1. Discuss the work of a teacher and administrator at various times of the year.
2. Reveal how both are performing properly.
3. Share why the individual student and the individual teacher must remain a priority of the administrator's leadership.
4. Discuss the statement, "We don't lead groups; we lead individuals."
5. Discuss the Law of Adjustment relative to the Law of Varied Thinking.
6. What adjustment can be made to help both administrators and teachers enjoy greater productivity?
7. How does the thinking of (students) (parents) vary from that of educators? Discuss.

THE
LAW OF
TRANSFERENCE

Rationale: To get the work of the classroom and school accomplished, specific methods and techniques must be employed to transfer the responsibility for the work being done from the leader to the people doing that work.

As leaders, we want control. We want power. We want to call the shots. On the other hand, we often complain that "everything" rests on our shoulders. As a result, we often feel the load is more than one can carry. Yet, the leadership objective is to get those being led to want and accept more work and more responsibility. This can occur only by transference. If we want all the power, transference cannot occur. If we want all the control, transference is impossible. Transference occurs via giving help and assistance to those being led—and by giving them as much authority, autonomy, control, and responsibility as possible.

If a leader ever gets to the point that those being led say, "My teacher or my principal or my superintendent gives me more help than I can use," the leader will have achieved a vital and necessary leadership feat. Why? He or she has taken the first step in getting those being led to accept responsibility for their work. When this law is combined with the Law of Total Responsibility and the Law of Top-Down Leadership, the leader should see the leadership task very easily.

The Law of Total Responsibility tells us we are responsible for everything that happens in our classroom and school—by contract and by law. The law also tells us we'll be blamed when things go wrong. The Law of Top-Down Leadership tells us leadership must come from us. The problem is, we can't get everything done alone. We have to work with, involve, and motivate a lot of people to get the work of the classroom and the school accomplished. Therefore, the more responsibility we can get those we lead to accept, the better our chances for success. And how much responsibility we can get people to accept has a great deal to do with how we choose to lead them.

For instance, if we believe that the people doing the work need a hand in what they do and how work is to be done, we will lead one way. On the other hand, if we believe that the leader should call all the shots, we will choose another course. Yet, if we want those we lead to accept responsibility, we must choose the former course—and for good reason. In order to accept responsibility, do the best job they can, and be successful—people need to be given help, responsibility, authority to do the job, and the credit for doing it. In addition, a close look will reveal that those being led also need vast amounts of information and autonomy if we expect to transfer responsibility for doing that work to them. That's why we ought to consider being a "point of reference" and "full disclosure" type of leader. After all, taking this stance allows transference to occur.

THOSE BEING LED NEED
INFORMATION TO DO THE JOB

The truth of the matter is that those being led will not accept responsibility without receiving information from the leader. This means, with the exception of knowledge regarding the salaries people receive—or the grades classmates earn—those being led should have all the information the leader does. The more information those being led have about what is being done, why it's being done, and how it might be done successfully, the better they can perform. And those being led will not accept responsibility to the degree we desire without this information. As long as the leader holds this information, he or she will also hold the responsibility. This principle applies on every level with everyone in the school.

For example, let's say a counselor has all the information about a student's situation at home, but doesn't pass it on to the teachers working with that student for fear the information will be misused. The counselor may have tied a teacher's hands, making it impossible for him or her to assume responsibility and help that student. Likewise, if a teacher is trying to initiate a plan that he or she wants students to accept, but doesn't use a full-disclosure policy because of fear that students may not understand a portion of the rationale, the action will cause a blockage when it comes to acceptance of the plan. Then, transference for the work at hand will not occur.

The rule of thumb is this: Whenever you fail to practice full disclosure and being a point of reference to those being led, an automatic blockage has been put in place to prevent transference—and getting those being led to accept responsibility. Worse, those being led will not accept responsibility for any failure if transference hasn't occurred, because they will believe they haven't received adequate help from the leader, weren't given any power, or didn't have essential information.

ALWAYS THINK "ADD ON" RATHER THAN "DELETE"

The best leadership plan is to give those being led more information than they can use in every single instance. Those who fail to use the information given to them or misuse information offered should be dealt with on an individual basis. Even when it comes to staff development and training, an administrator should always think "add on." That is, you should add to what you are doing rather than start something else and stop what you have been doing.

This action is true even when the constraints of time become a problem. Administrators must think "add on" rather than "delete." Remember, the idea is to give those being led more information—if you want them to accept responsibility rather than blame you for everything that goes wrong.

The leadership goal remains: to transfer responsibility from the leader to those actually doing the work. Without this action, the leader will always have to stay on square one. Make no mistake: A leader can move to higher levels of performance only when those being led do. And those being led will never move to higher levels of performance until they accept responsibility which is enhanced through the leadership technique of transference.

THE LAW: APPLIED

1. What individual needs are met by transference?
2. Share actions a leader can take to transfer responsibility for work to those doing the work.
3. Identify those responsibilities that a leader can't do as well as those being led.

4. What information can't be shared with those being led?
5. When transference occurs, what does a leader give up? Are these powers retrievable? Discuss.

THE
LAW OF
THE GRAPEVINE

Rationale:　The grapevine is a powerful and ever-present communication network vehicle in a classroom, school, and district which cannot be overlooked or discounted by the leader.

None can deny the existence of grapevines. And none can deny the power and efficiency of the grapevine in a classroom, school, or district. It can be the swiftest and most credible communicator of all. Sometimes, it carries the bulk of student, staff, and administrative communications—correct and incorrect, true and false, positive and negative, constructive and destructive. In case we don't believe that the rumor carried by the grapevine has power and influence, let us remember the times when rumor has altered our psyche as well as our course of action. How many times have we stopped something we were doing because of something we heard via this unofficial communicator?

Throughout history, the grapevine has been powerful. Heads have rolled when kings were told falsehoods by their confidants. Jobs have been lost when a grapevine of misinformation was set in motion and believed. Most of us can recall a reputation that was ruined by a grapevine rumor—which may have been true or untrue. Let's not think that the grapevine doesn't exist in our classroom, school, and district. It does—with students and staff alike. Likewise, let's not forget that every leader has to deal with the news carried by this form of communication. Let us also remember that most of us have used the grapevine to deliver a message that we wanted one or all to hear. It's not hard to use. Usually, we can tell one or two people and know that soon everyone will know.

NOT ALWAYS
NEGATIVE

The grapevine is always working. As leaders, we often overlook this reality. For instance, before a student or teacher ever comes to see us, he or she has probably already formed some kind of opinion about us from what he or she has heard from others. This is the grapevine at work. If we are fortunate, the opinion is favorable. Let us not forget that not all the information that travels by the grapevine is always negative or bad, just most of it. Humans seem to have a greater tendency to pass along the unpleasant. That's why leaders need to be careful about using the grapevine as a means of communication. After all, those we lead can come to expect bad news to come from us in this manner if we do.

What we need to remember is that our reputations almost always precede us. Students know teachers. Teachers know administrators. It's the business of those being led to know their leaders. They know a leader's likes and dislikes. They know how we think. They know how we communicate, what we expect, and what we will allow. They even know about our priorities and pet projects—or lack of both. As leaders, teachers and administrators need to be aware of how those being led know so much about us. The grapevine has given them information they need about us. In truth, if we had as much information about those being led as they have about us, we could be more effective leaders. On a daily basis, the grapevine gives people information as they arrive in school. And a close look will reveal that our personalities, behavioral traits, attitudes, and the way we normally function either confirm the "word" or dispel it as inaccurate.

Make no mistake: Our peers have our number too. They know if we're approachable or not. They know our pets and our peeves. They may even know how we will probably react to a new idea or a controversial issue in a meeting. That's the power of the grapevine. The question is: What should we do about it?

THE DECISION: HANDLE IT OR LEAVE IT ALONE

Once we know what message is being carried by the grapevine in our classroom, school, or district, we have a decision to make as leaders. As simple as it sounds, our action is vitally important. We'll have to decide whether it is best to handle the issue by using confrontation, discussion, and information—or whether this is a time that doing nothing is the best course of action.

After all, there will always be talk. There will always be rumors. Some have consequence and merit, and some do not. Some are just not worth bothering about, while others need to be dealt with to clear the air, calm fears, and restore stability. It's true that we can't control what people say about us and others, or what is going to happen—or not happen. However, sometimes a talk or discussion will curb people's beliefs and influence their actions in the future. Likewise, issuing official information can put an issue to rest. Most important, when we are on the hearing end of the grapevine, there is a professional stance we can take to help cut down the flow of rumors in a classroom or school. This action is important, for it can do much to establish the climate we need in order to operate successfully as educators.

We can say bluntly—even if the rumor appears to be absolutely true—that "Since this information is secondhand, it would be wise and beneficial for all concerned if we waited until we could check out this story ourselves before we pass it along or pass judgment." And we would be wise to teach this stance to students and everyone in a school. After all, a grapevine can't exist if we and others don't take part in it. We only need to remind ourselves that it's our weak and negative side that lets us or makes us want to participate in it.

We also need to remind ourselves and others that a grapevine only masquerades as a real power. It is not real power unless we let it be. It is hoped that we will deactivate it by knowing that rumor always wastes time, short-circuits progress, and cripples our ability to handle information. That's why we must check it out carefully, but fight our desire to perpetuate its existence. When we do, we are strengthened. So is everyone in the school and district. And this argument can work—if we are the kind of leader who refuses to use the grapevine ourselves. However, if we use it, those we lead will too.

THE ISSUE IS TO AVOID BEING GOVERNED BY RUMOR

We need to be aware that students, teachers, administrators, and parents are not immune to the destructiveness of the grapevine. Neither is the school or district. What is surprising is how often we, as leaders, are willing to accept hearsay as the absolute truth.

What is frightening is how often we do something wrong or how often we do nothing constructive after hearing a rumor.

However, we cannot allow ourselves to be governed by rumor. If we are, our interaction with those being led is impaired. That's why we need to share our feelings with others and keep the lines of communication open. To students we can say, "You've heard that we are cracking down on those who skip class. We are. But we will be fair. And I will do everything I can to ensure your success, rather than increase your chances of failure."

We can approach teachers and parents in the same manner. Most of all, we must trust others until we can clarify news carried by the grapevine. If we don't, rumors can become fact in the minds of those being led in our classroom and school. The grapevine can also become the primary source of information for students and faculty. Worse, it can become the primary determinant of negative attitudes, beliefs, and opinions for those we lead. That's the power of the grapevine. We can never discount its power. And if we are not a communicator, we aid its use and credibility. If we withhold information or use information as power, we guarantee the grapevine will get in the way of effective leadership.

THE LAW:
APPLIED

1. What individual needs are met by grapevine communication?
2. How can you meet these needs in appropriate ways? Discuss.
3. Discuss the kind of grapevine communication which should be handled by (confrontation) (discussion) (information).
4. Share ways a leader can handle rumors without putting anyone down.
5. Discuss ways to counsel (students) (peers) who use the grapevine extensively—as well as how to counsel those who use the people who use the grapevine as a means of getting information.

THE
LAW OF
TIMING

Rationale: Developing the art of timing is a key to leadership effectiveness, and it is based on the four-step process of *gauging, planning, waiting*, and *initiating*.

Some leaders have a knack for getting their own way. Everything they do seems to work out the way they planned. They have a golden touch with students, teachers, staff, administrators, and parents alike. There are many reasons for this reality. It might appear that their successes are primarily the result of their tact and diplomacy and intelligence. They probably are. Some might think it's simply their charisma and personality. Much of this logic may be true. Yet, the chances are that all these characteristics are combined with a very fine sense of timing. Developing the art of timing is an important leadership skill. In truth, a lack of timing skills can render us less effective than we can be and want to be.

TIMING GETS
AFFIRMATIVE ANSWERS

If we think timing is unimportant, we need simply recall how many times we have received a *no* to our request only to find out a short time later that another colleague received an affirmative answer to the same request. Likewise, how many times have we told one student or teacher yes on one occasion—and no on another? This law tells us that many leaders could get more of what they wanted if they would ask at the right time and the right place.

Picking the right time and the right place is the fundamental ingredient in developing the art of timing. It is not difficult. It requires but one guideline: looking through another's eyes with the same intensity that we look through our own. Some people find this very difficult to do. Their own wants and needs block their perceptions. They jump in, regardless of the situation. As a result, they ask the wrong thing at the wrong time in the wrong place—and their requests to get superiors and subordinates to do what they want them to do are usually denied. If we're having difficulty communicating with those being led, we may need to check our timing. It may be preventing our success.

Timing is essential in almost everything we do. There's a time to urge and a time to counsel. There's a time for talking to those being led about working more and taking work more seriously, just as there are times for not confronting about attitudes or behaviors. There are times to scold and reprimand—and times to wait until a better time. Whenever possible, we must look at the situation from the viewpoint of those being led *before* we act. The best time to talk to those being led is when they are ready or we can get them ready. That's when *we* must be ready—and not a minute before.

A FOUR-STEP
PROCESS

Contrary to popular belief, developing the art of timing is not a matter of manipulation.

It's a matter of consideration. A leader simply cannot pick the right time and the right place if his or her wants and needs must always be the first consideration. When such is the case, we function under the "bull in a china shop" syndrome. Developing the art of timing is based upon four proactive steps: *gauging*, *planning*, *waiting*, and *initiating*. All involve consideration for those being led.

To develop the art of timing, the leader must gauge the person and the situation. To do so, these questions should be addressed: What is the situation? What has happened in the past and the present, and what upcoming events should be considered in our timing? Answering these questions helps us gauge the person and the situation.

Second, a leader must plan his or her approach. What is the best way to deal with this person and situation? Who is involved? How will they react? What are the obvious positives and negatives contained in the attitude and ability of the person and in the situation?

Third, a leader must not plow ahead once he or she has gauged the situation and developed a plan. We must be patient. We must wait for the right time and place. If we do, our efforts will have a greater impact and a higher probability for acceptance. If the right time and place don't appear, we must set the stage by arranging a private meeting at a good time. However, if we perceive that the timing is poor at the meeting, we should simply tell the person we are talking to that "It doesn't appear to be the right time for taking up this matter. Let's wait until tomorrow." Such an act of consideration will be appreciated—and will probably work to our advantage. Remember, forging ahead, unless it is absolutely unnecessary, may not produce the results we desire.

Fourth, a leader must initiate action. We must know what we are talking about—and be prepared to deal graciously and professionally with both acceptance and rejection. We need to always keep in mind that how we respond to rejection affects the responses we will receive from others in the future.

NOT AN ART
OF DECEPTION

Some may think that developing the art of timing can be called the art of getting one's own way. It is. However, this is not an art of deception. It's an act of empathy. Empathy means understanding from the frame of reference of those being led. For instance, empathy means understanding the child from the child's own frame of reference. It is different from sympathy, but both imply caring for the child. When we have sympathy, we appreciate how the child feels, how things are for him or her—but we do not make the child's feeling or troubles our own in the sense that we are positioned to help a child solve his or her problems. Those leaders who have a knack for saying the wrong thing at the wrong time are usually void of this vital characteristic. That's why their timing is almost always bad.

A leader can't be oblivious to external forces and develop the art of timing. After a student has failed a test may not be the best time to talk. Likewise, after a teacher has had a bad day may not be a good time for him or her. We must know that if we give as much attention to our timing as we do to our wants, we will be more effective. Empathetic perceptions alone will tell us when to counsel those being led about attitudes or behavior and when to wait until a better time. We will see timing as one of our biggest advantages and motivators for urging those being led to perform at higher levels—or for initiating change through new ideas.

As leaders, we must realize that unless we can perfect the art of timing, we will never be as effective as we could be. And our actions are likely to cause a problem when we are actually trying to resolve one. Our leadership will neither be appreciated nor followed as readily by those being led. Worse, we are likely to think everyone is unapproachable—or against our ideas and plans when, in reality, others are simply offended by our timing—and our lack of consideration. That's why this law will serve us well, especially when we are upset, angry, and want to attack a problem immediately. And we all have many such moments.

**THE LAW:
APPLIED**

1. What emotions, such as anger, would indicate a leader's timing is not right?
2. List the kinds of situations which must be handled immediately.
3. List the kinds of situations which must not be handled immediately.
4. What days of the week might be (bad) (the best) to tackle a problem?
5. How do you like to be approached?

THE
LAW OF
CYCLES

Rationale: The only constant in the life of any organization is the recurring cycles of change. Only by being student-centered can a leader always be in tune with the current change cycle.

This is a valuable law because every leader wants to get things in place, smooth them out, and have them run well for a long time. Whether it's a procedure or a rule, we like to keep things as we arranged them. Yet, everything goes in cycles. What is a big priority this year will go away and be replaced by another. What *was* will return. And the pendulum will always swing to each extreme with time. Unfortunately, it never seems to stop in the middle.

Once a force begins to shift, however, it will move as far as it can in the opposite direction—until it goes too far and the forces develop to go in the opposite direction. Therefore, the focus will go from liberal to conservative, from strictness to permissiveness, from gifted to at risk, and from athletics to academics. Back and forth the priorities have gone in the past and will go in the future. And whatever *is* will be criticized. What *isn't* will be acclaimed. The forces for a new priority will be set in motion against the priority of the moment.

ONE GUIDE:
REMAINING STUDENT-CENTERED

If we lead by doing the right thing, for the right reason, in the right way, we will be the least affected by the realities of the Law of Cycles. If we produce results and are student-centered always—we will always be in tune with these cycles. And if our concern and consideration for people cannot be challenged, our leadership will be welcomed regardless of the cycle we are in.

However, if we fight the evolution of cycles, we will always be living in the past. Others will regard us as dated. They will think we are out of touch. As a result, during periods of change, the focus will constantly be on trying to take our leadership away from us. It may be our students who try. It may be a supervisor. It may be a parent or a citizens' group. Indeed, it may be a government mandate. At any rate, when you fight the current cycle, someone will try to take leadership from you in the classroom, the school, or the district. And whenever someone else steps in, the rules, regulations, procedures, and laws of others will play a larger role in governing our choices, our priorities, our work, and our focus.

THIS IS WHY A LEADER
MUST BE A VISIONARY

This reality never changes—*unless* those who plan the work, do the work, and are accountable for the work of others and the work of the institution become visionaries as well as practitioners. As teachers and administrators, we must do both—or the cycles of extremes will drive us crazy. Why? Because we can't stop change or all the various movements from moving too far in one direction for us to keep our balance. And this is the task: to keep the cycles from moving *all the way* in another direction. If we are not proactive, but we try to fight the cycle, this is exactly what will happen. We must also know that whenever the pendulum does hit the other extreme, it will start its return.

As leaders and educators, we must look to the future. We must be visionaries. We must grow and change continually to meet the changing needs of students and society for a simple reason: mandates will be thrust upon us if we don't. This leadership action is the only way we can maintain control of education. And we must carry out the day-to-day work in our classroom and school in agreement with the reason for our existence: the welfare of students. We must comply with sound leadership and educational practices and ethics if we hope to control our own destinies, the destinies of our schools and students, and the destiny of our profession.

Understanding the Law of Cycles can save us considerable grief. It tells us that change is inevitable. It tells us that if we fight the changing needs of students, parents, and communities, they will take our leadership away from us. They will tell us what to do. And they will go too far. Understanding and adhering to the Law of Cycles can keep our minds open and prepare us to take proactive action, rather than devote all of our efforts to fighting change and failing as we do.

**THE LAW:
APPLIED**

1. Identify all the cycles you have experienced as an educator.
2. Have any of the cycles returned? Discuss.
3. Share ways to prevent a current trend which is beneficial from going so far it becomes detrimental.
4. Discuss what you believe will be the priorities and focus of education in the future.
5. What changes will be required of educators in the future?

THE
LAW OF
FILTERED INFORMATION

Rationale: The more power and influence a leader possesses, the more the information he or she receives from those being led will be filtered.

The Law of Filtered Information relates that information received by a leader from those being led is filtered either by omission or distortion of the facts—especially if the information reflects negatively upon the one providing the leader with the information. Every teacher and administrator would be wise to remember this law, especially in problem situations. Generally speaking, this law holds true because subordinates can rationalize their actions out of self-preservation. When those being led are dealing with the leader, it is likely they will act out of three conscious or subconscious beliefs.

THREE REASONS LEADERS
DON'T GET THE WHOLE STORY

First, those being led do not feel it is their responsibility to tell the leader anything that would cause their own judgment, competency, or action to be revealed in an unfavorable light. People simply do not believe that it is their responsibility to make themselves "look bad." That does not mean those we lead will lie. It simply means they may omit some important facts that we might need to know so as not to reflect badly on themselves.

Second, teachers and administrators are the higher authority, and it is automatically assumed by those being led that the leader has more information than he or she does—maybe even more than he or she can or wants to tell those being led. Therefore, those being led can and will assume they are providing only a *part* of the information the leader needs or is requesting from them.

Third, those being led may assume that we are simply asking them for information in order to reinforce what we already know. Likewise, they may believe that we *should* already know the answers to the questions we are asking them, and if we don't admit that we do, then we are not being completely honest with them. Arriving at these assumptions allows those being led *not* to tell the leader "everything." This is especially true when telling would get them or someone else in trouble.

Remember, it is always assumed by those being led that the leader knows what is going on. It is taken for granted that the leader has vast sources of information which are not available to those being led. Furthermore, those being led will also believe that if we're obviously not worried about a situation, why should they be? This is not disloyalty. Neither should a leader think such attitudes and behaviors on the part of those being led are character deficiencies. They are not. They are normal human behavior.

THE NEED
FOR INFORMATION

This normal human behavior, however, makes the job of acquiring complete and accurate information, deciding issues, and solving problems more difficult. And, as we all know well, a leader needs information. The more and better our information is, the better are the decisions we can make. That's why we rely so heavily on information from reports, research, personnel data files, counseling with our colleagues, and any other source we can find—especially those we lead.

We all recognize that accurate information facilitates good leadership decisions. Computers, copiers, and communications equipment all exist because those in leadership and management positions want and need more accurate and detailed information as quickly as possible. Indeed, modern technology has provided us with electronic equipment that can give us every conceivable kind of information we need quickly and accurately. It has greatly aided the decision-making process. But computers are most often used in relation to the technical side of management. Yet, this law reminds us that a leader can't always expect this kind of complete and accurate information from those being led, especially if they have negative information to give about themselves. And we often rely on our students and teachers to give us valuable and necessary information on the human side of leadership and management. This law gives us a warning: Be careful.

It is also important to realize that a leader must not be disappointed in or offensive to those being led when they do not openly and completely answer every question we pose to them. A leader simply cannot let the need for information impair the relationship with those being led. Perspective can be maintained if we remember never to expect or demand one of our students or teachers to act against his or her own best interest. Our task remains: filtering, sorting, gathering, and evaluating information.

LEADERS MUST USE A BROAD
BASE TO GATHER INFORMATION

The problems come when a leader ignores the teachings of the Law of Filtered Information and acts and reacts out of information received from an individual or a small or select group of subordinates. To gain accurate and complete information, most teachers and administrators have found that an open-ended and open-door policy has proved to be very valuable. More often than not, however, we have a few "select" people whom we rely on to give us accurate, truthful, and objective information. This can be a help or a hindrance.

What we really need is a broad base of people from whom we can gather information. We must check and recheck. In problem situations, we must always talk to and listen to all parties involved. Please note: I said *talk to* and *listen to* all parties. If a leader talks to all, but listens only to a select few, he or she has not learned from the Law of Filtered Information and a mistake will, predictably, be made.

THE LAW:
APPLIED

1. Discuss the Law of Filtered Information relative to the Law of Survival.

2. Discuss the (ethics) (fairness) involved in gathering negative information from those being led.
3. How do you acquire information? What is your major source?
4. What steps can you take to employ a broad-based technique?

THE
LAW OF
RIGHT/WRONG CONFLICT

Rationale: The attitudes, opinions, and beliefs of those being led cannot be ignored, overlooked, or disregarded regardless of the opinion the leader holds concerning those attitudes, opinions, and beliefs.

Teachers and administrators are concerned with making good, fair, and sound decisions. We are very concerned about such things as right and wrong, good and bad, correct and incorrect. Unfortunately, our concern for right and wrong often leads us to do and say the wrong things in our leadership role.

Right and wrong, good and bad, correct and incorrect should have meaning only insofar as they indicate to the leader what adjustments one must make to change the attitude and behavior of those being led. A leader must never forget that "how people think" is always the real issue in any leadership situation and outweighs all other considerations. That is, it does if leadership beliefs, actions, and proposed actions are to be accepted and effective. Once a leader knows how those being led *think*, a plan or course of action can be initiated. Without such knowledge, we are likely to "plow ahead" without the support of those we lead. When we do, failure rather than success becomes the probability.

TRUTH IS WHAT OTHERS
PERCEIVE TO BE SO

Too often, a leader's judgment regarding the attitudes, opinions, and beliefs of those being led keeps him or her from approaching problems, much less solving them. Unfortunately, when a teacher or administrator judges a student or staff member's thinking as *wrong*, somehow he or she can walk away from that person and the problem with the rationalization that "I'm right—he or she is wrong." Then, the leader can even begin believing that he or she *can't* or *shouldn't* do anything about it. This is a leadership error.

What we have forgotten is that truth, in a leadership situation, is what those being led perceive to be so. This is the "truth" we must deal with. We have also forgotten that right or wrong is temporarily insignificant in comparison to understanding those being led, relating to them, guiding them, and solving the problem at hand. Right and wrong is simply not the issue for a leader at this point. Rather, we must deal with the perceptions of those being led.

If our students think we're unfair as teachers or administrators—we might as well be. If our students think we're mean and unprepared and don't like them, this is the "truth" we must deal with. Likewise, if teachers think we're weak and indecisive administrators, we must deal with this truth. For all leaders, it doesn't make any difference if the charges are untrue. We must take action to change these perceptions.

THE LEADER MUST
DEAL WITH THE PERCEPTION

Remember, your perceptions are not the issue. It does absolutely no good for a principal, for instance, to offer the staff a long list of his or her previous actions or decisions in an effort to prove that he or she is not unfair. Leadership action is only effective if the leader takes corrective action to treat the issue and change the perception. In the process, a leader must never say, "I can't help what they think." Yes, you can. And you must. If you don't, leading is going to be tough.

For instance, perceptions of right and wrong, as well as good and bad, are at the core of every movement or special interest group. If we reject the thinking of such groups and refuse to deal with the "truth" as they see it, we will never influence—and we will suffer the consequences. This law deals with respect for the opinions, beliefs, and perspectives of others. A close look will reveal that these people feel that if you reject their perspective, you also reject them.

Failure to accept the Law of Right/Wrong Conflict reflects an inability to accept many other management laws, such as the Law of Positive Reinforcement and the Law of Total Responsibility. Failure to recognize the importance of this law is often the beginning of the end to a satisfying teaching or administrative career. If leaders will remember to react professionally rather than personally to issues and criticisms and respond in proactive ways to how people think, always keeping in mind that what they believe personally to be right or wrong is not the issue, this failure can be avoided.

Because conflict plays such a huge role in the life of a leader, the dynamics of it are further explored in the Law of Conflict.

THE LAW:
APPLIED

1. Discuss the Law of Right/Wrong Conflict relative to the Law of Positive Reinforcement.
2. Discuss this law relative to the Law of Total Responsibility.
3. As a leader, what are the perceptions of those being led that you need to deal with?
4. What individual needs are met when you adhere to this law?
5. What individual needs are automatically left unmet when you violate this law?

THE
LAW OF
CONFLICT

Rationale: Conflict is inevitable and unavoidable and may have positive or negative results, but it does not have to result in dividing people.

Conflict can make us miserable. It can make us act poorly and unwisely. It can make us forget that we have a professional responsibility to handle conflict well—for our sake and the sake of everyone else—so as not to damage relationships or detract from the work and mission of the school. On the other hand, conflict can result in positives—and facilitate our bringing people together while producing growth as people and professional educators. The choices we make regarding how to deal with conflict are major determinants of whether conflict will stand in the way of success—or become a contributing factor in the search for better decisions, greater achievement, and more stimulation and satisfaction in working with others. Let's discuss how to handle conflict without creating division.

GOING INTO A MEETING "COLD"
CAN CAUSE DIVISION

First, if you intend to handle conflict without creating division, one action is mandatory. You must take the time to prepare to confront issues without accusing those being led. And your preparation must be both mental and emotional. If you approach those being led "cold," your chances of making a big mistake increase—dramatically.

Second, pick the time and the place for the approach—and make sure it's private. Please note: See only the person with whom you have the conflict. And see him or her as quickly as possible following the incident. The longer you wait, the more other people may become involved. Then, the person may become entrenched in a position from which it is hard for him or her to move. And if you are sincere in your desire to avoid division, you would be wise *not* to talk to anyone else about the issue or the person involved. It's vital to join only the key person with the key issues. Therefore, do not involve others. Do not elicit outside support. And do not bring any old issues to the table.

Third, approach the situation as a problem solver, not a gladiator. This is not a win/lose situation. Begin the discussion by restating the situation or issue as you understand it. Then, invite the other person to do the same. After all cards are on the table, identify the underlying needs and generate some options for satisfying them without regard to whether you or the other person is winning out. This is the only way you can work toward creating a mutual understanding of the conflict. Remember, once a mutual understanding is achieved, the outlines of possible solutions and restored good feelings can come back into focus.

WHAT YOU WANT MUST
SERVE BOTH PARTIES

Fourth, know exactly what you want in terms of the issue and the relationship. This action may seem self-serving, but it is not. This step serves both parties in three ways. It helps you stay focused. It gives you priorities. And it offers you the sense of control necessary to make the meeting go well from beginning to end.

Fifth, remember that you must find out exactly what the other person wants—and how strongly he or she feels about those wants. As you do, follow the three "don't do" rules: Don't guess, don't assume, and don't interrupt. If you expect to avoid or resolve a division, the other person *must* feel heard. If this requirement is overlooked, nothing positive will result. Remember, the conflict may be purely *personal*. It may be the result of *philosophical* differences. Or, it may be a *jurisdictional* conflict regarding who's in charge, who should be in charge, and who has what responsibilities. And it's not uncommon for all three types of conflict to be present in any given situation with adult and child alike.

Sixth, once you know what both you and the other person want and how badly he or she wants it, you are ready to begin moving toward closure. Simply propose action that you believe the other person can accept. To achieve the best results, find the highest common ground between you and the other person. In the process, don't be reluctant or afraid to bend. And if you find that you have been totally at fault, don't be afraid to capitulate. After all, during discussion it's not uncommon to find that the guilty one is *you*, not the other person.

Throughout the entire process, keep in mind that your intent is to handle the conflict without creating division. Your purpose is to achieve your goal, not to thwart the other person's. This stance represents the highest level of professional and ethical functioning. If you follow these guidelines, you're likely to come out of conflict with workable solutions, stronger relationships, and the respect of those being led.

CONFLICT CAN
CREATE OPPORTUNITIES

As leaders, we often go to great pains to eliminate the chances of conflict occurring within our classroom, school, and district. And we should. Yet, the truth of the matter is that when conflict is confronted promptly, directly, and appropriately, it can create opportunities for people and the organization. And when such is the case, a great deal of individual growth, progress, and achievement can occur in a short period of time. When a conflict's underlying issues are addressed and resolved, it releases a flow of pent-up energy and the path toward a quality outcome is much less obstructed.

That's why we need to recognize that conflict isn't always a bad thing for us or those being led. That is, it isn't when the leader is honestly trying to rejuvenate relationships and solve a problem. After all, a disagreement can bring a problem—even a hidden one—to the surface and help everyone focus on something that needs to be addressed. That's why we all need to be able to handle conflict in ways that bring us together with those being led, rather than use strategies that usually result in a division between us and those we lead.

THE LAW:
APPLIED

1. Discuss each of the six steps as they would apply to children and adults.
2. What individual needs are met in each of these six steps?

3. Give examples of personal conflict with (children) (adults).
4. Give examples of jurisdictional conflict with (children) (adults).
5. Give examples of philosophical conflict with (children) (adults).
6. What opportunities are often inherent in conflict for (the leader) (those being led)?

THE
LAW OF
CONFLICT RESOLUTION

Rationale: A leader can resolve conflict only by understanding it and dealing constructively with the emotions of those being led—first.

Is there a leader alive who loves conflict? I hope not. Yet, we need not hate or fear conflict as much as we do. And we won't, if we believe that the successful handling of conflict begins with making sure we understand it—rather than only knowing what someone is doing or what the conflict is causing. Therefore, let's begin by adding to our leadership understanding of conflict.

If we freely associate to the word *conflict*, it's likely that there would be three kinds of responses. One set of terms could have negative connotations: war, disdain, destruction, hate, disorder, aggression, and violence. On the other hand, a close look will reveal that a second set of terms could have positive connotations: adventure, opportunity, excitement, development, and growth. Finally, the third set of terms could be relatively neutral: mediation, bargaining, compromising, and reconciliation.

I won't summarize all of the propositions about conflict that find some support in the research and literature of the various social and behavioral sciences. However, a few propositions are very useful in thinking about valid and invalid strategies for handling conflict—and strategies that are and aren't likely to work.

CONFLICT ALWAYS OCCURS WITHIN
THE CONTEXT OF INTERDEPENDENCE

First and foremost, we must be aware that conflict *always* occurs within a context of interdependence rather than independence. Indeed, conflict results from a relationship between interrelated parts of an organization: a family, a classroom, a school, a district. If the "parties" in conflict were not interdependent in the sense that the actions of the one party had consequences for the other and vice versa, conflict could not occur. Nobody would care enough to create conflict.

This reality helps explain the strong emotions inherent in conflict—and the fear of conflict. Conflict disrupts our order and our work. It disrupts relationships. It alters our authority and power—and the productivity of the classroom, school, or district in which it occurs. It may even lead to the division, dismemberment, or destruction of the group. This reality also offers hope for the constructive resolution of conflict—if interest and the perception of the common values of maintaining an organization and its mission can be kept alive in all parties involved in the conflict.

THERE ARE TWO
TYPES OF CONFLICT

Second, we also need to be aware that there are two types of conflicts. One type of conflict grows out of *similarities* in the *wants*, *needs*, and *values* of parts of an organization in the presence of scarce and undistributed resources required to satisfy these wants, needs, and values. For instance, we share similar needs and values with those being led. However, there isn't enough money in the organization for us to have all the money we want for our classes or priorities. Or, we all have a 24-hour day—but someone may think a few of those being led are getting too much of our time and attention and others aren't getting enough.

The other type of conflict grows out of *differences* in *needs* and *values* among parts of a system. The needs and values of one part of a group, for example, may favor one direction of movement for the group, while the needs and values of another part of the group may favor another direction of movement. Perhaps one party wants to work while the other wants to play. On the other hand, the differences may not lie in another direction, but rather in the methods and means of moving toward the expected or the agreed-upon goal. It may be that both parties agree that discipline is the issue, but one favors punishment as the focus and the other does not. Regardless of the nature of the specific situation, we need to be aware that conflict results from needs and values, similarities and differences—and the availability of resources to satisfy these factors.

THE IDEAL SOLUTION
INVOLVES TWO REQUIREMENTS

The "ideal" resolution of either of these two types of conflict involves two requirements. First, both parties to the conflict must accept the right of the other party to have a claim upon the situation. This acceptance is mandatory. For instance, if we don't think a student has such a right, our solution cannot be ideal. If we think a colleague has overstepped his or her rights, an ideal solution will not be achieved.

Second, all parties must believe that all are capable of realistically and rationally locating the sources of the conflict and arriving at mutually acceptable solutions. This, of course, requires trust and confidence. Therefore, resolving a conflict is never a one-way street. It always involves both parties. It always involves granting rights. It always involves believing in the capabilities of others—and giving trust. When any ingredient is absent, the conflict will remain.

As leaders, we must keep in mind that conflicts occur between interested parties, not disinterested or apathetic ones. Conflicts occur between people who are stakeholders who care and are affected by the situation. It is not, as many think, a problem that results from disinterested, uncaring, and unconcerned parties. Because we are stakeholders, however, our drives in a conflict can be forceful. Emotions can run very high. And winning at all costs can become the motivation. Herein lies the real problem in conflict. After all, resolving conflict is not an ability problem. It is an attitude problem.

For instance, we can begin thinking something is none of another person's business. We can believe others have no rights, rather than as many rights as we do. And we can throw belief in the ability of others and "trusting" to the winds. Yet, common sense should really tell us that all the properties of conflict are already in place for resolution: interest, concern, desire, and caring. Our next step is to look at specific ways to handle conflict. After all, if one cannot handle and resolve conflict, it's very unlikely one will find much satisfaction being a leader.

THE FIRST GOAL IS TO
DEAL WITH EMOTIONS

To deal constructively with conflict, we must deal with emotions—including anger, distrust, defensiveness, resentment, fear, and rejection. And if feelings are intense, it's mandatory to deal with the emotional aspects of the conflict *first*. Remember, when feelings are running high, rational problem solving must be *preceded* by a positive or structured exchange regarding the emotional aspect of the controversy. This requires empathy and perspective because the rule of thumb is this: You must always deal with the feelings of people before you can deal with the issue causing those feelings. In the process, keep in mind that feelings or emotions are neither right nor wrong, good nor bad, correct nor incorrect. Also be aware that following specific guidelines enables conflict to be handled better in highly emotional situations.

First, we must identify the *interests* of everyone involved—including ourselves. We discussed this in the Law of Conflict. What do you want? What does the other person want? Identifying the interests and desires of both parties is paramount to resolution. Without this identification, the conflict may never get beyond the emotional state of those involved in the conflict.

Second, throughout the entire process, know that we must treat the other person with respect, and we must let him or her express truth as he or she sees it—and make sure that no one loses face in the situation. Respect is an attitude conveyed through certain behaviors: the way we listen, the way we look at others, our tone of voice, our selection of words, and our facial expressions. Mustering the will power needed to display these attitudes and behaviors may be tough—but it is mandatory.

YOU MUST UNDERSTAND THE CONTENT
OF THE OTHER PERSON'S FEELINGS

Third, we must listen until we can actually "experience" the other side. This action is vital. When feelings are strong regarding the issue, people are much more prone to misunderstand each other. Too many times we are listening—but also trying hard to get into the conversation with our interests, desires, and points of view. As a result, little accurate communication is expressed. Carl Rogers' rule is this: "Each person can speak up for himself or herself only after he or she has first restated the ideas and feelings of the other accurately—and to the other's satisfaction."

Remember, the goal in listening is to understand the content of the other person's ideas, the meaning that content has for him or her, and the feelings he or she has about it. This means being able to step into the other person's shoes and experience—insomuch as it is possible—his or her point of view. It's not enough to hear the other's emotion. That emotion needs to be understood and accepted. Sometimes it will appear that the other's feelings are a deliberate attempt to manipulate or hurt you. If you choose to resist the impulse to strike back and, instead, deliberately concentrate on reflecting the other person's feelings—right or wrong—you'll be amazed how quickly the other's negative feelings subside.

Fourth, after the other person feels heard, you have earned the right to speak your point of view and express your feelings. State your views, needs, and feelings. However, there are some guidelines to remember. State your point of view briefly. Say what you mean and mean what you say, and don't withhold information—especially your trump card. Avoid loaded words, and be careful not to use extreme statements, a common practice when we're in conflict. Disclose your feelings, but remember that until emotional issues are resolved, the conflict issues probably can't be settled.

Fifth, identify higher levels of common interest. This is best achieved by addressing the person's interests and desires regarding the issue and asking, "What does getting this mean to you? How important is this to you? Tell me." Then, create a framework for agreement by asking, "If I could show you how we can satisfy your interests, would you agree to...?" Remember, you have a "real want," and so does the other person—and by satisfying wants and interests, you will resolve the conflict.

Make no mistake: Conflicts are about needs and values. After value issues have been sorted out and the emotional components resolved, substance issues usually have to be solved. The bottom line of our conflict, however, is the conflict of needs. Problems are settled when they are approached in such a way that the needs of both parties are considered and met.

As leaders, we must know that "working things out" is a process. It requires defining the problem in terms of needs and feelings, not in terms of solutions. It requires brainstorming possible solutions together to find a win-win solution. We can't just hand a fantastic solution to the other person and expect him or her to accept it. He or she won't. Commitment to resolution is gained by getting people involved in the solution. Conflicts are resolved by selecting solutions that will best meet the needs of both or all parties—and checking out possible consequences. In the process, we must plan who will do what, where, and when—then agree to implement the plan. Finally, we must evaluate later to see how well the solution turned out. But all this can occur *only* after we deal with feelings. This is what this law teaches us.

THE LAW:
APPLIED

1. Reflect upon your last conflict. What were the (needs) (values) (feelings) on each side?
2. Discuss how conflict is about meeting needs.
3. Discuss the rationale for dealing with feelings first.
4. Discuss the steps in dealing with feelings, and offer your insights regarding each step.
5. What other laws are related to the Law of Conflict Resolution?
6. Which laws do you violate when you violate this law?

THE
LAW OF
REAL TRUTH AND TIME

Rationale: During the process of discovering and sorting out the "real truth" in
problem situations, the passage of time can magnify the problem.

One of the realities that make it difficult to be an effective leader is that it is so easy to be misled. For instance, if a leader could discover and determine the whole and real truth quickly in problem situations, making decisions and solving problems would be much easier. After all, we have the ability to solve problems—if we're not led astray.

However, a leader is dependent upon input. Through computers, we receive reliable technical information—in quantity and very quickly—which enables us to make good decisions rapidly and efficiently. But technology may not be able to give us the kind of input we need as we face those being led in the classroom or a faculty meeting and handle minute-to-minute problems on the human side of leadership. This fact presents a teacher and an administrator with a very real and formidable obstacle. Nevertheless, good leadership teaches that:

1.   A leader must know and influence the attitudes of the people he or she leads.
2.   A leader must determine the real truth in situations.
3.   A leader must be decisive and resolve problems efficiently and as quickly as possible.

THE TIME
LAG

At times, human behavior makes these three achievements difficult. That's even more reason that every leader must be aware of the "time lag" reality. This is the time between when a leader becomes aware of the problem and the time when the person or persons and the problem is dealt with and resolved. This time lag may result in larger problems—if the attitudes, beliefs, opinions, and actions of those being led are not dealt with swiftly.

Every leader must be cognizant of the fact that people form very firm opinions during a time lag. Worse, during the time delay, those being led can and do get personally committed by word and deed to firm courses of belief and action. Because there is often no communication or interaction with those being led until all the facts are known, this reality is intensified. Unfortunately, once an individual—or an entire staff, class, or student body—gets committed to certain beliefs about a situation, changing his or her strongly held attitudes regarding the situation may be very difficult.

In truth, those being led often form attitudes during the time lag without having complete information and without fully understanding situations. Then, unfortunately, even when they are exposed to more complete information, those being led can't find a way out of the attitudes, beliefs, and opinions they have formed and expressed to others during the time lag. Therefore, they hold to their judgments—even if they no longer agree with their own conclusion. In addition, many varied and complex individual commitments about a single issue can develop during the time lag, and a leader may be forced to deal with several problems rather than just one.

TAKE IMMEDIATE
ACTION

The Law of Real Truth and Time relates that problems should be dealt with as quickly as possible after they are identified. If they aren't, time can—and in all probability will—complicate, magnify, and intensify them. Problems do not go away. Even if people seem to have put them on the back burner, problems do not go away unless they are resolved. Quite the contrary. Rather, problems have a way of brewing—and resurfacing at a later time.

A leader also needs to be aware that the cumulative effect of such situations—even if the problems are small—can result in a complete breakdown in the acceptance of his or her leadership. That's why a teacher or administrator can never delay gathering truth about a problem and taking action immediately. When we don't, we are likely to end up dealing with several problems rather than one. This is the lesson taught by the Law of Real Truth and Time.

THE LAW:
APPLIED

1. If peers relate to and identify with peers, how does the time lag negatively affect a leader?
2. Those being led expect problems to be resolved by leaders. Identify the kinds of problems that (students) (staff) should expect to have resolved quickly. Discuss.
3. Identify the kinds of problems which require time to resolve. Discuss an approach which will give the leader an advantage, rather than always result in a disadvantage.

THE
LAW OF
BLAME

Rationale: If you try to pass the blame to those being led—even if it is fully deserved—they may not accept any of it. On the other hand, if you try to take all the blame, those being led aren't likely to let you shoulder all the responsibility—even if it's your fault.

To help remember both the Law of Blame and the one that follows, the Law of Credit, we might remember the words of Bear Bryant, the "immortal" football coach at the University of Alabama. He said, "I'm just a plowhand from Arkansas, but I know how to hold a team together. I know how to lift some men up, how to calm down others, until finally they've got one heartbeat together, a team. There's just three things I'd ever say: If anything goes bad, I did it. If anything goes semigood, then we did it. If anything goes real good, then you did it. That's all it takes to get people to win football games for you." This is a practical application of the Law of Blame as well as the Law of Credit. And it applies to our work with everyone we lead.

To be successful, administrators simply must know as much about human behavior as we know about budgets, ordering, scheduling, balancing classes, building buildings, and other tasks on the technical side of management. That's because we lead people. And teachers need to know as much about the behavior of students as we do about the academic subjects we teach. That's because we teach academics *to students*.

A KEY TO
ACCOUNTABILITY

Without question, we can't get enough advice or have enough information regarding how to pinpoint problems and the people who caused them—much less confront and correct those we lead. And our leading is facilitated when we can get those we lead to accept responsibility for what they have or have not achieved. That's why we spend so much time hoping and wishing that those being led will accept and fulfill their responsibilities—and urging and actually teaching them to do so. Yet, if we don't understand human behavior, we may find more failure than success when it comes to correcting problems and mistakes and leading the people who make them.

This law can be extremely beneficial in helping us get those we lead to admit mistakes as well as accept and fulfill their responsibilities and be accountable. After all, the immediate response many give when confronted with having made a mistake is, "It wasn't my fault." Without knowledge of and compliance with this law, we may approach our leadership responsibility in a way that turns those being led off to the error at hand—and to us. Worse, we may find that every effort to create a positive solution to a problem ends in a negative outcome. This is the lesson taught by the Law of Blame. This law tells us to take some or all of the responsibility for mistakes if we want those being led to accept responsibility as well. Even if a mistake wasn't our fault, this can be the best leadership stance to take.

Therefore, when a student or staff member misinterprets directions or performs a task incorrectly, the leader should simply refuse to blame—and openly accept all the blame for the failure. Why? More often than not, when we take the blame, the immediate response from the student or teacher is likely to be: "No, it wasn't all your fault; it was my fault too."

TRY TAKING
THE BLAME

If we want those being led to accept responsibility, we must try accepting total—not partial—blame for everything and anything that goes wrong within the realm of our leadership. We'll be surprised how much easier it is for people to admit that they were responsible when we take this stance. If we examine our own response when someone tried to blame us totally—or absolve us totally—we'll see why and how this law works so consistently.

There's another reason adhering to this law will almost always help a leader. The need for autonomy is within us all. We all have a need to control our own lives. Only the degree of this need varies within us. Therefore, when someone tries to take total blame, we often can't let him or her. To do so would infringe upon the need we all have to control our own lives.

Without accepting this law, you may automatically—and rightfully in some instances—take action which compounds the problem. For instance, a teacher may rightfully blame students for not listening or not following directions. An administrator may rightfully blame teachers for not putting forth the effort to get a job done. Remember, however, one of the hardest things for people to say is "I was wrong" or "It was my fault." And it often takes a special approach and unique action to get them to do so.

Remembering the Law of Blame will serve you well when you want to correct problems. It will help you when you want to get people to accept responsibility. It will help when you want to motivate those being led to positive and immediate action. Know, too, that when a leader tries to pass along or give the responsibility for failure to someone else, that leader gives up a measure of leadership control. In the process, those being led will not follow or have respect for the leader who takes such a stance. In addition, those being led may absolve themselves of all responsibility in the process—even for their own blatant mistakes. It's almost impossible to get those being led to want your leadership if you habitually place blame.

THE LAW:
APPLIED

1. Why do people hate admitting mistakes?
2. Why do people dislike taking the blame?
3. What individual motivators are behind such attitudes and behaviors?
4. How would you apply the law in the classroom after students have failed a test? What would you say to get them to accept responsibility?
5. Discuss how applying the concept of the Law of Blame would enhance your relationship with those being led.

THE
LAW OF
CREDIT

Rationale: If a leader does something extremely well or experiences a big success and tries to take all the credit, those being led may deny him or her any credit. If the leader tries to give those being led all the credit—even when deserved—they will not take it and will insist that the leader take a degree of the accolades.

A leader must handle success, achievement, and credit with extreme care. In truth, if you try to take all the credit—even when you've earned it—those being led may allow you to take bows, but they'll do so reluctantly. And they are very likely to do so with big reservations or outright disclaimers.

On the other hand, if you don't take any credit for an obvious success, those being led may actually force credit upon you. They may even give you *all* the credit. In the process, they may automatically diminish the contributions of others, including themselves.

Indeed, the human condition is often a predictable contradiction in thinking, emotion, and action. That's why a leader must understand human behavior and the responses that can be expected from those being led. Remember this law relative to your next achievement or success. It can serve you well.

COACHES GIVE US A
GOOD EXAMPLE

The Law of Credit is obvious in athletic situations. If, for instance, our coaches blamed the players rather than themselves after a loss—or tried to take all the credit for a win, we know what would eventually happen. They probably wouldn't have their jobs very long.

That's why, when the team wins, the highly-successful coach usually insists to reporters that "it's because of the character, commitment, hard work, selflessness, and dedication of the athletes." Then, all are allowed to arrive at the correct conclusion regarding the contribution of the coach when it comes to any success or failure: everyone involved was responsible to some degree. If, on the other hand, the coach took the credit for "making a team out of nothing" or "developing a superior game plan," we all know how people would respond, including the players.

Remember, if we put ourselves first and foremost when it comes to taking credit, we are making a mistake. We are not acting intelligently. When our need for achievement, recognition, and praise from others becomes a priority and we act out of it, our needs and our achievements are likely to be denied. Human behavior tells us why. And that's why the Law of Credit gives us the actions which are most likely to manage achievement and recognition appropriately. We would be wise to adhere to this law.

THE LAW:
APPLIED

1. What individual needs are met by adhering to this law?
2. When a leader takes all the credit, what reactions have you witnessed?
3. Did the response have long-term results? Discuss.
4. Discuss the expectations you hold for the behavior of leaders when success has been experienced.

THE
LAW OF
WORK SATISFACTION

Rationale: The perceptions that those being led have of their leader play a major role in determining the satisfaction they hold regarding their work.

Some of the keys to creating work satisfaction for those being led are found in lowering stress, decreasing friction, increasing morale, elevating competencies, and increasing productivity and achievement. Equally important, however, every teacher and administrator needs to be aware of and accept the fact that work satisfaction is also tied closely to the personal and professional perceptions those being led have of their leader. Unfortunately, these facts do little to lower the pressure and responsibility of being a leader in the classroom, school, or district.

FACTS ABOUT
WORK SATISFACTION

Management experts agree on two points. First, work satisfaction results from the pleasurable emotional state those being led experience as a result of their individual perceptions that work success is based upon specific characteristics which are achievable — and which those being led desire and value. Second, the more favorable the perception of the leader, the greater the satisfaction with work will be. Experts also agree that, of these two criteria for work satisfaction, the latter has the stronger direct influence on work satisfaction. Therefore, students' perceptions of teachers, teachers' perceptions of the principal, and the principals' perceptions of the superintendent influence work satisfaction more than any other single variable involved in working in a classroom, school, or district.

Without a doubt, management at any level of any organization plays a major role in determining work satisfaction for those being led. This reality proves the importance of teachers in the classroom and administrators in schools. Therefore, when it comes to leadership, we ought to look for ways to create a more favorable image — so that those being led have an increasingly favorable perception of us. The following recommendations can serve us well. Each of them will help a teacher or administrator be perceived more positively by students and the staff.

SIX WAYS TO ENHANCE OTHERS'
PERCEPTIONS OF US

First, teachers, principals, and superintendents should increase efforts to actively solicit opinions and thinking from those being led regarding work-related tasks, assignments, problems, and difficulties. Remember, one of a leader's primary tasks is to remove the obstacles and work on the wide range of problems experienced by those being led. Without such a stance, the leader may cause those being led to become frustrated by roadblocks and problems they don't have the time, know-how, responsibility, or authority to resolve. If we don't remove the roadblocks, we can't expect those being led to find satisfaction in their work.

243

Neither can we expect great effort or achievement by many.

Second, we should make every effort to continually improve and refine teacher-student and administrator-staff relations. And we should make those efforts visible to all. There is nothing more disconcerting to those being led than feeling like an "unknown" in the eyes of their leader. In addition, unknown subjective standards or shoddy evaluations make any leader appear as an enemy rather than an advocate.

Third, we should seek to discover the aspects of classroom and school management and decision making in which those being led want and need to become more involved and more successful. Then we should increase efforts to develop a plan which facilitates meaningful involvement and communicates to everyone our efforts to gain their involvement and enhance their success. In the process, we must never seek out just a few of our favorite students or teachers and involve only them. To the best of our ability, we must include everyone in some way. Some will refuse, of course. But the refusal should have to do with them, not us.

Fourth, we must magnify, glorify, and publicize the work, effort, and achievements of those being led. Furthermore, we should never give those we lead any reason to feel that they — or their work — are considered less important or less necessary than we, or our duties as a leader. Sometimes, for instance, administrators talk too much to teachers in faculty meetings or in the lounge about administrative work and pressures — and act as if there are no pressures on the staff. Likewise, administrators may excuse themselves to work in the office during an inservice day activity which teachers are required to attend. In the same vein, a teacher may act as if grading papers is more difficult than taking a test — or that a teachers' gathering is more important than conferencing with students. These are leadership mistakes. All say, "My work is more important than yours." It's difficult for students to find satisfaction in work when they receive such messages from a teacher.

Fifth, we should make the effort to increase our daily visibility and contact. Without question, "out of contact" can easily be "out of influence." This means administrators would be wise to get out of their offices, visit classrooms, and be in the halls between classes as well as before and after school. And it means a teacher must not stay behind a lectern or sit at a desk. Teachers must move around the room making continuous contact. Likewise, both students and staff need to see teachers and administrators in the cafeteria, on the playground, at practices, at rehearsals, at activities, and at other places where those being led congregate.

Sixth, a teacher, principal, or superintendent should do everything possible to increase awareness of the positive aspects of work. We must also emphasize the success that individuals and the school or district are enjoying. Remember, critics constantly tell people what the schools, including students and staff alike, aren't doing or can't do. Helping those being led recognize specific positive aspects of their work is vital to increasing work satisfaction. After all, people often look on the dark side. Frequently, they see only problems — and all too often people overlook their successes. As leaders, we must not let this happen — and for a very simple reason: People may not find satisfaction in the work we want them to do if we take such a course. Remember, satisfaction enhances work interest and effort too. Both work and satisfaction enhance the achievement of those we lead. And a great deal of this satisfaction is determined by how those being led perceive us as the leader.

MAKING ASPECTS OF
WORK MORE POSITIVE

Fortunately, there are specific actions we can take to help those being led hold a good perception of us and, as a result, increase satisfaction in work. Both teachers and administrators would be wise to look closely, use a little creativity, and see how many of those characteristics can be employed.

First, the leader must define responsibilities and possibilities as clearly as possible. Nothing reflects more poorly on the leader and work to be done than not being sure of what is required or the rewards that are possible.

Second, the leader should never, never give a person the responsibility to do a job without giving him or her a corresponding degree of authority to do the job successfully. Unless the responsibility and the authority go hand in hand, it will lower the opinions those being led have of the leader, create frustration, enhance failure, and decrease job satisfaction in the process.

Third, the leader must make sure those being led receive enough help to get the job done. At times, it may be necessary to alter the assignment or increase the number of people working on a task. Simply telling those being led to use their ingenuity and creativity to get a job done will not make them feel good about the work or the leader.

Fourth, the leader must make sure those being led have enough information to get the job done. If students or staff need more information in order to be successful with an assignment, the leader must see that they have it *before* they begin.

Fifth, the leader must make sure people have enough time to get the job done. In this regard, if we think we can assign a task and expect everyone to finish at the same time with the same degree of success, we are mistaken.

Sixth, whenever possible, the leader should make sure those being led have enough freedom to think and decide how to do the job. At times, tasks have to be done exactly the way we would do them. When such is the case, we should consider doing the task ourselves. Remember, our real concern is the end result. The process of doing the job should allow for some individuality. Therefore, our concern must be getting the job done, not always demanding that those being led follow step-by-step procedures which we have created. Of course, this is not always true regarding academic work in the classroom.

Seventh, the leader must help those being led avoid conflicting demands. Students and teachers can't be in two committee meetings at once. They can't work in their classrooms after school and meet responsibilities to an activity. There are countless examples of conflicting demands on students and teachers in a school. As leaders, we must establish priorities, respect the priorities of others, and resolve any time conflicts so that those being led can get certain jobs done—if we want to be perceived well and have work perceived well too. We must not, for instance, penalize a student for going to band and not to another activity.

Eighth, leaders must be very careful not to habitually ask those being led to do excessive amounts of work, including excessive busywork or paper work. An overabundance of such work will almost always result in job dissatisfaction. For instance, administrators must know when too much is being asked of the staff, and teachers need to know when they are piling work on students. And there are times when it is advisable to sit down and jointly determine what work can be done—and how it will be done. And, of course, there are times when leaders need to fight with superiors for those being led. Some of these battles may be lost, but they must still be fought.

If these actions are followed, the perception of the leader will be enhanced and satisfaction with work will increase. When these actions are ignored, those we lead are not likely to find satisfaction with us or their work. Worse, those being led will, in all probability, consider us to be a major cause of their dissatisfaction.

THE LAW:
APPLIED

1. How do you perceive yourself as a leader?
2. How do those you lead perceive you? How do you uncover the perceptions of those being led?
3. What do you expect of a leader? How do you model those expectations?
4. How do you enhance your perception in the eyes of those being led?
5. Discuss the eight actions a leader can take to enhance his or her perception in the eyes of those being led.

THE
MYTHS OF
THE PUT-DOWN, PUT-ON, AND PUT-OFF

Rationale: Leaders often inadvertently or purposely use three techniques—the *put-down*, *put-on*, and *put-off*—to handle people and problems, but all are guaranteed to magnify or perpetuate the problem and turn those being led away from the leader.

The *put-down*, *put-on*, and *put-off* are commonly used. And each ploy has its own properties and objectives. But they are more than behaviors. They are actually techniques that leaders choose to use against those being led. Unfortunately, they can become habits. They are easy traps, and the opportunity to fall into them exists daily in a classroom, school, or central office.

One reason it's easy to fall into the habit of using the *put-down*, *put-on*, or *put-off* is because we think each works. In fact, using these techniques may make us feel superior, smart, or clever. We may even think those being led feel the same way. And a close look will reveal that those being led use these techniques as well. In fact, they employ them against peers and leaders alike. Yet, close observation will reveal that these three techniques only allow leaders to fool themselves momentarily. These techniques are three bad habits that hold us back from success. We need to break these habits.

THE
PUT-DOWN

The put-down always has to do with victimizing others. It is used most often to show superiority. We employ it to ward off something that surprises or perplexes us or makes us angry. We also employ it to avoid dealing with an individual. Most often, the use of the put-down is spontaneous. It's a personal reaction in a professional situation.

Many teachers habitually use the put-down in discipline situations with students. Administrators use it when their authority is questioned or challenged by the staff. One thing is certain: it is used when a leader does not know what to do—or how to handle a person or situation professionally. Here, the leader can pretend superiority when inferiority is the real feeling or condition.

The put-down is often in the form of sarcastic comments and other words that degrade. Unfortunately, it tells those being led that we don't approve of or like them. It is an open show of disrespect in an uncaring and inconsiderate way. We know it violates, but the habit overtakes our intellect, and we use it. That's why we need to remind ourselves continually not to use the put-down. To demean any individual for any reason should be beneath our dignity and the dignity of those we lead—and against all of our own principles. This habit can be broken. We need only remind ourselves to say nothing unless we have something of value and relevance to offer—regardless of the situation.

THE
PUT-ON

The put-on has more to do with ourselves than others. It allows us to pretend we know something we don't or be someone we aren't. However, this technique, too, gives us the opposite of what we want. Usually, the put-on is used as a ploy to make us look good or raise our image in the eyes of others. Unfortunately, it may make us feel more important for the moment, but it does not make others feel the same way about us.

The put-on is used in many ways. We pretend to have knowledge we don't have or pretend that we are doing something important when we're not. We pretend we're listening and interested in what someone is saying when we're not. We indicate agreement when we really disagree. That's the key to the put-on. It has, in one way or another, an air of phoniness. This is one of the reasons it rarely works. It is never genuine.

We need to remind ourselves of one fact to gain the motivation needed to break this habit and eliminate it from our repertoire of techniques forever: people usually see through it immediately. Students do. Teachers do. Administrators do. Parents do. Those being led cannot and will not relate to its use or the leader who uses it.

THE
PUT-OFF

The put-off always has to do with getting out of something. Most of us have been guilty of using the put-off. Sometimes we use it simply to gain more time. Yet, it is often used to avoid doing a task, making a promise, or admitting that a job didn't get done. It is also used to avoid admitting failure. Sometimes it is used to pretend we are on top of a task when we are not.

The put-off can get the most conscientious leader into trouble. It can cause us to make promises to those being led that we can't or don't intend to keep. In using the put-off, we may use a wide variety of phrases. For instance, to a request we might say, "I haven't decided" or "I haven't made a decision yet." We might also say, "I'll think about it" or "I haven't had time to give it any thought yet." Or we might use comments such as "Let's visit and see;" "If I can find the time, I'll do it;" or "Maybe we will do it." For instance, I recently asked a young student when his class was going on its field trip, and he disappointedly replied, "The teacher said we aren't going." Surprised, I asked, "What did your teacher say?" To this, the youngster replied, "He said *maybe* we would go—but his *maybe* always means no."

The put-off can also allow us to pass the buck to someone else. This form of put-off is likely to hurt our relationships with students and staff members alike. Remember, leaders can't talk to those being led about meeting their responsibilities when the leaders don't meet their own. That's a fact. The put-off makes people doubt our ability and sincerity. It makes those being led question our honesty. That's why an open admission is always better than the put-off.

THREE
BAD HABITS

The put-down, put-on, and put-off are three bad habits leaders fall into for one reason or another—especially if they have lots of people to lead or loads of work to do. Using these techniques usually results in giving us the opposite of what we want and need as teachers and administrators. They make us look ignorant rather than intelligent, untruthful rather than truthful, incapable rather than capable, and unprofessional rather than professional. In the process, they drive people away from us rather than toward us.

In all of our methods and techniques—as well as attitudes and behaviors—we need to examine three leadership characteristics. First, we need to look at how we feel about people. Second, we need to examine how we treat people as a result of those feelings. Third, we need to know what kinds of behavior we project to students and staff when we are trying to get work done.

People are turned off by dishonesty and phoniness no matter what its form. Most will come to dislike anything or anyone who is phony. The put-down, put-on, and put-off are all based on dishonesty and phoniness. That's why we must fight falling into these three traps. After all, the put-down, put-on, and put-off may be easy traps to fall into, but they are hard traps for a teacher or administrator to get out of. Causing others to want your leadership is very difficult if you use those ploys.

THE LAW:
APPLIED

1. Identify the kinds of put-downs leaders use. What individual needs are denied with this ploy?
2. Identify the kinds of put-ons leaders use. What individual needs are denied with this ploy?
3. Identify the kinds of put-offs leaders use. What individual needs are denied with this ploy?
4. How do students use each with (peers) (teachers and administrators)?
5. Which of these actions do you use?

THE
PRINCIPLES OF
HANDLING ALIBIS, OBJECTIONS, AND COMPLAINTS

Rationale: Alibis, objections, and complaints from those being led are inevitable. However, all are different behaviors that must be treated in unique ways, or problems will not be resolved and may be magnified—and will result in creating additional problems with those being led.

If we have been a teacher or an administrator for any length of time, we have probably heard every alibi, objection, and complaint those being led can offer. And all can cause us a wide variety of emotions, from disgust to frustration to anger. Regardless of our response, we know that all are roadblocks to effective leadership. If we can't move past each of these behaviors, getting those being led to do what we want them to do can be difficult.

We first need to be aware that there are differences in these three behaviors. And in order to handle them successfully, we need to be able to recognize those differences. Furthermore, these behaviors can't be ignored if we want to decrease their frequency or handle the problems they can cause.

Without question, we must first listen carefully to determine which of the three problems we are dealing with. In handling each behavior, we need to use the analytical technique of listening to determine an appropriate response. And if we *listen*, we may find that a large part of each of these obstacles will begin to dissolve in the process. Conversely, none will disappear if we react angrily or defensively when they are offered. Let's talk about how to deal professionally and effectively with the alibis, objections, and complaints that remain after we have made it a practice to listen.

ALIBIS SHOW A
VOID IN INTENT

Alibis are quite different from objections and complaints. If they are not treated differently, big problems can result. It's easy to see why. Those offering alibis usually have *lost interest* in the activity related to the alibi. Administrators must remember this fact when handling teachers and their alibis. Teachers must remember this fact when handling the alibis of students. The alibi is expressed by such token offerings as, "I was too busy," "I'm going to do it tomorrow," "I didn't know what you wanted me to do," or "I didn't know we had decided to do it yet."

We must attempt to analyze the cause of the alibi—not the alibi itself. A series of questions can help us with this task: Can the person do the work? Is the assignment or task missing something in the eyes of the person? Would the person do something else better? After all, we might be much better off altering or changing the assignment rather than holding to a dead-end course. Remember, lack of interest is the primary reason behind most alibis.

Therefore, until we discover the reason behind the alibi, we can't employ these techniques to get the behavior we need: First, we must listen closely and respond quickly. If a student says, "I forget the directions," the teacher should say, "Here are notes." If a person offers the alibi, "I've been so busy," the leader should respond quickly with, "You can have more time." Then, we must ask to see the person later to find the real cause behind the alibi. When this action is taken, the leader is positioned to deal with the real problem: lack of interest.

OBJECTIONS INCLUDE "BUT"

Objections are easy to identify because they usually contain the word *but*. They are expressed by such phrases as, "But I don't know how to do it," "But you didn't say I had to do it immediately," or "But I didn't have time." In reality, however, the response is caused by those being led wanting or expecting *more*—whether it's more help, more prodding, more information, or more time to complete an assignment.

Of paramount importance is the fact that the objecting person may still have an interest in the project or task at hand. This is crucial to handling the objection. That's why a leader's proper analysis of the reason for the objection is vitally important. We need to ask ourselves four questions which will guide our approach with the objecting person: Is the objection intelligent? Is ignorance revealed by the objection? Is the objection emotional? Is the objection analytical?

To get answers to these questions, the leader must listen carefully to every objection. It's the failure to listen that gets a leader into trouble—because our response to objections is important. Remember, unlike the person who offers an alibi, the objector still has interest in the task, activity, or subject. If the objection has merit, the leader must share points of agreement. In the process, the benefits of the leader's rationale must outweigh the person's objections, or the objection cannot and will not be overcome. If the objector is wrong, the leader must educate him or her and let the person down gracefully. This is a must. In either case, however, the leader must ask questions rather than tell, give benefits rather than ultimatums, and relate assurances rather than demands. Using these three techniques will give the leader more success in handling objections—and make the task of teaching easier and more effective.

COMPLAINTS REVEAL UPSET

Complaints are usually the result of some kind of upset. They are expressed by those being led saying, "This is wrong," "This isn't fair," or "I don't think we should have to do this," or "What you're asking just isn't right." Because the leader is often annoyed or upset with complaints, there's one important facet of complaints a leader simply can't overlook: Inherent in complaints *is* interest. Furthermore, complaints usually indicate a certain amount of involvement in an issue. Otherwise, the person would not complain. That's why, if the leader ignores the complaint or the complaining person, the leader may change interest to apathy. And apathy is a huge problem. The wise leader will do anything to keep interest and avoid apathy.

Complaints require a full explanation on the part of the leader. For best results, the leader should always allow the person to say what is on his or her mind. If the person is totally or partially right, the leader should correct the situation immediately—and thank the person for bringing the matter to his or her attention. If the person is wrong, the leader should explain and give assurance in a caring and gentle way—without a hint of reprimand—in order to hold interest and involvement. Above all, the leader must not do anything that makes either the person or the complaint appear unimportant.

EVERY LEADER MUST HANDLE THESE THREE BEHAVIORS

Alibis, objections, and complaints are inherent in any leadership situation. They are normal. They should be expected—and even anticipated once we know our people. Teachers should know which students are likely to use which behavior. Principals and superintendents should have similar knowledge. Yet, all these behaviors are different in nature and need to be approached and managed differently. If we lump them together and try to treat all these behaviors in the same way, our chances for failure are greater than our chances for success.

All three behaviors require that the leader listen in order to analyze. However, each must be handled differently from this beginning point. The mistake is to take each personally and respond personally. If the leader responds in less than a professional way, the situation will not be corrected. Worse, the teacher or administrator's response can affect other students and other teachers in the school.

When students say teachers don't listen and when teachers say that administrators don't and won't listen, many other problems begin. And all leadership skills are of no avail unless the leader is positioned to lead. That's why we must handle alibis, objections, and complaints skillfully. And when we do, we can be confident that we will not find ourselves offering one of these roadblocks to others as the reason we can't be effective.

THE LAW: APPLIED

1. Identify the individual needs which are met by handling these three behaviors.
2. Discuss how these behaviors relate to the Law of Blame and the Law of Credit.
3. Can you identify those being led who use these ploys? If you can, discuss ways to counsel them at times other than when they are using these ploys.
4. Discuss leadership problems that result when interest is lost.
5. Discuss which is more difficult: creating interest or handling these behaviors. Why?

16

THE LAWS AND PRINCIPLES OF POWER AND CONTROL AND THE LEADERSHIP OF PEOPLE

Power and control are two advantages most leaders think they must have in order to lead effectively. And they must. Yet, two questions must be answered: What kind of control? What kind of power? To lead effectively, teachers and administrators must understand power and know how to use it to cause others to want their leadership. If they don't, they won't have influential power or control very long—because those being led will take it away from them.

The story of power has been the same since time began. Leaders want power. They fight to get power. They abuse power. They lose power.

The objective should be to want power, get power, manage power, share power, and keep power. Then, constructive leadership power and control can be maintained. These laws will serve us well when it comes to control and power—if we adhere to them.

The Law of Dominance
The Law of Power
The Principle of Sharing Power
The Theory of Power and Responsibility
The Law of Collaboration
The Law of Respect
The Law of Core Values
The Law of Problems
The Reality of Problem Existence
The Reality of Problem Solutions
The Law of Control
The Law of Self-Control
The Law of Morale Fluctuations
The Law of Disclosure

THE
LAW OF
DOMINANCE

Rationale: Dominance is a destructive leadership characteristic that results when management attempts to gain or keep control by making itself appear superior by attempting to make others appear inferior.

All leaders want to feel that they are on top of their jobs. Every leader wants to feel competent. All want to have a sense of control within a classroom, a school, or the school district—because they are responsible and accountable for all within the framework of their position. Yet, there is a vast difference between leadership control and leadership dominance. And all leaders need to know the difference. When they do not, leaders are likely to create a climate and culture that curtails individual growth, stifles the productivity of those being led, and is destructive to both leader and follower alike. In addition, dominance can also be destructive to the success of the institution.

DOMINANCE...
DEFINED

Literally, *to dominate* means "to name under." This fact should give teachers and administrators a linguistic as well as psychological appreciation of the word. Obviously, for one substance to be *under*, another must be *above*. It also means to "rule over." Therefore, if a leader feels a need or desire to dominate, at least part of that desire comes from wanting to be over someone else in a superior kind of way. Unfortunately, when a teacher or administrator dominates students or the staff, he or she usually considers himself or herself superior by finding others inferior—automatically. That's the ugly truth of domination.

Examples in life are countless. The misery of domination can be found anywhere. Husbands dominate wives, and wives dominate husbands. Governments may dominate people and may even try to dominate other governments. The results are always the same: attempts are made to gain the position of being over another. A close look will reveal that in almost every instance, a feeling of superiority is achieved by trying to prove that others are inferior. It is a sad reality, and little satisfaction is gained from knowing that selfishness, insecurity, or a need for power and control may be the forces that propel the desire to dominate into a real-life reality.

From experience, I have found that the feeling of insecurity is most often at fault. More often than not, the insecure leader will assume the mask of authoritarianism—or try to—with some or all of the people in his or her life. As educators, we should immediately recognize any insecurity found in domination. Recognition is not the only problem. Teachers and administrators sometimes fail to practice those principles they have learned regarding dominance, healthy leadership, and the formation of working partnerships. And sometimes teachers and administrators get these principles confused when applying them to their jobs as leaders.

For instance, teachers may believe that just because students are children, students are beneath them. We may not think students have certain rights. Administrators may think some things are none of teachers' business. The list goes on and on.

Facts are facts, and evidence assures us that insecurity can exist, even in the individual who seems and acts extremely secure—such as a teacher, department head, principal, or superintendent. Unfortunately, those leaders who dominate are seldom as competent or happy as they would like to be—even when their efforts to dominate appear to work for them. Their feelings of insecurity are ever-present and hound their every action, behavior, and decision. Insecurity even rules their appointments of subordinates and staff members.

THE TRUEST SYNONYM FOR INSECURITY

Insecurity is a vague description of several very well-defined feelings or emotions. Perhaps the truest synonym for insecurity is *unacceptability*. In truth, it is the conviction of self-unacceptability with which the insecure leader is struggling. This conviction is often expressed as a desire to dominate those being led.

As we well know, it is not uncommon to see a teacher or administrator who feels unacceptable to those being led. We've all heard, too, that the leader sits in a lonely chair. If he or she does, it's because the leader has made it that way. But the fact remains that if a form of dominance has been built, neither students nor the staff will be drawn to the leader. Dominance puts those being led in a different place and on a different level. It forces people away. In the classroom, young people are seldom drawn toward a dominating adult.

Perhaps history can furnish no better example of dominance in leadership than a Machiavelli or a Hitler. These individuals built empires out of the selfishness and insecurity which drove them to perfect their methods of dominating. On a lesser scale, the same type of domination occurs in homes as well as classrooms and administrative offices. Because of insecurity, people try to build their own little dynasties in which absolute control is maintained by domination. The result, unfortunately, is that superiority is always gained by making others appear inferior. It is never gained by acting in superior ways.

Proving others inferior is not our function or mission. Rather, we are star makers. And none can deny that some people are ideal victims for the unscrupulous teacher or administrator who is a dominator. If we, as leaders, recognize our own need to dominate, we can deal with these feelings. If we cannot recognize this need in ourselves, we teach others to operate in a similar manner—out of their weaknesses rather than their strengths.

DOMINANCE IS ALMOST ALWAYS A DESTRUCTIVE FORCE

The Law of Dominance teaches us that dominance is a force that is almost never constructive and almost always destructive in some way. The desire to dominate is strongest among those who have the least legitimate claim to adulation. They err in failing to realize that real power and authority can't be taken. They must be given. Those leaders who try to dominate often cling to the belief that the world is a savage place where the weak perish and the strong survive. They overlook the fact that if this is so, it is because of their own savagery. It is hoped that students and staff do not learn to dominate or be dominated from teachers or administrators. Instead, teachers and administrators must help those being led build human strengths, not nurture or capitulate to individual weaknesses.

The Law of Dominance tells us that the potential of students or the school team will never be reached with leaders who dominate. The law also tells us that, eventually, the dominator will succumb. Make no mistake: These leaders do not succeed over a long period of time. And in this era, those who dominate aren't likely to survive the short term. There is no way a teacher can beat down a roomful of students day after day and year after year without repercussions. There is no way a principal or superintendent can dominate an entire faculty and staff over the long term. Eventually, people will rise up and overthrow such a leader. They really should. After all, none of us want this kind of leadership. And in today's world, we don't have to accept it.

THE LAW: APPLIED

1. What approaches, such as shared decision making, are violated by dominance?
2. Identify all the laws that are violated by dominance.
3. Can a leader dominate even when he or she doesn't intend to? Discuss.
4. Assuming that insecurity is a major cause of dominance, discuss situations in which we might be prone to move in the direction of dominance.
5. What individual needs are denied by dominance?
6. What leadership laws are violated by dominance?
7. In what ways do you think "getting the job done" requires domination? Discuss.
8. Share experiences you have had under the leadership of a dominator. Include your feelings, your behavior toward the leader, and your level of achievement.

THE
LAW OF
POWER

Rationale: It's normal for a leader to want and need power and to take action to get it, but if a leader cannot manage and share power, he or she will lose it—and maybe all of it.

Educators often talk about needing control. They mean they want *power*. Students talk about wanting a voice. They are seeking a degree of power. Teachers express the need to give advice, have influence, and make decisions. They're talking about wanting some measure of power to determine the course of events and decisions which govern their professional lives. Teachers talk about receiving support. They are talking about receiving some power. Administrators talk about having their hands tied. They're talking about a loss of power.

The need for power is within us all. It's one of the secondary needs of human beings. In truth, this need varies from one person to another only in its intensity—and some of the intensity can be caused by the job we are held accountable to do. Whether a person is a teacher, a counselor, a nurse, or an administrator, he or she wants and needs a measure of power. Whether he or she is a cook, a custodian, or a secretary, he or she wants a degree of power. Students want power too—and so do parents. If any of us intend to get and keep a measure of power, however, we need to know its properties. It will also help us to know the value of empowerment.

HISTORY TEACHES US WHAT WE
NEED TO KNOW ABOUT POWER

Since the beginning of time, the story of the struggle for power has revealed the same message. People have wanted power and fought to get it. Once they obtained it, however, many of them abused it, and the results were inevitable. They lost much or all of their power. We can learn from this reality. After all, the idea is to want power, get power, manage and share power, and keep power. Unless we can manage and share power, we can be sure we will lose it—and for good reason. If we deny others power or abuse power, we actually open the door for those being led to try to take it away from us—with the blessing of everyone else, including those who have little desire for power.

All social movements have resulted from two factors: people's need to have a measure of control over their lives and the withholding or abuse of power by those who have it. The civil rights movement, the labor movement, the consumer advocate movement, the women's movement, and all others resulted because of a need for power and others' abuse of power. In regard to the labor movement, for instance, management had all the power in the first part of the 20th century. Yet management chose not to treat workers well. It refused to give labor any power. Working conditions, hours, and wages were determined without input from or consideration for labor. Management's abuse of power produced the inevitable result. Workers organized and took action to correct their plight. In most cases, they managed to take considerable power away from management, some of which management needed desperately in order to operate effectively and profitably. And when labor abused its newly

The Laws
and Principles
of Power and
Control and
the Leadership
of People

gained power and acted contrary to the welfare of companies and customers by restricting productivity, raising wages to record heights, and striking to get more and more benefits—thus contributing to higher prices of products and services—it lost much of its power. Why? Companies closed or moved to other places—or made moves to automate in the face of higher wages. And customers refused to pay higher prices and bought elsewhere, including products from other countries.

A similar situation once existed between teachers and administrators: administrators had all the power over teachers. And teachers would be the first to admit that they organized for the same reasons as did labor in industry. Clearly, with the power both teachers and administrators now have for the betterment of our schools, we must learn how not to abuse that power if we intend to cause others to want our leadership.

SHARING POWER IS THE BEST WAY TO MANAGE AND KEEP POWER

As teachers and administrators, we need to know that if we want the leadership and management power necessary to function effectively in a classroom or school, we must manage the power we have. Sharing power, unfortunately, is not easy for some leaders. But we must remember that not everyone in a school has a measure of power which can be used for or against our efforts to lead and manage effectively. Students have power. Teachers and administrators have power. Cooks, custodians, aides, and nurses have power. And parents have power. Therefore, if we intend to create a productive and satisfying school climate, we must pull people into our orbit and give them a measure of control over their own lives—which includes input into the decisions affecting the work they do. Recognizing this simple fact can make the task of leading easier. Fortunately, there are many ways in which administrators and teachers can share power.

For instance, we can involve those being led. We can take their input and use it. We can delegate the authority and responsibility to get specific tasks done. We can form advisory committees. We can ask those being led to be involved in certain decisions—within the parameters that we feel are reasonable and necessary to run a classroom, school, or district. We can suggest that those being led work with us and help decide the kinds of rules, regulations, and procedures needed in the classroom and the school. We can also pay attention to the feelings of people and respond in positive and proactive ways. We can make room for their ideas and opinions, because ideas are power. Most important, we can treat those being led in ways that show we intend to place their needs on a level equal with our own. This action, after all, is the ultimate act of sharing power as a professional.

HAVING FUNCTIONAL POWER IS A LEADERSHIP MUST

As teachers and administrators, we must have functional power in the classroom, school, and district. If we lose it, we're headed for certain trouble. That's why we must take great care to manage the power we hold. If we tell people, "Do it because I say so" or "Do it because I'm the boss," we are abusing power and negative results are inevitable. To hold power, we must adhere to four guidelines:

First, we need to decide how we can give those being led a measure of control over their work and their lives. Second, we need to decide what power we can share with various people throughout the school. Third, we must be careful to avoid trying to grab more and more power from wherever we can. Fourth, we must make sure we don't abuse the power we have.

We've all seen people who once had power and abused it—and became powerless in an instant. We must make sure we are never among these people. After all, as educators, we should be the first to agree that leaders who abuse power shouldn't have any.

THE LAW: APPLIED

1. To cause others to want your leadership, what kinds of power do you need?
2. What actions can you take to get these powers?
3. Discuss the various ways those being led take power away from a leader.
4. What powers do those you lead need in order to be highly successful (in school) (in life)?
5. How can you help those being led get those powers?
6. Discuss the statement, "If we wait until those we lead show that they can handle power, we will never give them any. That's why we must give them power first."

THE
PRINCIPLE OF
SHARING POWER

Rationale: Sharing power enhances meaningful involvement and achievement, but a leader's real and imaginary fears regarding sharing power with those being led can make a leader avoid even considering the practice.

When we think about sharing power with others, it's very normal for us to experience more fears and reluctance than we care to admit. These fears, real and imaginary, can prevent us from considering the notion of sharing power at all—or employing the practice to the full extent that we should. And when we initiate action to empower those being led, these feelings may intensify. In fact, we may lean in the opposite direction and believe we have to do all we can to protect the power we have. These normal tendencies reveal just how important power is to people, especially those who have it.

Thus, the leadership and management concepts regarding empowerment are often fought, rather than embraced and practiced. Yet, because we are told that all these concepts are coming to schools in the form of site-based management, shared decision making, and other innovations, every teacher, principal, and superintendent needs to look at these ideas closely before rejecting them. If we do, we will see that by empowering those we lead, we gain a great deal—and lose nothing.

POWER CAN BE
TYRANNICAL IN A SCHOOL

Without question, real leadership control is achieved by handling power appropriately to get high productivity and high satisfaction for everyone. Remember, when power is abused, management control can be lost—sometimes totally. Again, history gives us all kinds of examples to prove this point—from Hitler to Stalin to Mao Tse-tung. And when the abuse is political, sometimes the whole world has to pay the bill. But on any level, wherever there is a kernel of power, someone may benefit—or someone may suffer. This is the reality of holding power.

It may seem that this message doesn't apply to a teacher, principal, or superintendent. But it does. Abuse of power can be tyrannical in a classroom or an office. It can be tyrannical in a meeting of school board members. And someone can pay a huge price for the abuse of power in any of these settings. Many people have.

Despite all that we know, however, our hair may curl at the thought of sharing the power that we consider a part of our "leadership domain." As a result, we may fight sharing our power. Therefore, at the very least, we should know which kinds of power we have and may use—and which kinds of power we should avoid using unless we are on very firm ground. That's because we will, at various times, find it necessary to use all kinds of power. We need to make wise choices in employing these forms of power in different situations in the classroom and school. After all, even with plans for the empowerment of students, faculty, parents, and staff members, we will still have to use our own power. And we may have to use it more often than we like.

There are three approaches to the use of power, and we can define three categories of power based on those approaches: *guided power*, *restrained power*, and *raw power*.

USING GUIDED POWER

Whenever possible, *guided power* should be our first choice. When using guided power, we direct people toward a desired course. Guided power includes instructing, teaching, supervising, and influencing. It involves explaining and giving information. But the emphasis is on guiding—not demanding, forcing, or punishing. Using guided power is the best way to cause others to want our leadership.

There are many ways to use guided power. For instance, we can show those being led how to be successful. We can talk to a person about how his or her behavior is hurting others. Or we can point out how an attitude or behavior is self-destructive. We can use various techniques, such as reasoning, cajoling, or appealing to an individual's better self to bring about the attitudes or behaviors we desire. With all these approaches, the emphasis is on guiding.

USING RESTRAINED POWER

When it's necessary to use our leadership power, we should always use *restrained power*. Restrained power may be called for because the use of guided power may not be appropriate to the situation, or we may have already traveled the road of guided power to no avail. There is a difference between asking, reasoning, and explaining first—and jumping in and using restrained power immediately. And there's a difference between using restrained power and using raw power.

It may be a case of a teacher's being involved in a policy or procedure violation—or even a breach of ethics. It may be the case of a student's exhibiting disruptive or disrespectful behavior. Regardless of the situation, we subdue the desire to use force or punishment when using restrained power. We avoid excess or extravagance in any direction, including making our points. We keep power under control by holding back and refusing to use it—even though we have it and the other person is aware of this fact. With restrained power, we restrict the use of any kind of force by not going to extremes. We're firm, yes. Serious, yes. Direct, yes. Upset, yes. Angry, yes. But we're not hostile or out of control.

USING RAW POWER

Raw power is what the name implies. In this case, we are not necessarily teaching, counseling, or persuading. Neither are we concerned about holding anything back. The power we reveal is open, not tempered. It is power in a crude state, unmasked and unrestrained. Raw power may involve the use of coercion and may result in our inflicting some kind of pain.

At some point, we will all probably use raw power. It should be avoided, of course. After all, raw power can cause us to become everything we are criticizing—and even worse. That's why we should use guided and restrained power whenever possible. Even with our biggest issues, employee termination and student expulsion, we should avoid the use of raw power.

*The Laws
and Principles
of Power and
Control and
the Leadership
of People*

Using guided or restrained power always keeps us in control of ourselves and the situation. Using raw power does not. Raw power has a tendency to show observers that we have lost control. Raw power has widespread consequences and affects people in damaging ways. There's no doubt about it. Remember, our relationship with one staff member or one student affects our relationships with all employees or all students. And peers almost always identify with and relate to peers—not the leader with the power. Therefore, those being led will identify with anyone who has experienced our raw power. And they will come to one conclusion: "If the leader did something bad to my peer, he or she *can* and *will* do something bad to me."

In truth, raw power is a weapon of frustration and ignorance. We often see it used by parents in public. A child is physically struck or verbally whipped, slapped for crying, shaken fiercely for spilling milk, or threatened. When we witness such actions, we may feel disgust. We may even feel like using raw power ourselves on the parent. We can learn many lessons from this example. As teachers and administrators, we are in the same position every day. We have opportunities to inflict raw power upon those being led. The choice is ours. It's important that we choose to handle power responsibly and make sure the lessons we teach those being led about empowerment and about handling power are positive ones. One thing is certain: Unless we understand power, it is very unlikely that we will share it with those being led. In fact, we may vow to give them as little power as possible. And the cause is fear. This law teaches us that those being led will experience less involvement and achievement as a result of our fear.

THE LAW:
APPLIED

1. What are your fears regarding the sharing of power with (students) (teachers) (administrators) (parents)?
2. Which of those fears do you regard as "real" because you have "proof"? Which may be unfounded fears?
3. Reveal how you use guided power in (teaching) (correcting an attitude or behavior).
4. Reveal how you use restrained power in (teaching) (correcting an attitude or behavior).
5. Reveal how you use raw power in (teaching) (correcting an attitude or behavior).
6. Discuss the frightening aspects of raw power.
7. Do you witness raw power in others in your school? Discuss.
8. Is using raw power ever necessary? Discuss.

THE
THEORY OF
POWER AND RESPONSIBILITY

Rationale: To get those being led to be more responsible, we must first give them more power—and the more power we give them, the more responsible and accountable for performance we can expect them to be.

Behaviorists say that people want only one thing—their own way. Unfortunately, however, people can't have their own way all the time. Students can't, teachers can't, and neither can administrators. This need for our own way may be the reason many people believe and proclaim that they would handle power more skillfully and capably—if they had it. This reality may also explain why, even though those being led have made the same complaints and leaders have registered the same counter promises for centuries, the cycle continues. Indeed, the adage "Power corrupts and absolute power corrupts absolutely" seems to be the belief of many.

Make no mistake: Power is a big issue today. And it is certain that leaders who handle power well seem able to earn a special kind of loyalty and devotion from those they lead. That's why it's appropriate to talk about how we who have the power handle it as teachers and administrators. After all, everyone we work with or work for wants more power.

HAVING POWER IS
HAVING RESPONSIBILITY

First of all, we need to recognize that the more power we have, the more responsibility we have. If we want the people we are leading to be more responsible, we must give them more power—and the more power we can give them, the more responsible we can expect them to be. If we say "hogwash" to such a statement, we had better think again. The people within organizations who have the most power are the ones always held the most responsible and the most accountable.

When it comes to having power in a school system, the low people on the totem pole are students. Make no mistake regarding this fact: Students may be the entire focus of our work and our mission, but students are the least likely to have any real power. Teachers may also claim to be low on the totem pole with regard to power in the school. After all, the feeling of being powerless has long been a complaint of teachers. Yet, we all know that teachers often have *absolute power* when it comes to running the classroom. And is there an administrator alive who does not think he or she is powerless at times?

LOOKING AT POWER
FROM TWO VIEWPOINTS

That's why we must always look at power from at least two viewpoints: our own and that of those being led. As teachers and administrators, we should recognize that the management of

*The Laws
and Principles
of Power and
Control and
the Leadership
of People*

power is the measure of self-confidence, ability, and maturity. It is also a measure of the real esteem we have for others. True, we may occasionally have to exert power against the will of those being led. But we should do so only after we have spent a good deal of time thinking through various alternatives, including our approach to the two vital "p's"—people and power. Only when we understand the dimensions of managing power can we have good judgment in using it. If we don't have such knowledge, we are apt to misuse power—and become more dangerous than we will ever suspect.

We must always be aware of the positive and negative facets of having and using power. When we are forced to act against a consensus, we should be careful to explain our actions to those being led. Far too often, others think the people in positions of power look upon their positions in just that way—as positions. We need to look upon having power as a responsibility, a privilege, and a function. If we don't, we don't understand the concept of power itself. Worse, we will surely find that our power works against us and others.

Sometimes people—including groups—make a mistake in the person they choose as their leader. We've all seen students choose one of the most hostile or poorest students as a model. And we've seen the staff choose a leader whose biggest claim to fame was confronting or attacking every administrative decision. In those cases, an individual or a group has chosen to invest in a person with power. These leaders are often charismatic. Hitler, for example, mesmerized people and gained influence from them.

WE DESERVE
OUR LEADERS

A close look will reveal that this kind of leader seems to be everyone's friend and turns out to be no one's. When looking at the havoc engendered by such people (and we don't have to use the extreme of Hitler to make our point), we must remember that we deserve our leaders because we allow them to lead. When we watch one student, one teacher, one parent, or one administrator seize leadership without the consent of those being led, we are seeing a forfeiture of rights on the part of those who say nothing and make allowances.

Yet, the way is paved for such people by the leader who has the power and abuses it—for whatever reason—while those being led seemingly look the other way. Challenging a leader's power can serve a purpose. As school leaders, we ought to keep these realities in mind when someone opposes our leadership. After all, the objector can be right, just as he or she can be wrong. The mere fact that we are the leaders does not make us right and the objector wrong. Neither does it give us license to be a bad leader—even for a moment—or to abuse power or abuse the people who are causing us problems.

STUDENTS DON'T ALWAYS
GET TO CHOOSE

In education, there is a dichotomy with regard to leadership. Some of our leaders are chosen, and some are not. For instance, students in some schools do choose their teachers—but the vast majority do not. And students seldom get to choose their coach, counselor, or teacher in the visual and performing arts. The power inherent in the job is in the hands of whoever happens to be the classroom teacher of a grade or course—or coach or counselor. The implications of such a reality can be awesome. Because we are continually choosing leaders for students, however, we must take very seriously the responsibility that comes with our power over students if we want to understand power and make it work for us as leaders.

On the other hand, faculty committees are usually headed by colleagues who volunteer or who are elected or chosen. We should take these selections seriously too. And we who are the appointed leaders in the classroom, school, or district must always have compassion for the person in the leadership position—and compassion for each other. It's often easy for us to sit on the sidelines and make judgments about what we would do if we were the leaders in a given situation, when we are not. Sometimes, teachers judge other teachers, and principals judge other principals. And some principals are always second-guessing the superintendent. That is wrong, and it constitutes a misdirected use of power.

Our input about another's leadership should publicly support the positive and reasonably—but privately and professionally—object to the negative. If we can't object directly to the person responsible, then we ought not object at all. But we should never undermine leadership by pitting our own power against another's. To do so is to create an internal war and solves nothing. We must also be able to distinguish our personal biases from common sense that works for the good of all. If we can't, we shall again misuse power.

TEACHERS ARE IN CLASS BY MANDATE, NOT BY STUDENTS' CHOICE

We can never overlook the fact that teachers are in the classroom by mandate—not by students' choice. They create lessons, give or deny help, assign work, plan lessons, choose directions, grade papers, and do almost anything else they wish. But if teachers think of themselves as having only a *position* of power, they are headed for trouble. Teachers must recognize that their power comes from their function and their function brings with it privilege and responsibility. With this stance, they are more likely to be good learning leaders in the classroom and know how to handle well their almost absolute power over students. Even so, there are lessons about power that teachers and administrators need to learn.

Teachers and administrators also need to recognize that power in classrooms and schools should not be limited to a small circle of students or educators. If teachers and administrators give power only to their favorites, they are making a mistake. Power needs to be generously distributed to reap the benefits taught by this law. If leaders are unable to use power generously when it's difficult to do so, then using power generously when it's easy will make no mark at all. That's how people respond to power. Students, teachers, and administrators are no exception to this reality.

We must be aware that many people understand little about the problems and opportunities connected with managing power. In the classroom, students certainly have no real way of knowing about these problems and opportunities. But teachers can teach them. The best way to teach this lesson is to share power, because responsibility and experience are two excellent teachers of how to handle power constructively. Helping those being led to understand the responsibilities involved in the power of leadership is time well spent.

*The Laws
and Principles
of Power and
Control and
the Leadership
of People*

The more power we can give to students, the better. The same is true of giving the staff power. If administrators don't give staff members power, they may not be able to handle power when they do get it. Worse, they are very likely to mishandle the power they already have. And on some level, all the people in our schools today, from teachers to cooks to custodians, have considerable power. This law teaches us that the more power we can give to those being led, the better. And the more power we can give them, the more responsible we can expect them to be. This law is one of the foundations for greater achievement and accountability.

**THE LAW:
APPLIED**

1. Discuss how power and responsibility are linked.
2. Share powers that you believe should be given to (students) (teachers) (administrators).
3. Discuss powers that (teachers) (administrators) have — which should be given back to the other. Why?
4. Can those being led be given more responsibility without giving them power? Discuss.
5. What powers do students need in order to be more responsible?
6. How can we teach students how to handle these powers?

THE
LAW OF
COLLABORATION

Rationale: Collaboration is a multidimensional strategy which works only when the strategy is matched with the situation at hand and the goals to be pursued.

Leaders like the word *collaboration* when it is used to refer to a means to get support or to get jobs done. We don't like it when we think people, including those being led, are collaborating against us. Therefore, we need to be aware that collaboration has many contexts. It has multiple meanings and implications to us as well as those we lead.

Certainly, it's fashionable to collaborate. Organizations and units of government are doing it. Schools and businesses are doing it. Teachers and parents are doing it. Even regular and special education teachers are doing it. The real question is this: What does it really mean and, if it's so good, why do so many collaborative efforts fall apart or fail to have the impact we need and expect?

The fact is, like so many popular terms and concepts, collaboration suffers from misunderstanding as well as misuse. As a result, leaders often begin a project or attempt to solve a problem under the guise of collaboration, but find they can't get to the real issues, maintain momentum, or generate adequate commitment when using this strategy. As teachers and administrators, we need to understand collaboration if we intend to use it successfully.

SUCCESSFUL COLLABORATION
REQUIRES FIVE ELEMENTS

The dictionary defines *collaboration* as: "working jointly, especially in literary, scientific, or artistic work." The concept sounds simple and easy. However, the priorities, abilities, and relationships among those attempting to collaborate can vary widely—and make the strategy not so simple and not so easy. Therefore, the process requires clear understanding and careful attention—if the task or problem faced is even moderately complex.

We also need to know that collaboration for the sake of collaborating—without any investment made or significant outcome intended—is usually a waste of time and energy. Likewise, we need to be aware that successful collaboration requires at least five elements: trust, flexibility, shared resources, clear goals, and open communication. Fortunately, each of these elements is self-explanatory and doesn't require any explanation or clarification. But other aspects of collaboration do require clarification.

For instance, collaboration often is perceived as everyone participating in the effort. It's not uncommon to believe that everyone must meet and work together every minute and at every step of the process. While this is one way of collaborating, there are other effective and efficient options, depending on the tasks at hand and the goals involved. If we look at the dictionary definition of *collaboration*, we can see these differences.

For example, two scientists might work side by side as they conduct research. Each might check the other's work for accuracy and completeness. On the other hand, authors collaborating on a literary work might draft chapters or major sections of writing in isolation and later share the work with the other for critique and suggestions. Artists collaborating on the development of a play might discuss the concept, purpose, and setting of the work at the beginning, followed by one artist writing the play while the other later produces and presents the work. All of these applications include collaboration, but all present unique forms or faces of the concept.

*The Laws
and Principles
of Power and
Control and
the Leadership
of People*

THERE ARE DIFFERENT
FORMS OF COLLABORATION

Indeed, there are many faces of collaboration. The most common is characterized by partners to the collaboration defining the purpose, goals, and tasks together, working through the process in close contact, and facing and solving problems together. Often, this relationship requires the collaborators to give up a significant portion of their individuality in favor of the collaborative relationship. This form of collaboration works best when the object of collaboration requires a high degree of investment and represents a very significant goal for all involved. Coteaching a class of regular and special education students is an obvious example of this collaborative relationship.

Another somewhat less intense face or form of collaboration includes partners in the effort working closely at the beginning of the project to clarify goals and identify the investment and the interest of everyone involved—then working alone. The parties may set key points along the way where they will meet to review progress, address problems, and make adjustments. This approach to collaboration works best when the collaborators cannot work conveniently in physical proximity and the task does not require constant communication. Yet, each partner has an unique role and contribution in support of the collaborative goals. Often, effective collaboration between parents and teachers takes this form.

The third face of collaboration is characterized by initial goal setting and planning among all partners. However, each partner takes responsibility for completion of a portion of the whole. Communication is intense at the beginning of the relationship as details of the task and process are defined. However, collaborators may spend most of their time alone or in small groups, focusing on their part of the project. Communication and contact reintensify only when problems are encountered or the project is nearing completion and the parts are fit together. As in the previous faces of collaboration, partners each bring skills and resources to the relationship. Yet, the actual contribution may be made in a relatively collaborative framework. Schools experience this face of collaboration often in the development of curriculum, classroom management structures, and other similar efforts.

The source of collaborative success lies in our understanding and use of the key elements of trust, clear goals, shared resources, flexibility, and open communication. Without any or all of these elements, collaboration quickly becomes an activity without accomplishment. The predictable result will be confusion, disillusionment, and withdrawal.

Remember, there are many faces of collaboration. And when people work collaboratively, they must know the structure which will be used. If they do not, many may not understand the different forms of collaboration and, as a result, be critical of the way the leader is using the group. As the leader, we must be aware that all forms of collaboration have merit and usefulness, but only when matched with the situation at hand and the goals to be pursued. It is the match among circumstances, intentions, and approaches that creates the power and efficiency of collaboration. The experience of collaboration changes those involved. We learn from each other, we learn about ourselves, and we encounter the opportunity to create together what we cannot create alone. This is the value of collaboration. And every teacher and administrator must know this leadership strategy and be able to make it work.

THE LAW:
APPLIED

1. What efforts lend themselves to collaboration?
2. Identify tasks that should never be tackled with this strategy.
3. Discuss the elements of (trust) (flexibility) (shared decision making) (clear goals) and (open communication) that are needed for the following collaborative efforts:
   a. Team teaching
   b. Parents as teachers
   c. Handling discipline problems in a school
   d. Working with members of the community

THE
LAW OF
RESPECT

Rationale: Respect is multidimensional, and it significantly affects relationships within an organization as well as the productivity and satisfaction of the leader and those being led.

Respect comes in many forms. It is a prime ingredient in creating relationships. It also helps create a workplace where people fit in, belong, achieve to higher levels, and find satisfaction in the process. Unless a teacher or administrator recognizes these various forms, he or she is unlikely to take the steps necessary to get the responses and leadership rewards that come with a respectful climate and culture in a classroom, school, and district. Being respected can and will enhance both administrator and teacher influence, achievement, and professional satisfaction. Therefore, we need to understand the dimensions of respect, the relationship between giving and receiving respect, and how to establish respect for people in our schools.

Without question, respect includes consideration for the primary and secondary needs of people. We may say, "How do the primary needs of hunger, thirst, sex, air, rest, escape from pain, and the elimination of waste relate to respect?" If a teacher holds students in class before lunch or an administrator holds a roomful of teachers for a faculty meeting at dinner time, disrespect is likely to result. We must also respect the need for rest, including rest from work. If we, as administrators or teachers, pile on assignments or act without consideration for the work of teachers or students, we're not likely to be respected—because we have acted disrespectfully in the eyes of those being led. And when we take such actions, we contribute to the feeling of disrespect—and the feeling of powerlessness as well. In addition, there are many other dimensions of respect that we must reveal if we intend to give and get respect.

RESPECT FOR TIME

There is the respect for *time*. Administrators may feel that teachers are disrespectful of their time when the teachers make requests or demand another service. And teachers may think administrators are being disrespectful of teachers' time when they make intercom announcements, establish procedures, schedule meetings, or issue requests for another report. The same is true of students. Loading students up with homework is not showing respect for time. In secondary schools, should every teacher give assignments on every day of the week?

RESPECT FOR AUTHORITY

Another facet of respect is the respect for *authority*. Most teachers and administrators would feel a student or teacher was being disrespectful if he or she went "over their head" to talk to a higher authority about something they wanted. Yet, some of these same teachers and administrators may talk to parents or make plans and decisions before consulting a student or teacher who is directly affected by these plans and decisions. Such action makes people feel both disrespected and powerless.

THE
LAW OF
CONTROL

Rationale: Leadership control is established when responsibility is openly accepted and the role as point of reference for those being led is assumed, practiced, and achieved.

No one will deny that where the authority is, the control must be as well. That's why a leader must have control of what has happened, what is happening, and—as often as possible—what is going to happen or is likely to happen in the classroom, school, or district. This *does not* imply or remotely suggest that we should impose or dominate to get control. As we discussed earlier, force or dominance will not cause others *to want* what we are doing to get the work and mission of the classroom or school accomplished.

Having leadership control *does* mean we must accept responsibility—and we must be the point of reference for guiding, influencing, and showing the way. It does mean being the point of reference for teaching, giving authority, delegating power and responsibilities, and providing those being led with the attitudes, abilities, and motivation to achieve individually and as a group. It does mean we must be the point of reference for individual growth and for achieving the goals and objectives of the classroom and school.

A teacher must be the point of reference for students. The principal must be the point of reference for teachers. The superintendent must be the point of reference for principals and the entire district team.

GAINING CONTROL
REQUIRES POSITIONING

To gain the control necessary to be the point of reference we must position ourselves and act in a manner which conveys to all that we assume the responsibilities inherent in our leadership post. Remember, our title means nothing. The fact that we are the paid appointed leader is immaterial. It's our individual leadership attitude, stance, and function that count. Therefore, if we want to be the leader, we must demonstrate that we intend to be the point of reference for everyone. If we don't take such action, we simply cannot and will not be regarded as the point of reference and looked upon as the one in charge—and we will not gain the control necessary to lead effectively. This sounds simple. Yet, while many leaders want control, some abandon the leadership attitudes and stances which allow it. They want to be the leader, but don't want to do the things a good leader is supposed to do.

A close look will reveal that while all leaders want control, some give their point-of-reference control away in a wide variety of ways. They enter the faculty meeting or classroom thinking only in terms of what those being led ought to be doing. They think primarily in terms of the responsibilities of those being led. Worse, they think in terms of correcting rather than helping—and many quickly give up on those being led. Some teachers may even tell students that the office sets all the rules and has all the control—then, in the next breath, complain that they can't control some student attitudes and behaviors.

In addition, some leaders don't want problems. Some administrators refuse to tackle certain problems. Rather, they appoint a committee to look at every issue. Yet, it's the top-

RESPECT FOR COURTESY

There is also respect revealed in *courtesy*. When we do something for someone, we expect to be thanked. Yet, leaders may make demands of students, teachers, secretaries, custodians, cooks, and others every day without even thinking of saying please or thank you. In truth, courtesy is a two-way street and a catalyst for respect. We need to remember this fact as we work with those we lead. We simply cannot do anything that might be regarded as demeaning or discourteous and expect those being led to show respect for us by being courteous or showing courtesy to one another.

RESPECT FOR FEELINGS, THOUGHTS, AND IDEAS

We must also show respect for the *feelings* and *thoughts* of those being led. In problem situations, if we don't care how those we lead feel or what they think, we have bypassed a vital dimension of respect—and people will end up feeling demeaned. If we think we can create respect even though we tell a student to "shut up" or imply to a teacher that we'll handle the decisions and he or she should take care of the work, we are mistaken.

In the same vein, there is also respect for *ideas*. If we cannot respect the ideas of those being led, it's impossible for these individuals to believe that we respect them. Generally speaking, people tend to feel worthless if their ideas are treated as worthless. While we may not be able to accept all ideas, we can always show respect for those ideas as well as the people who offered them.

RESPECT FOR BELIEFS

Likewise, there's respect for *beliefs*. If we respect only those who think and act as we do, we shall live in a very limited world. Again, we may or may not change our beliefs, but if we want those being led to respect our beliefs, we must show respect for theirs. If we don't, the people with those beliefs will feel no sense of influence in our classroom or school.

RESPECT FOR KNOWLEDGE

There is also respect for *knowledge*. Most certainly, without a scholarly approach to teaching, learning, and leadership, we are unlikely to be respected. Yet, if we are arrogant, our knowledge works against us and others. If we can respect only our own knowledge, it won't be long before others will begin to resent our knowledge—or resent us for having the knowledge and gloating over it. We must respect the knowledge of others—and realize that everyone has some knowledge that we don't have.

RESPECT FOR PRIVACY

It's impossible to earn or show respect without thinking in terms of *privacy*. Most of us would be outraged if our shortcomings were discussed with anyone, especially our

*The Laws
and Principles
of Power and
Control and
the Leadership
of People*

superiors. That's why we must be careful when we talk. Some teachers will discuss the faults of students with anyone who will listen. In fact, some enter the teachers' lounge daily talking about the character deficiencies and lack of intelligence of their students—by name. One thing is certain: If this type of talk ever got back to students, these teachers would not be respected. We can learn a lesson from this reality—and never talk about anyone except in a professional setting for professional reasons in a professional manner.

RESPECT FOR POSITION

There is also respect for *position*. A close look will reveal that when we cannot or will not show respect for all, our leadership is in trouble. Indeed, we may sometimes find it impossible to respect a person. It's just not possible. Nevertheless, we must always show respect for the position he or she holds. This is true whether the position is that of student, teacher, administrator, parent, board member, or citizen. If we expect to gain respect because of the professional position we hold and the expertise we have, but don't see our obligation to respect the positions of others, we have entirely missed the meaning of respect for the position and function people hold.

It would be a mistake not to admit that some leaders try to demand respect. Some leaders also try to pressure or force those being led into showing respect for them—and punish those who don't. Forcing respect doesn't work. Respect cannot be demanded or forced. And, just as it's difficult to obtain, once respect is lost, it is very hard to regain.

Teachers and administrators who show respect by the way they treat those being led and the way they handle the responsibilities of teaching and administration are the most likely to be respected and liked by all. A close look will reveal that we'll seldom find a teacher or administrator who is respected by students and not by colleagues. This isn't necessarily true of the teacher or administrator who is merely *liked* by students. That's why we must know that respect comes from giving. We earn it by managing responsibility in a competent and considerate way—and by encouraging others to do the same. We get respect by respecting people. Therefore, earning others' respect requires more than just being a *skillful* person. It comes from being a *better* person as well. And when we are successful on both fronts, we will position ourselves to empower those being led.

THE LAW:
APPLIED

The various dimensions of respect are shown in the diagram on the next page. Add to the listing in the diagram and answer these six questions presented for your consideration.

1. How do teachers reveal (respect) (disrespect) for administrators in each area?
2. How do administrators reveal (respect) (disrespect) for teachers in each area?
3. How do teachers and administrators reveal (respect) (disrespect) for support staff in each area?
4. How do administrators, teachers, and support staff reveal (respect) (disrespect) for students in each area?
5. How do educators reveal (respect) (disrespect) for parents in each area?
6. What dimensions of respect can you add to the wheel?

VARIOUS DIMENSIONS OF RESPECT

THE
LAW OF
CORE VALUES

Rationale: If leaders and those being led share the same core values, relationships—
as well as a higher level of achievement and satisfaction—will result with
significantly fewer conflicts between the leader and those being led.

If we're teaching a class and place a heavy value on students' paying attention and
students place a heavy value on paying attention as well, teaching is a whole lot easier.
Likewise, if we go into a meeting with colleagues and everyone shares the value that he or
she will do whatever it takes to get the job done, we're apt to get the job done extremely
well. On the other hand, if some students don't place a value on paying attention, our
teaching task is made more difficult—and if some colleagues will do anything to get the job
done, but others think they are doing too much already, an uphill road lies ahead. Herein lies
the significance of core values.

When the leader and those being led hold the same values, how to get the job done
may be an issue—but whether or not we should get the job done is never an issue. When
everyone holds the same values, differences are professional—and seldom personal. The
sailing is always smoother. In the process, people focus on the task and mission at hand
rather than secondary issues, conflicting priorities, or personal agendas.

WE ALREADY TEACH VALUES
WHETHER WE INTEND TO OR NOT

Unfortunately, the word *values* has been deemed a bad or scary word in schools and
has been avoided by many of us in recent years. We think it has too many negative
connotations, including *what* values and *whose* values to teach. Yet, values are vital to
achieving both the highest levels of functioning and the success of any organization,
including classrooms, schools, and districts. For instance, if we can't accept the core value
that schools exist to meet the needs of students, leading is impossible.

In truth, we teach values continually whether we think so or not. In everything we do
or say, we are teaching a value. And, of course, some of the values we teach by word or deed
are good ones—and some are not good for us or those we lead. However, a close look will
reveal that it's very difficult for a leader to gain the influence and meaningful control to lead
successfully in a classroom, school, or district without identifying, adopting, and teaching
core values in both informal and formal ways. The question is this: What kinds of core
values must we teach in order to gain influence and to establish control, create a proactive
culture, lead effectively, increase productivity, and enhance work satisfaction in the
classroom, school, or district? The answer is that we must teach those core values that
facilitate the success of those being led which are in agreement with the Law of Origin.

Here is a partial listing: hard work, fairness, focus, professionalism, ethics, effort,
consistency, cooperation, caring, trust, consideration, courtesy, patience, self-control, and
honesty. As a leader, you can easily add to the list.

This law tells us that as we teach the core values that lead to success—and those being
led begin to accept and practice those values—leading and being led become a lot easier and

enormously more productive. The law also teaches us that if people don't hold the same values or if they have conflicting values, every task is made harder—and maybe impossible. It's hard to gain influence and meaningful control without teaching values—and teaching values is part of the leadership responsibility. But we must be sure that the core values we are teaching do, in fact, contribute to the success of those being led and the work and mission of the schools we serve.

TEACHING VALUES IS A LEADERSHIP PROCESS

To teach these core values, four steps are necessary. First, we must identify the core values we believe those being led must acquire in order to be successful. Second, we must relate to those being led the benefit of accepting and adhering to these values. Third, we must reveal the consequences or problems that those being led can expect to have in school and in life if they reject a specific value. We can say, "If you don't accept the core value of (honesty) (hard work) (self-control), this is how it can work against you." Fourth, and absolutely mandatory, we must model the core values being advocated.

Teachers need to take this action with students. Administrators need to take this action with the staff. Some leaders might say, "I can't do that. I wouldn't have time to do anything else—such as teach academic content." Yet, we must know what often happens when we don't teach core values: Those being led pull in opposite directions. Every issue brings on a fight. Teaching those being led to achieve to potential—or building a team—is a constant struggle. We'll have as many core values in our school or district as we have teachers. Unless we identify core values and teach them to those being led, the leader will never be the point of reference or have the meaningful control necessary to lead. This is true for a teacher. It is true for a principal and superintendent. And, of course, teachers and administrators must model these values for those being led. Remember, leadership is showing the way to be successful.

PROACTIVE LEADER OR CUSTODIAL CARETAKER?

If we fail to teach core values, we will be forced to simply accept the condition that exists in a place—and that condition will remain. Then, we are not proactive leaders, we are only custodial caretakers. Worse, we may think we have to dominate or capitulate to do any leading at all. Then, giving orders or throwing up our hands in despair is the only door open to us. We will have to walk away from having meaningful influence or professional control—or we will have to continually keep our heavy foot on those being led in order to feel that control will not surely be lost. This is not a leadership role that we or those being led will find productive or satisfying. It is not a management behavior which fosters high levels of cooperative effort or achievement. That's why we ought to opt for the kind of influence and control that makes us the accepted and respected leader in the classroom, school, and district.

Teaching the core values moves the leader and those being led toward success. It enhances and elevates leadership influence and control. Teaching core values does not make

The Laws
and Principles
of Power and
Control and
the Leadership
of People

those being led act *less* responsibly, but helps them act *more* responsibly on a higher plane. It puts everyone on the same wavelength with the same priorities which go hand in hand with achievement. And teaching core values allows teachers and administrators to enrich the lives of those being led.

When the leader and those being led hold the same values, higher productivity and satisfaction become much more probable. Differences and disagreements are professional, not personal. We are still hard on problems, but we aren't hard on people. And the functions of leading and being led are a whole lot more pleasant and rewarding. This is what the Law of Core Values teaches us.

THE LAW:
APPLIED

1. Share the core values you believe a leader (should) (should not) teach.
2. Which of those values facilitate the success of leaders and those being led? Explain.
3. Identify the conflicting core values that hinder the work of leaders and those being led.
4. Which of the laws are (violated) (supported) by the values you identified?
5. Because a leader cannot impose truth, what course of action should be taken when those being led reject a value?

THE
LAW OF
PROBLEMS

Rationale: Problems are normal, inevitable, and continuous. Failing to expect
problems is abnormal, and failing to face them is fatal.

We don't awake in the morning, put our feet on the floor, and say to ourselves, "Oh, what a great day this will be. I get to handle so many different kinds of problems today." We're more likely to get up in the morning hoping we won't have any problems—and we won't have to see anyone today who has a problem—and that nobody will lay an unexpected problem at our doorstep.

But life doesn't work that way. And it never works that way for a leader. Understanding and accepting this simple reality is the first step toward developing the professional attitudes and actions that allow us to be the point of reference for solving problems and helping those we lead who have them.

PROBLEMS ARE
OUR LIFEBLOOD

This law reminds us that whenever people gather, problems are inevitable. It reinforces the fact that problems are normal and continuous. Everyone experiences problems. This law also tells us that it is abnormal not to expect problems. And if we don't even want to hear about anyone having problems, we can't function as a leader. Therefore, we must know and accept the fact that problems are the lifeblood of a leader.

Indeed, problems are one of the major reasons for our existence as leaders. If those being led never had any problems, the need for our services would be lessened. If we can't face and handle problems, we ought not be the leader. If we can't or don't want to help those who have problems, we don't stand a chance of causing others to want our leadership. It's impossible.

Does this mean we should grow to love problems? No. But it does mean we can't think that we, those being led, and the organization itself are terrible because we have problems. It does mean that we must acquire a realistic perspective and develop our skills so that we handle problems more successfully as we gain knowledge and experience. Remember, if we look down on problems, we automatically look down on the people who have them. And a leader can't look down on people and lead them effectively.

Shouldn't we try to eliminate problems? Yes. If we face problem situations quickly and squarely—and teach others how to resolve problems—we will cut down on the number of problems both we and those being led have to handle. In the process, we will also have fulfilled our leadership responsibility and function.

A leader must hold a functional and professional leadership stance toward problems, rather than one which causes us to react personally to problems and the people who have them. We must acquire the professional attitudes and skills to handle problems and the people who have them—including ourselves. We must teach those being led to do the same. And we must be proactive rather than passive when it comes to problems. If we aren't, there is no need for us to be a leader.

GOING INTO THE
LION'S DEN

*The Laws
and Principles
of Power and
Control and
the Leadership
of People*

The six biggest mistakes you can make with problems are to treat them with disdain, get angry at the problems and the people who have them, feel diminished because problems arise, avoid them, ignore them, or walk away from them. In many cases, we often take one or more of these actions, whether we intend to do so or not. After all, problems can upset our whole psyche. They can make us angry. They can make us physically and psychologically distraught. Problems can make us rant and rave at the problems and the people who have them or cause them. Problems can make us feel inadequate. These realities are the reasons that we must understand the Law of Problems.

We also need to know what to do when we have made a mistake and caused a problem. Here's an approach we can use. If you have made a mistake and it seems as though the whole world is mad at you, don't cower or hide. Rather, go "into the lion's den" immediately. Face those who are angry with you. Even let them air their upset if they must. But don't avoid them or your mistake. And don't try to hide from them or the mistake. Don't try to let some time pass before facing those being led. If you wait, matters will get worse.

You'll find that just seeing you physically as well as seeing you are willing to face the music is very beneficial. It will help those being led see you as the leader—acting like a leader. And if someone else is at fault, go to him or her—immediately. But don't go as a lion. Rather, go as a leader who intends to attack the problem, not the person who caused the problem.

A FEW RULES
TO FOLLOW

There are a few rules that it makes sense for a leader to follow in regard to problems. First, don't act as if problems are abnormal. Second, never act as if the people who cause them are bad, evil, dumb, or incompetent. Attack the problem with diligence, but not the person. Third, assist rather than criticize.

Fourth, never make the problem larger than life. Fifth, bring calm and feelings of competency to the problem. Resolve to make every situation better, not worse. Sixth, think like the leader, and take the action you think a good leader and a good person would take. Seventh, teach—and model the way a professional should behave when the problem is identified, during its solution, and after it has passed.

Remember, if you can control your own attitudes and actions toward problems and the people who have them, you can meet the lifeblood responsibility of a leader when problems arise. If you can't, you will become part of every problem. In the process, you will make every problem worse. It's guaranteed. As a result, you will never get those being led to want your leadership. In fact, you and your leadership may be the last thing they want when problems arise. And this law teaches us that problems will arise.

THE LAW:
APPLIED

1. Discuss the statement: Problems are the lifeblood of a leader.
2. A leader must be a visionary. Therefore, what problems can you expect from those being led?
3. At what time of the (day) (month) (year) can you expect specific kinds of problems in the (classroom) (school) (district)?
4. How have you prepared to (handle them) (ward them off)?
5. Discuss the six biggest mistakes we can make with problems—and how to keep from making them.

THE
REALITY OF
PROBLEM EXISTENCE

Rationale: Problems *do not* exist until they are identified, defined, and described by people.

In addition to fully recognizing and accepting the Law of Problems and the leader's role as the agent for handling problems, a teacher or administrator must understand two other significant aspects of people problems. Without this understanding, we may never be able to practice preventive leadership when it comes to problems. First, *we must recognize that problems do not exist until they are identified, defined, and described by someone.* A teacher or administrator who understands this reality is able to look at a situation which may, indeed, soon be identified by others as a problem if nothing is done—and take action to eliminate a potential problem before it ever becomes one.

WHEN THE SIGNS
APPEAR, ACT

Many, many, many times we see all the *signs* of a problem. We see a situation developing before those being led do. Experience tells us that all the signs are present for the development of a situation which will, indeed, soon be identified, defined, and described by others as a problem. Here are some of the signs: Students are abnormally restless. Administrators are criticizing teachers too much. Too many students are unhappy with a school rule or policy. Teachers are spending too much time out of the classroom, or administrators are out of the building too much. The staff is quarreling frequently. Administrators are wasting too much time or not seeing each staff member frequently enough.

Rather than face these danger signs and correct the situation, we do nothing. In fact, we may ask someone how he or she feels about one of these situations, and if *he or she doesn't see* a problem, we may say, "Well, I've got enough problems to worry about. I'm not going to make a problem." This is a mistake. In time, others will make this a problem we have to handle. But if we take action at the point at which *we* see the danger signs, preventive leadership action is possible. Therefore, if a leader intends to manage situations which may become problems, he or she must take immediate action—and for good reason. This proactive move is preventive leadership which prevents problems from occurring—and automatically reduces problems.

THE REAL
TRUTH

The second significant aspect of solving people problems involves the ability to discover the "real truth" about a given situation. The Law of Filtered Information, the Law of Real Truth and Time, and the Law of Right/Wrong Conflict can serve us well. When a leader develops a professional attitude that allows seeking out and accepting the real truth, problem solving is easier. Remember, real truth is not only what we think—it's what others think as well. Until we can discover truth from other points of view as well as our own, problems are not resolved. They may be buried or sidetracked. They may be ignored. They may explode. But they don't get resolved. For instance, a student may not be upset simply because a teacher denied a request. The real truth may be that he or she thinks the teacher dislikes him or her. A teacher may not be angry because an administrator disagreed, but because he or she really thinks the administrator put her down in the process. Never forget, truth is the important issue in resolving problems, and it has two sides—yours and the other person's.

A teacher or administrator must discover the real truth and take action quickly, because after problems are identified, people may become committed to a way of thinking. They may become entrenched in a position. Consequently, they may do and say things they normally would not—if they knew all the facts. This is the point at which rumors flourish, misunderstandings develop, and "mountains are made out of molehills." Yet, the fact remains that if people can't find a graceful way out of their position, they may never back off. Examples in a school are countless, with students and educators alike. We have all witnessed such examples. The result is that several problems develop rather than one.

THE REALITY:
APPLIED

1. Identify situations in the (classroom) (school) (district) which will be identified as problems.
2. Discuss reasons that we don't correct a situation before it is labeled a problem.
3. Discuss the ways to practice preventive leadership in the (classroom) (school) (district).
4. Discuss how problem situations are really opportunities for insightful leadership.

THE
REALITY OF
PROBLEM SOLUTIONS

Rationale: Problems get resolved more consistently and effectively when a leader has a process for accepting, analyzing, and resolving them.

Our level of success as leaders will be determined by how well we teach those we lead to solve problems and how well we resolve problems ourselves. That's why it helps to develop a logical and effective method of resolving each difficulty faced. This can be accomplished only by adjusting our attitude, behavior, or action in order to get others to adjust their attitude, behavior, or action. One way that a leader can neutralize negatives and change them into positives is called Situation Management. Situation Management has multiple objectives.

THE OBJECTIVES
OF SITUATION MANAGEMENT

First, we want to change problem situations into positives.

Second, we want to learn how to prevent these problem situations from occurring again. The question is this: What are problem situations? They are negative occurrences which cause us to be faced with the need to take corrective action. Our objective may be to correct a situation, to improve a situation, or simply to return our life and the lives of those we lead to normal—or at least to the status which existed prior to the negative occurrence.

We should recognize that negative situations are opportunities for leadership failure or success. Because we are human beings, however, in every negative situation, we are likely to encounter at least three personal and professional reactions and behaviors which hinder our ability to achieve positive outcomes. First, we often have a tendency to react defensively. This is a common human response. It is not abnormal. However, it is not professional either. When we automatically think that negative occurrences or problems reflect upon us personally, our efforts as teachers or administrators can easily be devoted to trying to absolve ourselves of the responsibility for the situation and everything related to it. Unfortunately, we automatically abandon and withdraw ourselves from our leadership positions when we do. Remember, we must react professionally toward problems and the people who have them, including ourselves.

Second, many leaders have a tendency not to face the reality that many adverse situations are, at least partially, created by them. Teachers and administrators are not the exception to this reality. However, if a leader accepts the definition of leadership which includes "causing others to want your leadership," then he or she can accept the damage this common human tendency can cause both to himself or herself and to those being led. When we refuse to accept the reality that many adverse situations are partially caused by us, problems don't get solved, they just get blamed on someone else—usually the follower. When this occurs, those being led will ultimately turn and blame the leader. For instance, if students can't read and a teacher blames students for this reality, what usually happens? You're right. Parents and students alike blame the teacher.

Third, many leaders fail to know, understand, or appreciate their own behaviors and motivations or those of the people they lead. That's why a brief study of the wants, needs, and motivations of human beings is included in this book. Before the rationale for the laws and principles of leadership and management can be fully grasped and applied, we must come to a greater appreciation of not only what motivates other people to act as they do, but also of what motivates us, as leaders, to think, believe, and act as we do.

PROBLEM SOLVING THROUGH SITUATION MANAGEMENT

The responsibility of leadership dictates that leaders take all negative situations and problems seriously and then act on them quickly. But knowing how to take action is just as important. One of the most workable techniques for problem solving is Situation Management. The technique of Situation Management is the *modus operandi*, the *vehicle*, the *procedure* through which our understanding of the motivations of people and the laws and principles of human management can be molded into a variable leadership plan of action. Situation Management has a proven track record of success in business, industry, government, and all professions.

Situation Management is a step-by-step process used to solve problems effectively. Using the laws and principles of human management and the understanding of human motivation as the foundation for our beliefs, we simply use a three-step process of problem solving to ensure that objective thinking replaces subjective, emotional, erroneous, or incomplete thinking.

One primary objective of Situation Management is to prevent leadership overreaction and misdirection. In addition, Situation Management forces a leader to deal with only the specific problem situation and include only the parties involved in that specific problem in the problem-solving process. It seldom allows magnification, and the process facilitates the discussion of real truth and feelings.

A CASE STUDY

Situation Management can be applied to any situation. Pick any problem you wish: a board member is openly criticizing teachers or administrators, a few teachers are absent frequently, student failures are high, teachers are unhappy about a policy, or teachers are quarreling with other teachers or the principal. The following is a simple, real, school incident. It is typical of the kind we have all experienced sometime in our careers.

Situation: You are happy. Everything is going well. You see (a colleague) (the principal) (the superintendent) (a parent) (a board member), and he or she says, "What's the matter? All I have been hearing lately is that the kids in your (classroom) (school) are out of control." End of incident. (For the completion of this Situation Management case study, let's use the principal as the recipient of the comments from the superintendent.)

Your whole psyche is upset. You are angry. You are worried. You are concerned. What do you do? Do you...

> ...rush back, call a staff meeting, and discuss the situation?
> ...call certain teachers to your office and question, accuse, or reprimand them in an
> effort to see if they talked to the superintendent or can shed any light on the
> situation?

*The Laws
and Principles
of Power and
Control and
the Leadership
of People*

...come to an immediate decision as to who, what, and why someone talked to the
  superintendent?
...see counselors and assistant principals?
...call an assembly and talk to students?
...call in student leaders and discuss the situation with them?
...send a letter to parents about student behavior, and write a note to the staff for inclusion
  in the teachers' bulletin?

Don't laugh. Situations like this have caused principals to take these kinds of actions.
Later, we might say, "Impossible" or "Unbelievable." Yet, hindsight often gives us
conclusions different from those provided by foresight.
  Of course, the question is: What should you do? Here is the answer. First, retire to a
quiet spot, and ask yourself some questions—and answer them truthfully.

  Q. Why am I concerned?
  A. I believe the superintendent is upset.

  Q. Why is he or she upset?
  A. He or she is upset because he or she believes the kids are out of control.

  Q. Is that what he or she said?
  A. No. He or she said, "All I have been *hearing* is that the kids are out of control."

  Q. Do I think that is true?
  A. No.

  Q. Where did he or she hear it?
  A. He or she didn't say.

  Here is the point at which our use of Situation Management can give us the objective
answers we really need to solve problems. And this is what we often need because situations
like these cause our imaginations to run wild—and cause us hurt, anger, grief, and turmoil in
the process. However, we must use objective questions like the ones offered—along with
others, such as: Who does the superintendent talk to? When and where might the
superintendent have heard such talk? How do I dispel such misinformation? By answering
these questions, we can move toward solutions rather than remain upset and anxious.

PROBLEM
ANALYSIS GUIDE

  The Problem Analysis Guide for Situation Management is composed of three parts:
Problem Awareness, Problem Assessment, and Problem Action. Remember, problem
situations cause us to make whatever decisions are necessary to return our life to its status
prior to the occurrence. These problem situations are opportunities for both success and
failure. Here are questions to ask in each of these areas:

Problem Awareness

1. What seems to be the situation?
2. How did I find out the situation existed?
3. What is the potential effect of this situation?
4. How serious is it?
5. How much time do I have to extricate myself?
6. Who is involved at this point?

Problem Assessment

1. What evidence leads me to believe that the situation exists?
2. What is the specific source of this evidence?
3. Do I know that the evidence is factual?
4. Could I list steps or events that created the situation?
5. Whose mind must I change in order to resolve the problem?
6. What does that person think now?
7. How will I know when the situation is resolved?

Problem Action   (Whether the problem is real or exists only in the mind of someone else, use the same questions. When answered honestly, they lead us to take action to solve the problem.)

1. Match the key individuals in the situation with the key issues. Note: Do not include those who are not involved, or you enlarge the problem.
2. State specifically: Who believes what?
3. Why do they believe this? Is there a difference between reality and perception?
4. How can I change their beliefs?
5. What is the best method to use to gain this change?
6. How do I implement this method?
7. Once the problem is resolved, what steps can I take to ensure that it will never happen again?

You may, of course, add to these three sets of questions. However, I think you will find that it usually isn't necessary. Through Situation Management, we not only apply our practical understanding of human motivation and the laws and principles of human management, we also avail ourselves of a workable technique through which we may implement our leadership plan with students and staff alike.

Without such a guideline, a teacher or administrator may be able to identify problems. But he or she may not be able to resolve them. And, of course, we may find that we are consumed by problems and the people who have them for a very simple reason: The people we lead have problems. They will always have problems. And many will need us to help them. After all, we are the chief executive officer in the classroom, school, or district. Therefore, problems are our lifeblood. Problems provide us with the opportunity to make a difference.

THE REALITY:
APPLIED

*The Laws
and Principles
of Power and
Control and
the Leadership
of People*

1. Discuss a leader's role in problems.
2. Identify situations which have not yet been labeled a problem by others, but may in the future.
3. Present three problem situations, and use the Problem Awareness, Problem Assessment, and Problem Action Guide of Situation Management.
4. What (primary needs) (secondary needs) (people motivators) did you use in your action plans?
5. Identify the laws and principles you applied in solving the problems.

*The Laws
and Principles
of Power and
Control and
the Leadership
of People*

down/bottom-up interaction synergy that creates exceptional commitment and facilitates outstanding accomplishments. A bottom-up leadership stance *only* leads to chaos. No effective teacher or administrator can avoid doing what those being led expect a leader to do. Nor can they permit responsibility or blame to be passed or ignore the problems those being led are experiencing. Remember, we can never abandon the leadership function. We'll lose control if we do. We will cease being the point of reference for those we lead. This is an important law in managing people—and in managing the work we want them to do.

CONTROL MEANS
BUILDING A TEAM

Being the point of reference and team builder helps us think and act in terms of "we" and "our." It gives those being led a sense of place. It gives importance, worth, and dignity to work, achievement, and the people who do it. It gives them feelings of ownership. It promotes cooperation.

Building a team helps prevent leaders from making common mistakes caused by the need for control. We hear these mistakes daily when leaders say *I, me, my, mine* and *I did, I want, I need,* or *I don't allow.* We say *my office, my school, my classroom, my staff, my student, my project, my budget, my schedule, my test, my lesson,* and *my plan.*

Undoubtedly, the fewer leadership skills we have, the more likely we are to revert to self-ownership, self-direction, and raw power. After all, we do have the power to pressure, force, and instill fear. Yet, the leadership control necessary to get high productivity and high satisfaction comes from working with people, showing the way, and giving people the attitudes, tools, knowledge, and authority to be successful. The control we need most is to take action designed to help and include—to make others productive, successful, and accountable—all of which are more difficult for a leader to achieve without being the point of reference and the team builder. Make no mistake: If we intend to be a successful leader, those we lead must be able to look to us at any time, especially when they need help. When they do, we must do the things a good leader is supposed to do.

THE LAW:
APPLIED

1. What does being the point of reference mean to you?
2. Identify the attitude and behavior a leader must assume to be the point of reference for those being led.
3. As the point of reference, do we "do for" those being led, teach them how to do, or both? Discuss.
4. Is being the point of reference limited to the math student—or the whole student? Discuss.
5. Discuss the areas of (shared decision making) (empowerment) (critical thinking skills) (cooperative learning) relative to team building in a (classroom) (school).
6. Discuss being the point of reference relative to being a star maker. Share your conclusions.

THE
LAW OF
SELF-CONTROL

Rationale: The control needed to start, continue, and complete work has more to do with managing and controlling ourselves than it does with controlling those we lead.

It may seem trite, but the fundamental professional control we need to lead any activity to completion may have absolutely nothing to do with those being led. Rather, it has to do with our ability to control and manage ourselves. And leaders must have self-control in order to achieve three vital powers if they are going to find leadership success. A leader must continually develop, exercise, and refine these three basic powers. This action is impossible without self-control.

THE POWER
TO START

The first self-control we need is *starting power*. It takes an open act of leadership determination to begin something significant in a classroom or school. Whether we're trying to turn a student around, counseling parents to take advice, or attempting to encourage the staff to a higher level of functioning—we must have starting power. It takes commitment and an expression of vested power to make the move to begin. It is not easy. But everything we do requires a beginning. As teachers and administrators, we are the ones with the power to begin.

Unfortunately, there are times when we fail to take that first step, and we can usually offer all kinds of reasons that we didn't. For example, our whole attitude may shift into negative when we see students failing to act appropriately or staff members acting negatively about taking on a new task. This is where many leaders falter. They lack the self-control to ignite the power to start themselves because they have made no allowance for the fact that those being led enter the classroom and school with interests, intents, priorities, motivations, abilities, and skills that are different from their own.

The list of ways in which those being led may differ from the leaders is endless. As a result, many leaders continue to measure where those being led are now—then throw in the towel when it comes to trying for higher standards or greater achievements. Some say things such as "Nobody will do anything" or "Nobody is interested in anything." Yet, these comments tell us that we have a leader who is being led—because of his or her lack of starting power. That's comparable to a teacher saying, "I'm not going to teach this year because the students aren't where they should be academically." Remember, a teacher must pick students up wherever they are and take them as far as they can go. He or she can do this only by beginning. Administrators must do the same for staff members. This requires the self-control of starting power.

WE NEED
STAYING POWER

We also need self-control to maintain *staying power*. It's one thing to make the move which gets things on the road. It's quite another to stay focused, keep on top of events, and keep everything moving on a productive course. In truth, this secondary thrust requires both a strong will and artistry. This is the point at which we must motivate and inspire to keep progress going—and draw upon more and more leadership skills to get the job done. Too, some leaders believe that once they get those being led started, they can move on to other tasks. But this belief is not true.

Staying power often requires that we support and reinforce what is being attempted by being creative, making adjustments, and offering additional information, ideas, and suggestions. We must have skills to encourage those being led to continue or join the effort to see the project through to completion. This almost always involves helping those being led through problems—and actually taking care of some of the more extraneous problems while those being led keep working on the central issue. We can keep momentum going and enthusiasm high only if our own momentum and enthusiasm remain high. This requires self-control and staying power rather than quitting. Nothing will dampen morale more than to find out that the leader has quit, shifted gears, moved on to a new priority, or tried to shove all the problems and hard work off on those being led.

Staying power is plain hard work. It's no easy task to help a roomful of students or an entire faculty and staff that have different skills and backgrounds work to the best of their abilities and achieve the goals and objectives of the school. Without self-control and staying power, we are likely to give up and quit on some teachers, some students, and many projects. And a great many hopes and dreams for what we have started will go down the drain.

THE FINAL POWER

Finally, we need the self-control necessary for *finishing power*. We need it each day, each week, and each month. We need it to help people progress and move to the successful completion of tasks and projects. We need the ability to get people to work on plans until the objective is met. The days will go by automatically, but finishing a task or project doesn't just happen.

The self-control of finishing power is the vital bow on the package. It's the necessary wrap-up. It's the finale. Without finishing power, most undertakings result in loose ends, work without achievement, and few meaningful successes. We need to remember that we need to tie the bow on each day and each project—as well as on the whole year. This requires self-control—and it is vital to acquiring finishing power. You can go into any classroom, school, or district, and you'll be told about all the marvelous projects that are under way. You can return two years later and inquire about these projects. And you'll be surprised by the number that have fallen through the cracks or been discarded for a wide range of reasons. If you analyzed each case, you would be amazed by the number that failed because finishing power was lacking. In each case, a lot of time and effort was expended—with no results.

Make no mistake: Most of the major controls we need in order to lead effectively have nothing to do with those we lead. They have to do with us. This is the reason we need not worry about putting those we lead in positions in which we can control them. Our biggest task is to manage ourselves—and use our starting, staying, and finishing powers to help those we lead achieve.

If we see those we lead and their differing abilities, interests, and needs as possibilities, rather than as problems, we will see ourselves in the same light. It's the possibilities that will give us the enthusiasm, excitement, and stamina to generate self-control—and to develop these three necessary powers every day, all year long. If we don't have the self-control to manage ourselves or these powers, we will not find a high level of success—and neither will those we lead.

THE LAW: APPLIED

1. Identify why self-control is a prerequisite for successful leadership.
2. Discuss what you believe is involved in starting power, staying power, and finishing power.
3. What leadership challenges are a part of each stage?
4. Discuss actions a leader might consider taking in each stage if faltering occurs.
5. Identify common attitudes of leaders which prevent them from beginning.
6. Identify major projects in your (classroom) (school) (district) for years past. Which ones are still going strong? Which ones have been discarded? Why?

THE
LAW OF
MORALE FLUCTUATIONS

Rationale: A pattern of fluctuation in morale exists in all situations involving change—and it's normal and predictable.

A few years ago, the world-famous Menninger Foundation in Topeka, Kansas, was involved in a study regarding the stages of morale. As teachers and administrators, we should have no problem recognizing each of these distinct stages. We should also have no problem seeing that the ongoing changes that occur in schools may have varied effects on the morale of those being led—and the leader as well. We need to understand these stages so that we can make change productive rather than destructive.

THE FOUR STAGES
OF MORALE

The Menninger Foundation found that there are four stages of morale that a person or group goes through with each new activity encountered. The first stage is the *arrival* stage. It is characterized by mixed individual or group feelings: anxiety, high motivation, apprehension, and enthusiasm. The second stage of morale is *engagement*. It's characterized by feelings of inadequacy, depression, frustration, and a realization of losses—either real or imagined. The third stage is *acceptance* and is characterized by awareness, activism, and realistic understanding of the situation. The final stage is called *re-entry* and is characterized by a sense of completion and satisfaction. It's also characterized by an increased anxiety about any possible impending change.

Teachers and administrators need to realize that the timespan for the occurrence of these four stages of morale—whether in regard to a new schedule, a new activity, new rules, new procedures, new requirements, or a new curriculum—can be minutes, hours, weeks, or years. For illustration purposes, let's consider your possible response to taking on a new project.

You're eager to get started, and you begin thinking about what to do. Your anticipation is high. You arrive at the first meeting and discuss the issue; everything sounds great. But when the time comes to do the work, the project doesn't look quite as good as you had expected. In addition, you begin thinking about the other work you have to do—or the golf or tennis game you could be playing—and you wish you could change your mind. Then you accept the situation and get the job done—with satisfaction. However, as you go home late to dinner, you remind yourself not to be so quick to endorse the next new idea or volunteer for another assignment. This is the range of the stages of morale.

A PATTERN OF FLUCTUATION
EXISTS FOR ALL

This pattern of fluctuation of morale exists for administrators, teachers, students, and parents in all situations involving change. Awareness of these predictable stages can be very helpful in approaching change with those being led as well as in maintaining balance in classroom, school, and district projects and activities. Being mindful of these stages also

292

saves the leader considerable frustration. Every teacher and administrator can be better positioned to lead by understanding the stages of morale as well as the mixed and contradictory feelings inherent in each new activity encountered. In the process, we can realize that the fluctuations in morale of those being led affect our attitude, outlook, and mental health.

Remember, even new friendships that students, teachers, and administrators develop are affected by this reality. For instance, a new relationship is often met with great enthusiasm and high expectations. In the beginning, everything about the other person seems wonderful. Then, as we begin to get better acquainted, a slight disappointment creeps in. We arrive at the realization that the person isn't quite everything we imagined. Finally, however, acceptance of both the positive and negative characteristics takes over, and the stages of morale are completed.

We must be aware that these stages of morale cannot be avoided. And, in each of the stages, there is a potential crisis that must be managed. Unless teachers and administrators are aware of this reality and prepared to confront these crises, we may not be able to pick up a slumping student or teacher. Likewise, we may not be able to pick ourselves up and go on when engaging in change.

OCCASIONAL PERIODS
OF LOWS...

We must also be aware that the importance of morale can be overstated. Neither the school nor the classroom will automatically fall apart because of occasional periods of low morale. After all, life does not run on a continuous high, as so many people seem to expect. However, continuous low morale can bring an organization to its knees.

Too, every leader needs to be aware that if the high morale that leads to productivity is to be present, some ingredients are necessary. For instance, justice, order, input, involvement, challenge, and freedom must be present. And without question, empowerment—through such means as shared decision making—helps in each of these areas.

Once these ingredients are present, significant achievements can begin to happen. That's why we need to understand the stages of morale. With this understanding, we have a better chance to make good things happen in our classroom, school, and district.

THE LAW:
APPLIED

1. Identify a project; then reveal the emotions you experienced in the four stages of morale.
2. Perform the same exercise, but identify the (emotions) (behaviors) of those being led in each stage.
3. What leadership action should accompany change? Discuss.
4. Share how understanding the stages of morale helps a leader know what is normal during change.
5. Have you ever seen a change falter because leaders thought the change was the problem—when, in reality, those being led were in a normal stage which was not recognized? Discuss.

THE
LAW OF
DISCLOSURE

Rationale: The more information and knowledge given to those being led, the more equipped they are to find success on progressively higher and higher levels.

Executives in every profession have long felt that they continually face a great dilemma: What types of information should they give to those being led—and how much should they tell them? Whether these executives were in business, industry, or schools, the question regarding what and how much to tell those being led about plans, priorities, decisions, events, circumstances, budgets, costs, and expenditures caused them considerable consternation. And the experiences of many leaders have also caused them to come to some very definite conclusions about what and how much to tell employees—as well as when to offer information.

It may be simple and obvious, but teachers and administrators need to appreciate that this dilemma is "part of the leadership territory." It is derived from the leadership position and function and the power held. Teachers and administrators usually get information first in a classroom, school, and district. Leaders always have more information than those being led. In addition, leaders always have the prerogative to decide what information to share with those being led.

A MILITARY
ORIGIN

Unfortunately, many leaders come to the ill-conceived conclusion that those being led don't want to know, don't need to know, and shouldn't have access to the majority of information available to the leaders. And many leaders think those being led should never have access to very much privileged information—even though such information can and does affect the productivity and success of individual employees as well as the entire organization. School leaders are not the exception to this reality. As a result, teachers are often kept in the dark regarding finances, negative issues facing the organization, the details of decisions, the ranking of priorities, and plans to solve problems. In the classroom, a teacher can adopt the same belief: some things are none of a student's business, including what we will do in the classroom tomorrow.

This thinking has origin in the old military style of management. The military style of management was an extension of the blue collar vs. white collar mind-set which many traditionalists held in the '20s, '30s, and '40s. Some leaders still hold to this style today—and plan to hold it in the future.

This style was standard operating procedure for most leaders after World War II. In fact, the military style is a legacy of World War II. Men and women used what they learned in the service to run companies, schools, and classrooms. Bureaucracies were built on a chain of command. The objective was command and control—with orders coming from the top. Subordinates were supposed to follow. And, of course, rank had many privileges, including the privilege of information and disbursement of information. The leader called the shots. At best, the leader was a benevolent dictator. In classrooms and schools, we could hold our heads high if we were benevolent teachers, principals, or superintendents. And, without question, those being led were truly grateful if we were.

This management style is fading fast. Today, leaders are trying to make their organizations less bureaucratic and more responsive to those who work with the client being served. They are trying to create teamwork rather than blind compliance. Leaders now know the advantages of requiring those being led to be involved in—as well as to actually make—some decisions. Leaders are also trying to create trust and cooperation in order to increase involvement and achievement. Today's executives realize that they must ease the stress and pressure within the organization. Unfortunately, it's not possible to relieve the fear and pressure for those who haven't been given enough knowledge and information to do the job as easily, efficiently, and productively as possible. Above all, leaders recognize that those being led cannot make wise decisions without good and complete information.

The management beliefs of the military style worked 50 years ago. In recent years, however, these management beliefs have given way to a new openness. It's easy to see why: new levels of skill are required of workers in business, industry, classrooms, and schools. Today's workers have more education, stiffer standards, and more complicated and comprehensive work. And, of course, today we live in a high-tech, information-based society. We have more information, and it is easily accessed. We deal with a marketplace that is competitive on a worldwide basis. We now know that complete information needs to be given to and received from those who have to do the work. Our beliefs have been expanded to encompass the idea that the process of deciding how to do the work should involve those being led.

AN OPEN-BOOK STANCE
CREATES A BETTER WORKER

Adopting an open-book stance has a very practical application in a professional and results-oriented workplace. A teacher or administrator simply can't treat those being led as second-rate when it comes to knowledge and information—and create first-rate students and schools. We can't have those being led trying to function with varying levels of information and expect them to achieve all that is required of them. It's impossible.

An open-book stance has many advantages. First, it allows those being led to work smart. Whenever a leader decreases ignorance, he or she has the best chance to improve understanding and acceptance as well as the quality of the work itself. Second, access to information helps those being led do a better job and be more productive. Third, it allows people to take the initiative and to show innovation and commitment individually and as a group. This is reason enough to bring the inner workings of a classroom, school, or district out into the open. When information is lacking, everyone usually has to get more information or the approval of the leader before thinking or acting. And, if people don't know, they are likely to fill the gaps with speculation. On the other hand, when information is available, the best thinking is always more likely to surface.

Fourth, information makes those being led think and act more like managers and leaders. Fifth, it allows every person in the organization to give both input and support to plans, decision making, and action—and to find more success and less failure in the process. Obviously, it's very difficult for those being led to support what they don't know or understand. It's also hard for anyone to do a job well without total information.

*The Laws
and Principles
of Power and
Control and
the Leadership
of People*

Unfortunately, many educators at the elementary, middle, and high school levels know very little about the academic teaching their colleagues do. And this is a condition that needs changing. We all need to know the curriculum taught in our schools. Sixth, information fosters cooperation because it encourages the understanding and empathy that comes from knowing what challenges and accomplishments others are experiencing.

Seventh, an open-book stance promotes trust between leaders and those being led, whereas the traditional white collar vs. blue collar type of management promotes division. Eighth, an open-book stance helps people recognize mistakes sooner. Ninth, it puts the success of the organization up-front for all to see. Tenth, information helps those being led consider new ideas that affect the whole and alleviate pressure and responsibility. Finally, the open-book stance gives those being led a sense of worth and dignity.

INFORMATION: A KEY TO
SUCCESS AT EVERY LEVEL

Having comprehensive and accurate information is a prerequisite to a leader's success. The more information a leader has, the more successful he or she can be. The reasons are obvious. We have to make good choices. We have to make good decisions. We have to get others to take action and *achieve* when they do. We can do none of these things without information. Having information is also a prerequisite to the success of those being led. And there is one reality that many traditionalists forget regarding giving information to those being led: When the leader protects, withholds, or hides information and keeps those being led in the dark, those being led will do the same with their leaders. Therefore, when those being led don't get the information they need to do a better job—neither does the leader. And students have vital information that a teacher needs. Likewise, teachers have information that administrators need.

Holding to the belief that people can't handle information responsibly is nonsense. However, so is believing that nobody will misuse the information. They will. And certainly we must be prepared to deal with that inevitability. However, keeping everyone in the dark because someone may misuse information is a self-destructive stance for a teacher or administrator.

We also need to take a close look at *how* we give those being led information. Leaders use many ways of doing so. We send them notes. We issue reports. We conduct meetings. We call people in for conferences. We use chalkboards, bulletin boards, newsletters, and weekly bulletins to impart information. We use assemblies, clubs, and staff development sessions to deliver messages and information. However, too much of the information leaders give is shallow and incomplete—intentionally.

Remember, the key to proper dispensing of information is to believe that those being led need to know *everything* that contributes to the whole of the classroom, school, and district—with only two notable exceptions: First is the salary of an employee or the grades of an individual student. Second is the handling of a personnel problem or a matter which is protected by ethics and law. All other information, from priorities to finances, needs to be given openly and freely.

THE DIFFERENCE BETWEEN
SUCCESS AND FAILURE

Make no mistake: You can't give those being led too much information—unless, of course, the disclosure of such information is prohibited by ethics or law. More often than not, you will find that information is the difference between exceptional attitudes and achievement and mediocre attitudes and achievement for those being led. It is often the difference between growth and sluggishness of students and educators alike. It can be the difference between a person coming to school and simply doing a job—and doing a job intelligently and being totally committed to the work. That's why wise leaders today accept several beliefs.

First, open-book leaders believe all have a right to know anything and everything. Second, they believe all have a responsibility to know everything. Third, open-book leaders believe that keeping people in the dark is a form of misused power which is detrimental to everyone. Fourth, open-book leaders hold to the belief that those being led also have a responsibility to give information. They know the transmittal of information is not a one-way street. Fifth, open-book leaders believe that everyone has a responsibility to give information which identifies problems and offers possible solutions. This belief prevents problems from being hidden or being laid at someone else's door.

As we look to the future of schools, we should also see that we must use all the resources of a school if we expect to get the job done. If we think it can be done with a division of labor, we are mistaken. It will take all of us working cooperatively to create better schools. And the best way to get cooperation is to be cooperative ourselves. Being an open-book leader will give us the best chance of success on all fronts.

THE LAW:
APPLIED

1. What kind of information is required in order for students to be high performers? Discuss.
2. What kind of information is required in order for (teachers) (administrators) to be high performers? Discuss.
3. What kind of information do teachers need to receive from students in order to be high performers? Discuss.
4. What kind of information do administrators need to receive from teachers in order to be high performers? Discuss.
5. What information must remain confidential?

THE LAWS OF COMMUNICATING TO LEAD

If you can't communicate, you can't lead. Indeed, because of the importance of communication to leadership effectiveness, volumes have been written on the subject. And all of this material could probably help us—and we could study the subject the rest of our lives. Six laws are presented in this section. Knowing and remembering the content of these laws can help all of us in our jobs as educators.

The Law of Persuasive Communication
The Law of Listening
The Law of Proactive Listening
The Law of Leader-Follower Relationships
The Law of Group Communication
The Law of Confronting

THE
LAW OF
PERSUASIVE COMMUNICATION

Rationale: Persuasive leadership involves both ideas and feelings, verbal and nonverbal communication, and the use of all three styles of communication: action, senses, and scholarly.

A leader must be aware that every communication has two *basic components*: *ideas* and *feelings*. Ideas are the words people say. Feelings are the emotions they have about what they are saying. What those being led say, of course, is important—but so is how they feel about what they are saying. Those being led may have strong feelings about what they say—or have little intensity at all. However, a lot of good ideas, as well as bad ideas, are accepted because of how strongly a person feels about what he or she is saying. Too, a lot of good ideas are rejected because of how someone is communicating.

For instance, you may think someone is not very serious when he or she is—or vice versa. Therefore, you will almost always misread people if you don't link ideas and feelings. Most important, when feelings are missed, you are not likely to communicate persuasively or effectively. Remember, some people can't explain or relate ideas well. Regardless of what someone says, however, a leader must acquire the ability to perceive the message accurately. This task is difficult if words and feelings are not linked.

A leader also needs to know that every communication has *two distinct channels*: *verbal* and *nonverbal*. Verbal is what is being said. Nonverbal is the body language being used. Nonverbal includes tone, posture, mannerisms, and habits. Without question, a leader must know that nonverbal communication is the most powerful. Of equal importance, a leader must be aware that when nonverbal communication contradicts the verbal, the nonverbal will be believed—always. As a result, you may tell those being led "Yes," but if your nonverbal communication indicates "No," the latter will be believed. That's why we must be aware that we always send both verbal and nonverbal messages with every message to those being led—and a nonverbal message may support or contradict the words we use.

WE EACH HAVE A DOMINANT
COMMUNICATION STYLE

How people communicate tells you a lot about them. It can reveal their personality as well as their values. It tells you what they like and dislike. It even reveals what they trust and distrust. And how people communicate always tells you the way that they need you to communicate with them. That's because everyone has a dominant or preferred communication style which usually matches his or her personality. The leader is not the exception to this reality. Knowing our communication style can help us understand ourselves and the communications we send—as well as those we receive from others. Without question, our style can affect our ability to reach and influence those being led. If others are like us, they may relate to our style of communication. However, if they aren't like us, we may have to make some adjustments or we may have trouble relating to and persuading these people—and they will have difficulty communicating with us.

There are three communication styles: *action*, *senses*, and *scholarly*. We need to

300

understand these styles. Above all, we need to utilize all three styles as often as possible when communicating—if we intend to effectively reach *all* the people we are leading. If we do not utilize all three styles, we will probably only be highly effective with people who have a communication style which matches ours.

Generally speaking, the styles of communication used by a school population are evenly mixed. Probably one-third of all people are action-style communicators; one-third are senses-style communicators; and one-third are scholarly-style communicators. Therefore, if we communicate only in our preferred style, we may be effective with only one-third of those being led—or one-third of our colleagues. And this reality spells trouble no matter how we look at it. Therefore, let's take a look at the three styles of communication.

THE ACTION-STYLE COMMUNICATORS

Action-style communicators are easy to identify. They are direct, abrupt, and to the point. These communicators place emphasis on speed, productivity, getting started, and getting things done. They communicate in brief terms. They will usually emphasize objectives, goals, and immediate needs. They address accomplishing tasks—always. They have a sense of urgency—with a no-nonsense approach. Action-style communicators do not like red tape, structure, bureaucracies, treading water, attending meetings that don't result in immediate action, worrying about the past, or trying to foresee the future. They are uncomfortable with anyone who is not like them.

To senses- and scholarly-style communicators, however, action-style communicators are thought to be cold, hard, ruthless—and without regard for people. Scholarly-type communicators are likely to believe action-style communicators rush to action without having any facts or figures to back them up. In fact, both senses- and scholarly-type communicators tend to believe action-style communicators are only concerned with getting what they want and reaching goals—and would "walk over" anyone to be successful. As a result, they fear action-style communicators and don't relate to them or their urgings very well.

Do action-style people make good educators? Indeed they do. Do we need them among the ranks as leaders and those being led? Absolutely. These are the people we count on to get things done.

THE SENSES-STYLE COMMUNICATORS

Senses-style communicators are also easy to identify. They are warm, friendly, sympathetic, empathetic, and concerned with human feelings, conditions, and emotions—always. They speak and write in a highly personalized manner. They are openly and freely humorous, caring, and loving. They often dress flamboyantly. They are prone to keep—and display on their desk or wall—every momento they have ever received, including any evidence of close relationships with other people.

They often sign notes and letters in flowery or flamboyant ways with closings such as "Have a happy day" or "Enjoy," or with a picture of a smiling face. Without taking any action, senses-style people can talk all day about caring and be very happy and uplifted. Yet, any idea, suggestion, or action—no matter how good or how well documented with facts— that doesn't contain the dimensions of consideration and caring will make senses-style communicators uncomfortable and bring about their suspicions or rejections.

To some, senses-style communicators are regarded as caring and considerate. To others, however, they are regarded as weak, having no substance and no facts to base decisions upon—only emotion. Nevertheless, senses-style communicators expect a degree of humanism from those who communicate with them. If they don't receive it, they perceive others to be cold, hard, or noncaring. Remember, senses-style communicators are very suspicious of both action- and scholarly-style communicators. Why? They do not believe that those people really care about people.

Do senses-style people make good educators? Absolutely. Do we need them on the team? Yes. Do we need them in the classroom? Absolutely. They keep everyone focused on caring for students and each other.

THE SCHOLARLY-STYLE COMMUNICATORS

Scholarly-style communicators are cool and objective. They view everything constructively. They want to look at the whole picture—and all the details as well. They want to see the evidence that what the leader is suggesting will work. Their style always involves objectivity and logic.

Scholarly-style communicators stress working toward individual and institutional goals, but only with facts, proven concepts, and research. They like evaluations of the past, present, and future. They promote systematic investigations regarding anything new. These are the people who will always suggest that a committee be formed to study any issue. Likewise, they are the people who are reluctant to do anything that is not in the book of time-tested practices. They are business-like and highly professional. Their communication is specific, organized, and usually undeniable. They do not make decisions quickly. In fact, quick action makes them feel irresponsible and unprofessional.

Scholarly-style communicators don't use emotion; they just use evidence. Action-style people don't like them for a very simple reason: They believe they are long on talk and study and short on action and achievement. And senses-style communicators feel the devotion of scholarly-style communicators is for facts, not people—and view them as cold and distant.

Do scholarly-style communicators make good educators? I hope so. If not, we're all in trouble because we should all be scholars. Do we need them in the classroom? Absolutely—and we need more of them.

USING THE THREE STYLES OF COMMUNICATION

While each of us is predominantly one of these types of communicators, we need to use all three types of communication in the classroom, school, and district when we communicate with those being led—if we want to influence them. And when we are giving a group presentation, we must use all three styles in every presentation.

Individually, we need to match the style of the person with whom we're talking. This means we ought to consider whom we are talking with before we deliver our ideas, suggestions, or message. Does this mean we totally shift gears when talking with someone different from us? No. It simply means, for instance, if we are an action-style communicator, we must insert or add to our message the appeals that will allow the senses- and scholarly-style communicators to listen and accept what we are saying. Taking this action should not be hard for one reason: Every message we deliver should contain action, a regard for people, and a carefully researched and studied proposition. And in every action, our goal should be to cause others to want our leadership.

If we don't use all three styles as we communicate, a big dimension of leadership is missing. It's hard to create an effective classroom or school without these three forces— because it would mean that we have only similar kinds of people in our classroom or school which, of course, is not the case. We need to use all three dimensions to be whole. And there is a big leadership dimension missing in us if we don't—or can't—use all three styles in communicating with those being led.

SIMPLE GUIDELINES TO BECOMING A BETTER COMMUNICATOR

Following a few simple rules can make every teacher or administrator a more persuasive communicator. First, be open. Keep in mind that when your communication is guarded, you will be regarded as less than truthful. Second, be confident, honest, and empathetic. Always consider everyone, and make sure you tell everyone the same story. Third, know yourself and how you affect others. In the process, be sure to use all three styles of communication, especially in group meetings. Fourth, know your message. And make sure that the facts you raise are rational and accurate.

Fifth, be consistent and persistent—and never "blow like the wind" in varied directions. In the same vein, don't talk just to be talking. Sixth, keep your verbal and nonverbal messages consistent with each other. Seventh, increase the impact of your message by repeating key points and using nonverbal and verbal skills to supplement each other.

Eighth, try to establish and maintain trust and warmth with people so that you are a credible communicator—and those being led feel that you are. Ninth, make sure your ideas are reasonable so that people can accept you as believable. Tenth, be crystal clear about the intentions of your message. Do not try to be clever. And never, under any circumstances, try to manipulate. Eleventh, show responsibility by using the pronouns, *I, my, mine,* and *me* to indicate personal involvement when it is appropriate. By using these eleven guidelines, you will adhere to the Law of Persuasive Communication.

THE LAW: APPLIED

1. If you were explaining a new problem to (students) colleagues), how would you utilize (ideas) (feelings)?
2. If you were explaining a new procedure to (students) (colleagues), how would you match verbal and nonverbal communication?
3. If you were explaining a new procedure to (students) (colleagues), how would you use

all three styles of communication?

4. Look at your classroom rules. How would you present these rules using all three styles of communication?

5. Identify your dominant style of communication. How could a mentor help you avoid obvious professional voids? Discuss.

THE
LAW OF
LISTENING

Rationale: Listening is always as important to influencing and persuading those
being led as speaking is.

Listening is something we do every day, but we may not do it as well as we could—or as well as we should. We know its importance, but often find it a very difficult task. After all, a leader has many people to listen to. And, in truth, we may not hold some of the people who are talking to us in very high regard. Couple these realities with the fact that we may know very little about either the skills or the leadership benefits of listening, and the stage is set for trouble.

If we're good listeners, it's probably because of our personality rather than our knowledge about listening in ways that help us be influential and persuasive. In fact, we may think we have to talk to achieve these goals and get those being led to want our leadership. But we don't. In fact, this law teaches us that listening is always as important as talking when it comes to leadership effectiveness.

YOU CAN'T INTERACT, EXCHANGE,
AND COMMUNICATE WITHOUT LISTENING

We should all believe that when we talk, someone should be listening. And when others talk, we ought to believe that we should be listening—and for good reason. You can talk without listening, but you can't interact, exchange, and communicate with those being led without listening. Listening is, without reservation, a key to communication, human relationships, drawing those being led toward you, being influential, and persuading those we lead. If you can't listen, you can't know people. You'll miss strengths. You won't know what they want or what they are saying. You can't give them respect. Worse, without listening you can work on the wrong problem.

When a leader doesn't listen, those being led always know it. Make no misjudgment regarding this fact. As a result, they will react differently toward us and our leadership. They may also stop talking to us. Worse, they may go around us. Students will go around teachers to another teacher, principal, or counselor. Parents will go around the teacher to the principal. Parents will go around the principal to the superintendent. Board members may go to teachers, principals, and anyone else if the superintendent will not listen to them.

It's simple, but if you want to become a better communicator, there are some realities you must accept and practice. Unless you do, you may not be able to listen accurately or to be highly influential. That's because there are some distorters of listening and communication which can get in the way and actually prevent you from listening to the communications those being led try to give you. And those distorters are within us all. They are common. They are normal. But they must be overcome.

OVERCOMING THE DISTORTERS
OF LISTENING

The most common and natural distorters of listening and gaining accurate communication are hearing the words, but missing the feelings of people. The distorters also include stereotyping and labeling the person talking to you. Having information in advance can distort your ability to listen. So can making premature decisions or failing to get feedback as you communicate. And, of course, trying to talk when someone is talking to you will always eliminate your ability to listen and gather information. And remember, a leader must have information to be effective. One can lead without many things, but one cannot lead effectively without extensive and accurate information.

There are other distorters that get in the way of our listening. If we don't overcome them, we will not listen accurately. For instance, we often think the issue or subject being discussed is too elementary—or we're simply not interested. Or we may have other things on our mind and develop the habit of mentally tuning in and out when people talk to us. Too, psychologists claim we see and hear only what we expect to see and hear. We turn off people we don't like—and we turn off facts we don't like. Sometimes, especially if we're an action-style communicator, we only want to hear main points. We let our mind wander. After all, we can listen to 500 words per minute—while we can speak only 200-250 per minute. During a speech or lecture, only 100-125 words are spoken per minute.

There is also competition when we want to listen: interruptions, the phone, the person next to us, people entering and leaving the room. Mostly though, we are reluctant to listen because it requires a highly active role and it's hard work—physically and mentally. And sometimes when others talk to us, we use the time to rest. Yet, if we intend to be an effective leader, we need to be aware that those we lead have a very strong desire to be listened to—and we have a big need to hear what they have to say.

WE RELY ON PEOPLE
WHO LISTEN TO US

In truth, a close look will reveal that we begin early in life to rely upon those who listen to us. Why? It enhances our self-worth and gives us pleasure and prestige to be listened to. It makes us feel important. It gives us power. Therefore, leaders who cannot or will not listen reduce their chances of causing others to want their leadership because they automatically demean those being led whether they intend to or not. We also learn quickly that withholding listening is a form of punishment. We must ask ourselves "Why do some students refuse to listen to some teachers? And why do some teachers refuse to listen to some administrators?"

Unfortunately, one of the biggest of all problems is that leaders like to talk. Leaders like to talk for many reasons. We talk for attention. We talk for power and control. We talk to get our way. We talk to get people working. We talk for self-confidence.

Talking is freeing. Talking is relaxing. Talking is a way to reveal as well as conceal our real selves. Talking is a way to show our abilities to others. It is a means of seeking recognition. That's why we often talk more than we listen. If we intend to be an effective leader, we must listen first. That's why this law reminds us that listening is always as influential and as persuasive as talking.

THE LAW:
APPLIED

1. How much should a leader talk in a meeting?
2. How much time should a teacher spend each hour teaching by lecture? Discuss.
3. Are there any people you never listen to? Why?
4. Identify other distorters which prevent communication.
5. Identify situations where the leader should listen first, talk second.
6. Identify situations where the leader should talk first, listen second.

THE
LAW OF
PROACTIVE LISTENING

Rationale: The most effective method of achieving understanding and preventing breakdowns in communicating with those being led is proactive listening.

Proactive listening aids clarity. It can assure understanding. It nurtures involvement. It requires participation. It meets the communication needs of the leader and those being led. It provides various checks to make sure we are receiving accurate information. And it prevents misunderstandings and breakdowns in communication.

Without doubt, proactive listening helps the leader to bring ideas and feelings together. It clarifies and connects verbal and nonverbal communication. It actually forces or creates interaction between the leader and the person with whom he or she is talking. And it provides the person we are talking to with proof of listening and understanding via proactive feedback. Passive listening does not offer these leadership benefits. In fact, passive listening is the same as silence.

HOW IT
WORKS

Proactive listening is a trait every teacher and administrator must acquire. Let's use an example to see how proactive listening works, why it works, and how it differs from passive listening. For illustration purposes, let's say a student walks into class and immediately asks, "Are we going to have a test today?" Or let's say a teacher or administrator asks, "Do we have to turn in our reports this week?"

When the leader receives this kind of message, his or her mind must go through a quick decoding process—before he or she can react. The leader has to figure out the meaning of the person's message—and what's going on inside him or her. For instance, is the student unprepared and afraid of the test? Is the student going to claim that he or she wasn't told about having a test today? Or is the student prepared and really saying he or she wants to take the test quickly—before he or she forgets the material covered on the test? In the example of the teacher, does the teacher have the report done? Is the teacher trying to get an extension of time for turning in the report? Or is the teacher eager to turn in his or her report? Obviously, how we decode and respond is important.

Therefore, the decoding process must be a guess or an inference, because we can't see inside the person. If we guess one way in this case, our decoding process may tell us "He or she is worried." Or our decoding guess might produce: "He or she isn't ready for the test," "He or she hasn't finished the report," or "He or she forgot that the reports were scheduled for next week."

THE DECODING PROCESS
IS VITAL, BUT INCONCLUSIVE

While the decoding process is critical in the communication process, we don't know whether we are right or wrong. Equally important, the person can't know whether we have decoded his or her message correctly either. He or she can't read our mind any better than we can read his or hers. Therefore, we must have a way to check the accuracy of our decoding effort—before we respond to his or her message.

All we need to do to make proactive listening a part of our decoding is to always respond with a question. We can ask, "Are you worried about getting the report completed on time?" The person may say "Yes." Both of you now know you heard and understood. This process of "feeding back" is part of the process we call proactive listening. It's the step that puts an effective communication process in action. If the person had said "No," we would have had to ask another question, such as "Are you ready to turn it in?"

This may sound trite, but it is not. Without such a procedure, a leader is going to misinterpret the words of those being led often. We're going to jump in and put our foot in our mouth frequently. Whether it's one sentence or a long conversation, the process of decoding and proactive listening is a must.

THREE LEVELS
OF LISTENING

There are three levels of listening—and only one of them is good. One level is not hearing at all what is being said. Another level is that we listen or hear, but we don't process the communication. The highest level is proactive listening. We hear, we process, and we use the information that we have heard accurately.

To be a proactive listener, you must be people-oriented. You must be able to show those being led that you are willing and able to receive a message from them. Unless people feel the lines of communication are open between you and them, they are less likely to talk. Therefore, you must want to meet the needs of other persons. You must be willing to give them time. You must be able to be inviting when those being led are talking to you. Above all, however, you must be able to prove that you have the ability to understand both verbal and nonverbal messages.

Make no mistake: Listening in silence will not work. It is passive listening. It proves nothing. You signal your readiness to listen by being actively engaged in the conversation. And being engaged requires specific action.

First, you must stop what you are doing—and focus only on the person talking to you. It's true, you can do two things at once. You can continue to grade papers and listen to what a student says to you. But you'll never convince a student that you were listening if you do.

Second, you must make eye contact. Focusing on the person's eyes or slightly below them is necessary. Even if the person does not look at you, eye contact is vital. Why? The other person is aware when you are not making eye contact—and will not think you are proactively listening unless you are looking at him or her.

Third, you must keep the body quiet. Mannerisms and fidgeting affect the person adversely. In addition, you must face the person or sit or stand near him or her. Equally important, you must lean or bend slightly toward the person—and never lean away from him or her.

Fourth, to be a proactive listener, you must determine what the person is saying to you—and how he or she feels about what he or she is saying. You can use the person's words, plus some of your own, to help you decode. You must ask questions to indicate you understand the person's words and to clarify the meaning of the message for both of you.

To facilitate proactive listening, the technique of paraphrasing is encouraged. When you paraphrase, you indicate that you are listening, understanding, and caring about the person talking. You can lead into a paraphrase with such phrases as:

1. Do you mean that...?
2. Do I understand correctly that...?
3. I read that you....
4. What I hear you saying is that....
5. In short, you're saying that....
6. The essence of your point is that....
7. Are you saying that...?

Speak your own thoughts only after you have paraphrased the speaker's message.

In addition, perception checking should be used. This strategy is a means of checking your perception of what another person is saying. You indicate your interpretation of both his or her words and feelings—and intensities. You check the words of the message, the tone, and the hidden agenda of the message. You can lead into a check of your perceptions with such phrases as:

1. You seem to be....
2. I get the impression....
3. You appear....
4. It sounds to me as though you are....

This technique demonstrates that you are listening, understanding, caring, and responding accurately, especially to an emotionally loaded and challenging message. The booming business of professional listeners—psychiatrists, psychologists, counselors, and therapists—tells us of the need people have to talk and to be listened to. Those being led want to be listened to—and not just heard. After all, talking to a wall doesn't help any of us. However, listening proactively adds to personal worth, importance, and dignity. Proactive listening helps people fit in and belong and develop a sense of ownership. Above all, it facilitates accurate communication.

Proactive listening is a skill that has to be learned—and a leader has to work at it constantly. It is not easy. It is not simple. It is complex. And it's not always enjoyable. However, a sincere and empathetic listener can draw anyone out of his or her cocoon—and cause those being led to want his or her leadership.

LISTEN DURING
PAUSES

Proactive listening is aided by technique. For instance, whenever the talker pauses, wait. The talker may get uncomfortable. But if you let him or her break the pause, he or she may open up. Therefore, don't "jump in" the first chance you have. And don't be quick to terminate a conversation. Rather, keep in mind that there is a human fellowship in the insecurity we all share.

Remember, closed questions, which require only a yes or no answer, finish any conversation. If you don't know what the other person means, ask. He or she will be grateful or flattered that you care enough to ask. However, be careful that you do not show interest only in what you want to hear, what makes you feel good, or what agrees with your own ideas. Too many times, psychologists claim, we see and hear only what we expect to see and hear. We mentally tune in or out. We turn off people as well as facts we don't like.

You will never be rejected, isolated, left out, ignored, or bored if you proactively listen to those being led. Everyone needs at least one dependable sounding board. Remember, talking to people is not the problem in the world today. Not talking to people is the problem. It's such a problem that many people can't express themselves. They haven't had enough practice because nobody wants to listen. Worse, nobody will listen to them.

THOSE BEING LED NEED A LEADER WHO WILL LISTEN

A leader must become a proactive listener for a very simple reason: Those being led must have a leader who will listen to them without judging instantly or coming to the wrong conclusions immediately. They need a leader who knows and understands them. And, of course, the leader must understand those being led in order to lead them successfully. Without this proactive listening approach, a leader can easily make a mistake. For instance, we might have responded, "You know the test is today—I've told you fifty times," or "If you don't have your report, you're in big trouble because it's due today."

Remember two realities: Many good things happen because teachers and administrators do listen—and many good things don't happen because we fail to listen. Therefore, when you are being bombarded from all directions to listen, remember to check for understanding. It takes only a moment when you do so from the other's frame of reference, rather than yours. This can occur only via proactive listening. When you are a proactive listener, you are in a positive listening mold. If you're judging and arguing, you're not listening. Rather, you are coming to conclusions—and many of them will be wrong. Coming to the wrong conclusions will not cause others to want your leadership.

THE LAW: APPLIED

1. Discuss the differences between proactive listening and passive listening.
2. Share ways to use paraphrasing in proactive listening.
3. Share ways to use perception checks in proactive listening.
4. Pick a partner and let him or her tell you "anything he or she has been wanting to tell someone." Say nothing as your partner talks for three minutes. Then, start again and use proactive listening techniques. Discuss your observations together.
5. Use the same exercise, but reverse roles.

THE
LAW OF
LEADER-FOLLOWER RELATIONSHIPS

Rationale: Your relationship with one person affects your relationships with all being led—and peers always identify and relate to peers.

A teacher's relationship with one student affects his or her relationship with all students. An administrator's relationship with one teacher or one staff member affects his of her relationship with all teachers and all staff members. In addition, peers always identify and relate to peers. Therefore, one must never forget—even for a minute—that leadership action or nonaction taken with one student or one teacher affects the relationships with all being led.

HOW WE TAKE
ACTION ALWAYS COUNTS

We need to be aware of the reality that how we take action counts at all times—and especially when taking any corrective or disciplinary action against a person being led. We must be aware that it's not only *what* we do, but *how* we do it which will be judged by all. For instance, let's consider the most disrespectful student in class. If the teacher kicks him or her out of class and treats him or her in a harsh and disrespectful way, this law teaches us that other students will side with their classmate. If, in a harsh and uncaring way, an administrator terminates the worst teacher in school, the one everyone dislikes and thinks is worthless, the administrator can expect the following to be said by others: "You mean they let him go?" "After fifteen years, they fired him?"

Remember, when leaders take harsh, inconsiderate, or uncaring action with those being led—no matter what the reason—they damage relationships with all students and staff because peers relate to peers. Consciously or subconsciously, the normal response is this: "If the leader did it to him, he or she can do it to me. If the leader did it to her, he or she will do it to me." Thus, the key is not just doing what we have to do. Rather, it's how we do it that counts. Remember, we said there are only two ways to lead people: being pleasant or being unpleasant. We said the leadership objective should be to do the right thing, in the right way, for the right reason. This is why we must opt to function on the highest level. We must never forget that concern, caring, and consideration must be part of our action because it puts "pleasant" as well as the leadership objective into the most unpleasant situations. And there are students who will have to be removed from class. And there will be teachers and administrators who must be confronted and even terminated. When these actions are necessary, this law tell us that our actions should not turn others away from us.

CHOOSING TO BE PLEASANT
ALWAYS PAYS OFF

Unfortunately, any leader who has led very long has had a bad experience in his or her efforts to make it pleasant for people to do what he or she wants them to do. Some have had many bad experiences. As a result, many have come to believe and practice the "you can't be nice to people" philosophy. They believe a leader must carry a big stick and use or threaten to use it often in order to lead people. When this is the adopted leadership attitude and action, the leadership personality automatically becomes punitive. It takes on an unpleasant demeanor. One simply begins leading toward the negative and away from the positive and productive with everyone. The Law of Leader-Follower Relationships reminds us that this is a dangerous road to take. It tells us our relationships with all those being led will be altered as a result.

Fortunately, successful leaders know this kind of leadership is not good for them, the institution, or those being led. Not only does it make being led a terrible experience, it makes leading even more miserable—and it pushes those being led away. Those leaders who choose to abuse the power delegated to them and who then adopt a leadership philosophy and direction based on mistreatment seldom find any degree of happiness and satisfaction in their life's work. More important, they seldom survive in their positions of leadership over the long term. In the years ahead, they will find survival almost impossible. The only way they will manage to stay in leadership positions is to move continually from job to job and district to district.

When you're dealing with those being led, be aware of the teaching of this law continually. Your relationship with one affects your relations with all. And when push comes to shove, those being led always identify with each other. It's easy to see why. In the final analysis, they are all in the same boat—and they know it. So should you. The truth of the matter is that treating the worst student or teacher in a considerate, concerned, and caring way while you take the action you must take can "make" your relationship with everyone else. And when a leader tries to make an example out of a person, he or she usually impairs his or her relationships with everyone else.

THE LAW:
APPLIED

1. Share ways to counsel those being led without jeopardizing the relationship with the group.
2. Discuss leadership behaviors which should never occur publicly.
3. Discuss why fear may be a counterproductive behavior.
4. Discuss the value of due process.
5. Why will the behavior of the leader ultimately be judged?
6. Discuss the danger in using one person as an example or creating a standard by treating him or her harshly.

THE
LAW OF
GROUP COMMUNICATION

Rationale: Leadership communication should be arranged and presented in such a manner that the messages offered impact personally upon the listener—or only partial listening will result.

I have stated repeatedly that listening and achieving understanding is a constant leadership responsibility. And a close look will reveal that everyone says that he or she listens and understands, but the other person doesn't listen and understand. Students say they listen and understand, but teachers don't. Administrators say they listen and understand, but teachers don't. Boards of education say they listen and understand, but educators don't. If we understand this law, however, we know it's *not odd* to think the problems of listening and understanding lie with those being led.

Yet, all leadership laws relate emphatically that the responsibility for achieving understanding lies at the top. It rests with the teacher in the classroom. It rests with the administrator in a school or district. However, there are two primary reasons those being led do not understand the communications from the leader. First, they aren't interested. Second, they don't listen.

PERSONAL IMPACT PLUS...
RESPECT

Most certainly, it is recognized that a leader can't force those being led to listen or be interested. Too, we all know that no leader can influence everyone in every place all the time. Teachers can't. Administrators can't. Yet, we also know that every leader can change both the communication approach and technique to gain a better success average for arousing interest, listening, and understanding. Herein lies the key to gaining the listening and the understanding of those being led.

What every leader must know and appreciate is that if he or she wants someone to listen and understand something, he or she must work hard and smart to explain it—and take definite steps to make sure he or she is reaching those being led with his or her message. This is not as difficult as one might think, because some important facts are known about communication. In relation to the Law of Group Communication, there are two very important facts that a leader must be aware of when planning to talk to groups. These facts constitute the primary reasons people often don't listen to a speaker in group situations. A leader cannot ignore or discount the existence of these realities:

1. People don't listen to the speaker because they believe what is being discussed doesn't pertain to or affect them personally.
2. People don't listen because they believe their own opinions, beliefs, or judgments are superior to those which are being offered by the speaker.

That's why the following leadership techniques facilitate group listening:

- Arranging the message so that is has as much personal impact on the listener as possible.
- Making every effort to gain the respect of students and staff by planning, preparing, and knowing what you're talking about—and knowing whom you are talking to.

THREE VITAL FACTS ABOUT COMMUNICATION

The Law of Group Communication teaches us three basic concepts that cannot be forgotten. First, we are always speaking to *individuals*—even when talking in group situations. Second, people are concerned about what affects them in a direct way. Therefore, when the leader's communication has personal impact and reliable subject matter, interest in listening and understanding is enhanced. That's why it's wise to offer "cause and effect" messages whenever possible. And we must offer both the direct and indirect impact on each person in the audience. Third, when those being led don't listen, the leader can—in many ways—either command listening or deprive those being led of a secondary need such as power, status, or autonomy. That's a hard statement, but a truthful one. And leaders do it consciously or subconsciously daily when those they lead do not listen to their urgings and follow their directions—or work to accomplish tasks or achieve goals. We pull away; we focus on others; we give our attention elsewhere. Make no mistake: We must not revert to being unpleasant.

Most certainly, a leader can't deprive those being led of a primary need like food or shelter because of a reluctance to listen and act on requests. But we can withhold a secondary need such as status, power, autonomy, affiliation, praise, and recognition. This, of course, is dependent upon how much those being led care whether we love, praise, or honor them.

THE LAW: APPLIED

1. What is the personal impact for each student in not completing an assignment?
2. Share the issues you have faced in the (classroom) (school) (district). How have these subjects impacted personally on those being led?
3. Share ways we withhold a secondary need.

THE
LAW OF
CONFRONTING

Rationale: A leader must confront both people and problems if success is to be
achieved, but those who confront by attacking or accusing will fail.

All our lives, we have been taught that honesty is the best policy. We believe it's
always the best course of action. Yet, when it comes to confronting another person about
something that is wrong or something we dislike, we can often rationalize talking to
everyone else about the problem, but not confronting that person. In the process, we can
convince ourselves that *not* confronting is the caring and wise thing to do. There may be
many good reasons we choose this course. And, as leaders, we need to look at those reasons
because certain beliefs can affect our success.

A DIFFICULT
MOVE

None can deny that it's easier to write about confronting than to do it. In the first place,
many of our experiences with confronting or being confronted have been negative ones.
That's why we can think of all kinds of reasons not to confront. Therefore, when we feel the
need and urge to confront, all kinds of personal emotions are brought into play. One is fear.
We may fear the other person and his or her reaction. We may not know how to confront,
not be able to find the right time and place, not want to take the time, or not really care
enough to take such an unpleasant and threatening action as confronting.

Regardless of the reason we might have for our reluctance to confront, if teachers and
administrators cannot and will not perfect the art of productive confrontation, few problems
will be resolved. As a result, we will have difficulty being effective leaders. The plain truth
is that if we can't confront successfully, we can't always help those being led improve or
change. Likewise, if we can't confront, we might not get some of the work of the classroom
or school accomplished—or get it done very well. That's why confrontation is often the best
course of action. Sometimes it's the only one.

Of course, there are different kinds of confrontations. Obviously, a duel with swords is
one kind. An honest, open, and gentle exchange of differences is quite another. One is a
war, the other is not—and there are few situations in our lives that call for action as strong as
war. Unfortunately, however, we often think of confrontation as being just that—a war.

Once we eliminate this myth from our minds, we can begin to learn to use
confrontation as a valuable and necessary leadership tool. If we still question the wisdom of
confronting, we should ask ourselves whether the decision not to confront can be called a
genuine solution or simply a shallow avoidance of responsibility.

A WAY
TO BEGIN

Confronting may not be something you like to do as a teacher or an administrator, but it is something you have to do. And you need to do it well. Therefore, realize that there is no such thing as the right time or place—but there may be the wrong time and place. For instance, *public* confrontations with anyone about anything should be avoided. In the classroom, this may be difficult. But if there is a way to move to the back or a corner of the room or into the hall and lower your voice, you must. When you know you must confront, be aware that people don't confront people or situations that they don't care about. Quite the contrary. Herein lies the key to your leadership attitude, approach, and action when confronting.

First, always talk about caring when you confront. Convey the fact that things don't get resolved unless they are talked out and worked out. And be sure you tell the person you are talking to that you know he or she can handle the truth of your thinking better than the deceit of your saying nothing. Let the person absorb what you are saying—and never force or demand a response. Often, it's wise to make your first discussion short. But always make plans to talk again soon. Never let the matter hang for days before you talk again.

Second, be sure to use tact and diplomacy. If you attack, you will take ten steps backward. As a result, the healing may take a long time.

Third, confront without accusing. All you need to do is ask questions which require a constructive response rather than a defense. This is easier to do if you act like a leader rather than a boss.

Fourth, be aware that a common mistake made in confronting is talking about everything but the real, core subject that led you to confront in the first place. Remember, you must touch the hurt. Therefore, don't skirt or talk around it. If you do, people will know what you're doing—and they'll resent it. Simply confront the issue in as gentle, caring, and considerate way as possible. You will find that you can confront almost any problem if those being led know you like and care about them. On the other hand, it's difficult to confront if those being led think you don't care about them. That's why you must lay a caring foundation. It's as important to you as the person you are confronting. After all, caring and love are the basis for human acceptance. And that's not surprising. Of all the emotions, it's the one we cannot seem to live without.

A NECESSARY SKILL

Make no mistake: Developing the skill to confront is easier if we look upon confrontations as an act of caring, rather than an act of reprimand or hate. This attitude alone will guide our approach. It will determine what we say and how we say it. It will also guarantee that we address the real issue rather than talk around it. Remember, we can't convince anyone that we care by playing games.

Confronting must be more than private. It must also remain confidential. It's the only way future caring and productive confrontations are possible. People don't want to hear how successfully a leader confronted those being led for fear that their own future confrontations with that leader will be made public. Leaders also need to realize that a reluctance to confront may say something about how they feel about being confronted themselves. As we speak, we may fear that the person we are confronting has some disclosures to make as well. Therefore, some attitude change may be necessary on our part. And if we can allow them, we'll find it quite a helpful and healing act.

Teachers and administrators know we do not reside in Utopia. We reside in classrooms and schools where the density of the population is probably the highest in town. That's why we always have people problems. We can't leave problems alone and help those we lead achieve. Our success in leading will never result from avoidance.

APPROACHING THE UNAPPROACHABLE

Unfortunately, there are some people we will always be reluctant to approach. In fact, we may be afraid to approach them—much less confront them to resolve a problem. And if we are afraid of them, we can be certain others are as well. And the unapproachable include more than the professional staff. Sometimes, custodians, clerks, secretaries, and others qualify for the title. Or it may be a student or parent. We all know who they are. We avoid them. We may never think of questioning them. Yet, whether we have thought about it or not, two questions remain. First, what are we doing to change or cope with them? Second, is it possible that the person is counting on being unapproachable? We've all experienced the foot-dragger and the obstructionist. We also know the hard-nosed person who stands firm, rejects, and has the fortitude to make it stick. When it comes time to adjust or change, this person won't budge. It doesn't take long to identify these derailing people—and label them *unapproachable*. And that ends that—maybe.

If we aren't observant, we may fail to notice that the staff in a school and the students in the classroom may be grateful for them. After all, these students and educators can be depended on to veto any new plan and influence enough people to cancel almost any new idea. Therefore, they save others work. With them around, others can settle for the status quo. Others can even be lazy. Others don't have to worry about measuring up to standards with them around. They don't have to propose anything new. They can pass along the responsibility for failure. Others are even saved from contributing anything negative. More than anyone may care to admit, others may use unapproachable people as a crutch. And if a leader chooses a hands-off approach in response to the actions of the unapproachable, he or she actually reinforces this behavior.

Usually, the entire staff or the entire class knows that Mr. Smith or Donald Jones is always tagged as the culprit. And if it's a lazy staff or class, the members will never confront the unapproachable. They will be content with saying, "It's wrong or sad that we can't do anything because of Mr. Smith or Donald Jones." If we're honest, we know this stance isn't good enough. That is, it isn't if we are leaders who hold ourselves responsible.

DEALING WITH ISSUES

If someone breaks his or her leg, does a doctor choose to do nothing to avoid hurting the leg further? Of course not. Neither does the doctor choose to treat our arm to avoid touching our injured leg. Yet, this is what leaders often do. When we have a personality conflict with a staff member, we may criticize his or her technique or competency, rather than deal with the real issues. If an entire class fails a test, we may say the students didn't study, rather than confront the teacher. We may even skirt the real issues in faculty disagreements and devote much time and energy to countless side effects. And that's the problem. We don't touch the hurt where the pain and injury are—and nothing gets resolved.

Like the doctor, we must deal with the issues gently and directly. A doctor can't set a broken leg without touching it. The doctor knows it will hurt. The doctor's responsibility is to touch the hurt in a caring way and cause as little pain as possible in the process so that the healing can begin. Our responsibility as teachers and administrators is the same.

Unfortunately, many people were taught as children to avoid issues. It was part of their upbringing. Even if we were hurting ourselves, we may have learned it was best to keep it buried within ourselves. Telling adults about our problems only brought more problems. Mother would say, "If you can't get along with Johnny, don't play with him." So we learned to make choices. We decided that the best rule for survival was not to touch our own hurts—much less those of others.

If we have managed to come to adulthood through this system of ignoring our hurts, then we may function the same way as adults. This presents a formidable problem—especially if we are in a position of working with people. Such is the case for teachers and administrators. After all, it's impossible to lead in a responsible way without confronting.

Hopefully, we recognize that there is something we can do. We can change. Admittedly, this is a difficult thing to do. We may not know how to go about changing, much less approaching our hurt and the hurts of those we lead in a caring way. But we will be very effective if we refuse to attack—and we refuse to accuse.

THREE THINGS
TO REMEMBER

As leaders, when we decide to touch the hurt, we need to remember three things. First, we must make sure we are dealing with the real issues in a professional, rather than a petty way. We cannot allow ourselves any "game playing" here—for this is a serious business. Second, we need to deal quickly and honestly with problems, rather than let them grow. Third, we need to deal in a caring way with the hurts of those we lead, trying to cause the least amount of hurt in the healing process. This is our challenge as professionals. It is not one we can avoid.

Remember, the hurts of people do not dissipate like morning dew on a leaf. Just as some people do not want to go to the dentist for fear of pain, many teachers and administrators do not look forward to meeting issues head-on. People often delay going to the doctor or dentist until the pain of not going is greater than the anticipated pain of going. This is a mistake. In truth, dealing with the hurt often causes less pain than anticipated. Indeed, it may cause less pain than all the things we may do to avoid it. And our professional position dictates that we treat issues. It is our responsibility to touch the hurt in a caring way—remembering that some of the hurt may have to do with us.

We humans too often function out of our reluctance, when we ought to be functioning out of our love. The times that we will be rebuffed for offering love are so infrequent that they are hardly worth mentioning. This is particularly true in the administrator-teacher and teacher-student relationship.

THE LAW:
APPLIED

1. Share ways to confront without accusing.

2. Discuss common fears related to confronting the unapproachable.
3. How can you reveal caring when confronting?
4. Discuss (words) (phrases) to avoid using when confronting.
5. Using failure as the topic, share gentle and caring ways to touch the heart.

A LEADERSHIP OBJECTIVE: MOVING PAST OBLIGATION TO COMMITMENT

All of us came to our schools and our responsibility as teachers and administrators from different families with different backgrounds and for different reasons. We have different strengths, weaknesses, positions, functions, and academic disciplines. We have so many different life experiences that we can honestly say we are all totally different human beings—even though we are all educators. In reality, there are probably as many different lifestyles and life experiences among the people in a school as there are people in a school. And yet, it can be accurately stated that we are more alike than unlike each other. This truth is vitally important to us and our success as leaders because we all have the same basic human wants and needs, such as the need for security, the desire to avoid fear, and the need to be wanted and loved and successful.

Even our strengths and weaknesses as human beings are more alike than different. It's only their degrees of intensity which vary among us. For instance, we all have fears and problems—they differ only in how big or small they are. It's very likely that we've even thought the same thoughts and shared the same dreams. Yet, we all need the same professional foundations to be successful. Two of those professional foundations are obligation and commitment.

YOUR FOUNDATIONS MUST BE OPERATIONAL

To be successful leaders, we must fulfill our obligations. If we don't, we will fail. But we also need to think and function in terms of commitment if we want to operate on the highest level. Unfortunately, we may avoid these two issues. In fact, we may regard such issues as just another attempt made to get us to do more without paying us any more money to do it. Yet, if we are serious about being the best leader we can be and finding more and more satisfaction in being a leader, these are the kinds of issues we need to address.

When we discuss personal and professional foundations, simply talking about being good is not a very good foundation. Nor is the ability to quote the latest trends or priorities in education. It's a good beginning. But to be a successful leader as a teacher or an administrator, one must have an operational foundation. Our professional foundations must work for us in a practical and living way, because we need our foundations often in the classroom and the office. If our foundations aren't workable, we won't use them.

Worse, if our foundations aren't used often, we'll feel clumsy when we want to use them. That's the way we humans are with the unfamiliar and uncomfortable.

Unfortunately, many leaders don't understand the importance of good foundations. And some of those people are teachers and administrators. But one foundation that we all need in order to find success and satisfaction as leaders is to come to our jobs with a greater sense of commitment than obligation.

As human beings, we are reminded often of our obligations as well as our commitments. We are told frequently of our obligations as a wife and mother, husband and father, employee and employer. We are also told of the commitments we must make on all fronts in order to be productive, successful, and good people. That's why we need to know the difference between obligation and commitment. Such an understanding can give us direction. It can help us make good decisions. It can move us to the highest level of personal and professional functioning. It can enhance our happiness, satisfaction, and effectiveness in life with ourselves, our colleagues, and our students.

BECAUSE WE HAVE TO—
BECAUSE WE WANT TO

If someone does favors for us, we usually find ourselves obligated to return them. Likewise, if we incur a financial debt, we are obligated to repay it. In other words, we are responding because we feel we must—and so do others. As educators, we understand the importance of obligations very well. We must. After all, we will feel the weight of obligation frequently in our role as a teacher or administrator.

Commitment, on the other hand, is an emotional pledge that we choose to make because we want to. It has an entirely different weight. It has an entirely different intention. While obligation is often imposed or demanded by position and circumstances, commitment is a free decision to invest effort or time. Transposing this into specifics is easy. We all know the person who acts only out of some kind of obligation and the one who is motivated by commitment. They are two different people. One thinks in terms of what he or she must do. The other thinks in terms of what he or she can do. Can we possibly think the person who operates under obligation is achieving his or her potential as a person? I think not. This person will not achieve his or her potential with his or her family, friends, or work.

Make no mistake: These people will get by—because they meet their obligations. But they'll never find the quality of life that commitment offers. Remember, obligation is a duty. Commitment is a free choice to invest. Therefore, commitment is always a positive. Obligation is often a negative. And positives are very important in our lives. The motivation, stimulation, and confidence needed to live productive and rewarding lives are impaired by the negative. One negative person can ruin your whole day. Commitment guarantees you a positive relationship with ideas, goals, work, and people. Obligation just gives you another duty, and it may be one you don't want to perform.

A WAY
OF LIFE

Living and leading only out of obligation can make you go through life never knowing who you are, much less being all you can be. With commitment, you don't have to bear any crosses, for you have made a free choice. You bear a cross only under obligation. Commitment is made out of love and desire. Obligation, unfortunately, can be out of fear or guilt.

Commitment allows you to easily and openly admit when you're wrong—to yourself and to others. Obligation does not. In fact, a close look will reveal obligation can promote offering excuses, alibis, and rationalizations when you are wrong. Commitment allows you to use your strengths. Obligation can exploit your weaknesses. In many ways, obligation is a form of slavery. Commitment is a natural self-motivator. Obligation is not. Rather, it forces compliance. Obligation is also one of the biggest producers of dislike, dissatisfaction, and unhappiness.

There are many people out there who hate their jobs because of forced obligations. They avoid commitment because they think it only involves giving. It doesn't. You get back much more from commitment than you give, for it's commitment that allows a person to reach for his or her potential in a complete and embracing kind of way—whether it's at home or at work.

I like commitment because it is simple, natural, intelligent, enjoyable, and a profound way to be totally involved in each day and each relationship—and to try to make each day and relationship count for something. Lack of commitment puts the heaviest restrictions on us because it usually makes us put limitations on what we will or will not do. And that's a heavy burden. It makes living up to what we want to be and what we should be almost impossible. As leaders, we should easily see why commitment is one of those vital factors which determines the success and the satisfaction we get out of being a teacher or an administrator.

WE CHOOSE HOW
WE WILL FUNCTION

Make no mistake: Our choice to function out of obligation or commitment permeates our entire lives—both personal and professional. We cannot act out of commitment at school and obligation at home and function very successfully. At least, I've never known anyone who has. From experience, I have come to believe that when we are functioning out of commitment, we are usually happy. When we are functioning out of obligation, we may be angry and resentful—and sometimes we don't even know why.

It's easy for the rest of us to criticize the person who operates only out of obligation. But our sense of obligation has been with us for a long time. It has been drilled into us. And it's not bad. But people will continue to hammer us with obligation because it helps them control us. That's why we can't easily move away from the moral burdens of obligation that are placed on us.

We are taught, for instance, to do a fair day's work for a fair day's pay whether we want to do that kind of work or not. So we stay in jobs we shouldn't be in. We tell young people not to quit what they begin even if their reasons for quitting are both good and healthy. We tell women they are not good wives or mothers for countless reasons—if dinner isn't ready, the laundry isn't done, or they want to pursue a career. We tell husbands they are bad if they don't fix the faucet or play with their children every day.

All along the way, obligations are put upon us. Unfortunately, trailing after our obligations often seems to be the easiest course, until we realize—if we ever do—that avoiding a head-on experience with our own feelings is not a resolution of anything. It turns out to be a most miserable postponement. That's the way it is with obligation. How different it is to come to our jobs out of a sense of wanting to rather than a feeling that we must. We cannot be made victims out of commitment, because we approach our job with the most solid and sound foundations. This is the only way we, as leaders, should come to our jobs if we expect to cause others to want our leadership.

THE DIFFERENCE NEEDS
OUR CONSIDERATION

A Leadership Objective: Moving Past Obligation to Commitment

The lessons inherent in the difference between commitment and obligation need to be considered by every leader. It's important to understand that our whole lives can be shaped out of whether we initiate what we do as leaders out of obligation or commitment. Very often, leaders settle for being obligated because they don't want to think their way through to feeling committed. We shouldn't make this mistake. There are at least three things we can do to make commitment a bigger part of our lives.

First, we can get our priorities straight. Schools were created to meet the needs of students. They were not created to employ secretaries, bookkeepers, custodians, principals, teachers, superintendents, or anyone else. As the Law of Origin teaches us: A person or institution must operate in agreement with the reason for its existence, or failure rather than success becomes the probability. Maybe if we started approaching leadership out of a sense of what we want to do for students rather than ourselves, we wouldn't be so burdened with obligation.

Second, we can keep our perspectives straight. We shouldn't expect bands to play when we meet our obligations and do what we should. Operating from the level of obligation is not functioning from the highest of levels. Nobody reaches any kind of mountain top through obligation. And those being led aren't grateful when we do only what we have to do—or what we are paid to do. If we started approaching leadership in terms of what we can do, rather than what we don't have to do, we wouldn't feel the negative weight of our duties so heavily. And we would, most certainly, experience a new level of leadership success and satisfaction.

Third, we can keep our vision. Maybe if we had the vision to know what business we're in, we wouldn't have any trouble making decisions or serving the needs of students. A lot of major businesses, institutions, and professions have gotten into trouble because they forgot what business they were in. If we view ourselves as teachers, principals, superintendents, or specialists of some kind, then our leadership course and action will most likely be both individual and limited. In truth, if we hold such a vision, we are job-oriented rather than student-oriented. That's why the need to sit down and examine what business we are really in is a vital leadership priority. After all, we're not in the teacher or administrator business. We're in the business of enriching lives. We're in the business of preparing students to learn and live better today—and tomorrow. And once we decide what business we are in—and should we decide that we're in the business of learning for today, learning for tomorrow, and enriching lives—our options for leadership are wide open.

A CHECKLIST FOR UNDERSTANDING
AND APPLICATION

1. What obligations do you have as (a teacher) (an administrator)?
2. Discuss the good and necessary aspects of obligation.
3. Share your beliefs regarding commitment.
4. What is preventing you from functioning out of commitment?
5. Discuss the advantages of functioning out of commitment.

CHAPTER 19

BECOMING A STAR—AND A STAR MAKER

There isn't any doubt as to who has already reached "star status" in the school. Teachers have. Principals have. Superintendents have. We have already been able to raise our own star. This is evident by the fact that we have been named the appointed leader and chief executive officer in the classroom, school, or district. However, this is not the real issue when it comes to being an effective leader. To lead for results in any organization, the leader must look upon himself or herself as a star maker and continually think and act accordingly. This includes developing a plan of training in the classroom, the school, and the district so that success becomes a higher probability for everyone we lead.

The reason for this leadership stance is obvious: When it comes to success in a classroom, school, or district, a bell curve of performance does not create highly productive and fulfilled people or a good organization. Rather, we must make *everyone* productive and successful. And the more stars we can make out of those being led, the more successful we will be as leaders.

This principle applies to every level of appointed leadership. A teacher is a star maker. A principal is a star maker. A superintendent is a star maker. The members of the board of education are star makers. This means we can't just sit back on our own stardom and hope that the cream of those being led will rise to the top and that we will be successful leaders.

MANY LEADERS FOCUS
ON THEIR OWN STAR

One of the reasons that this concept isn't practiced faithfully is that an appointed leader is already looked upon as the star—and often looks at himself or herself as the only one who is supposed to be the star. Many appointed leaders even tend to think in terms of how they *should* be the big star—and how those being led exist only to help make them even bigger stars. Unfortunately, many leaders work very hard to raise their own star even higher and don't give too much consideration to trying to make stars out of those being led.

If you're an administrator, your job is to become a teacher of teachers. And everything you ask teachers to be to students, you must be to teachers. Teachers must take a similar stance with students. If you don't take this stance, then there's no reason for you to be the appointed leader for those being led. The idea is for the appointed leader to bring everyone in the school to a higher level of functioning.

As long as the goal of each appointed leader is to facilitate the success of those being led, the right steps can be taken. Remember, those being led aren't apt to fight leaders who are helpers and advocates. They aren't likely to resist or reject leaders who are trying to help them be successful and find satisfaction. Why? People don't ignore or fight advocates—and for good reason. Those being led don't have a world full of leaders—or anyone else—who are committed to their success and welfare. That's why those being led are prone to follow leaders who are advocates trying to help them be successful. In fact, those being led are likely to "go along with" and follow such a leader even if they aren't completely sure that they should, simply because they trust the leader and don't want to risk losing an advocate.

YOU MUST FIND THE GIFT
IN EACH PERSON YOU LEAD

I have said it before, but it needs to be said again and again. Everyone you lead has talent. Everyone being led has strengths. If you want to reach goals, get results, and experience achievement, your job as a leader is twofold.

First, you must find the talent and gift in each person being led, and then magnify, glorify, and perpetuate that strength to its fullest. Without doubt, many leaders fail to take this course. They can find weaknesses in people, but they can't find and utilize strengths. The weaknesses of those being led "hit them in the face" quickly. Worse, some leaders find such a weakness and repeatedly use it to beat to death those being led with their shortcomings. They tell those being led what they aren't rather than what they are and can be. They don't increase productivity and effectiveness or create many stars as a result.

Remember, it is via the strengths of individuals that you will be able to gain participation, reach goals, and create stars. This reality applies to students, teachers, principals, superintendents, and the board of education. Therefore, the real leadership task is to know those being led, to be a talent finder, and to develop talent to the highest level possible.

If you're a weakness finder and have a tendency to focus on weaknesses rather than strengths, you will quickly and easily discover the shortcomings of all. It's easy. It requires no special expertise. And whether you intend to or not, you will magnify, glorify, and perpetuate weakness and failure. You will end up with people who don't feel very good about themselves—and don't do very well either. You will be surrounded by people who don't think they can achieve—so they won't. Then, it is very unlikely that your leadership will produce results for those being led in the classroom, school, or district.

Your second task, of course, is to detect the weaknesses and help people minimize, neutralize, overcome, or compensate for these weaknesses. In the process, you need to be aware that a leader will never build a star by focusing on the weaknesses of an individual. Yet, we all have weaknesses. That's why leadership efforts, if we intend to get results, must teach to correct shortcomings while focusing heavily on the strengths of the individual and the group.

FOCUSING ON STRENGTHS
ALLOWS WEAKNESSES TO BE APPROACHED

"But," you say, "we can't let weaknesses go unchecked." No, we can't. In truth, it is by focusing on strengths that we are allowed to approach weaknesses in a constructive way. Why? Because once people have the competency, success, and security that come from their strengths, they are much more willing and able to work on their shortcomings.

People have an easier time working on their weaknesses when their strengths are producing success. When the focus is only on weaknesses, however, strengths may not be used—or even seen as much of a value. That's why recognizing and developing strengths must be the primary objective of the leader—whether that person is the leader of the classroom, the school, or the district.

Remember, no student, no teacher, and no administrator will ever have every strength that he or she needs without also having some weaknesses. Therefore, when we tackle weaknesses, we must position ourselves to do so without "tearing down." For instance, we must give those being led constructive criticism whether they want it or not. The idea, however, is to have those being led receive what we say without lowering their motivation and productivity. This means offering correction in such a way that those being led accept it without feeling degraded—or without feeling angry, resentful, or embarrassed. We want those being led to receive our criticism, learn, and, if possible, be grateful that we cared enough and were capable enough to help them. Believe it or not, there are actions we can take when we criticize to build up those being led rather than tear them down—if we focus on strengths. By learning and mastering these techniques, we can help those we lead deal with their shortcomings and learn from their mistakes.

CRITICISM IS AN EVALUATION OF BOTH THE POSITIVE AND THE NEGATIVE

We need to know—and teach those being led—what criticism is by definition and design. It may surprise us to learn that criticism is the evaluation of both positives and negatives. Make no mistake: Criticism is not reserved for the negative. And this is where many leaders err. They don't know criticism as a positive—and, therefore, use criticism only for the negative. That's why it usually tears down rather than builds up.

We can begin by teaching that criticism is a method of developing and teaching ideas, concepts, and skills. Then we can make sure that criticism is no longer used only as a negative form of feedback or corrective instruction. We can help those being led experience criticism as a positive if we employ these ten actions.

First, we must focus on the *delivery* more than we focus on the *content* of our criticism. When it comes to constructive criticism, *how* we say it can be as important as *what* we say. Second, we must *always* place the heaviest emphasis of any corrective effort on protecting the self-esteem of those being led. Third, we must remember that labeling a person as *dumb*, *foolish*, or *lazy* will not help us achieve our objective—but will cause anger and resentment. When correcting a person, we must remember that we can never develop or build up a person by accusation or attack.

Fourth, we must design our approach to fit the individual, not the criticism or the condition. To build people up, we can't handle a failure the same way with everyone we lead and expect the same outcome. Those we lead are different. Some are sensitive—others have a thick skin. And some of those we think have a thick skin really don't. Therefore, we must know people thoroughly, consider the personality of the person we are correcting, and be flexible and creative in how we approach each person.

Fifth, we must realize that criticism needs a carefully planned time and place to be constructive and effective. Seldom, if ever, will public criticism make anyone feel good about us or our words of advice. Likewise, a blanket criticism of the whole class or the entire staff is a waste of time and a breeder of discord. It has one probability: it will tear

Sixth, to build people up, we must know that criticism requires two-way conversations rather than one-way judgments. Rather than just saying what's on our mind, we need to focus on getting those being led involved in the conversation. Our goal must be to find out what happened, what those we lead were thinking, and what they think can be done to improve or change the situation. Just telling those being led that they're wrong does little to develop their strengths or teach them anything, except that we don't think they're very good or very smart—and that we lack good manners.

Seventh, to engage people in positive conversations, we need to abandon the *you did* approach. Instead, we should use the *I-you-I* technique. With this technique, we say, "*I* think you calculated incorrectly. What do *you* think? *I* can't figure out how you arrived at this answer." Above all, we should avoid starting any sentence with *you*. It only serves to accuse, rather than to teach or show the way. That's why using the *I-you-I* technique works.

Eighth, criticism becomes constructive only when options or solutions are offered or help is given to find options or solutions. If we start with pointing out the errors or faults, our words never proceed to the positive or constructive. And when we just criticize and then walk away and let those being led *hang*, they aren't apt to feel good about themselves or us. To build people up with criticism, we must guide them to options, choices, or possible answers to the problem. It's that simple.

Ninth, we must remember that *destructive* criticism is confrontational. It's unpleasant. It's harsh. In contrast, *constructive* criticism is calm. It's helpful. It employs concern and caring. It is sensitive and positive.

Tenth, constructive criticism requires follow-up—including the offer of more help. As a form of teaching, only follow-up lets us know if our effort to guide, help, and show the way was successful—and gives us another chance to give positive guidance and input. It also allows us to build strong and enduring relationships with those being led.

As leaders, we can't develop the art of showing the way without developing the art of correcting and criticizing. Like the art of teaching, the art of constructively criticizing requires that we pick people up wherever they are and take them as far as they can go. Both require developing and employing leadership skills as an advocate, not as a critic.

Nothing is gained if our criticism makes those being led angry or causes them to pull away. Likewise, all is lost if our efforts to correct cause embarrassment and resentment, damage self-worth, or jeopardize relationships. When our efforts produce such results, we can't build until we rebuild. However, when we keep the definition and design of criticism in mind, we are best prepared to proceed successfully. Criticism is, after all, an evaluation of the positive *and* the negative. And only by recognizing the positive aspects of every negative situation can we build up those being led.

LEADERS CAN'T BE EFFECTIVE UNLESS THEIR PEOPLE ARE

It's a teacher's task to make stars of his or her students. Principals must make stars of teachers. Superintendents must make stars of principals. And the board must make a star of the superintendent. And all of us will be stars only when we are successful at doing the work we are supposed to do. This is one of the primary objectives and functions of the appointed leader. Why? There is no way a teacher can be successful unless students are successful. The principal can't be successful unless teachers are. Likewise, a superintendent can't be successful unless principals are—and the board can't achieve success unless the superintendent does.

Will everyone we lead achieve to the same level? No. Some will achieve far more than others, but the goal should be for each person to achieve to the level of his or her abilities and the standards necessary for the organization to be successful. And each should reach for his or her potential. And, of course, some of those being led should achieve beyond us. Therefore, we must be committed to helping some of those we lead reach heights beyond our own attainment.

The problem is that people love looking for weaknesses in others. After all, weaknesses and flaws are so easy to find. And creating stars is more difficult because it requires that the leader make an investment. And, of course, some leaders are afraid someone will be a bigger star than they are. Yet, we can't achieve or be effective with weakness as our focus. Strengths, ours and everyone else's, are the key to leading successfully. Therefore, if we want to be a significant star, we must start making significant stars out of those we lead by making sure they are successful with work and relationships. That's what effective leadership is all about—and it's the only way we will raise our own star any higher. In addition, to be a highly effective leader, we need at least four competencies which are discussed in the next chapter.

A CHECKLIST FOR UNDERSTANDING AND APPLICATION

1. Identify the various talents of those being led.
2. How can a person literally find success and "live off" one talent?
3. Discuss the ten recommendations for correcting or criticizing. How do those apply to your leadership?
4. Discuss the statement: There's no way a leader can be successful unless those being led are successful. Next, discuss success relative to this statement.
5. Share the special insights needed for teachers, principals, and superintendents who wish to make stars out of those being led.

THREE KINDS OF LEADERS

A close look will reveal that leaders function predominantly in certain ways. In this regard, there are only three kinds of leaders anywhere—including in the classroom, and the office, and the student body:

1. The Creators
2. The Maintainers
3. The Destroyers

The creators are proactive. They are the catalysts for achievement. They think in terms of making things happen for people and the institution. Creators are always trying to "make a better mousetrap." They are positive, progressive, and forward-looking.

Maintainers do not think in such ways. They do not think in terms of "making a better mousetrap." Instead, they think, "If I already have a mousetrap and it is working, why would I try to make a better one?" In a school, the maintainers will keep doing what they have always done—in the same way and with the same intensity. If they have a lesson that works, they will keep using it. If they sponsor a club, they will use the same activities year after year.

The destroyers are easy to identify. They have but one answer to any situation: "The less I have to do the better." They are always in search of the things they believe shouldn't be required or the things that could be eliminated from the workload. And they are almost always negative.

THE
CREATORS

Only the creators function proactively, generate positive and constructive energy, instill a desire to fulfill obligations, and inspire functioning out of commitment. They operate from a platform of total acceptance of responsibility and adhere to the Law of Proactive Leadership and the Law of Origin.

Only the creators accept the reality that it is their responsibility to make things happen. They are proactive. Only the creators know that the moral, ethical, and professional tone of an institution is established to a large measure by the chief executive officer. Time and time again, it has been proven that those being led will achieve in accordance with the pace and example of the leader. In many ways, those being led cannot be any better than their leader.

Neither can the classroom or institution.

For instance, we've known for a long time that there can be superb teachers in a school that has an ineffective principal, but we've also known that it's not possible to have a good school without an effective principal. And we've also known for a long time that the classroom teacher is the most significant factor in giving students a quality education.

The creators who lead our classrooms, schools, and districts are those who set the tone, climate, and pace for achieving and for enriching life. Teachers are the creators who instill enthusiasm and generate achievement in the classroom. Administrators are the creators who instill enthusiasm and generate the professional attitudes which promote a positive approach to teaching and accomplishing all the work of the school and district. First and foremost, those who are creators accept their position and function as the leaders. They make decisions out of strengths rather than capitulate to weaknesses. They never lose sight of the fact that the fundamental value in a school is the well-being of students. Every action and decision supports this fundamental value.

THE MAINTAINERS
AND DESTROYERS

In many ways, the maintainers and destroyers are alike. One difference, however, is that the maintainers erroneously think that the status quo will hold a classroom, school, or district on course and generate good leader-follower relationships in the process. Make no mistake: It will not. In truth, the achievement, competency, and efficiency in a classroom, school, or district must increase continuously just to keep pace with the natural evolution of new information and new needs. Status quo in any organization—be it a family, church, business, or school—almost guarantees regression. All it needs to go downhill is the passage of time.

The maintainers and destroyers do not adhere to the Law of Proactive Leadership or the Law of Origin. For example, a maintainer or destroyer might not always ask of a new idea, "Is it good for students?" Rather, he or she would more likely be concerned with whether or not staff members would accept or reject the offering. Before taking action on an idea, he or she might ask, "Will teachers like it or not?" "Will it cause teachers more work?" "Is it good for the administration?" or "Will it be easy or difficult to do?"

The leadership decisions and actions of the maintainer and destroyer focus on either continuing what is being done now or eliminating what is being done now. They usually end up with few followers—and none who don't hold views similar to their own. Good students and teachers tend to dislike or have little respect for the destroyers. Unfortunately, the destroyers don't know why. Yet, the answer is obvious.

We do, however, need maintainers in our organizations. Once something is started, we need people who will keep it going. Maintainers won't add anything or delete anything, but they do keep things going. They make excellent aides, but poor classroom teachers. They make good assistants, but ineffective principals or superintendents. They are maintainers, not proactive leaders. They are not good chief executive officers.

The big difference between the maintainer and the destroyer is that the destroyer is always looking for work, programs, and activities to eliminate. The destroyer believes the answer to every problem is elimination. If a fight occurs at a school party, his or her solution to the problem is to stop having school parties. He or she is always looking for less to do— and doesn't want to do what he or she is already doing. Unlike the destroyer, the maintainer is not an eliminator. However, neither is he or she adding to the services offered in the classroom or school. The status quo is his or her goal.

If we intend to be successful leaders, we must be creators. We must also be maintainers. We should never be destroyers.

THREE GUIDELINES FOR BEING A CREATOR

Being a creator is not an easy task. But this level of functioning should be our goal. If we remember three realities of being a highly effective leader, we are more likely to function as a creator. First, a leader must never forget that every person being led has the right to ask, "What is my leader doing for me—personally—to help me become successful?" Therefore, every student has the right to ask, "What is my teacher doing to help me be successful in this class?" Every teacher has a right to ask, "What is my principal doing to help me be successful in my classroom?" Every principal has the right to ask, "What is my superintendent doing to facilitate my professional success?" All those being led have a right to look for tangible evidence of their leader's concern for their success. As long as the leader's words and actions are providing an answer to this ever-present question being asked individually and collectively by those being led, the leader is functioning as a creator.

Second, we must recognize that, in truth, a leader does not have the right to criticize, judge, or evaluate anyone being led until he or she has first fulfilled the leadership responsibility of helping, guiding, and assisting through instruction. This means an administrator who evaluates teachers without first having a planned program of staff development in place has the "cart before the horse"—and will pay the price for the leadership mistake. And anything teachers require of students must first be taught to them—everything. For instance, if we want students to take notes in class, we must first teach them how to take notes successfully. This truth is also revealed in the Laws of Management. Effective leadership can only be achieved by showing the way. As long as we are facilitating the work of those being led, we are functioning as a creator.

Third, a teacher or administrator must accept the fact that when help is absent from leadership, then, as far as those being led are concerned, there is no leadership at all. When leadership help is nonexistent, those being led must depend on self-help and trial-and-error knowledge. Giving approval and appreciation of leadership efforts is difficult. Worse, negative attitudes and credibility gaps become the probability. In fact, those being led are likely to believe that the leader is incompetent. Truly, when this happens, leadership is no longer a function in the eyes of the followers. It is merely a position. Therefore, as long as we are trying to help, we are functioning as a creator. When we give up, quit, or let those being led try to be successful without us, we are functioning as a maintainer or destroyer.

A CHECKLIST FOR UNDERSTANDING AND APPLICATION

1. Discuss the need to be a maintainer.
2. When is eliminating appropriate in the leadership role?
3. To the fullest extent possible, list the attributes of a creator.
4. Compare these attributes with those of a (maintainer) (destroyer).

21

YOUR LEADERSHIP COMPASS

Demonstrating leadership is not being passive or defensive. Neither is it being protective of the status quo or searching for work or people to eliminate. There is nothing in the word *leader* that even hints that any of these stances hold the key to a leader's success. However, by both definition and intent, the words *leader* and *leadership* indicate that our words and deeds must be proactive and pull people and the institution toward success by meeting the needs of those being led—so that they can meet the needs of those being served.

However, if we are to be highly effective and take some of the trial and error out of the leadership experience, we will benefit from having a personal and professional compass. It's also helpful to have a moral compass. And our compass needs to point continually in one direction—at meeting the needs of students and getting the work and mission of the school accomplished. In our roles as leaders in the classroom, the school, and the district, we must use our compass to give us the mind-set, the understandings, the skills, and the passion needed to get the job done—and our professional foundations must be firm. We must commit to understanding the wants, needs, and motivations of human beings. And we must adhere to following the laws and principles of leadership and management when tackling work and leading people.

If every issue, every decision, and every action is made with our compass pointed toward our pursuit of and support for student learning and the welfare of students, we can take the right action, in the right way, for the right reason. In the process, we can monitor our direction and adjust our course with confidence. When the Law of Proactive Leadership and the Law of Origin are our foundation guides, all the laws and principles of leadership and management will, without reservation, give us the knowledge, expertise, and resolve to be extremely successful. One thing is certain: We will feel secure—and those being led will feel secure with us. And we won't make many mistakes—and we will draw those we lead toward us and our leadership.

But the choice of setting and using our compass is ours alone. The decision regarding how we lead is easier when one looks at the times we live in and the needs and opportunities facing the leader as well as those being led in the 21st century.

A NEW
ERA

We are on the brink of a new era. We are presiding over change in our society far greater than that which occurred during the era when we moved from an agricultural-based to an industrial-based economy. Our task in the 21st century involves educating all of our young people. Our task involves easing the pain of change. It also includes reducing the problems of our young people left behind in the industrial era while capitalizing on the new opportunities of the future. Make no mistake: We must make the problems arising out of the computer era easier to endure while success is being achieved. We must also deal with the challenges of those we lead as they compete in a global economy which is being driven and defined by the computer age. If the real test of learning is applying what has been learned to new and unfamiliar situations, both we and our students face the ultimate test. After all, change as well as working in new ways will be the ever-present conditions in the world of work in the 21st century.

The questions are these: What does the current leadership in classrooms and schools tell us about the new world our students are entering? Do we represent the leadership of the new era—or are we trying to operate out of the past? Are our leadership foundations and strengths innovating and exciting and designed to pull those being led toward us and build greater learning for students and greater support from parents and public alike? Are our leadership foundations and strengths designed to pull all students, teachers, and administrators to new heights—or is our leadership leaving many behind? And if our leadership is being ignored or rejected, we must know that something is wrong.

If we are destined to be effective leaders in the 21st century school, we must be proactive. We must be innovators. We must openly and freely challenge our own ways as well as the wisdom of what we are doing in classrooms and schools. We must be willing and able to take those we lead down new roads to meet new opportunities. We will, if we remember the words of Francis Bacon, "He that will not apply new remedies must expect new evils, for time is the greatest innovator."

In being proactive, we must trust the need as well as the readiness of those we lead to reach for success. In the process, we must be ready to expect resistance from those who want to hold on to the status quo and those who want to eliminate services which meet the needs of students. What we cannot do is abandon our professional compass, become paralyzed, and fail to act. Rather, we must dedicate ourselves to lifelong learning on both the technical/academic and people sides of our job. In the process, we must develop and reveal a spirit and an enthusiasm for each day and for each new task and hold firm to our mission of meeting the needs of students. To do so, however, we must also know and understand the rules of the game.

KNOWING THE RULES OF THE GAME

There are a lot of people in leadership positions who simply don't know the rules of the game. Yet, if you intend to play the game, you've got to know the rules—and you've got to play by the rules, or you'll fail. And if you're a teacher, principal, or superintendent, you're already in the game. In fact, you're already the captain of the team. You can try to ignore the rules or minimize them, but you won't be effective if you do. You can think you can make your own rules and play by your own rules, but you can't. You can try to change the rules of the game to meet your desires, but it won't work. And, of course, you can try to fight the rules of the game, but you will lose if you do. The rules are firm—and they are the same for all of us who are in positions of leadership.

The rules include what leadership is and is not. The rules include the primary needs, secondary needs, and people motivators. The rules include the Foundation Laws, the Laws and Principles of Self-Management, the Laws and Principles of People Management, the Laws and Principles of Power and Control and the Leadership of People, and the Laws of Communicating to Lead.

If you study and adhere to the rules, your professional compass will serve you well. If superintendents will hold regular study groups with principals and principals will hold regular study groups with teachers and teachers will hold study groups with students, you'll see big changes in schools. A new level of functioning with work and people will occur—and good experiences will become the norm. That's not just a promise. It's a guarantee.

"THE BUCK STOPS HERE"

There was a well-known sign on President Truman's desk. It read, "The buck stops here." Although it explains itself, we might note that on every teacher's, principal's, and superintendent's desk resides such a sign, whether actual or symbolic. Indeed, our leadership position dictates that the buck stops at each of our desks. After all, we are the chief executive officers in our classroom, in our school, and in our district. And with leadership comes large responsibility—and much greater opportunity.

In a school setting, there are what we might call levels of leadership. Students have responsibilities. In a sense, they could have "the buck stops here" signs on their desks, for they are responsible to lead and manage themselves. Assignments belong to them, and it's up to them to see that these assignments are carried through. Teachers and principals have responsibilities. Superintendents have responsibilities too. So do cooks, custodians, nurses, paraprofessionals, aides, secretaries, and everyone else on the school team. All these people must lead themselves. All of these people have a responsibility for work as well as the responsibility to work with and serve others. And we all need a professional compass for doing our work. But none of these people will have a compass until they are taught.

So to whom does the major responsibility belong in a school setting? It belongs to all of us. And we should know that all responsibility is major, no matter how minor it may seem, for every small move affects the whole. At every step, the buck keeps stopping along the way. But it really has its final home in the classroom with teachers, in the office with principals and superintendents, and in the board room with members of the board of education. Those being led are counting on us as professional leaders to develop firm foundations which hold student welfare supreme—and to acquire the methods, techniques, and skills to cause others to want our leadership. This book was written to help meet those needs—and to make the journey of success as gratifying as the destination—and for good reason.

If you don't lead well, those you lead will not do well—and neither will you. Whether you are a teacher, principal, or superintendent, your ability to lead is the single most important factor affecting your success and fulfillment as a person and as a professional educator—and the success and fulfillment of those you lead. It is my belief that you have the most important leadership job in the world. You also have one of the most difficult.

YOU NEED TO
BE NOURISHED TOO

Leadership is a nurturing function. We are continually nurturing others. Yet, a leader needs to be nurtured too. We need everything that those being led need. We need to learn. We need to grow. We need to be confirmed. We need support. We need to network and develop collegial relationships. Yet, we can't meet these needs without being proactive—and acting selfishly on our own behalf. We can do so by taking several steps—and add some of our own.

First, we need to surround ourselves to the greatest degree possible with proactive and successful people. We're not going to be nurtured very much by people who are without passion and without significant success. And the people we surround ourselves with need not be just educators. They can be people from all walks of life—from bankers to insurance salespeople to plumbers.

Second, we need to know what we believe—and make it a point to learn from those who hold the beliefs we do about creating and maintaining student-centered classrooms and schools. If our primary associations are with people interested only in feathering their own nest, we're not likely to get much nurturing.

Third, we need to develop close personal and professional relationships inside the school with progressive and positive people. When it comes to nurturing ourselves, we need to stay away from those who are negative—and for a very practical reason: We'll not get any rejuvenation or nurturing from them. Therefore, we should consider socializing as well as having breakfast, lunch, or dinner with positive and proactive people on a regular basis. We should form study groups with them. The group need not be large. A handful of people—even one or two—can have a significant beneficial influence on our life.

Fourth, we need to read. In truth, it is almost impossible to learn and grow without reading. To be nurtured, however, we need to measure the words of those who are only critical. Instead, we should read the words of those who can identify the problem and offer possible solutions. And, of course, we should include in our reading material from those who are being successful—and are sharing ways we can be successful.

We can add to this list. But the point is simple: You must be nourished too. You have to take care of your own state of mind and grow professionally. You have to develop your own support system in order to experience a high level of success and satisfaction as a teacher or an administrator. Without nurturing, you are not likely to be all you are capable of being. This book is intended to nurture you and serve as your compass. It is hoped that it will serve you well.

APPENDIX

About the Author
The MASTER Teacher Story
The Leadership Plan for Administrators
The Best Kind of Training

ABOUT THE AUTHOR

Bob DeBruyn was born in Chicago and raised in an area called "The Region" in Northwest Indiana in the suburbs of Chicago. He went to Indiana University and began a business career with Standard Oil. Then he joined the internationally famous Dun & Bradstreet. He received extensive training from each organization, which helped mold his leadership and management beliefs. He was drafted into the U.S. Army and moved to Manhattan, Kansas, where he got involved in summer baseball and a youth organization called Teen Town—and then he decided to return to college for a teaching certificate.

Bob received a B.S. from Kansas State University in 1961 and an M.S. from Kansas State University in 1963. He went directly to Manhattan High School as a classroom teacher. Five years later, he went to Manhattan Junior High as an administrator. In 1969, while he was at Manhattan Junior High, he founded The MASTER Teacher.

During college and while he was teaching, Bob retained his business interests. He worked with a CBS radio and television affiliate in Topeka, Kansas, for 13 years. And he served on the board of directors of a bank and was an owner or a partner in other businesses while teaching and serving as an administrator.

We tell you this because the continued business exposure—along with the Standard Oil and Dun & Bradstreet training has, without reservation, influenced the philosophy of The MASTER Teacher. Bob carried many firm business beliefs into his teaching career. Since his first week in education, Bob has believed that both teachers and administrators operate under a tremendous handicap. Why? When Bob worked for Dun & Bradstreet and Standard Oil, he learned that both companies had excellent records for hiring the best people. Yet, neither company would consider putting these people on the job immediately after they were hired. Even though those hired had the educational background, the credentials, and the potential for a successful career, both companies believed new employees couldn't hold their own with their secretaries, much less their customers, until they were thoroughly trained to think professionally about themselves, their colleagues, the company, their career, their customers, and the products and services of the company.

Bob did not find this thorough training to be the case when he entered education. In fact, what he found was quite the contrary. In early 1969, new teachers were given student teaching experience in college. After they were hired, they were given a brief orientation the week they started their careers—and handed a gradebook, textbook, class roster, and policy manual. Then they were placed in classrooms with between 25 and 125 different kinds of students and asked and expected to be master teachers. In effect, they were told to learn to become good teachers by trial and error. It was a very difficult way to learn. Worse, during their careers, most teachers were "on their own" to refine and perfect the science of teaching.

To compound this problem, the structure, function, physical makeup, and the time schedule in a school almost prevent administrators from giving teachers professional assistance. Administrators can't talk to a teacher anytime they wish because teachers are in classrooms with students. Neither can a teacher leave the classroom after a bad experience to relax or have a cup of coffee before facing the next task as professionals do in business, industry, and other professions. Teachers are confined to the classroom—sometimes all day long. It's even hard for administrators to find time for meeting before or after school to help teachers solve a problem or improve their performance.

Yet, this is a handicap inherent in teaching for which principals and superintendents *must compensate. For if they don't—who should? If administrators are not responsible for helping teachers find success in a school and district—who is? In truth, principals and superintendents must accept this responsibility. If they don't—then, in reality, there is a void of leadership in schools or districts.*

As a school administrator, Bob firmly believed there was a tremendous need for an administrator to deliver a planned and comprehensive program of teacher training on a continuous basis. He became more and more aware of the fact that teachers had the right to look to their administrators for two things:

1. *Job security. The best security any of us can have is to be very good at what we do.*
2. *Help in achieving success as a teacher. This expectation is very important to principals and superintendents. After all, consciously or subconsciously, we all ask the same question about our leaders: What is he or she doing to help me find success and satisfaction in this job? If the answer is "Nothing," an administrator is in a very precarious position—and he or she should be.*

Bob firmly believes that school administrators must be able to meet these two basic expectations of those being led. If they do not, teachers may begin to think principals and superintendents serve no useful function that couldn't be delivered by anyone. In fact, teachers may begin believing that administrators are incompetent regarding the art of teaching. In the process, of course, teachers may also believe that they are more competent, more intelligent, and more significant to the work and achievement of the school than administrators. When this happens, administration is no longer a function. It is merely a position. Worse, the leadership of principals and superintendents to influence and motivate the staff is rendered ineffective.

Bob saw a lot of things happening in education—on a nationwide basis—which convinced him that creating a program of training that principals and superintendents could give to their teachers was necessary.

First, he saw schools becoming more teacher-centered than student-centered. That's a violation of the Law of Origin. This law relates that institutions and the people who work in them must operate in agreement with the reason for their origin and existence, or failure rather than success becomes the probability.

Second, he saw many master teachers doing a great job—but he also saw leadership on school faculties emerging from the negative members of the staff. Their negative voices were telling other teachers what they should not do for students and the school—rather than what they should be doing for students as well as what they should be doing to accomplish the work and mission of the school.

Third, he saw a gap developing between teachers and administrators that was unhealthy—to say the least. He believed one reason for this reality was the fact that many teachers did not see their principal or superintendent as a source of security or as a resource in achieving personal and professional success in the classroom and school.

Fourth, he saw administrators offering hundreds of rationalizations for not helping teachers do a better job in the classroom—especially limited funds. He also believed this was a response to the fear to lead, feeling inadequate with the people side of management, and not viewing teacher training and growth as an absolute necessity.

Fifth, he believed being a successful teacher, principal, or superintendent was a difficult and demanding achievement—and required special professional attitudes and talents which needed to be acquired and then reinforced continually.

These were some of the reasons Bob began thinking seriously about developing a *program like **The MASTER Teacher**. The motivation was a simple truth: Success or failure as a teacher—and happiness as a human being—is almost totally dependent upon the ability to develop relationships and work effectively with students, colleagues, staff, and parents. A teacher teaches more than academic subjects. A teacher teaches people.*

Bob recognized that teachers must have a tremendous number of methods, techniques, and skills which can be employed in an instant. They have to have a vast understanding of human behavior—including their own. They have to acquire the ability to develop rapport with students, administrators, counselors, cooks, aides, parents, and the rest of the school team. If teachers can't relate to these people, if they can't understand them, if they can't cause students to behave in a manner that enables individual and group instruction to occur, they will not find very much success in this profession. And in teaching—when you don't find success—failure keeps knocking at your door. It comes in the form of frustration, inadequacy, hopelessness, anger, and feelings of powerlessness. Bob believed that anytime a teacher said he or she felt powerless, a lack of training was obvious. And continuous professional training was the only power that created a feeling of competency.

Bob also noted that teachers are likely to direct any personal or professional failures back at students, parents, colleagues, and administrators. They are also prone to become a negative influence on other members of the staff. When failure hits a teacher, it's easy to rationalize all our failures away by blaming kids and parents and colleagues and administrators and even society itself. All this happens primarily because teachers want so badly to be good teachers, but they don't have the professional foundations or the vast repertoire of methods, techniques, and skills to deal with all these people—and the problems people have and cause.

As a school administrator, Bob was convinced that the vast majority of teachers were academically prepared to teach. He could count on one hand the number of teachers he knew who were academically incompetent. Those he knew who were not successful had people problems—with themselves or others.

He believed there was a giant need to help teachers strengthen their own attitudes toward their work as classroom teachers and the work of the school. He also believed it was important to add to teachers' human relations skills while helping them acquire the vast array of methods and techniques necessary for effective teaching and learning. From these perceptions and beliefs, The MASTER Teacher was founded.

The difficult part of his task was overcoming the fact that inservice training and staff development were not common practices in 1969. And the notion that principals and superintendents were responsible for teacher success was almost unknown. Robert L. DeBruyn was one of the pioneers of this movement in education. He was also one of the most successful. Just nine weeks after publishing the first issues, The MASTER Teacher was one of the largest educational publishers in the world. It still is today.

THE MASTER TEACHER STORY

The MASTER Teacher is the name of a company and its original publication—a program of weekly inservice training for teachers. The program is purchased by principals and superintendents and given to the professional staff each week. Many administrators even give it to cooks, custodians, bus drivers, aides, secretaries, and the rest of the school team. They do so out of the belief that all of us teach—and the more all of us know about the work and mission of the school, the better we can all do.

Designed to be read and studied individually by teachers in five to eight minutes, the writing can serve as a topic for individual teacher counseling and group sessions. One of the primary objectives is to give teachers volumes of practical and professional information in small segments throughout the 36-week school year.

The MASTER Teacher *covers the broad spectrum of teacher needs and concerns. It addresses both the professional attitudes and the skills needed to find success in teaching. As a comprehensive and continuous program, the publication addresses teaching methods, techniques, and skills as well as professionalism, ethics, discipline, motivation, public relations, student relationships, communication skills, parent relationships, staff relationships, grading, testing, and mastering meetings.*

Supplementary materials for the program's introduction, reinforcement, and follow-up are provided at no cost. The program is new each year.

CREATED SOLELY TO HELP
TEACHERS FIND MORE SUCCESS

The year was 1969, and any professional training a teacher or administrator received was on his or her own. Staff development was not in vogue. Even inservice days were rare. Every teacher and administrator, however, had to return to a college or university every few years and take a small number of graduate hours to remain certified.

*The decision to create **The MASTER Teacher** came at a social gathering. We had a group of teachers and administrators who not only worked together, but socialized together as well. And even during social gatherings, the conversation always turned to "shop talk." We had what I called "define the problem" discussions. We defined the problem—then talked about what we needed, what was wrong with education, and what should be changed—then we went home. The next time we gathered, the discussion format was repeated. In many ways, our discussions were like the local, state, and national meetings we attended. Everyone identified what needed to be done, but no one had any good ideas or suggestions for how to do it. Everyone just defined the problem and provided input to enlarge the problem.*

It was during one of our "define the problem" talks that I vowed to stop engaging in such conversations and try to do something about it. I did believe the professional help had to be provided on a weekly basis. And I did have the firm belief that training had to cover the professional foundations which included the professional attitudes, methods, techniques, and skills that would give teachers a high probability of success in working with students, colleagues, and parents. And I believed that teachers had to have a multitude of techniques to draw upon in the many and varied situations they face. The question was how to do it.

Even though I was an administrator, I was also working for a CBS affiliate in radio and television. In the search for a way to deliver training, I considered audiotapes. But I *thought such a vehicle was too cumbersome and hard to use. It involved finding a tape recorder and the time to listen to a tape. And it would be too costly—about $6 per tape, which was too much money for a principal or superintendent to spend who had 20, 50, or 500 teachers.*

I considered videotapes. But, again, I ruled it out as being too expensive for schools to purchase—and too hard for every teacher to use on a weekly basis. Finding time for everyone to meet to view such tapes would be almost impossible. Admittedly, in the case of most video presentations, it's not necessary for everyone to view them together. But in the ongoing and comprehensive staff training I was planning, it would be.

I also considered books, but ruled them out for several reasons. First, I felt that teachers needed volumes of material in small segments that they could read in five to eight minutes—or they wouldn't have the time to use the resource. Second, I believed it had to be a training vehicle that principals and superintendents could give every teacher. In the media, I had been taught that "read and route" or "pass along" materials contained too many negatives: Who gets it first? Who gets it last? Who gets it late? Who forgets to pass it along? What is the condition of the "pass along" material when it is received by another person? How is it delivered to a teacher by another colleague? All these questions affect readership and attitudes toward such communication. And in my media training, I had also been taught that help and assistance should be given to everyone simultaneously—as a gift with no strings or demands attached.

I chose the brochure format for several reasons:

First, it was the most practical vehicle. It would allow weekly training over the entire 36 weeks of the school year.

Second, it best lent itself to comprehensive training on the wide front of teacher needs and concerns.

Third, it was individual and private.

*Fourth, it allowed volumes of materials to be presented and absorbed in short doses. I was taught that **short** was more effective than **long** when it comes to professional learning.*

Fifth, it was a device that lent itself to an ongoing program—not only from week to week but from year to year.

Sixth, teachers could use the training as they saw fit, when they saw fit, when it was needed—and save the brochures for future reference. In a period of time, a teacher could develop a professional library on a wide range of topics with quick and easy access.

Seventh, the brochure format was inexpensive and allowed administrators to give every teacher a personal copy. It was easy for a principal or superintendent to give one to everyone—and also to make sure that nobody was ever left out. And the total cost for each teacher was minimal. For just pennies a week, a principal or superintendent had a total foundation of staff development which could be reinforced and added to without additional cost.

Eighth, the brochure format is easy to administer. All an administrator has to do is place a copy in each teacher's mailbox every week. Because of time demands on both administrators and teachers, the best-laid plans, I knew, could be easily derailed. For an administrator, it is very difficult to uphold a promise to help every teacher every week of the year. And I wanted administrators to be able to make this promise to teachers—and keep it.

It was my belief in 1969 that teachers had to learn far too much by trial and error. I believe they still do today. Likewise, I believed then—and still believe now—that teachers need continuous and comprehensive training in two areas: the academic side and the people

344

side of being an educator—with heavy emphasis on the latter for a very vital reason. Regardless of our academic competence, if we can't work cooperatively with people and teach students, we aren't likely to be very effective.

OUR BELIEFS ARE PROBABLY YOUR BELIEFS TOO

*The MASTER Teacher is one of the few professional organizations whose primary purpose is to support all who are engaged in the educational process. We don't pit teacher against principal or principal against teacher. We don't support boards of education over educators. We support the college of education and the job it is doing. We believe that it is preparing people to **enter** our profession just as well as the college of engineering, business, or architecture does. We don't advocate any job in education as being more important than another in meeting the needs of students.*

We function from the following beliefs:

First, we believe that we're all on the same team with the same mission, whether we are teachers, administrators, board members, cooks, custodians, nurses, or secretaries. Only our functions differ. But each of our contributions to the whole is vital.

Second, we believe that the student is the fundamental value in a school. Therefore, the welfare of students must be our primary consideration—always. This means, while we are striving to help educators find the highest level of achievement and satisfaction in their work, we do not place the welfare of teachers, principals, superintendents, or anyone else above the welfare of students. All of our positions exist to meet the needs of students, and the only security any of us have as professionals is to meet the needs of the clientele we serve.

Third, we believe that it takes a quality teacher to give students a quality education. It's not books, materials, overheads, gyms, cafeterias, or playground equipment that gives students a quality education. There is no research or experience that supports anything being more important in giving students a quality education than a quality teacher. In the classroom, the teacher is the chief executive officer.

Fourth, we believe that we can have good teachers in a school without a good principal, but that we can't have a good school without a good principal. In addition, the teacher is the chief executive officer in the classroom. The principal is the chief executive officer in the school. The superintendent is the chief executive officer of the district. This supports what we have known in business and industry for years: management is the single most important factor in the success of the institution—and the teacher is the most significant factor in the success of students in the classroom.

Fifth, we believe professional growth is a process, not an event. It is never-ending. Acquiring and maintaining the professional attitude as well as the methods, techniques, and skills to be a highly effective teacher or administrator doesn't happen because of one or two inservice days each year. Training must be constant—and must begin on the first day of a career and not end until we retire.

Sixth, we believe excellence cannot be achieved until it has been experienced. Until that time, we may not even know what it is. And if our only contact with excellence is in our classroom, our school, or our community, we may never know the real possibilities.

Seventh, we believe excellence is a vicinity, not a destination. The idea is to get in the vicinity—and stay there. This requires lifelong learning. And we believe all educators have to grow 15 percent a year just to stay even with last year.

*Eighth, we believe the quality of human relationships that exist in a school determines the quality of life that exists in a school. We believe human relationships are the single most important factor in determining the productivity and satisfaction—which are the two goals of climate—for students and educators alike. It is out of these beliefs that **The MASTER Teacher** was started and continues to this day. The training holds to three objectives:*

1. *To give principals and superintendents an effective way to help teachers develop a positive and professional attitude toward teaching, students, colleagues, and administrators. This includes developing a positive approach toward their individual work as classroom teachers and their contribution toward getting the entire work and mission of the school accomplished.*

2. *To give teachers something new and practical that they can apply in their daily work with human beings.*

3. *To remind teachers to use the knowledge and skills they know but fail to apply in getting the work of the school accomplished.*

No educational organization reaches more teachers, administrators, boards, support staffs, parents, or college people than The MASTER Teacher.

INPUT FROM EDUCATORS HAS CONTINUALLY IMPROVED THE PROGRAM

While delivering an inservice presentation in a school district, I was told by a superintendent that he prepared "questions for discussion" to go with each weekly brochure. He used those questions for discussion in his staff newsletter and urged principals to use them in weekly bulletins as well as in individual teacher conferences, small group discussions, and faculty meetings. This was a good idea—except it was work that we should have been doing. Result: We now write "Questions for Discussion" for you and give them to administrators free to use with their teachers.

Later, while I was attending a national conference, several principals told me that they wrote or found a "Thought for the Week" that would correspond to each brochure—and used it in their weekly bulletin or as a poster or bulletin board in their school. This was another good idea—and one that we should have been doing. Result: We write "Thoughts for the Week" to correspond to each weekly brochure and urge administrators to use it as a beginning in the weekly bulletin. And we also suggest administrators do what other administrators have told us they do: begin their weekly bulletin with the "Thought for the Week"—and end their weekly bulletin with "Questions for Discussion."

*While I was working with teachers at an inservice day workshop, a teacher told me that while she liked **The MASTER Teacher**, she didn't like the way her administrator used it. I asked, "Why?" She said her principal highlighted specific sentences in each copy and read the highlighted sentences at faculty meetings. Consequently, the principal used it more as a "club" rather than as a helpful and caring aid. Very good input. Result: We write an introductory greeting card and give it to principals and superintendents every year to be used to introduce **The MASTER Teacher** to teachers. In addition, we have a special introductory brochure to be given to each teacher. A card is provided for each teacher—free of charge. It sets the tone for positive acceptance by offering the training as a gift to teachers from the principal or superintendent—with no strings attached—to help them find more success and satisfaction as teachers.*

We receive countless letters from teachers inquiring about past brochures. They are usually looking for specific writings and can't find them. Result: We now write an index for each year of **The MASTER Teacher** *and give it to every teacher at the beginning of the year to facilitate quick and easy reference—and to promote saving each issue of* **The MASTER Teacher**.

In the same vein, teachers told us they put a rubber band around their copies of **The MASTER Teacher**—*or put them in some kind of box for storage. Result: We make a storage box and sell it for a nominal fee.*

In recent years, our incoming mail has revealed another need: finding a way to keep teachers abreast of the research regarding teaching, learning, and schools. And this is a need we know is growing rapidly. Result: We publish **The 3R's for Teachers: Research, Reports, & Reviews** *and send it to administrators quarterly. If a principal or superintendent orders* **The MASTER Teacher** *for ten or more teachers, we allow him or her to photocopy* **The 3R's for Teachers: Research, Reports, & Reviews** *and give all teachers a copy. The cost is only $10.00 annually for administrators who subscribe to ten or more copies of* **The MASTER Teacher**.

ANOTHER ADDITION

Beginning in the 1993-94 school year, we developed a poster with the same theme as the first brochure of the year. Administrators can buy posters, one for every classroom if they choose, for $5.00 each. And for students, they can buy ribbons to go with the theme.

Most important, all these additions, including the new posters and ribbons, have come about as the result of ideas, suggestions, and input from educators. These ideas have helped us give principals and superintendents an ongoing program of staff development—and the privilege of promising their teachers they can and will help them every week of the year—no matter how busy they get or what new priority gets in the way.

Now principals and superintendents can help everyone without leaving anyone out. **The MASTER Teacher** *even allows principals and superintendents to address issues which might be difficult or awkward to approach. Equally important,* **The MASTER Teacher** *gives administrators the much needed third-person support for everything they are doing every day by both word and deed to help teachers be more successful and to motivate them to want to get the work and mission of the school accomplished—in the most professional, effective, and satisfying way.*

EVERYTHING WAS THE
RESULT OF A PERCEIVED NEED

In the process of meeting one need, we discovered other needs revealed. The MASTER Teacher now has a total of ten different publications for teachers, administrators, board members, support staff, and the public. They are:

► **The MASTER Teacher** *(weekly for 36 weeks of the school year) for teachers*
► **The Board** *(semimonthly) for the board of education*
► **Views, Ideas, & Practical Administrative Solutions** *(monthly) for administrators, department heads, and team leaders*
► **About Our Schools** *(monthly for 10 months of the year) for public relations programs for a school or district*

▶ *Leadership Vision/Professional Vision* (semimonthly) for support staff
▶ *The 3R's for Teachers: Research, Reports, & Reviews* (4 issues per year) for teachers
▶ *Superintendents Only,* (monthly) for superintendents and assistant superintendents
▶ *The Professor in the Classroom,* (semimonthly for 9 months of the school year) for professors and graduate assistants
▶ *Technology Pathfinder for Administrators* (monthly) for administrators
▶ *Technology Pathfinder for Teachers* (monthly for 9 months of the school year) for teachers

In addition to these publications, The MASTER Teacher has nine divisions:
▶ *Publications*
▶ *The Academy—six, one-week courses*
▶ *Technology*
▶ *Videotape*
▶ *Book*
▶ *Awards*
▶ *Cards, Posters, and Ribbons*
▶ *Apparel*
▶ *Educational Publishers—to print publications and promote products of the organization*

Almost 800 products and services have evolved since 1969. The vast majority of publications, as well as the vast majority of products and services are conceptualized, created, manufactured, sold, and delivered from the Manhattan, Kansas, location on Leadership Lane.

The staff has grown to over 50 full-time employees, several part-time employees, a professional cadre of 24 superintendents, principals, and teachers in schools throughout the United States and Canada, and 12 to 18 mentally or physically impaired adults with two professional trainers.

Cadre members, all of whom work in schools, are involved in writing many MASTER Teacher publications. They are also involved in planning, writing, or delivering presentations periodically throughout the year at inservice day activities, state and national conventions, or The MASTER Teacher Academy. Each of the week-long courses at The Academy offers three hours of graduate credit from Kansas State University. Today, of the 93,000 schools in the United States, 66,000 use the publications, products, and services created by The MASTER Teacher each year.

THE LEADERSHIP PLAN FOR ADMINISTRATORS

One of the highest priorities for every administrator should be the continuous objective of improving teacher performance and developing master teachers. This means every administrator must establish and initiate both short-term and long-range leadership plans designed exclusively to help teachers on both the academic and human side of teaching. The plans should utilize both internal and external resources to ensure breadth and depth. After all, excellence can be achieved only if it has been experienced. Until the time we experience excellence, we may not really know what it is.

Both internal and external resources must also be used to make sure our definition of excellence meets world-class standards. Remember, the school of the 21st century will not be localized. In the past, we talked about Canadian schools, Japanese schools, German schools, and Russian schools. Now, we are in global competition, and our students will be in the global work force. Therefore, teacher training needs to include external input to make sure we have the proper standards and broad-based input.

PRINCIPALS AND SUPERINTENDENTS HAVE THE POWER TO HELP TEACHERS

If a principal or superintendent does not provide ongoing training, he or she is not living up to his or her leadership responsibilities. After all, facilitating the work of the classroom teacher is the fundamental definition of administration. The function is to give teachers the foundation necessary for success—and to do everything possible to prevent teachers from failing. This means it's the principal's and superintendent's job to help teachers think and act professionally toward themselves, students, other teachers, parents, cooks, custodians, secretaries, and everyone else they work with—as well as the work and mission of the school.

There are two people in the entire system with the power and authority to help teachers and staff get better at what they do—the principal and the superintendent. The real questions are: If management doesn't help teachers develop positive and professional attitudes toward students, teaching, and the work of the school, who should? If principals and superintendents don't help teachers acquire the knowledge and skills to be exceptional educators, who should? The answers are obvious. Yet, the answers may not be so obvious to the administrator who is only a manager.

TWO STAFF DEVELOPMENT PLANS ARE A MUST

A principal or superintendent should include two distinctly different types of programs of staff development in the leadership plan. The two programs are:

1. *Foundation Program or Continuous Program*
2. *Special Events Program or Inservice Day Program*

The principal or superintendent who doesn't use both programs is at a disadvantage. And, as we all know well, many administrators are operating with this disadvantage. The deeper we move into the 21st century, the more many will wish they had both programs in place a long time ago. Too, many superintendents leave this decision to the building principal. This is a mistake.

The foundation program must be continuous. It must also be comprehensive and cover the wide spectrum of needs necessary to be successful in the classroom and school. An ongoing foundation program of staff development is a leadership and teaching absolute. It sets the tone for constant growth and improvement—and is continuous evidence of leadership assistance from administrators. It not only reinforces the need to grow, but also complements and reinforces special events such as inservice days. Furthermore, it establishes the climate and culture that support school goals and objectives on both the technical and the human side of education in order to meet the needs of students and get all the work of the school accomplished.

*The ongoing foundation program should meet some very definite criteria. The criteria and rationale which are vital considerations as a foundation program are offered in the remaining pages of this appendix. If principals and superintendents have the time, money, and ideas to create and administer their own continuous program of teacher training—they should. If they don't have those resources, they must look to an established program like **The MASTER Teacher.** This is not a commercial message. But please do allow me to say that a lot of people can define the problems related to helping teachers find success in the classroom—but few give administrators any practical, concrete, and workable suggestions that can be carried out effectively and economically to meet those needs every week of the school year. I firmly believe that a program like **The MASTER Teacher** must be inherent in the leadership plan if principals and superintendents are to fulfill their functions as the leaders and operate in agreement with good management practices.*

To develop your plan, make a list of competencies teachers need to be successful. As you do so, remember that whatever competencies teachers need to be successful, administrators need as well if they intend to be proactive teaching leaders. Make a chart from your list of competencies. Then look to see how you are training all teachers in the school or district to acquire these skills. The following are some of the items that ought to be on your chart:

▶ *Positive and professional attitudes, beliefs, and practices that enhance success*

▶ *Teaching techniques designed to produce results*

▶ *Professionalism and ethics*

▶ *Preventing and handling discipline problems*

▶ *Techniques for motivating students*

▶ *Grading, testing, and homework*

▶ *Dealing effectively with change*

▶ *Student relationships*

▶ *Parent relationships*

▶ *Staff relationships*

▶ *Functioning successfully in groups, teams, and meetings*

▶ *Creating better public relations*

▶ *Developing skills to enhance communication*

▶ *Creating the climate and culture necessary for teaching and learning*

▶ *Creating a safe environment*

These are the areas of teacher needs. They need to be addressed continually to improve teacher performance and enhance teacher motivation and satisfaction.

THE BEST KIND OF TRAINING

In this section of the appendix, you may say that my biases are revealed. And they are. After all, I have spent since 1969 developing **The MASTER Teacher** *Program. It contains all the features described in this section.*

1. THE BEST TRAINING IS CONTINUOUS... EVERY WEEK OF THE YEAR

A staff development program must be continuous because the work of the school is constant. The pressures are constant. The challenges are constant. The problems are constant. And the demands are constant. That's why inservice training for teachers is an administrative process that should begin on the first day of a teacher's career and not end until retirement. And everything an administrator expects a teacher to be to students, the administrator must be to teachers.

The best kind of staff development is continuous. Teachers and administrators don't develop positive, professional, and proactive attitudes in one or two meetings a year. Teachers and administrators can't pick up all the methods, techniques, and skills they need to lead people during a couple of inservice days each year. Day in, day out, year after year, leadership is an ever-present task for teachers and administrators. That's precisely why a teacher, principal, or superintendent needs a continuous program of staff development throughout the year. We need ask ourselves but a few questions to fully realize how vitally important an ongoing foundation program of training is to both teachers and administrators:

- *How vital is teacher attitude and performance in a classroom? Administrator attitude and performance in a school or district?*
- *How important are teaching methods, techniques, and skills to student success? To teacher success? To administrator success?*
- *Should administrators and teachers be partners in professional learning and getting the work of the classroom, school, and district accomplished?*
- *Is helping students be successful the function of being a teacher? Is helping teachers find success one of the functions of being a principal or superintendent?*
- *Will one or two inservice days each year keep a teacher or administrator current and growing professionally to the levels needed?*
- *Without ongoing training designed to help teachers be more successful, can teachers see administrators as leaders who are advocates?*

A principal's or superintendent's plan always includes provisions for the physical things teachers need such as rooms, desks, equipment, and books. The administrator's plan includes balancing classes, purchasing supplies, and scheduling buses but, far too often, ignores giving teachers help in acquiring competencies in their relationships with other people. This is paradoxical—because people are always more vital to success than are things.

In truth, a principal or superintendent can work diligently to secure new books, new desks, and any other physical objects for teachers. Yet, these administrative efforts may never change a negative teacher attitude into a positive one. These efforts may not add one professional competency. These efforts may never make teachers feel any differently toward students, administrators, or their role in creating a better school. The perceptive leader learns quickly that people growth is the vital aspect in developing the school and district team.

In any profession, you get better or you regress. You grow—or those around you grow past you. That's a fact. Teachers and administrators need continuous help and constant encouragement. The highest level of functioning can be achieved only through continuous administrative efforts to help teachers be successful.

A foundation plan of teacher development—designed as an aid and not a "club"— should offer assistance to teachers on a regular basis throughout the entire school year. If administrators don't think so, they have been out of the classroom too long. They have forgotten how hard and how demanding it is to teach and how many skills are needed to be a good teacher every day. Only through a continuous program of staff development can administrators fill this staff need—and fulfill their responsibility to help teachers find more success in the classroom.

2. THE BEST TRAINING IS COMPREHENSIVE AND COVERS THE BROAD SPECTRUM NEEDED FOR SUCCESS

Sometimes I think even we in the profession forget how complex education is—and how many different kinds of competencies we need to do well. To have 30 or more students in a room hour after hour and day after day—with the responsibility of providing individualized instruction, motivation, and nurturing—is not an easy task. In addition to being able to do the common things uncommonly well, a teacher must have a wide range of academic and human relations methods, techniques, and skills to be highly successful.

*Teachers face more kinds of people problems and make more instant decisions in a day than some professionals face in a month. Teachers must wear many hats and be a "jack of all trades" as well as a master of relating to everyone they work with—from students to colleagues to parents. That's why the foundation program of staff development must be comprehensive and deal with the whole range of professional needs that are of concern to teachers. Inservice days may deal with a specific area. But the ongoing foundation program must be broad-based and comprehensive in nature, because a teacher's work is so diversified. Therefore, administrative assistance must be comprehensive and deal with the wide range of areas that help teachers with the **wholeness** of their perceptions and their work. This includes current teaching techniques, discipline, staff relationships, student motivation, parent relationships, professionalism, ethics, public relations, working in groups, and communication skills. And help also must provide practical and workable methods and techniques that teachers can grasp and use immediately.*

Principals and superintendents must never forget that, in many ways, teachers teach alone. They must operate daily as a separate entity in the classroom within the whole of the school and district. They are adults who work in a child's world. They are confined to the classroom. They face problems alone. Yet, they work in a situation in which teamwork and cooperation are asked for and even required. All too often, they are required to acquire much of their professional knowledge without assistance. They gain much of their expertise by trial and error. It is a very difficult way to learn—and a costly way to learn as well. Without feeling the presence of administrative concern along with tangible evidence of assistance, teachers may develop strong resentments. Yet, with comprehensive administrative assistance, teachers can develop strong professional competencies and loyalties.

A weekly foundation program of training with a wide base meets a big need—while inservice day programs give special offerings at specific times in the year. Both programs serve to reinforce each other. The advantages are obvious. The entire spectrum of professional needs are covered all year long—and select training is offered during inservice days.

3. *THE BEST TRAINING IS INDIVIDUALIZED AND PRIVATE— BUT CAN BE USED FOR GROUP STUDY AND INTERACTION*

To promote and facilitate maximum teacher learning and acceptance, a staff development training program must be individualized and private—and for good reason. Professional learning is individual. Teachers do not grow professionally en masse. Rather, they grow one teacher at a time.

Individual help answers the Primary Question, "What's in it for me?" on an individual teacher basis before group work begins. Individual teacher help must present high professional standards. It must share rather than tell, persuade rather than demand, and suggest rather than insist. All these aspects of training require privacy.

Training must be offered as a private aid, not as an administrative "club." Administrators are partners with teachers in the education process—not opponents. That's why a staff development program should privately provide direction and assistance—not criticism or pressure.

For maximum acceptance and productivity, large group meetings may follow the individualized plan. After private training is provided, small groups or the entire staff ought to be able to discuss the material, offer additional suggestions, and apply the material to various situations. If possible, however, large groups should be avoided for initial presentations of the training in favor of individualized and private inservice.

This aspect of the foundation plan is tremendously important. The individualized and private aspect of teacher development eliminates the need to react negatively or defensively to the inservice offering and to affect others in a negative way. Instead, a teacher can just absorb the instruction. Remember, good training is not entertainment. Good training tells people what they need to hear to be successful—rather than what they want to hear. It focuses on the knowledge, skills, values, standards, and character needed to find a high level of achievement.

Private and individualized inservice practices also help build administrator-teacher rapport on a one-to-one basis. Those who are positive and proactive are better equipped to neutralize those who are always negative toward training.

Even when group discussion follows individualized private training, an administrator need not be drawn into any differences which may arise. Rather, it is an opportunity to simply observe teacher attitudes and listen to teacher comments as a third person. Never forget, just listening and asking questions helps teachers begin to change—and gives teachers the support they need to develop professional attitudes. It provides an opportunity for them to begin thinking about what really is working and what isn't working for them as educators.

4. THE BEST TRAINING SERVES AS A FOUNDATION FOR ACCOUNTABILITY

Any administrative-sponsored program must contain the foundation for the measurement of performance. It must serve as a guideline for accountability because management does not have the right to evaluate, criticize, judge, or reprimand any teacher until management has first fulfilled its function of instruction. This is a law of leadership that cannot be violated if good administrator-teacher relations are desired.

When administrators evaluate teacher attitude or performance without first providing tangible help and assistance for the standards being evaluated, they are likely to be regarded as enemies by those they lead. It's not difficult to see and understand why. This is probably the most common mistake made by administrators in schools today. And it probably creates the most problems between administrators and teachers. With the authority of administration comes the responsibility to evaluate. But the responsibility to help those being led always comes first. The responsibility to help those being led always precedes the responsibility to evaluate. We are the professional partners of those we lead—not just their judges. Our task is to develop the talents of the staff to the fullest. Therefore, like testing in the classroom, the process of evaluation is twofold: first, to find out how well our staff has learned, and second, to find out how well we have taught.

That's precisely why a wide variety of specific teaching and human relations methods, techniques, and skills must be offered in a foundation program of staff development. These methods, techniques and skills must be designed to help teachers cope with their day-to-day work with students, colleagues, parents, and anyone else they touch in their work. The foundation program of training must help teachers sort out and deal with their own attitudes, behaviors, and beliefs—as well as develop the professional attitudes and beliefs necessary to be successful and accomplish the work of the school. It is the providing of professional, practical, and workable assistance that creates acceptance of the leader and his or her leadership. And it is the foundation program of training provided by principals and superintendents which promotes the administrator-teacher relationship as a partnership and team endeavor—and allows those being led to see the leader as the point of reference for finding success.

Remember, there aren't opposing teams in education. We are all on the same team whether we are administrators, teachers, secretaries, nurses, aides, media specialists, curriculum directors, or custodians. We must all have the same goals and educational philosophies. We must all have the same professional core values. We must all have the same mission. Only our individual functions differ. We all need to be aware of these vitally important facts. Without a foundation program of training provided by principals and superintendents, many of those we lead will never come to know and accept this truth.

Teachers don't need another critic. They don't need a noncontributing administrator to evaluate them. They need someone they can turn to and rely on for professional teaching— to show the way to being successful. If continuous help is given by principals and superintendents, then and only then is management leading—and does management have the right to evaluate. When management fulfills this teaching function first, they are likely to find that their suggestions are appreciated and their leadership welcomed. And when administrators teach first, evaluation takes on a positive, constructive, and productive tone.

Teachers have the right to expect help from their leader in finding success. A foundation plan of training adds administrative weight to recognition of the need for continuous teacher growth and improvement. The plan reflects administrative willingness to *help teachers find and enjoy professional success **with** their leader and with their work.*

5. THE BEST TRAINING SUPPORTS EDUCATIONAL GOALS, SCHOOL GOALS, AND ADMINISTRATIVE GOALS

A staff development program should support both educational goals and the leadership actions necessary to maximize staff performance, create a good school, and maximize the abilities of each teacher and student. Without reservation, the administrative goals should be the creation and maintenance of student-centered schools and the accomplishment of all the work of the school. Too, a part of these goals should be to effect positive leadership by example as well as to generate good administrator-staff-student relationships in the process.

To achieve these necessary objectives, a staff development program sponsored by the administration must adhere to what is known about teaching and learning. It must advocate the characteristics of a good school and a good teacher. It must include both theory and practice. It must include research and the application of research. And it must have continuity and professional direction.

It must be honest. It must be teaching that is attainable. It cannot be training that "blows like the wind" in one direction and then another. It can't reveal one educational philosophy, then another. The administrative-sponsored staff development program must contain the common thread of being results- or outcomes-driven. It must show teachers how to achieve goals and why they need to be achieved. It must deal with both the specific work and the entire spectrum of being a teacher. This includes understanding the needs of students and society and designing training that helps teachers know and understand change in education and change in the world, know how to make adjustments, and know how to adapt and change. The objective: to help teachers be successful. The approach: to introduce sound professional foundations as well as methods, techniques, and skills that work—and that can be used immediately.

6. THE BEST PROGRAMS COMMUNICATE THE SAME TRAINING TO ALL TEACHERS AT THE SAME TIME

*A staff development program must allow all-inclusive communication to all staff members simultaneously. It's called **total penetration**. Make no mistake: Partial or selective communication to teachers is a leadership error. In truth, it is one of the basic mistakes many principals and superintendents make which causes leadership problems. Unfortunately, this is a hard point to get many principals and superintendents to accept. Yet, the rule for leadership is: communicate, communicate, communicate. Communicate with everyone at the same time—without ever leaving anyone out. This action is a must when it comes to teaching the standards, establishing the values, and creating a professional climate for high performance and acceptance of the leader.*

When principals or superintendents fail to utilize total communication to every teacher simultaneously, misunderstandings, feelings of unimportance, divisions of labor, varied loyalties and priorities, isolation, and lack of unified effort become the probability. That's why total penetration offers a vital leadership advantage and is a must for any ongoing program of staff development.

Believe it or not, the continuity and total penetration feature of a staff development

355

program is an aspect that an administrator should never discount, minimize, overlook, or ignore. We must do all we can to make sure we reach and influence everyone. No teacher should ever be left out—or feel left out. No teacher should ever feel that some colleagues are favored over others—or get more help than others. None should ever think the squeaky wheel is getting the grease. Principals and superintendents often get discouraged because these kinds of teacher thoughts and feelings are often hard to prevent. Yet, the failure to utilize total penetration is often the cause of this dilemma. Partial penetration often lies at the root of a wide assortment of administrative problems. A leader's responsibility is to all. That's why an administrative-sponsored program should include every member of the staff.

Total communication with everyone is the responsibility of the administration. It is the duty of management. Administrative leadership help cannot be reserved for a select few— such as new teachers, those who request help, those experiencing problems, or those who are favorites. This is true regardless of any situation or circumstance. That's why total penetration is mandatory for an effective administrative-sponsored program of staff development.

7. THE BEST TRAINING IS DESIGNED TO BE EASILY AND CONVENIENTLY ADMINISTERED

A foundation plan of staff training should be designed so that it can be easily and conveniently administered in a school or an entire district. Administrators are busy. So are teachers. Nevertheless, the training must be carried out—and used extensively by the staff.

Ongoing staff development is not easy for principals or superintendents to deliver. Giving private and individual help on a regular basis is not an easy accomplishment. Neither is administrative follow-up. Therefore, any staff development foundation plan has a good chance of getting shelved, delayed, postponed, or discontinued simply because of a lack of available administrative and staff time. The truth of the matter is that principals and superintendents can start the year with good intentions only to be derailed shortly after school starts because finding the time for training is impossible. That's why the ease of administering a program of training must be a primary consideration. It's simply a reality of life in a school or district.

As we all know well, a staff development program cannot distract principals or superintendents from other leadership and management endeavors. The program must be carried out no matter how busy an administrator is or what other priorities are on the table. A training program should not be delayed, postponed, or canceled. This is only possible, of course, if the program is available and easy to implement. In truth, ease of administering is just as important to teachers—for the same reasons.

8. THE BEST TRAINING FACILITATES PERSONAL FOLLOW-UP BY PRINCIPALS AND SUPERINTENDENTS

To maximize the benefits, all staff development plans must contain a follow-up feature. If they don't, the training effort is limited to the action time of the training. Good staff training has the expansion feature facilitated by follow-up. The follow-up feature also strengthens and reinforces all administrative leadership urging and efforts. Follow-up also adds more weight, significance, and meaning to initial training. Therefore, if the foundation

356

plan of training has follow-up features, it has added training value.

Equally important, the foundation plan which contains follow-up goes one step further in communicating to teachers, "Your work is important, and you are important to students, this school, and this district." Make no mistake: Follow-up is a vital consideration of the staff development plan, for it strengthens both the inservice program and the teachers' attitudes toward the administrative offering. It will also facilitate the development of positive teacher attitudes toward the administrator.

9. *THE BEST TRAINING AIMS TOWARD EXCELLENCE, BUT IT ALSO SUPPORTS EXISTING EXCELLENCE*

A good program of staff training focuses on what's right as well as what needs improvement. It makes sure that teachers receive the support to hold on to certain attitudes and skills while abandoning others. This is best done by delivering training in a professional, no-nonsense, direct way while being respectful and acknowledging existing excellence. This is important for several reasons.

Often, administrative efforts are necessarily devoted primarily to teachers who are experiencing problems. This is where the bulk of administrative time and energy must be spent. Yet, one of the biggest errors a leader can make is to believe that some staff members need help and others do not—and that leaders need only to correct the mistakes rather than acknowledge and extend recognition for what is being done superbly. All teachers need help to maintain state-of-the-art practices—and the best of teachers will be the first to admit that they want help the most.

In truth, those teachers who day after day demonstrate master teacher performance are often ignored—or they believe they are. This reality does not strengthen administrator-teacher relationships with those a leader needs allegiance from the most—the best teachers. And these teachers are the standard-bearers for any good school. The good teacher is the backbone of the teaching staff. Administrators' success in accomplishing the work of the school is dependent to a great extent on the quality of the relationship created and maintained between the administrator and the best teachers.

Therefore, a foundation program must serve as a constant support system and recognition vehicle for the master teachers on the staff. This positive reinforcement and administrative acknowledgment for existing excellence is vitally important to the satisfaction of the teacher as well as to the success of any leadership plan. If this feature is lacking, teachers may not think a principal or superintendent knows anything about good teaching—and couldn't even recognize it if he or she saw it. That's why the foundation plan of staff development should aim at excellence and give recognition to the excellent methods, techniques, and skills demonstrated by the master teachers on the staff. And a close look will reveal that good staff development has a two-sided benefit. It actually develops administrators at the same time it is developing teachers. It allows both to stay in touch with the issues and with excellence.

10. *THE BEST TRAINING IS EASILY SUPPLEMENTED... FOR STAFF AND ADMINISTRATOR ALIKE*

To be widely accepted and meet the specific needs of individual teachers or the entire faculty, the foundation plan of training should lend itself to easy supplementation. The training should not be so rigid or narrow that it keeps principals and superintendents from making additions, adding dimensions, or supplementing the effort with related training—including inservice day programs. Rather, the foundation program should give a leader more room to operate and more opportunities to improve the performance of the staff.

Just as one academic class leads to another and one year leads to the next, the ongoing program of training should do the same. When the foundation program can be supplemented, it is automatically enhanced. And other efforts are enhanced by the foundation program. When the supplemental feature is not included in the program, educators tend to switch from one training program to another. Sometimes, such decisions are made just for the sake of **change**. *Yet, all students of management would agree that this is a mistake. Once a foundation program is in place, it should be continued. We can add to the program, but we should not change programs. To do so simply for the sake of change is foolish. Why? Such a change reflects a leadership change in philosophy or direction. Again, that's why the feature of* **easy supplementation** *is so important to both the foundation and ongoing program of training.*

11. AN EFFECTIVE PROGRAM OF TRAINING MUST HAVE STAFF ACCEPTANCE

Even with the advent of shared decision making, site-based management, and school restructuring, I continue to believe that it is both the responsibility and the prerogative of management to identify the professional foundations, attitudes, disciplines, methods, techniques, and skills required for success in teaching, then put into place a training program which enhances teacher competencies to get the work of the school accomplished successfully. It is vital to put into place training that meets the needs of teachers and gains their support, of course. But if principals or superintendents are waiting for 100 percent staff acceptance, they will never do anything. Unfortunately, it is doubtful that any administrative-sponsored program will be received, accepted, and approved by the entire staff with 100 percent acclaim.

Regardless of need, some teachers will use and appreciate the assistance more than others. Some will drag their feet. Remember the Myth of the Perfect Plan. It tells us that no training plan is without flaws. Remember also, however, that administrators are the appointed leaders of the school or district. They should know what needs to be done to meet their responsibility to create the climate for teaching and learning. They must be concerned with fulfilling their responsibilities as the leaders in a school or district. They can't choose to do nothing simply because not everyone will appreciate what they are doing.

Certainly, every principal or superintendent wants to plan a program of training that will be received favorably by the staff—and grow in acceptance. This can be the case if the planned program is carefully presented to suggest rather than dictate, praise rather than condemn, appeal rather than command, share rather than impose, and counsel rather than tell—while holding to the highest standards of professionalism. Too, we must make sure the plan is in agreement with sound educational philosophy and practices.

12. TRAINING MUST BE CONSISTENT TO REFLECT POSITIVELY ON PRINCIPALS AND SUPERINTENDENTS

It's one thing for a principal or superintendent to start a program of training for everyone. It's quite another to carry it out week after week, month after month, and year after year. It is, indeed, hard work. Yet, an administrative-sponsored program must be consistent. If it isn't, it reflects negatively on principals and superintendents in countless ways.

Most often, because of lack of time and countless other school events, the best-laid plans never get off the ground or are found too difficult to perpetuate. Yet, "spotty" or inconsistent training reflects bad management. Likewise, announcing big plans at the beginning of the year—then halting or postponing planned training for any reason automatically casts shadows on the ability and integrity of a leader. In the process, it diminishes the value of training. Remember, if training is halted because of other necessary tasks, then training is automatically viewed as being less important than those tasks. In the same vein, it needs to be said that principals and superintendents who introduce speakers at inservice day activities, then excuse themselves because of "work in the office," send a wrong and terrible message to the faculty. In the process, they miss a big opportunity. After all, principals and superintendents have few days in the school year that they get to spend all day observing, learning, and working side by side with their teachers.

The ongoing foundation program of staff development must be consistent. It must reveal the stability of management. It must be dependable and give teachers security. Remember, enhancing the administrator-teacher partnership is one of the purposes behind the establishment of the program. A special events program offered during inservice days twice each year will not give the image of consistency that must be a part of any leader's plan. Only a continuous and comprehensive program of training—delivered consistently—will achieve this goal.

13. A GOOD TRAINING PROGRAM OFFERS THIRD-PERSON SUPPORT TO PRINCIPALS AND SUPERINTENDENTS' URGINGS

A leader must teach. A leader must motivate people to achieve and reach goals. Above all, a leader must help people achieve to new levels of performance that they have not experienced before. And it is extremely helpful if someone else is confirming what a leader is teaching and urging those being led to do. This is called **third-person support**. Third-person support is a very beneficial leadership tool. It is probably the most significant asset overlooked by many leaders.

Third-person support offers an immeasurably valuable leadership reinforcement. This support can always be used to uphold everything we are asking teachers to do for students and the school. It can be used to support decision-making actions. Third-person support also paves the way for new ideas and the acceptance of new ways of doing things. Third-person support lets a leader approach sensitive issues or say things that he or she often can't.

A leader needs to ask but one question to see how vitally important third-person support can be: "Can you imagine how valuable it would be to have someone else constantly confirming what you are telling the staff?"

Business and industry use third-person support extensively. It is used to create staff acceptance, pull people together in cooperative ways, and build trust and confidence in management. It shows employees what others are doing to support what they have decided to do. It relates what other business people say about vital issues ranging from increasing productivity to training to wages. Often, business executives cite trends from the economists, changes in customer habits, and statistics to support their decisions and pave the way for staff acceptance of their leadership ideas.

*Leaders in education need the same advantage. Without third-person support, we stand alone and lead alone. That's why the foundation program of ongoing staff development should reinforce and strengthen the administrative actions for creating successful schools. The third-person support feature included in the staff development program can pave the way to easier management with fewer conflicts. Third-person support aids acceptance of a leader's course of action—and lessens the chance of second-guessing, constant challenges, and automatic rejections. In truth, third-person support **proves the boss is right** and facilitates following.*

14. *A CONTINUOUS PROGRAM OF TRAINING MUST BE ECONOMICAL—OR IT WILL NOT BE ADOPTED AND EMPLOYED*

The linkage between training teachers and the cost of that training is a reality that cannot be overlooked. No matter how great the need, ongoing training will not happen if the cost is more than principals and superintendents can afford. What is more, some principals and superintendents continue to look upon training as a perk and a luxury, rather than a necessity. Until all teachers, administrators, and boards of education realize that teachers' knowledge and skills need continuous upgrading if continual improvement is expected, this reality will not change.

*That's why staff development must be economical. It must cost $20 or less per teacher per year. If it costs more, ongoing training will not occur individually or privately. Rather, "passing along" and "reading and routing" will be employed, even though it is known that these are poor management practices because such factors as who gets the material first and last, the condition the material is in when it is received, and **how** it is delivered from one teacher to another minimize the efforts of the training. These communication practices say everything to teachers from "You're not important enough to get personal help" to "This training isn't that important" to "Your training is last on the list of our priorities."*

We might say, "But we don't have the funds to spend $20 per year per teacher for an ongoing program of teacher training." And, in many cases, this is true. When it is true, we're in big trouble. Building a better school is going to be very difficult for such schools in the 21st century. Teachers will not be trained adequately. I would suggest that the schools seek funds for training from the PTA, PTO, or a service club in the community.

*I believe that a school or district cannot afford to spend less than one day's wage per teacher per school year in upgrading a staff on **both** the human and technical sides of staff development. Equally important, I believe the expenditure should contain both a weekly foundation program and an inservice day program. Once- or twice-a-year programs of staff development alone are not adequate. Teachers need continuous help throughout the year. If they don't get it, it is very difficult for them to move to higher and higher levels of performance.*

*As I said in the beginning, I am biased. **The MASTER Teacher** program of staff development is designed to meet all fourteen of these criteria.*